WORK ENGAGEMENT

T0341400

This book provides the most thorough view available on this new and intriguing dimension of workplace psychology, which is the basis of fulfilling, productive work.

The book begins by defining work engagement, which has been described as "an opposite to burnout," following its development into a more complex concept with far-reaching implications for work life. The chapters discuss the sources of work engagement, emphasizing the importance of leadership, organizational structures, and human resource management as factors that may operate to either enhance or inhibit employees' experience of work. The book considers the implications of work engagement for both the individual employee and the organization as a whole. To address readers' practical questions, the book provides in-depth coverage of interventions that can enhance employees' work engagement and improve management techniques.

Based upon the most up-to-date research by the foremost experts in the world, this volume brings together the best knowledge available on work engagement, and will be of great use to academic researchers, upper level students of work and organizational psychology, as well as management consultants.

Arnold B. Bakker is Full Professor at the Department of Work and Organizational Psychology at Erasmus University Rotterdam, The Netherlands. His research interests include positive organizational behavior (e.g., flow and engagement at work, performance), burnout, crossover of work-related emotions, and serious games on organizational phenomena.

Michael P. Leiter is Canada Research Chair in Organizational Health and Professor of Psychology at Acadia University and Director of the Center for Organizational Research & Development (http://cord.acadiau.ca) that applies high-quality research methods to human resource issues. He is actively involved as a consultant on occupational issues in Canada, the USA, and Europe.

Work Engagement

A Handbook of Essential Theory and Research

Edited by Arnold B. Bakker and Michael P. Leiter

Psychology Press
Taylor & Francis Group

HOVE AND NEW YORK

Published in 2010
by Psychology Press
27 Church Road, Hove, East Sussex BN3 2FA

Simultaneously published in the USA and Canada
by Psychology Press
711 Third Avenue, New York, NY 10017

First issued in paperback 2015

Psychology Press is an imprint of the Taylor & Francis Group, an informa business

Typeset in Times by RefineCatch Limited, Bungay, Suffolk

Cover design by Jim Wilkie

British Library Cataloguing in Publication Data
A catalogue record for this book is available from the British Library

Library of Congress Cataloging-in-Publication Data
  Work engagement : a handbook of essential theory and research / edited by Arnold B. Bakker
    and Michael P. Leiter
      p. cm.
  Includes bibliographical references and index.
  ISBN 978-1-84169-736-9 (hb)
  1. Employee motivation. 2. Psychology, Industrial. 3. Work—Psychological aspects.
  4. Employees—Attitudes. I. Bakker, Arnold B. II. Leiter, Michael P.
  HF5549.5.M63W667 2010
  158.7–dc22
                                                                        2009033356

ISBN13: 978-1-138-87763-4 (pbk)
ISBN13: 978-1-84169-736-9 (hbk)

Contents

Contributors

Arnold B. Bakker
Erasmus University Rotterdam
Institute of Psychology
PO Box 1738
T12-47 3000 DR Rotterdam
The Netherlands

Russell Cropanzano
Department of Management and Organizations
University of Arizona
Tucson, AZ 85721–0108
USA

Evangelia Demerouti
Eindhoven University of Technology
Department of Industrial Engineering and
Innovation Sciences
Human Performance Management Group
PO Box 513
5600 MB Eindhoven

Christian Dormann
University of Mainz
55122 Mainz
Germany

Charlotte Fritz
Department of Psychology
Bowling Green State University
Bowling Green, OH 43403
USA

Jari J. Hakanen
Centre of Expertise for Work Organizations
Finnish Institute of Occupational Health
FI-00250 Helsinki
Finland

Jonathon R. B. Halbesleben
Department of Management and Marketing
University of Wisconsin-Eau Claire
PO Box 4004
Eau Claire, WI 54702
USA

Chak Fu Lam
Department of Management and Organizations
Ross School of Business
University of Michigan
Ann Arbor, MI 48109-1234
USA

Michael P. Leiter
Centre for Organizational Research and
Development
Acadia University
Halifax, NS B4P 2R6
Canada

Fred Luthans
Department of Management
University of Nebraska-Lincoln
Lincoln, NE 68588-0491
USA

Christina Maslach
Department of Psychology
University of California
Berkeley, CA 94720-1650
USA

Gert Roodt
Centre for Work Performance
Department of Industrial Psychology and
People Management
Faculty of Management
University of Johannesburg
South Africa

Marisa Salanova
Department of Social Psychology
Universitat Jaume I
12071 Castellón
Spain

Wilmar B. Schaufeli
Department of Work and Organizational
Psychology
Utrecht University
PO Box 80.140
3508 TC Utrecht
The Netherlands

Akihito Shimazu
Department of Mental Health
The University of Tokyo Graduate School
of Medicine
Tokyo 113-0033
Japan

Arie Shirom
Faculty of Management
Tel-Aviv University
POB 39010

Tel Aviv 69978
Israel

Sabine Sonnentag
Department of Psychology
University of Konstanz
PO Box 42
78457 Konstanz
Germany

Gretchen M. Spreitzer
Department of Management and Organizations
Ross School of Business
University of Michigan
Ann Arbor, MI 48109-1234
USA

David Sweetman
Global Leadership Institute
Department of Management
University of Nebraska-Lincoln
Lincoln, NE 68588-0491
USA

Toon W. Taris
Department of Work and Organizational
Psychology
Utrecht University
PO Box 80.140
3508 TC Utrecht
The Netherlands

Despoina Xanthopoulou
Department of Work and Organizational
Psychology
Institute of Psychology
Erasmus University Rotterdam
PO Box 1738
T12-56 3000 DR Rotterdam
The Netherlands

Work engagement: Introduction

Michael P. Leiter and Arnold B. Bakker

William loves his work and can talk about it really enthusiastically. Every day he feels driven to excel and he throws himself into work passionately. He finds his job challenging, exciting, and enjoyable, and does much more than is requested, just for the fun of it. William has the autonomy to be creative, and has the feeling that he learns new things all the time. Although he is always busy and is usually completely immersed in his work, he rarely feels tired or exhausted. Instead, work seems to give him energy, and every day he feels happy to start working again. Even if he sometimes faces difficulties, William persists. He is really dedicated to his work and finds that he deals with interesting and important issues. Nevertheless, he can relax and disengage from work and he knows how to downplay his work. Although he often gets totally absorbed by his work, there are also other things outside work that he enjoys to the fullest. William's motto is: work is fun!

(Anonymous engaged worker)

Employees' psychological connection with their work has gained critical importance in the information/service economy of the 21st century. The contemporary world of work thrives on creativity. In the current economy, advances in quality or efficiency occur through new ideas. To compete effectively, companies not only must recruit the top talent, but must inspire employees to apply their full capabilities to their work. Otherwise, part of that rare and expensive resource remains unavailable. Thus, modern organizations expect their employees to be proactive and show initiative, take responsibility for their own professional development, and to be committed to high quality performance standards. They need employees who feel energetic and dedicated – i.e., who are engaged with their work. As we will see in this book, work engagement can make a true difference for employees and may offer organizations a competitive advantage (see Demerouti & Cropanzano, Chapter 11).

What is work engagement?

Work engagement is a positive, fulfilling, affective-motivational state of work-related well-being that can be seen as the antipode of job burnout. Engaged employees have high levels of energy, and are enthusiastically involved in their work (Bakker, Schaufeli, Leiter, & Taris, 2008). Most scholars agree that engagement includes an energy dimension and an identification dimension. Thus, engagement is characterized by a high level of vigor and strong identification with one's work.

The perspective of this book is that the field is best served by a consistent construct for work engagement, one that focuses on employees' experience of work activity. Unfortunately, the broad exploration of constructs over the past decade has not produced consensus about its meaning. In contrast, a recent review by Macey and Schneider (2008) documented the proliferation of various definitions of engagement, many of them being old wine in new bottles. These authors try to "solve" the conceptual problem by proposing employee engagement as an all-inclusive umbrella term that contains different types of engagement (i.e., trait engagement, state engagement, and behavioral engagement), each of which entails various conceptualizations; e.g., proactive personality (trait engagement), involvement (state engagement), and organizational citizenship behavior (behavioral engagement). In contrast, we advocate the use of engagement as a specific, well-defined and properly operationalized psychological state that is open to empirical research and practical application.

We define work engagement as a motivational concept. When engaged, employees feel compelled to strive towards a challenging goal. They want to succeed. Work engagement goes beyond responding to the immediate situation. Employees accept a personal commitment to attaining these goals. Further, work engagement reflects the personal energy employees bring to their work. Engaged employees not only have the capacity to be energetic, they enthusiastically apply that energy to their work. They do not hold back. They do not keep their energy in reserve for something important; they accept that today's work deserves their energy. In addition, work engagement reflects intense involvement in work. Engaged employees pay attention. They consider the important details while getting to the essence of challenging problems. Engaged employees become absorbed in their work, experiencing flow in which they lose track of time and diminish their response to distractions.

Work engagement pertains to any type of challenging work. It describes employees' ability to bring their full capacity to solving problems, connecting with people, and developing innovative services. Management makes a difference as well. Employees' responses to organizational policies, practices, and structures affect their potential to experience engagement. In a stable work environment employees maintain a consistent level of work engagement. Work engagement thrives in settings that demonstrate strong connections between corporate and individual values. On the one hand, companies promote their values with employees, inspiring their allegiance. On the other hand, companies are responsive to the values employees bring to their work. They maintain sufficient flexibility to accommodate a variety of approaches to their complex challenges. They manage human resources in a responsive way that appreciates employees' distinct contributions to the enterprise. As we will see throughout this book, work engagement has implications for performance, both individual and corporate. While engaged employees find their work more enjoyable, they turn that enjoyment into more effective action.

When do people experience work engagement?

Previous studies have consistently shown that job resources such as social support from colleagues and supervisors, performance feedback, skill variety, autonomy, and learning opportunities are positively associated with work engagement (Halbesleben, Chapter 8, this volume; Schaufeli & Salanova, 2007). Job resources either play an intrinsic motivational role because they foster employees' growth, learning and development, or they play an extrinsic motivational role because they are instrumental in achieving work goals. In the former case, job resources fulfill basic human needs, such as the needs for autonomy, relatedness and competence (Van den Broeck,

Vansteenkiste, De Witte, & Lens, 2008). For instance, proper feedback fosters learning, thereby increasing job competence, whereas decision latitude and social support satisfy the need for autonomy and the need to belong, respectively. Job resources may also play an extrinsic motivational role, because work environments that offer many resources foster the willingness to dedicate one's efforts and abilities to the work task (Meijman & Mulder, 1998). In such environments it is likely that the task will be completed successfully and that the work goal will be attained. For instance, supportive colleagues and performance feedback increase the likelihood of being successful in achieving one's work goals. In either case, be it through the satisfaction of basic needs or through the achievement of work goals, the outcome is positive and engagement is likely to occur (Schaufeli & Bakker, 2004; Schaufeli & Salanova, 2007).

Job resources become more salient and gain their motivational potential when employees are confronted with high job demands (Bakker & Demerouti, 2007; Hakanen & Roodt, Chapter 7, this volume). Hakanen, Bakker, and Demerouti (2005) tested this interaction hypothesis in a sample of Finnish dentists employed in the public sector. It was hypothesized that job resources are most beneficial in maintaining work engagement under conditions of high job demands. The results were generally consistent with this hypothesis. For example, variability in professional skills boosted work engagement when qualitative workload was high, and mitigated the negative effect of high qualitative workload on work engagement. Conceptually similar findings have been reported by Bakker, Hakanen, Demerouti, and Xanthopoulou (2007) in their study of Finnish teachers. They found that job resources act as buffers and diminish the negative relationship between pupil misbehavior and work engagement. In addition, they found that job resources particularly influence work engagement when teachers are confronted with high levels of pupil misconduct.

These notions and findings are compatible with the idea of a "fit" between a person and a job or organization. Person–job fit is conceptualized as having two aspects: (1) the fit between an individual's knowledge, skills, and abilities on the one hand, and the demands of the job on the other hand (i.e., demands–abilities fit; Cable & Judge, 1996), and (2) the fit between the needs and desires of an individual and what is provided by the job (needs–supplies fit; Cable & DeRue, 2002). Research has indeed shown that employees who perceive a high level of congruence between their personal characteristics and the requirements of the job experience a high level of job satisfaction (Brkich, Jeffs, & Carless, 2002). Person–organization fit is defined as the compatibility between people and entire organizations (Lauver & Kristof-Brown, 2001; Sekiguchi, 2007). A person may fit in the organization because they hold the same values (i.e., supplementary P-O fit) or because the person and the organization meet each other's needs (i.e., complementary P-O fit) (Carless, 2005; Sekiguchi, 2007).

Work engagement thrives in settings that demonstrate strong connections between corporate and individual values. On the one hand, companies promote their values with employees, inspiring their allegiance. These companies reflect seriously on their values, articulate them clearly, and enact policies to assure that their values direct important decisions. On the other hand, companies are responsive to the values employees bring to their work. They consider employees' professional values as assets that assure responsible dedication to work. Employees do not arrive with identical values, so companies support engagement by accommodating a variety of approaches to work. In this way, a clear and responsive approach to the congruence of individual and corporate values encourages diverse perspectives from employees to converge on major objectives reflecting core corporate values.

The importance of engagement

Work engagement has far-reaching implications for employees' performance. The energy and focus inherent in work engagement allow employees to bring their full potential to the job. This energetic focus enhances the quality of their core work responsibilities. They have the capacity and the motivation to concentrate exclusively on the tasks at hand.

Further, work engagement supports extra-role performance. The complexity of contemporary workplaces works against specifying every detail of an employer's expectation. In addition to a position's core responsibilities, employers hope that incumbents go beyond the formal structure of their positions to take initiative. A proactive approach to work includes developing new knowledge, responding to unique opportunities, as well as going the extra mile in supporting the company's community through mentoring, volunteering, or attentiveness to colleagues. With initiative, employees anticipate new developments in their professions and strive to position themselves as leaders in their fields. Through their actions, they go beyond living within the confines of their job description to craft their job into something that dynamically adapts to the ever-changing worklife that has become the norm.

Work engagement resonates with the broaden-and-build perspective of Fredrickson and her colleagues (Fredrickson, 1998, 2001). Cognitive broadening lies at the core of this perspective. It builds on research demonstrating that positive emotions increase the flexibility (Isen & Daubman, 1984), creativity (Isen, Daubman, & Nowicki, 1987), integration (Isen, Rosenzweig, & Young, 1991), and efficiency (Isen & Means, 1983) of thought. In contrast to the narrowing focus of the stress experience, positive emotions go beyond neutral states of mind to inspire wider perspectives on the self and the situation. Isen and colleagues (Ashby, Isen, & Turken, 1999; Isen, 2002) have proposed dopamine circulation as a physiological basis for the observed broadening that accompanies positive emotions (Fredrickson, Tugade, Waugh, & Larkin, 2003).

Evidence for the broadening hypothesis has been reported by Fredrickson and Branigan (2005) and by Isen (2000). Accordingly, positive affect produces a broad and flexible cognitive organization as well as the ability to integrate diverse material. The question is now whether this "broaden-and-build" effect will manifest itself in enhanced job performance, as one would assume because of the accumulation of personal resources. Fredrickson (2001) has argued that we need to investigate how (and whether) broadened thought–action repertoires are translated into decisions and actions. In an organizational context, Fredrickson and Losada (2005) showed that when the ratio of managers' positive to negative emotions is relatively high during business meetings, they ask more questions, and their range between questioning and advocacy is broader, resulting in better performance.

Evidence for the build hypothesis has been reported by Xanthopoulou, Bakker, Demerouti, and Schaufeli (2009). Their diary study revealed that daily job resources generate positive emotions that, in turn, have a positive impact on employees' personal resources. In addition, in an innovative experimental study, Fredrickson, Cohn, Coffey, Pek, and Finkel (2008) used a manipulation to increase positive emotional experiences. The employees who participated in this experiment either attended a loving-kindness meditation workshop or had no intervention. Results indicated that meditation practices increased the daily experience of positive emotions, which in turn produced gains in personal resources 8 weeks later, including gains in mastery and self-acceptance. Consequently, these increments in personal resources predicted increased life satisfaction and reduced depressive symptoms (see also Salanova, Schaufeli, Xanthopoulou, and Bakker, Chapter 9, this volume).

Fredrickson's theory gives additional substance to the concept of work engagement. It goes beyond the general notion that a positive affinity with work increases employees' attachment to the setting or its activities. Broaden-and-build proposes cognitive mechanisms underlying that general affinity, translating it into cognitive processes and perspectives. That is, positive emotions go beyond the general motivating properties of pleasant feelings. They change cognitive processes in ways that open possibilities that people overlook when under pressure or experiencing distress. Positive emotions encourage the integrative, creative perspective that adds value to enterprises in the information/service economy of the 21st century. This specific mechanism increases confidence in the connection between efforts to develop supportive work environments and enhancing individual performance that will contribute to corporate success. In short, work engagement is both efficient as well as fulfilling.

The social context of work engagement

The social context of work engagement emphasizes the concept's importance, as it has relevance for the primary relationships of employees. Collegial relationships hold the potential for social contagion in which employees not only respond similarly to their shared work environment but also influence one another's experience of engagement (Bakker & Demerouti, 2009; Bakker, Van Emmerik, & Euwema, 2006). Colleagues as well are potential resources – as sources of knowledge, emotional support, materials – that pertain to the engagement experience. Both first-line supervision and senior management define leadership within the organization. They symbolize the values of the organization, determine the flow of organizational resources, and model to employees' ways of thinking, feeling, and reacting to important events in organizational life (Schein, 1985). Senior management plays an important role in articulating the core values of organizations, translating them into formal mission statements and policies, while front-line supervisors enact these values through their day-to-day actions and interactions with employees. Finally, work engagement translates into performance in many industries through employees' interactions with customers, clients, students, or patients. It is in these interactions that the energy, dedication, absorption, or efficacy that lie at the heart of work engagement turn into action.

Although work engagement is a personal experience of individual employees, it does not occur in isolation. A thorough consideration of the sources, experience, and consequences of engagement go beyond the individual to consider the social dynamics among individuals as well as the larger institutional dynamics reflecting an organization's culture.

The conceptual models presented in this book that guide research on work engagement consider the experience as embedded in organizational cultures. The focus on work resources in these models acknowledges an intrinsic quality in people to make full use of their skills and abilities in their careers. Unfortunately, many work situations fail to provide the resources, leadership, or guidance that would permit employees to fulfill their aspirations. These gaps between potential and reality reduce an organization's capacity to fulfill its mission while discouraging employees' dedication to their roles.

Work engagement presents as serious a challenge to individuals as it does to organizations. In the first instance, employees' opportunities for secure employment rest on their employers' productivity. In competitive global markets, companies that cannot make effective use of their employees have a dim future. But engagement remains important to individuals beyond their contribution to their current employer. Career tracks in the 21st century anticipate many more changes and larger shifts than was the case in the 20th century. As active participants in the job market, individuals benefit from demonstrating their personal productivity. Demonstrating one's personal energy, dedication, and efficacy will open more and better opportunities while building a dynamic and rewarding career.

In conclusion, work engagement is not solely a concern for management, it matters to each employee. It is not enough for employees to respond to management initiatives regarding workplace resources or corporate values. Everyone shares responsibility for developing vibrant, engaging work environments.

Structure of the book

We hope that this book will contribute to that goal. The scope of the book includes a serious reflection on the concept of work engagement. We consider the source of the term, its position in the complex world of organizational psychology, and its distinguishing qualities. We devote considerable attention to identifying the qualities of work environments that contribute to the experience of engagement and that help employees avoid its negative alternative, burnout. Most importantly we consider work engagement as subject to change. The lack of work engagement today does not condemn an individual, a work group, or an organization to a dull worklife forever. We consider how engagement fluctuates from day to day in response to events, as well as the potential of concerted effort on the local or organizational level to support a more engaged approach to worklife. Together, the chapters in this book present work engagement as an important focus for study and a vital target for organizational development.

Work engagement and neighboring concepts

The book begins by pinning down the concept of work engagement. While acknowledging a diversity of perspectives as a healthy sign in the early years of an idea, these chapters reflect on the current state of things. In Chapter 2, Schaufeli and Bakker address the question of measurement. The capacity to derive a credible quantitative indicator of work engagement provides a necessary prerequisite for assessing a work setting's current state and to evaluate the impact of initiatives designed to enhance work engagement. The chapter considers current measures and notes the virtues of the Utrecht Work Engagement Scale (UWES).

In Chapter 3, Sonnentag, Dormann, and Demerouti consider how engagement varies over short periods of time. They review research that identifies workplace events that precede changes in work engagement as well as downstream consequences of these changes. This perspective underscores the extent to which work engagement is a variable quality of worklife rather than an enduring characteristic. It is a perspective that encourages definitive action to build work engagement among employees.

In Chapter 4, Taris, Schaufeli, and Shimazu contrast work engagement with other constructs with more mixed implications for the quality of worklife. By positioning work engagement in contrast to workaholism, burnout, and rust out, the chapter clarifies the core elements of the concept, contrasting the positive qualities associated with work engagement against the negative end of those same continuums. Defining the position of work engagement in this conceptual space supports the concept's distinct contribution to organizational psychology.

Chapter 5 by Sweetman and Luthans considers work engagement as a vital concept within the domain of positive psychology. The chapter presents the core rationale for positive psychology to provide a framework to consider work engagement's place within that domain. The authors consider the quality of psychological capital as a fundamental resource in developing fulfilling and productive lives at work. Positive psychology legitimizes the focus on energy and dedication as fundamental dimensions of existence. Rather than focus on the problems that arise when these qualities break down, positive psychology considers in depth the psychological benefits derived when these qualities are working well.

In Chapter 6, Shirom extends this perspective in his chapter on vigor. The chapter provides a far-reaching consideration of the centrality of subjective energy in personal experience at work and beyond. The chapter considers a diverse range of research and conceptual work to support the central role of energy. In addition, the chapter gives a strong consideration to the health implications of work engagement.

The organizational context of work engagement

The second part of the book considers the organizational context in which work engagement thrives or fails. Chapter 7 presents the job demands-resources (JD-R) model of work engagement. This perspective has emphasized the important role of resource access at work to the development and sustaining of work engagement. It provides a direct contrast to models of job burnout that place a greater emphasis on demands such as work overload, unresolved conflict, and values conflict. In this chapter, Hakanen and Roodt examine research to demonstrate the model's viability.

In Chapter 8, Halbesleben extends this perspective by conducting a meta-analysis of work engagement research. Although the research record remains somewhat modest at this time, there are sufficient studies to identify persistent patterns across samples and occupations. The review supports core aspects of the JD-R model while bringing fresh perspectives to the concept. The analysis emphasizes both the quantity of organizational resources and the diversity of resources in sustaining the various components of work engagement.

Chapter 9 considers the self-sustaining quality of work engagement. Salanova, Schaufeli, Xanthopoulou, and Bakker consider longitudinal research that affirms the long-term impact of resource enrichment on employees' experience of engagement and the complementary relationship of work engagement and the ongoing enhancement of resources. This perspective reflects upon the conceptual challenges in untangling causal pathways in complex social systems in which major experiences have multiple influences and multiple outcomes. The chapter's encouraging message is that efforts to enhance work engagement through enriched resources have a potential to sustain over time.

Chapter 10 by Spreitzer, Lam, and Fritz positions engagement in relation to thriving as an alternative perspective on positive connections with work. Their perspective emphasizes organizational learning as a critical dimension of employees' developments through their careers and in their tenure in a job. The chapter provides a thoughtful consideration of leadership as a definitive quality of engaging work settings. This chapter emphasizes the importance of both senior leadership and first-line supervisors in developing a workplace culture conducive to engagement and thriving.

In Chapter 11, Demerouti and Cropanzano examine the evidence for the crucial relationship of work engagement with performance. In contrasting work engagement with job satisfaction, the authors demonstrate robust relationships between employees' thoughts and feelings about their work with the behaviors on the job. In their review of the engagement–performance relationship, the authors acknowledge the scope of unresolved questions that require extensive and rigorous research to address.

In Chapter 12, Leiter and Maslach consider the design and efficacy of interventions to enhance work engagement. This chapter provides an overall conceptual model for considering intervention while giving specific direction on the design of effective organizational action. Through a case example, the chapter reviews the specific points of assessment, planning, action, and evaluation. The chapter argues for management interventions as a means of having the greatest impact on a workplace.

In Chapter 13, we reflect on the diverse perspectives included in the book and describe our expectations for the future of work engagement. We also present a research agenda that identifies seven key research questions that would extend our perspectives on work engagement, its relationship to other constructs related to the quality of worklife, and strategies for increasing the prevalence of work engagement in organizations.

Throughout the book the authors have provided specific points on their chapters' practical implications. While we intend to provide the state of the art on high quality work engagement research, we also intend to present engagement as a practical idea. All of the research in this book has occurred in collaboration with people working in real organizations facing the challenges of productivity, health, and well-being. We are constantly considering ways in which organizations can apply new ideas to their challenges.

References

Ashby, F. G., Isen, A. M., & Turken, A. U. (1999). A neuropsychological theory of positive affect and its influence on cognition. *Psychological Review*, *106*, 529–550.

Bakker, A. B., & Demerouti, E. (2007). The Job Demands-Resources model: State of the art. *Journal of Managerial Psychology*, *22*, 309–328.

Bakker, A. B., & Demerouti, E. (2009). The crossover of work engagement between working couples: A closer look at the role of empathy. *Journal of Managerial Psychology*, *24*, 220–236.

Bakker, A. B., Hakanen, J. J., Demerouti, E., & Xanthopoulou, D. (2007). Job resources boost work engagement particularly when job demands are high. *Journal of Educational Psychology*, *99*, 274–284.

Bakker, A. B., Schaufeli, W. B., Leiter, M. P., & Taris, T. W. (2008). Work engagement: An emerging concept in occupational health psychology. *Work & Stress*, *22*, 187–200.

Bakker, A. B., Van Emmerik, I. J. H., & Euwema, M. C. (2006). Crossover of burnout and engagement in work teams. *Work and Occupations*, *33*, 464–489.

Brkich, M., Jeffs, D., & Carless, S. A. (2002). A global self-report measure of person-job fit. *European Journal of Psychological Assessment*, *18*, 43–51.

Cable, D. M., & DeRue, D. S. (2002). The convergent and discriminant validity of subjective fit perceptions. *Journal of Applied Psychology*, *87*, 875–884.

Cable, D. M., & Judge, T. A. (1996). Person organization fit, job choice decisions, and organizational entry. *Organizational Behavior and Human Decision Processes*, *67*, 294–311.

Carless, S. A. (2005). Person-job fit versus person-organization fit as predictors of organizational attraction and job acceptance intentions: A longitudinal study. *Journal of Occupational and Organizational Psychology*, *78*, 411–429.

Fredrickson, B. L. (1998). What good are positive emotions? *Review of General Psychology*, *2*, 300–319.

Fredrickson, B. L. (2001). The role of positive emotions in positive psychology: The broaden-and-build theory of positive emotions. *American Psychologist*, *56*, 218–226.

Fredrickson, B. L., & Branigan, C. A. (2005). Positive emotions broaden the scope of attention and thought–action repertoires. *Cognition and Emotion*, *19*, 313–332.

Fredrickson, B. L., Cohn, M. A., Coffey, K. A., Pek, J., & Finkel, S. M. (2008). Open hearts build lives: Positive emotions, induced through meditation, build consequential personal resources. *Journal of Personality and Social Psychology*, *95*, 1045–1062.

Fredrickson, B. L., & Losada, M. F. (2005). Positive affect and the complex dynamics of human flourishing. *American Psychologist*, *60*, 678–686.

Fredrickson, B. L., Tugade, M. M., Waugh, C. E., & Larkin, G. R. (2003). What good are positive emotions in crises? A prospective study of resilience and emotions following the terrorist attacks on the United States on September 11th, 2001. *Journal of Personality and Social Psychology*, *84*, 365–376.

Hakanen, J. J., Bakker, A. B., & Demerouti, E. (2005). How dentists cope with their job demands and stay engaged: The moderating role of job resources. *European Journal of Oral Sciences*, *113*, 479–487.

Isen, A. M. (2000). Positive affect and decision making. In M. Lewis & J. M. Haviland-Jones (Eds.), *Handbook of emotions* (2nd ed., pp. 417–435). New York: Guilford Press.

Isen, A. M. (2002). A role for neuropsychology in understanding the facilitating influence of positive affect on social behavior and cognitive processes. In C. R. Snyder & S. J. Lopez (Eds.), *Handbook of positive psychology* (pp. 528–540). New York: Oxford University Press.

Isen, A. M., & Daubman, K. A. (1984). The influence of affect on categorization. *Journal of Personality and Social Psychology*, *17*, 1206 1217.

Isen, A. M., Daubman, K. A., & Nowicki, G. P. (1987). Positive affect facilitates creative problem solving. *Journal of Personality and Social Psychology*, *52*, 1122–1131.

Isen, A. M., & Means, B. (1983). The influence of positive affect on decision-making strategy. *Social Cognition*, *2*, 18–31.

Isen, A. M., Rosenzweig, A. S., & Young, M. J. (1991). The influence of positive affect on clinical problem solving. *Medical Decision Making*, *11*, 221–227.

Lauver, K. J., & Kristof-Brown, A. (2001). Distinguishing between employees' perceptions of person-job and person-organization fit. *Journal of Vocational Behavior*, *59*, 454–470.

Macey, W. H., & Schneider, B. (2008). The meaning of employee engagement. *Industrial and Organizational Psychology*, *1*, 3–30.

Meijman, T. F., & Mulder, G. (1998). Psychological aspects of workload. In P. J. D. Drenth & H. Thierry (Eds.), *Handbook of work and organizational psychology, Vol. 2: Work psychology* (pp. 5–33). Hove: Psychology Press.

Schein, E. (1985). Organizational culture and leadership: A dynamic view. San Francisco: Jossey Bass.

Schaufeli, W. B., & Bakker, A. B. (2004). Job demands, job resources, and their relationship with burnout and engagement: A multi-sample study. *Journal of Organizational Behavior*, *25*, 293–315.

Schaufeli, W. B., & Salanova, M. (2007). Work engagement: An emerging psychological concept and its implications for organizations. In S. W. Gilliland, D. D. Steiner, & D. P. Skarlicki (Eds.), *Research in social issues in management* (Volume 5): *Managing social and ethical issues in organizations*. Greenwich, CT: Information Age Publishers.

Sekiguchi, T. (2007). A contingency perspective of the importance of PJ fit and PO fit in employee selection. *Journal of Managerial Psychology*, *22*, 118–131.

Van den Broeck, A., Vansteenkiste, M., De Witte, H., & Lens, W. (2008). Explaining the relationships between job characteristics, burnout, and engagement: The role of basic psychological need satisfaction. *Work & Stress*, *22*, 277–294.

Xanthopoulou, D., Bakker, A. B., Demerouti, E., & Schaufeli, W. B. (2009). *A diary study on the happy worker: How job resources generate positive emotions and build personal resources*. Manuscript submitted for publication.

2

Defining and measuring work engagement: Bringing clarity to the concept

Wilmar B. Schaufeli and Arnold B. Bakker

Engagement has become a rather popular term, first in business and consultancy, and recently also in academia. The origin of the term "employee engagement" is not entirely clear, but most likely it was first used in the 1990s by the Gallup organization (Buckingham & Coffman, 1999). Although the phrases "employee engagement" and "work engagement" are typically used interchangeably we prefer the latter because it is more specific. Namely, work engagement refers to the relationship of the employee with his or her *work*, whereas employee engagement may also include the relationship with the *organization*. As we will see in the section on "Engagement in business", by including the relationship with the organization the distinction between engagement and traditional concepts such as organizational commitment and extra-role behavior gets blurred.

The current popularity of engagement is illustrated by Table 2.1. An internet search yielded almost 650,000 hits though narrowing the search down to only scholarly publications – many of them from the gray area (e.g., white papers, fact sheets, and consultancy reports) – reduced the number of hits to less than 2000. These impressive numbers stand in sharp contrast to the dearth of publications on engagement that are included in *PsycINFO*, the leading database of academic publications in psychology. The most comprehensive *PsycINFO* search revealed one hundred publications with either "employee engagement" or "work engagement" in the title or in the abstract

TABLE 2.1

The popularity of engagement (state: March 2008)

	The internet		*PsycINFO*	
	Google	**Google scholar**	**Anywhere**	**In title**
Employee engagement	626,000	1120	35	12
Work engagement	21,400	785	66	20
Total	645,130	1898	100	32

of any publication. The most restrictive search with either "employee engagement" or "work engagement" in the title of any peer-reviewed international journal yielded only about thirty hits. If anything, Table 2.1 illustrates that compared to the popularity of engagement in business and among consultants there is a surprising scarcity of academic research.

Moreover, almost all scientific articles appeared after the turn of the century. This recent academic interest in engagement links in with the emergence of the so-called Positive Psychology that studies human strength and optimal functioning, instead of the traditional four D's: *D*isease, *D*amage, *D*isorder, and *D*isability. A telling example is the switch from job burnout to work engagement (Maslach, Schaufeli, & Leiter, 2001).

This chapter presents an overview of the way engagement is conceptualized and measured, particularly in academia but also in business. Our purpose is not only to present a state-of-the art review of current scientific knowledge, but also to link this with notions of engagement that are being used in business contexts, particularly by leading international consultancy firms. In doing so, we focus on work engagement across all kinds of jobs and not on such specific types of engagement as school engagement, athlete engagement, soldier engagement or student engagement that have been described in the literature as well.

The chapter sets out with an overview of various concepts of engagement, including a discussion of related concepts such as extra-role behavior, personal initiative, job involvement, organizational commitment, job satisfaction, positive affectivity,

flow, and workaholism. Next, various engagement questionnaires are presented and their psychometric quality is discussed in terms of reliability and validity. The closing section attempts to integrate the various conceptualizations of engagement into a more comprehensive model of employee motivation and engagement.

The concept of work engagement

Everyday connotations of engagement refer to involvement, commitment, passion, enthusiasm, absorption, focused effort, and energy. In a similar vein, the Merriam-Webster dictionary describes engagement as "emotional involvement or commitment" and as "the state of being in gear". However, no agreement exists among practitioners or scholars on a particular conceptualization of (work) engagement. Below the major business and academic perspectives on engagement are discussed in greater detail.

Engagement in business

Virtually all major human resources consultancy firms are in the business of improving levels of work engagement. Almost without exception these firms claim that they have found conclusive and compelling evidence that work engagement increases profitability through higher productivity, sales, customer satisfaction, and employee retention. The message for organizations is clear: increasing work engagement pays off. However, with the exception of the Gallup Organization (Harter, Schmidt, & Hayes, 2002) this claim is not substantiated by publications in peer-reviewed journals. Instead of presenting scientific *evidence* it is merely *stated* in reports that a positive relationship between employee engagement and company's profitability has been established. Nevertheless because of the major impact of consultancy firms in business we present some examples of the ways in which engagement is conceptualized:

- *Development Dimensions International (DDI)*: "Engagement has three dimensions: (1) cognitive – belief in and support for the goals and values of the organization; (2) affective – sense of belonging, pride and attachment to the organization; (3) behavioral – willingness to go the extra mile, intention to stay with the organization" (www.ddiworld.com).
- *Hewitt*: "Engaged employees consistently demonstrate three general behaviors. They: (1) Say – consistently speak positively about the organization to co-workers, potential employees, and customers; (2) Stay – have an intense desire to be a member of the organization despite opportunities to work elsewhere; (3) Strive – exert extra time, effort, and initiative to contribute to business success" (www.hewittassociates.com).
- *Towers Perrin*: Employee engagement is considered an affective state that reflects employees' "personal satisfaction and a sense of inspiration and affirmation they get from work and being a part of the organization" (www.towersperrin.com).
- *Mercer*: "Employee engagement – also called 'commitment' or 'motivation' – refers to a psychological state where employees feel a vested interest in the company's success and perform to a high standard that may exceed the stated requirements of the job" (www.mercerHR.com).

Although these descriptions may differ at first glance, a closer look reveals that, in essence, engagement is defined in terms of: (1) organizational commitment, more particularly affective commitment (i.e., the emotional attachment to the organization) and continuance commitment (i.e., the desire to stay with the organization), and (2) extra-role behavior (i.e., discretionary behavior that promotes the effective functioning of the organization). Hence, the way these leading consultancy firms conceptualize engagement comes close to putting old wine in new bottles.

Gallup uses a slightly different conceptualization which, instead of the organization, refers to the employee's work: "The term employee engagement refers to an individual's involvement and satisfaction with as well as enthusiasm for work" (Harter et al., 2002, p. 269). Like the definitions of other consultancy firms, Gallup's engagement concept seems to overlap with well-known traditional constructs such as job involvement and job satisfaction.

In conclusion: because in business and among consultants engagement is used as a novel, catchy label that in fact covers traditional concepts, it has the appearance of being somewhat faddish. However, the popularity of engagement in these circles signifies that "there is something to it". Therefore, academic scholars have begun to define and study work engagement as a unique construct.

Engagement in academia

The first scholar who conceptualized engagement at work was Kahn (1990), who described it as the "harnessing of organization members' selves to their work roles: in engagement, people employ and express themselves physically, cognitively, emotionally and mentally during role performances" (p. 694). In other words, engaged employees put a lot of effort into their work because they identify with it.

According to Kahn (1990), a dynamic, dialectical relationship exists between the person who drives personal energies (physical, cognitive, emotional, and mental) into his or her work role on the one hand, and the work role that allows the person to express him or herself on the other hand. Later Kahn (1992) differentiated the concept of engagement from psychological presence or the experience of "being fully there", namely when "people feel and are attentive, connected, integrated, and focused in their role performance" (p. 322). Or put differently, engagement as behavior – driving energy in one's work role – is considered as the manifestation of psychological presence, a particular mental state. In its turn, engagement is assumed to produce positive outcomes, both at the individual level (personal growth and development) as well as at the organizational level (performance quality). Rothbard (2001), who was inspired by the work of Kahn (1990, 1992), took a slightly different perspective and defined engagement as a two-dimensional motivational construct that includes attention ("the cognitive availability and the amount of time one spends thinking about a role"; p. 656) and absorption ("the intensity of one's focus on a role"; p. 656).

A quite different approach is followed by those who consider work engagement as the positive antithesis of burnout (Maslach et al., 2001). Contrary to those who suffer from burnout, engaged employees have a sense of energetic and effective connection with their work, and instead of stressful and demanding they look upon their work as challenging. Two different but related schools of thought exist that consider work engagement as a positive, work-related state of well-being or fulfillment.

According to Maslach and Leiter (1997) engagement is characterized by energy, involvement, and efficacy – the direct opposites of the three burnout dimensions. They argue that in the case of burnout energy turns into exhaustion, involvement turns into cynicism, and efficacy turns into ineffectiveness. By implication, engagement is assessed by the opposite pattern of scores on the three dimensions of the Maslach Burnout Inventory (MBI; Maslach, Jackson, & Leiter, 1996): low scores on exhaustion and cynicism, and high scores on professional efficacy.

The alternative view considers work engagement as an independent, distinct concept that is negatively related to burnout. Consequently, work engagement is defined and operationalized in its own right as "a positive, fulfilling, work-related state of mind that is characterized by vigor, dedication, and absorption" (Schaufeli, Salanova, González-Romá, & Bakker, 2002b, p. 74). That is, in engagement, fulfillment exists in contrast to the voids of life that leave people feeling empty as in burnout. Rather than a momentary, specific emotional state, engagement refers to a more persistent and pervasive affective-cognitive state. Vigor is characterized by high levels of energy and mental resilience while working, the willingness to invest effort in one's work, and persistence even in the face of difficulties. Dedication refers to being strongly involved in one's work, and experiencing a sense of significance, enthusiasm, inspiration, pride, and challenge. Absorption is characterized by being fully concentrated and happily engrossed in one's work, whereby time passes quickly and one has difficulties with detaching oneself from work. Accordingly, vigor and dedication are considered direct opposites of exhaustion and cynicism, respectively, the two core symptoms of burnout (Schaufeli & Taris, 2005). The continuum that is spanned by vigor and exhaustion has been labeled "energy", whereas the continuum that is spanned by dedication and cynicism has been labeled "identification" (González-Romá, Schaufeli, Bakker, & Lloret, 2006). Hence, work engagement is characterized by a high level of energy and strong identification with one's work, whereas burnout is characterized by the opposite: a low level of energy and poor identification with one's work. In addition, based on in-depth interviews (Schaufeli, Taris, Le Blanc, Peeters, Bakker, & De Jonge, 2001) absorption was included as the third constituting aspect of work engagement.

By way of conclusion it is important to note that the key reference of engagement for Kahn (1990, 1992) is the work *role*, whereas for those who consider engagement as the positive antithesis of burnout it is the employee's work *activity*, or the work itself. As we have seen above, in business contexts the reference is neither the work role nor the work activity but the organization. Furthermore, both academic conceptualizations that define engagement in its own right agree that it entails a behavioral-energetic (vigor), an emotional (dedication), and a cognitive (absorption) component.

Related concepts

Because no agreement exists on the meaning of engagement and because in many cases descriptions of engagement look like putting new wine into old bottles, it is imperative to discuss similar, alternative concepts – to taste the old wine, so to speak. The crucial question to be answered is: Has the concept of engagement – as defined in academia – added value over and above traditional, related concepts? Eight such concepts can be distinguished which either refer to behaviors (extra-role behavior, personal initiative), beliefs (organizational commitment, job involvement), or affect (job satisfaction, positive affectivity) that are considered prototypical for work engagement, or refer to comparable, more complex psychological states (flow, workaholism).

- *Extra-role behavior.* Although it is common to define engagement in terms of discretionary effort, "giving it their all", or "going the extra mile" it is limiting to consider engagement solely in terms of extra, voluntary effort. First, engaged employees bring something *different* to the job (e.g., creative problem solving) and do not just do something *more* (e.g., work longer hours). Second, the boundaries between in-role behavior – the officially required behavior that serves the goals of the organization – and extra-role behavior – discretionary behavior that goes beyond in-role behavior, also called organizational citizenship behavior (Organ, 1997) – are weak at best. Since engaged employees might or might not exhibit extra-role behavior this should not be considered to be a constituting element of work engagement.
- *Personal initiative.* According to Frese and Fay (2001), personal initiative comprises self-starting behavior, proactivity, and persistence. As a specific kind of behavior, personal initiative goes beyond what is normal, obvious, or ordinary in the job. Rather than referring to the quantity of behavior, personal initiative is about the quality of the employee's work behavior. As such, it is related to the behavioral component (vigor) of the broader concept of work engagement.
- *Job involvement.* In their classical article Lodahl and Kejner (1965) define job involvement as: "the degree to which a person is identified psychologically with his work, or the importance of work in his total self-image" (p. 24). Clearly, job involvement –

being the opposite of cynicism – is closely related to the engagement construct but not equivalent to it.
- *Organizational commitment.* Similar to job involvement, organizational commitment is a psychological state of attachment and identification, but unlike job involvement it is a binding force between individual and organization. Or as Mowday, Steers, and Porter (1979) put it: "the relative strength of an individual's identification with and involvement in a particular organization" (p. 226). In contrast, work engagement, as defined in academia, is about being involved in the work role or in the work itself. When engagement is considered to be equivalent to organizational commitment, as in some definitions that are used in business, the very notion of engagement is superfluous.
- *Job satisfaction.* Perhaps the most widely cited definition of job satisfaction comes from Locke (1976) as "a pleasurable or positive emotional state resulting from the appraisal of one's job" (p. 1300). In contrast to engagement that is concerned with the employee's mood *at* work, job satisfaction is concerned with affect *about* or *toward* work, which probably has more cognitive underpinnings. Moreover, engagement connotes activation (enthusiasm, alertness, excitement, elation), whereas satisfaction connotes satiation (contentment, calmness, serenity, relaxation).
- *Positive affectivity.* Work engagement can be considered a domain-specific psychological *state* that corresponds with positive affectivity, being a context-free dispositional *trait*. For instance, markers of positive affect in the Positive Affectivity scale of the PANAS (Watson, Clark, & Tellegen, 1988; p. 1064) include, among others, *attentive* (absorption), *alert* (absorption), *enthusiastic* (dedication), *inspired* (dedication), *proud* (dedication), *determined* (vigor), *energized* (vigor), and *strong* (vigor). Hence, it is to be expected that some employees are dispositionally more prone to being engaged at work than others.
- *Flow.* According to Csikszentmihalyi (1990),

flow is a state of optimal experience that is characterized by focused attention, clear mind, mind and body unison, effortless concentration, complete control, loss of self-consciousness, distortion of time, and intrinsic enjoyment. Clearly, being fully absorbed in one's work comes close to this description of flow. Yet, flow refers to rather particular, *short-term* "peak" experiences – also outside the realm of work – whereas absorption refers to a more *pervasive* and *persistent* state of mind. Moreover, flow is a more complex concept that may also include specific antecedents such as immediate (performance) feedback.

- *Workaholism.* Although at first glance there might be some similarities between workaholics and engaged employees, it has been argued elsewhere that engaged employees lack the compulsive drive that is typical for work addicts (Schaufeli, Taris, & Bakker, 2006). Engaged employees work hard because work is challenging and fun, and not because they are driven by a strong inner urge they cannot resist. A similar distinction is made by Vallerand et al. (2003) who discriminate between *harmonious* passion (akin to engagement) and *obsessive* passion (akin to workaholism).

Although a partial overlap is observed between work engagement and personal initiative, job involvement, positive affectivity and flow, the concept of engagement cannot be reduced to any of these. Furthermore, work engagement is conceptually distinct from extra-role behavior, organizational commitment, job satisfaction and workaholism. Hence, it is concluded that work engagement has added value over and above these related concepts.

The assessment of work engagement

Based on different kinds of conceptualizations, various instruments have been proposed to assess work engagement, both for applied research in organizations as well as for scientific purposes. In this section the psychometric quality of these instruments is discussed in terms of reliability and validity. Since no psychometric data are available from engagement questionnaires that have been used by consultancy firms in business contexts, these instruments cannot be reviewed. However, one exception exists: Gallup's Workplace Audit (GWA) or Q^{12}. Furthermore, a distinction can be made between questionnaires that assess work engagement as a separate construct in its own right and questionnaires that assess engagement as the opposite scoring pattern of burnout.

The Gallup Q^{12}

After an iterative process of item formulation and testing that took several decades, the final wording of the Gallup questionnaire was established in 1998. It was dubbed Q^{12} since it includes 12 items (see Table 2.2). Meanwhile, the Q^{12} has been administered to more than 7 million employees in 112 countries (Harter, Schmidt, Killham, & Asplund, 2006). The Q^{12} has been explicitly designed from an "actionability standpoint". This means that in the development of the instrument, practical considerations regarding the usefulness of the Q^{12} for managers in creating change in the workplace have been the leading principle. In other words, the Q^{12} has been designed as a management tool.

The Q^{12} items are scored on a 5-point rating scale ranging from 1 ("strongly disagree") to 5 ("strongly agree"). In addition a sixth, unscored response option is included ("don't know/does not apply"). A closer look at the content of the items reveals that, instead of measuring engagement in terms of an employee's involvement, satisfaction, and enthusiasm as is claimed by Harter et al. (2002), the Q^{12} taps the employee's perceived job resources (added by the authors of this chapter in italics and within brackets in Table 2.2). In other words, the Q^{12} assesses the perceived level of resources in the employee's job and not his or her level of engagement. As such, rather than the *experience* of engagement in terms of involvement, satisfaction and enthusiasm, the *antecedents* of engagement in terms of perceived job resources are measured. This is also acknowledged by Harter et al. (2002), who write that the Q^{12} assesses "antecedents to positive affective

TABLE 2.2

Gallup's Q[12©]

1. Do you know what is expected of you at work? (*role clarity*)
2. Do you have the materials and equipment you need to do your work right? (*material resources*)
3. At work, do you have the opportunity to do what you do best every day? (*opportunity for skill development*)
4. In the last seven days, have you received recognition or praise for doing good work? (*social support, positive feedback*)
5. Does your supervisor, or someone at work, seem to care about you as a person? (*supervisor support*)
6. Is there someone at work who encourages your development? (*coaching*)
7. At work, do your opinions seem to count? (*voice*)
8. Does the mission/purpose of your company make you feel your job is important? (*meaningfulness*)
9. Are your associates (fellow employees) committed to doing quality work? (*quality culture*)
10. Do you have a best friend at work? (*social support*)
11. In the last six months, has someone at work talked to you about your progress? (*feedback*)
12. In the last year, have you had opportunities at work to learn and grow? (*learning opportunities*)

constructs as job satisfaction" (p. 209). It is somewhat awkward that in Gallup's definition job satisfaction is considered a hallmark of engagement (see "Engagement in business" above), whereas the Q^{12} measures the *antecedents* of job satisfaction.

Things get even more complicated because of the very high correlation between the Q^{12} and overall job satisfaction as assessed with a single item: "How satisfied are you with <name of company> as a place to work?"). The observed correlation at business-unit level is .77, which increases to .91 after controlling for measurement error (Harter et al., 2002). Moreover, in a study of about 8000 business units with nearly 200,000 employees, the observed correlations with a composite measure of business unit performance were identical for satisfaction and engagement ($r = .22$) (Harter et al., 2002). This means that Gallup's employee engagement concept is virtually identical with overall job satisfaction. As a matter of fact, this is illustrated by the fact that the authors write about "employee satisfaction-engagement" (Harter et al., 2002, p. 269).

Except for the excellent internal consistency at the business-unit level ($\alpha = .91$; Harter et al., 2002) and at the individual level ($\alpha = .88$; Avery, McKay, & Wilson, 2007) no other psychometric data are available for the Q^{12}.

The Utrecht Work Engagement Scale (UWES)

Based on the definition of work engagement that includes vigor, dedication, and absorption, a three-dimensional questionnaire has been developed (Schaufeli & Bakker, 2003; Schaufeli et al., 2002b). Meanwhile, the Utrecht Work Engagement Scale (UWES; see Table 2.3) is available in 21 languages and an international database exists that currently includes engagement records of over 60,000 employees (see www.schaufeli.com). In addition to the original UWES that contains 17 items, a shortened version of 9 items is available (Schaufeli, Bakker, & Salanova, 2006a), as well as a student version (Schaufeli, Martínez, Marques-Pinto, Salanova, & Bakker, 2002a). The UWES items are scored on a 7-point frequency scale ranging from 0 ("never") to 6 ("always").

Factorial validity

Confirmatory factor analyses convincingly show that the hypothesized three-factor structure of the UWES is superior to the one-factor model that assumes an undifferentiated engagement factor. This has been demonstrated in samples from different countries such as China (Yi-Wen & Yi-Qun, 2005), Finland (Seppälä et al., 2009), Greece (Xanthopoulou, Bakker, Kantas, & Demerouti, in press), Portugal (Schaufeli et al., 2002a), Spain (Salanova, Agut, & Peiró, 2005a),

---

TABLE 2.3

The Utrecht Work Engagement Scale (UWES)©

1. At my work, I feel that I am bursting with energy* *(Vi)*
2. I find the work that I do full of meaning and purpose *(De)*
3. Time flies when I'm working *(Ab)*
4. At my job, I feel strong and vigorous *(Vi)**
5. I am enthusiastic about my job *(De)**
6. When I am working, I forget everything else around me *(Ab)*
7. My job inspires me *(De)**
8. When I get up in the morning, I feel like going to work *(Vi)**
9. I feel happy when I am working intensely *(Ab)**
10. I am proud on the work that I do *(De)**
11. I am immersed in my work *(Ab)**
12. I can continue working for very long periods at a time *(Vi)*
13. To me, my job is challenging *(De)*
14. I get carried away when I'm working *(Ab)**
15. At my job, I am very resilient, mentally *(Vi)*
16. It is difficult to detach myself from my job *(Ab)*
17. At my work I always persevere, even when things do not go well *(Vi)*

Note: * Short version; Vi = Vigor; De = Dedication; Ab = Absorption.
Copyright © 2003 Schaufeli & Bakker. All rights reserved.

South Africa (Storm & Rothmann, 2003), Sweden (Hallberg & Schaufeli, 2006), and The Netherlands (Schaufeli & Bakker, 2004; Schaufeli, Taris, & Van Rhenen, 2008; Te Brake, Bouwman, Gorter, Hoogstraten, & Eijkman, 2007). However, it appears that the three dimensions of engagement are very closely related. Usually correlations between the three observed factors exceed .65, whereas correlations between the latent factors range from about .80 to about .90 (e.g., Schaufeli et al., 2002b, 2008; Schaufeli & Bakker, 2004; Hallberg & Schaufeli, 2006; Seppälä et al., 2009). Seen from this perspective, it is not very surprising that Sonnentag (2003), using explorative factor analyses, did *not* find a clear three-factor structure and decided to use the total, composite score of the UWES as a measure for work engagement. In conclusion, work

engagement as assessed by the UWES seems to be a unitary construct that is constituted by three different yet closely related aspects. For that reason Schaufeli et al. (2006a) recommend, particularly for practical purposes, the total score on the UWES as an indicator of work engagement.

Factorial invariance

Confirmatory factor analyses using the so-called multiple group method in which samples of two or more countries are simultaneously included showed that the three-factor structure of the UWES is invariant across nations such as Spain and The Netherlands (Llorens, Salanova, Bakker, & Schaufeli, 2006), Greece and The Netherlands (Xanthopoulou et al., in press), Spain, Portugal and The Netherlands (Schaufeli et al., 2002a), and Australia, Belgium, Canada, Finland, France, Germany, The Netherlands, Norway, South Africa, and Spain (Schaufeli et al., 2006a). More specifically, the three-factor *structure* of the UWES is similar and does not differ between countries but the *values* of the factor loadings and the correlations between the latent factors slightly differ across nations. In a similar vein, Storm and Rothmann (2003) concluded that the equivalence of the UWES is acceptable for White, Black, Colored, and Indian members of the South African Police Service, and that no evidence was found for item-bias in these race groups.

In addition to cross-national invariance, factorial invariance was also demonstrated between various occupational groups, such as Dutch (Schaufeli & Bakker, 2004) and Japanese (Shimazu et al., 2008) white collar employees and health care professionals; Spanish workers and students (Schaufeli et al., 2002b); and Finnish health care workers, educators, and white and blue collar workers (Seppälä et al., 2009). Finally, the last mentioned study demonstrated that the correlated three-factor structure of the short version (but *not* of the original version) of the UWES was invariant across a time interval of 3 years.

In conclusion: the factorial structure of the UWES with three strongly related underlying factors seems to be invariant, both across nations as well as across occupational groups. In addition, as far as the short version of the UWES is concerned this factor structure is also invariant across time.

Internal consistency

Meta-analyses[1] of the original and the short versions of the UWES indicate very good internal consistencies for vigor, dedication, and absorption. More particularly, analyses across thirty-three samples (total N = 19,940) from nine different countries (i.e., Australia, Belgium, Finland, Greece, The Netherlands, Norway, Spain, South Africa, and Sweden) revealed that sample weighted values for Cronbach's α of all three scales of the original and short versions of the UWES exceeds .80. Moreover, Cronbach's α for the composite score exceeds .90.

Hence, it can be concluded that the three scales of the UWES as well as the composite questionnaire are sufficiently internally consistent.

Stability

An analysis[1] across five samples from three countries (i.e., Australia, The Netherlands and Norway; total N = 1057) revealed that the mean stability coefficient of the original and short versions of the UWES across a 1-year time interval is .65 (ranging between .56 and .75). Similar stability coefficients have been observed for burnout (Schaufeli & Enzmann, 1998, pp. 51–52). Recently, Seppälä & Schaufeli (2009) studied the rank-order stability of the UWES that reflects the degree to which the relative ordering of individuals within a group is maintained over time. They found high standardized stability coefficients for the three scales of the short version of the UWES across a 3-year time interval, ranging from .82 to .86. Since the factor structure of the original version of the UWES did not remain invariant across time (see above), its rank-order stability was not assessed.

In conclusion: consistent with the definition of work engagement as a persistent psychological state, UWES scores are relatively stable across time periods up to 3 years.

Discriminant validity

Various studies have been carried out to investigate the extent to which work engagement can be discriminated from related concepts such as:

- *Burnout.* In accordance with the assumption that work engagement is the positive antithesis of burnout, the three dimensions of the UWES are negatively related to the three defining characteristics of burnout as measured with the Maslach Burnout Inventory (MBI; Maslach et al., 1996). Typically, correlations between the engagement and burnout scales range between −.40 and −.60, whereby the correlations of absorption with the MBI scales are occasionally lower and the correlations of lack of efficacy with the UWES scales are occasionally higher (e.g., Andreassen, Ursin, & Eriksen, 2007; Bakker, Van Emmerik, & Euwema, 2006; Te Brake et al., 2007; Durán, Extremera, & Rey, 2004; Jackson, Rothmann, & Van de Vijver, 2006; Langelaan, Bakker, Van Doornen, & Schaufeli, 2006; Salanova, Bresó, & Schaufeli, 2005b; Schaufeli et al., 2008).

Studies using confirmatory factor-analyses showed that, instead of loading on the second-order burnout factor, reduced professional efficacy loads on the second-order engagement factor (Salanova et al., 2005b; Schaufeli et al., 2002b; Te Brake et al., 2007; Schaufeli et al., 2006a; Schaufeli et al., 2008). In these studies the correlations between the latent burnout and engagement factors ranged from −.45 to −.66. One possible explanation for the "wrong" loading of lack of professional efficacy is that it is measured with *reversed positively* formulated items. This explanation is supported by a study of Schaufeli and Salanova (2007) who showed that a factor-analytic model with *in*efficacy (i.e., the negatively reworded MBI-efficacy scale) loading on burnout, and efficacy (i.e., the original MBI-efficacy scale) loading on engagement fit the data of two samples of employees and students from both Spain and The Netherlands.

In sum, as expected, engagement is negatively related with burnout, whereby the unexpected results regarding professional efficacy are likely to (at least partly) result from an artifact caused by the reversing positively phrased items.

- *Personal initiative*. Using a within-group design, Sonnentag (2003) showed that the effect of today's recovery on next day's personal initiative was mediated by the employee's level of work engagement. In a similar vein, Salanova and Schaufeli (2008) provided evidence for the discriminant validity by showing that work engagement fully mediates the relationship between job resources and personal initiative. Observed correlations between personal initiative and engagement ranged in both studies between .38 and .58.
- *Job involvement*. Using confirmatory factor analyses, Hallberg and Schaufeli (2006) showed that engagement and job involvement represent two distinct, weakly related ($r = .35$) concepts. Moreover, work engagement is strongly negatively related to various health complaints and positively related to job resources, whereas job involvement is not, or significantly less strongly related to these variables.
- *Organizational commitment*. The study of Hallberg and Schaufeli (2006) also confirmed the discriminant validity of engagement vis-à-vis organizational commitment. Not only did organizational commitment constitute a separate latent factor that correlated only moderately with engagement ($r = .43$), also a differential pattern of correlations with health complaints and job factors was found. For instance, engagement correlated more negatively with health complaints, whereas organizational commitment showed a higher negative correlation with turnover intention. Typically, observed correlations between the UWES scales and organizational commitment range between .45 and .55 (Demerouti, Bakker, De Jonge, Janssen, & Schaufeli, 2001; Hakanen, Bakker, & Schaufeli, 2006; Jackson et al., 2006; Llorens et al., 2006; Schaufeli et al., 2008).
- *Job satisfaction*. So far, no studies have been carried out on the discriminant validity of engagement and job satisfaction. However, the correlations that have been reported seem to suggest at least some overlap between the two constructs (Schaufeli et al., 2008; Vansteenkiste, Neyrinck, Niemiec, De Witte, & Van den Broeck, 2007).
- *Workaholism*. Confirmatory factor analysis showed that engagement and workaholism (operationalized by working excessively and working compulsively) are two distinct constructs (Schaufeli et al., 2006b; Schaufeli et al., 2008). However, the absorption scale of the UWES has a weak double loading on the latent workaholism factor. This might indicate that absorption could also entail obsession that is characteristic for workaholism. Moreover, Schaufeli et al. (2008) showed that work engagement and workaholism are related to different variables: both types of employees work hard and are loyal to the organization they work for, but in the case of workaholism this comes at the expense of the employee's mental health and social contacts outside work, whereas engaged workers feel quite well, both mentally as well as socially. Finally, Andreassen et al. (2007) found that work engagement is predicted by enjoyment but *not* by drive, being the more typical workaholism component.

In sum: although a partial overlap seems to exist with some elements of workaholism (particularly absorption), it is concluded that engagement can be discriminated from work addiction.

In conclusion: work engagement is negatively associated with burnout. Moreover, it can be clearly distinguished from personal initiative, job involvement and organizational commitment. Although some overlap seems to exist with job satisfaction and workaholism this does not seriously call into question the conceptual distinctness of work engagement.

Questionnaires with limited application
Three questionnaires have only occasionally been used to assess engagement:

- Based on Kahn's (1990, 1992) conceptualization of engagement May, Gilson, and Harter (2004) developed a 13-item scale that consists of three dimensions: cognitive, emotional, and physical engagement. The items of these three scales show a striking resemblance with those included in the absorption, dedication, and vigor scales of the UWES, respectively (see Table 2.3). For instance: "Performing my job is so absorbing that I forget about everything else" (cognitive engagement); "I really put my heart into this job" (emotional engagement); and "I exert a lot of energy performing my job" (physical engagement). Unfortunately instead of three factors only one factor emerged from factor analysis, but the total scale is sufficiently internally consistent ($\alpha = .77$).

- Saks (2006) distinguished between job engagement and organizational engagement that are described as employees': "psychological presence in their job and their organization" (p. 608), respectively. Job engagement is measured with five items (e.g., "Sometimes I am so into my job that I lose track of time"; $\alpha = .82$) and organization engagement is measured with six items (e.g., "One of the most exciting things to me is getting involved with things happening in this organization" $\alpha = .90$). Both aspects of engagement are moderately highly related with each other ($r = .62$) and show different patterns of relationships with antecedents and outcomes, thus suggesting conceptual distinctness.

- Also basing herself on the work of Kahn (1990, 1992), Rothbard (2001) distinguished two separate but related components of role engagement: attention and absorption. Attention refers to cognitive availability and the amount of time one spends thinking about the work role, whereas absorption means being engrossed in the work role. Attention is measured with four items (e.g., "I spend a lot of time thinking about my work"; $\alpha = .74$) and absorption is measured with five items (e.g., "When I am working I am totally absorbed by it"; $\alpha = .65$). Although both aspects of engagement are moderately correlated ($r = .56$) they seem to play a different role in the dynamics of engagement in work and family roles.

All three operationalizations agree that engagement is a multidimensional construct and that it includes absorption as its common denominator. Tellingly, absorption is also included as a separate dimension in the UWES, which is the most widely used engagement questionnaire.

Towards an integration

As we have seen in this chapter, work engagement has been conceptualized and operationalized in several different ways. Unfortunately, these differences do not permit the formulation of a synthetic definition of work engagement which includes all major elements that have been proposed. Instead we suggest a model that integrates our notion of work engagement with several related, overlapping concepts that have been discussed previously. Recently, in an attempt to "untangle the jangle", Macey and Schneider (2008) took a quite different approach. They used a very broad description of engagement as "a desirable condition [that] has an organizational purpose, and connotes involvement, commitment, passion, enthusiasm, focused effort, and energy" (p. 4). Their conceptual framework for understanding employee engagement includes: (1) trait engagement (e.g., conscientiousness, trait positive affect, proactive personality); (2) state engagement (e.g., satisfaction, involvement, empowerment); (3) behavioral engagement (e.g., extra-role behavior, proactivity, role expansion). Consequently, as Saks (2008) has criticized, "engagement" serves as an umbrella term for whatever one wants it to be, In contrast, we propose a model of employee motivation with work engagement as a psychological state that mediates the impact of job resources and personal resources on organizational outcomes (see Figure 2.1; see also Bakker, 2009). So unlike Macey and Schneider (2008), who present a taxonomy that covers a wide range of concepts which – in one way or another – refer to engagement, we present an integrative model of work motivation in which engagement – as defined in this chapter – plays a key role.

In fact, Figure 2.1 represents the motivational process of the job demands-resources (JD-R) model, which assumes that job resources have

FIGURE 2.1

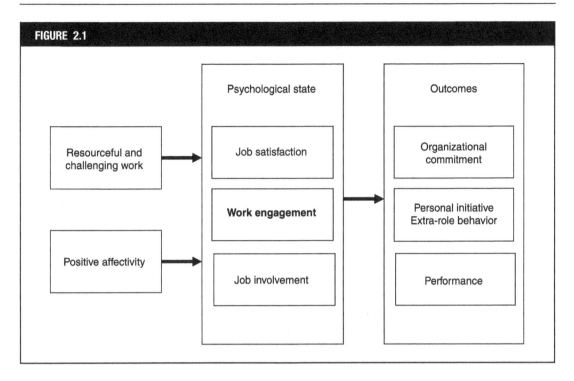

An integrative model of work motivation and engagement.

motivational potential and lead to high work engagement and excellent performance, respectively (Bakker & Demerouti, 2007). According to the JD-R model job resources may either play an intrinsic motivational role because they foster an employee's growth, learning, and development, or play an extrinsic role because they are instrumental in achieving work goals. Recently, Xanthopoulou, Bakker, Demerouti, and Schaufeli (2007) extended the JD-R model by including personal resources such as optimism, self-efficacy, and self-esteem that are assumed to have similar motivational potential.

The focal psychological state in Figure 2.1 is work engagement, which includes a behavioral-energetic (vigor), an emotional (dedication), and a cognitive (absorption) component. It seems that – despite minor differences – the two academic approaches that are discussed in the section "Engagement in academia" agree on this three-dimensional conceptualization of engagement. Job satisfaction and job involvement are psychological states that show some conceptual as well

as empirical overlap with work engagement and are therefore likely to play a similar mediating role. Job satisfaction and work engagement share positive affects, but in the former case they refer to low intensity affect (e.g., contentment), whereas in the latter case they refer to high intensity affect (e.g., excitement). Job involvement and work engagement are both defined in terms of identification. In sum, job satisfaction and job involvement share some meaning with work engagement but cannot be reduced to it.

According to the JD-R model, both job resources and personal resources foster work engagement. The Gallup Organization defines employee engagement in terms of resourceful work, considering it an antecedent for both positive affective outcomes such as job satisfaction as well as business-unit performance (Harter et al., 2002). Thus Gallup's conceptualization of engagement fits into Figure 2.1, namely as resourceful and challenging work. Being a personal resource, positive affectivity includes similar affects as work engagement, but at a dispositional rather than a state level. This means that employees who are characterized by positive affectivity are more likely to be engaged with their jobs. For instance, Langelaan et al. (2006) showed that work engagement is positively and substantially related to extraversion, commonly considered an indicator of positive affectivity.

Studies using the JD-R model showed that work engagement is associated with organizational outcomes such as organizational commitment (Hakanen et al., 2006; Schaufeli & Bakker, 2004), extra-role behavior (Bakker, Demerouti, & Verbeke, 2004), personal initiative (Salanova & Schaufeli, 2008), and performance (Salanova et al., 2005a; Xanthopoulou, Bakker, Demerouti, & Schaufeli, 2009). So it appears that both theoretically – based on the JD-R model – and empirically work engagement can be distinguished from various organizational outcomes. This is at odds with the view of most major consultancy firms who define engagement simply in terms of such outcomes as commitment and/or extra-role behavior. In contrast, we maintain that work engagement is the psychological state that accompanies the behavioral investment of personal energy, but does neither coincide with the (extra-role) behavior itself nor with the concomitant attitudes (organizational commitment).

We believe that our approach to define work engagement as a *specific* psychological state that is related to *specific* antecedents and outcomes is superior to other approaches that either serve old wine in new bottles (as in business) or serve a rather undefined cocktail (i.e., use engagement as a general umbrella term). The reason for this is three-fold: (1) theoretically speaking, our model identifies an underlying motivational process; (2) empirically speaking, our model allows us to formulate and test specific hypotheses, for instance about similarities and dissimilarities of work engagement with other related concepts; (3) practically speaking, based on our model specific kinds of interventions can be envisaged, for instance about ways to increase the resources of employees' jobs.

Note

1. Details of the meta-analyses can be obtained from the first author of this chapter.

References

Andreassen, C. S., Ursin, H., & Eriksen, H. R. (2007). The relationship between strong motivation to work, "workaholism", and health. *Psychology and Health*, *22*, 615–629.

Avery, D. R., McKay, P. F., & Wilson, D. C. (2007). Engaging the aging workforce: The relationship between perceived age similarity, satisfaction with coworkers and employee engagement. *Journal of Applied Psychology*, *92*, 1542–1556.

Bakker, A. B. (2009). Building engagement in the workplace. In R. J. Burke & C. L. Cooper (Eds.), *The peak performing organization* (pp. 50–72). Oxon, UK: Routledge.

Bakker, A. B., & Demerouti, E. (2007). The Job Demands-Resources model: State of the art. *Journal of Managerial Psychology*, *22*, 309–328.

Bakker, A. B., Demerouti, E., & Verbeke, W. (2004). Using the Job Demands-Resources model to predict burnout and performance. *Human Resource Management*, *43*, 83–104.

Bakker, A. B., Van Emmerik, H., & Euwema, M. C. (2006). Crossover of burnout and engagement in work teams. *Work and Occupations*, *33*, 464–489.

Buckingham, M., & Coffman, C. (1999). *First, break all the rules: What the world's greatest managers do differently*. New York: Simon & Schuster.

Csikszentmihalyi, M. (1990). *Flow: The psychology of optimal experience*. New York: Harper & Row.

Demerouti, E., Bakker, A. B., De Jonge, J., Janssen, P. P. M., & Schaufeli, W. B. (2001). Burnout and engagement at work as a function of demands and control. *Scandinavian Journal of Work, Environment and Health*, *27*, 279–286.

Durán, A., Extremera, N., & Rey, L. (2004). Engagement and burnout: Analyzing their association patterns. *Psychological Reports*, *94*, 1048–1050.

Frese, M., & Fay, D. (2001). Personal initiative: An active performance concept for work in the 21st century. In B. M. Staw & R. M. Sutton (Eds.), *Research in organizational behavior* (Vol. 23, pp. 133–187). Amsterdam: Elsevier.

González-Romá, V., Schaufeli, W. B., Bakker, A. B., & Lloret, S. (2006). Burnout and engagement: Independent factors or opposite poles? *Journal of Vocational Behavior*, *68*, 165–174.

Hakanen, J. J., Bakker, A. B., & Schaufeli, W. B. (2006).

Burnout and work engagement among teachers. *Journal of School Psychology, 43*, 495–513.

Hallberg, U., & Schaufeli, W. B. (2006). "Same same" but different: Can work engagement be discriminated from job involvement and organizational commitment? *European Journal of Psychology, 11*, 119–127.

Harter, J. K., Schmidt, F. L., & Hayes, T. L. (2002). Business-unit-level relationships between employee satisfaction, employee engagement, and business outcomes: A meta-analysis. *Journal of Applied Psychology, 87*, 268–279.

Harter, J. K., Schmidt, F. L. Killham, E. A., & Asplund, J. W. (2006). *Q¹² meta-analysis*. Princeton, NJ: The Gallup Organization.

Jackson, L. T. B., Rothmann, S. R., & Van de Vijver, F. J. R. (2006). A model of work related well-being for educators in South-Africa. *Stress and Health, 22*, 263–274.

Kahn, W. A. (1990). Psychological conditions of personal engagement and disengagement at work. *Academy of Management Journal, 33*, 692–724.

Kahn, W. A. (1992). To be fully there: Psychological presence at work. *Human Relations, 45*, 321–349.

Langelaan, S., Bakker, A. B., Van Doornen, L. J. P., & Schaufeli, W. B. (2006). Burnout and work engagement: Do individual differences make a difference? *Personality and Individual Differences, 40*, 521–532.

Llorens, S., Bakker, A. B., Schaufeli, W. B., & Salanova, M. (2006). Testing the robustness of the Job Demands-resources model. *International Journal of Stress Management, 13*, 378–391.

Locke, E. A. (1976). The nature and causes of job satisfaction. In M. Dunette (Ed.), *Handbook of industrial and organizational psychology* (pp. 1297–1349). Chicago: Rand-McNally.

Lodahl, T. M., & Kejner, M. (1965). The definition and measurement of job involvement. *Journal of Applied Psychology, 49*, 24–33.

Macey, W. H. & Schneider, B. (2008). The meaning of employee engagement. *Industrial and Organizational Psychology, 1*, 3–30.

Maslach, C., Jackson, S. E., & Leiter, M. P. (1996). *The Maslach Burnout Inventory* (3rd ed.). Palo Alto, CA: Consulting Psychologists Press.

Maslach, C., & Leiter, M. P. (1997). *The truth about burnout*. San Francisco, CA: Jossey-Bass.

Maslach, C., Schaufeli, W. B., & Leiter, M. P. (2001). Job burnout. *Annual Review of Psychology, 52*, 397–422.

May, D. R., Gilson, R. L., & Harter, L. M. (2004). The psychological conditions of meaningfulness, safety and availability and the engagement of the human spirit at work. *Journal of Occupational and Organizational Psychology, 77*, 11–37.

Mowday, R. T., Steers, R. M., & Porter, L. W. (1979). The measurement of organizational commitment. *Journal of Vocational Behavior, 14*, 224–247.

Organ, D. W. (1997). Organizational citizenship behavior: It's construct cleanup time. *Human Performance, 10*, 85–97.

Rothbard, N. P. (2001). "Enriching or depleting?" The dynamics of engagement in work and family roles. *Administrative Science Quarterly, 46*, 655–684.

Saks, A. M. (2006). Antecedents and consequences of employee engagement. *Journal of Managerial Psychology, 21*, 600–619.

Saks, A. M. (2008). The meaning and bleeding of employee engagement: How muddy is the water? *Industrial and Organizational Psychology, 1*, 40–43.

Salanova, M., Agut, S., & Peiró, J. M. (2005a). Linking organizational resources and work engagement to employee performance and customer loyalty: The mediation of service climate. *Journal of Applied Psychology, 90*, 1217–1227.

Salanova, M., Bresó, E., & Schaufeli, W. B. (2005b). Hacia un modelo espiral de la autoeficacia en el estudio del burnout y engagement [Towards a spiral model of self-efficacy in burnout and engagement research]. *Estress y Anxiedad, 11*, 215–231.

Salanova, M., & Schaufeli, W. B. (2008). A cross-national study of work engagement as a mediator between job resources and proactive behavior. *International Journal of Human Resources Management, 19*, 116–131.

Schaufeli, W. B., & Bakker, A. B. (2003). *Utrecht Work Engagement Scale: Preliminary Manual*. Department of Psychology, Utrecht University, The Netherlands (available from www.schaufeli.com)

Schaufeli, W. B., & Bakker, A. B. (2004). Job demands, job resources and their relationship with burnout and engagement: A multi-sample study. *Journal of Organizational Behavior, 25*, 293–315.

Schaufeli, W. B., Bakker, A. B., & Salanova, M. (2006a). The measurement of work engagement with a short questionnaire: A cross-national study. *Educational and Psychological Measurement, 66*, 701–716.

Schaufeli, W. B., & Enzmann, D. (1998). *The burnout companion to study and research: A critical analysis*. London: Taylor & Francis.

Schaufeli, W. B., Martínez, I., Marques Pinto, A., Salanova, M., & Bakker, A. B. (2002a). Burnout and engagement in university students: A cross national study. *Journal of Cross-Cultural Psychology, 33*, 464–481.

Schaufeli, W. B., & Salanova, M. (2007). Efficacy or inefficacy, that's the question: Burnout and work engagement, and their relationship with efficacy beliefs. *Anxiety, Stress, & Coping, 20*, 177–196.

Schaufeli, W. B., Salanova, M., González-Romá, V., & Bakker, A. B. (2002b). The measurement of engagement and burnout: A confirmative analytic approach. *Journal of Happiness Studies, 3*, 71–92.

Schaufeli, W. B., & Taris, T. W. (2005). The conceptualization and measurement of burnout: Common ground and worlds apart. *Work & Stress, 19*, 356–362.

Schaufeli, W. B., Taris, T. W., & Bakker, A. B. (2006b). Dr. Jekyll or Mr. Hyde: On the differences between work engagement and workaholism. In: R. Burke (Ed.), *Work hours and work addiction* (pp. 193–252). Northampton, MA: Edward Elgar.

Schaufeli, W. B., Taris, T. W., & Van Rhenen, W. (2008). Workaholism, burnout and engagement: Three of a kind or three different kinds of employee well-being? *Applied Psychology: An International Review, 57*, 173–203.

Schaufeli, W. B., Taris, T., Le Blanc, P., Peeters, M., Bakker, A., & De Jonge, J. (2001). Maakt arbeid gezond? Op zoek naar de bevlogen werknemer [Does work make healthy? In search of the engaged worker]. *De Psycholoog, 36*, 422–428.

Seppälä, P., & Schaufeli, W. B. (2009). The construct validity of the Utrecht Work Engagement Scale: Multisample and longitudinal evidence. *Journal of Happiness Studies, 10*, 459–481.

Shimazu, A., Schaufeli, W. B., Kosugi, S., Suzuki, A., Nashiwa, H., Kato, A., et al. (2008). Work engagement in Japan: Development and validation of the Japanese version of the Utrecht Work Engagement Scale. *Journal of Applied Psychology: An International Review, 57*, 510–523.

Sonnentag, S. (2003). Recovery, work engagement, and proactive behavior: A new look at the interface between non-work and work. *Journal of Applied Psychology, 88*, 518–528.

Storm, K., & Rothmann, I. (2003). A psychometric analysis of the Utrecht Work Engagement Scale in the South African police service. *South African Journal of Industrial Psychology, 29*, 62–70.

Te Brake, J. H., Bouwman, A. M., Gorter, R. C., Hoogstraten, J., & Eijkman, M. A. J. (2007). Professional burnout and work engagement among dentists. *European Journal of Oral Science, 115*, 180–185.

Vallerand, R. J., Blanchard, C., Mageau, G. A., Koestner, R., Ratelle, C., Léonard, M., et al. (2003). Les passions de l'âme: On obsessive and harmonious passion. *Journal of Personality and Social Psychology, 85*, 756–767.

Vansteenkiste, M., Neyrinck, B., Niemiec, C. P., De Witte, H., & Van den Broeck, A. (2007). On the relationship between work value orientations, psychological need satisfaction and job outcomes: A self-determination theory approach. *Journal of Occupational and Organizational Psychology, 80*, 251–277.

Watson, D., Clark, L. A., & Tellegen, A. (1988). Development and validation of brief measures of positive and negative affect: The PANAS scales. *Journal of Personality and Social Psychology, 54*, 1063–1070.

Xanthopoulou, D., Bakker, A. B., Demerouti, E. & Schaufeli, W. B. (2007). The role of personal resources in the Job Demands-Resources model. *International Journal of Stress Management, 14*, 121–141.

Xanthopoulou, D., Bakker, A. B., Kantas, A., & Demerouti, E. (in press). The measurement of burnout and work engagement: A comparison of Greece and The Netherlands. *New Review of Social Psychology*.

Xanthopoulou, D., Bakker, A. B., Demerouti, E., & Schaufeli, W. B. (2009). Work engagement and financial returns: A diary study on the role of job and personal resources. *Journal of Organizational and Occupational Psychology, 82*, 183–200.

Yi-Wen, Z., & Yi-Qun, C. (2005). The Chinese version of the Utrecht Work Engagement Scale: An examination of reliability and validity. *Chinese Journal of Clinical Psychology, 13*, 268–270.

Not all days are created equal: The concept of state work engagement

Sabine Sonnentag, Christian Dormann, and Evangelia Demerouti

Work engagement is a broad concept, comprising a variety of multidimensional constructs and experiences, including affects, cognitions, and behaviors. The concept of work engagement has also been characterized by using a variety of time perspectives ranging from trait concepts (comprising stable positive views of life and work), to state and state-like concepts (e.g., feelings of energy or absorption; e.g., Schaufeli & Bakker, 2004; Macey & Schneider, 2008). In the following, we will delineate how, in our view, state work engagement (SWE) is best conceptualized. We will do so by briefly reviewing different conceptualizations of SWE and different perspectives on time-related issues. Afterwards, we continue our introduction by explaining why a state perspective of engagement is important and by summarizing existing evidence that supports such a state perspective. In subsequent sections, we will address methodological issues that pertain to the study of state engagement, and we will summarize existing evidence from diary studies in order to finally come up with a comprehensive model of state work engagement, its potential antecedents, and its consequences.

Conceptualization and definition

To illustrate the importance of focusing on SWE let us think how we would answer the question "How do you do at work?" The answer to this question may reflect temporal reports regarding recent personal experiences rather than one's past general status. The trait-level or between-person view answers questions like why one person feels engaged at work while other persons do not. The state-level or within-person view answers questions like why one person feels more engaged at work on specific days and on other days not. Building on the existing knowledge of trait work engagement, our aim is to introduce SWE and its conceptualization, to review the piecemeal evidence on SWE, and to suggest a framework that may facilitate future studies on SWE.

In their review of several conceptual definitions, Macey and Schneider (2008) portrayed engagement as an attitude-like construct. Opposed to the tripartite model of attitudes but in line with other job-related motivational concepts (e.g., job satisfaction), they distinguished between the attitudinal component (i.e., cognitions and affects) of engagement and its behavioral consequences (e.g., extra-role activities). In addition, most definitions of engagement can comprehensively be described as made up of attitudes (or their components) plus some additional features. These additional features frequently encompass the energetic aspect and the involvement of the self. For instance, in his seminal work, Kahn (1990, p. 692) proposed that "People can use varying degrees of their selves, physically, cognitively, and emotionally, in the roles they perform . . . the more people draw on their selves to perform their roles . . . the more stirring are their performances." Thus, the conceptual space in which engagement is located comprises a motivational dimension including an energetic/activation facet and a self-involvement facet, and an attitudinal dimension including a cognitive facet and an affective facet. In line with Macey and Schneider, we do not include a behavioral facet in our concept of engagement. Behaviors should be seen as potential outcomes of work engagement and not as constituent parts.

As with positive affect (PA) and negative affect (NA), where studies have distinguished between a trait and a state perspective (e.g., Niklas & Dormann, 2005), a similar distinction can be made with regard to work engagement. This is not commonly done yet, however. For instance, Macey and Schneider describe state engagement as "relatively durable over time" (p. 13) and thereby explicitly neglect more transient forms of work engagement that fluctuate within persons within relatively short periods of time (as do Schaufeli, Salanova, González-Romá, & Bakker, 2002). Others viewed work engagement as a state that can vary within persons over short periods of time (Dalal, Brummel, Wee, & Thomas, 2008; Sonnentag, 2003). This characterization mirrors other descriptions of the state–trait continuum. In line with other descriptions of trait–state continua (Luthans, Avolio, Avey, & Norman, 2007; cf. also Chen, Gully, & Eden, 2001), we want to focus on state work engagement as transient experiences that fluctuate within individuals over time.

We believe that a state perspective on work engagement is particularly worthwhile. Following the three-dimensional conceptualization of Schaufeli and colleagues (e.g., Schaufeli & Bakker, 2004; Schaufeli et al., 2002), work engagement is defined as a state characterized by vigor, dedication, and absorption. Similar to this definition of work engagement, definitions of many constructs frequently leave open the question as to whether they describe a phenomenological experience (experiential state) or a hypothetical concept. To reflect an experiential state, ideally all three facets of work engagement should be *simultaneously* present (i.e., vigor *and* dedication *and* absorption at the same time). However, when individuals recall their experiences over an extended time period in the past (e.g., a couple of days), they could possibly score high on all three facets of engagement without ever having experienced them simultaneously. Hence, if one aims at investigating the full phenomenological experience of work engagement, one has to focus on state work engagement as a rather momentary and transient experience that fluctuates within individuals within short periods of time (i.e., from minute to minute or from hour to hour, perhaps from day to day). In the present chapter, we follow such a state perspective.

Relevance

Although the general approach of examining fluctuations of experiences and behaviors within persons (e.g., Bolger, DeLongis, Kessler, & Schilling, 1989; Hormuth, 1986) is not new, in recent years researchers in work and organizational psychology and related fields became increasingly interested in such within-person processes (Beal, Weiss, Barros, & MacDermid, 2005; Ilies, Schwind, & Heller, 2007; Weiss & Cropanzano, 1996).

Most important, however, are the conceptual and theoretical prospects associated with such a within-person perspective. First, the within-person approach allows for a closer look at temporal patterns of work-related experiences and behaviors. As demonstrated in the previous section, individuals are not equally engaged at work across all days. There are days (or weeks) on which employees feel more vigorous, absorbed and dedicated than on other days (or weeks). As explained above, "averaging" across these situations by assessing a general level of work engagement (i.e., by asking individuals to provide retrospective reports over the previous months or even the year and providing summary accounts of their psychological states) ignores the dynamic and configurational part of the work engagement phenomenon.

Second, the within-person approach enables us to examine – in addition to general predictors such as stable resources specified in the job demands-resources model (Bakker & Demerouti, 2007) – the more proximal predictors of work engagement. Thus, this approach promises answers to the question: when do people feel work engagement? Are there specific situational features that have to be present during a specific day in order to feel engaged? For example, one could imagine that not only a generally high level of resources such as appreciation by one's co-workers (Bakker, Hakanen, Demerouti, & Xanthopoulou, 2007), but also a supportive comment and encouraging feedback from one's co-workers or supervisor on a specific day increases work engagement. Similarly: are there person-specific states that foster work engagement during a specific day or week? For example, it might be that not only generally high levels of self-efficacy are

important for work engagement (Schaufeli & Salanova, 2007), but that a person has to be self-efficacious about his or her task on a specific day in order to feel engaged during that day.

Third, as an experiential state, SWE is probably much more causally tied to real work-related events and behavioral outcomes than a judgment that requires aggregating previous experiences over an extended period of time. Consequently, investigating SWE may yield much stronger evidence of its antecedents and consequences than investigating its trait-like counterpart. Investigating SWE may, additionally, provide evidence for different causal antecedents and consequences because it might involve fewer human judgmental processes and errors than more trait-like conceptualizations and, therefore, might better reflect true causal relations. Investigating SWE is perhaps even more important than investigating trait engagement; while SWE as an experiential state is a continuous stream of reflections on our work-life and, thus, part of our very existence, trait engagement is perhaps only present in those few times when we actively reflect on our past work experiences. In other words, trait work engagement might be seen as a cognitive construction of a not really existing phenomenon, which is based on a bias-prone recall of previous experiences. Probably, trait work engagement reflects more of an attitude, whereas SWE reflects a vivid experience.

Thus, from a conceptual and theoretical point of view, the within-person approach is essential for developing a more comprehensive understanding of the work engagement phenomenon. In addition, research following this within-person approach is also practically relevant. In many work settings there are specific times and periods when it is necessary that employees are particularly engaged at work, for example when making an important presentation to a potential future customer, when entering a critical stage in a difficult project, or when facing other novel and challenging job requirements. Knowledge about the more proximal situational and person-related predictors of work engagement is crucial to create a setting that optimally supports work engagement during such critical times and periods.

Moreover, investigating the determinants of daily or weekly fluctuations of work engagement allows us to uncover whether theoretical models used to explain trait work engagement are also applicable when adopting a micro-level (i.e., within-person) perspective. There is a strong need to theoretically and empirically investigate the structural similarities of state- and trait-engagement models. A failure to demonstrate such structural similarities might evoke the necessity to develop new theories and models when studying SWE.

In our view, the state approach to work engagement should complement – rather than replace – the more traditional trait approach that analyzes a person's more general level of work engagement. Both approaches are necessary and provide unique perspectives on a complex phenomenon.

Empirical evidence

Diaries represent a proper method to collect information about within-person experiences. In particular, quantitative diary studies have become popular research methods in order to collect frequent reports on the events and experiences of people's daily lives (Bolger, Davis, & Rafaeli, 2003). Such studies have demonstrated that work engagement fluctuates substantially within individuals. For example, Sonnentag (2003) assessed work engagement in 147 public service employees over the course of five working days and found that 42% of the overall variance was at the day (i.e., within-individual) level and 58% of the overall variance was at the between-individual level. Similarly, Xanthopoulou, Bakker, Heuven, Demerouti, and Schaufeli (2008), who studied 44 flight attendants during three flights to intercontinental destinations, reported that 41% of the overall variance in work engagement was attributable to within-person variation. A slightly smaller percentage was found by Xanthopoulou, Bakker, Demerouti, and Schaufeli (2009) in their study of 42 employees of a fast food restaurant (31%). Empirical research suggests that work engagement not only fluctuates from day to day, but also from week to week. Bakker and Bal (in press) examined work engagement in 54 teachers over the course of five working weeks and took

weekly measures on work engagement on Friday. Here, 35% of the total variance was attributable to within-person variation. Taken together, these studies show that at least one third of the total variance in day-specific and week-specific work engagement is within-person variance. Thus, although individuals clearly differ in their overall level of work engagement (also expressed in the 58 to 69% of total variance that is attributable to between-person variation), day-level and week-level studies suggest that individuals do not engage in their work to the same degree on every day; work engagement shows substantial variation across time.

At first glance, this finding might contradict findings from longitudinal research on work engagement that reported within-person stabilities of work engagement ranging between $r = .45$ and $r = .74$ (Mauno, Kinnunen, & Ruokolainen, 2007). These two sets of findings, however, do not necessarily contradict each other. Whereas results from the longitudinal studies show that the general level of a person's work engagement is relatively stable, day-level and week-level studies demonstrate that there is systematic fluctuation around the person-specific general work engagement level within the person. The high stability of work engagement in longitudinal studies is probably due to the fact that people tend to report the levels of work engagement they *normally* experience (which differs from person to person, cf. 58% between-person variation) and not their work engagement on a specific day. Furthermore, we have to explicitly take into account that even when fluctuations in SWE exist, SWE is also affected by trait work engagement. Consequently, trait work engagement has to be statistically partialled out when changes in SWE are used to estimate the natural variability within persons across time.

Methodological issues

Researchers examining engagement as a state have to address a number of methodological issues. The most important ones refer to the measurement of state engagement and to issues of study design and data analysis.

With respect to the measurement of state

engagement, it should be taken for granted that work engagement is assessed as a state (i.e., an experience present during a specific moment or even a day) – as opposed to work engagement experienced over longer periods of time. In most studies, items used in research on trait engagement are modified to make them applicable for measuring day-specific levels of engagement. For example, items used in studies examining state engagement explicitly refer to a specific day ("today", Sonnentag, 2003; Xanthopoulou et al., 2009) or even shorter time frames (i.e., several hours, Bledow, Schmitt, & Frese, 2008). Although this measurement approach seems rather straightforward, it is not without problems as so far it remains largely unclear to what extent the experience of work engagement at the day level, for instance, mirrors work engagement as assessed as a trait. Some items of the existing scales capturing trait work engagement might be inappropriate to be answered on a daily basis. People may have different experiences on a certain day than over a longer-term time frame; for instance, they can be enthusiastic about a specific work task (daily basis) but not about their work tasks in general (longer-term). More research is needed that examines whether the quality and configuration of state engagement is identical to the quality and configuration of trait engagement. This raises also the issue of the content and factorial validity and reliability of modified trait work engagement scales to SWE measures. Interestingly, studies that assessed SWE used an overall measure of work engagement and did not differentiate between the three components vigor, dedication, and absorption. Clearly, additional work on the construct validity of SWE is needed.

Studies that examine fluctuations of work engagement within individuals assess work engagement along with its predictors and outcomes multiple times, for example once every working day over the course of one or two weeks. Here, more frequent assessments are possible and often desirable. With respect to study design, it is important to keep in mind that assessing work engagement, its predictors and outcomes at the same point in time (e.g., in the evening at the end

of the working day) still is a (within-day) cross-sectional design. Thus, no conclusions can be drawn if the (assumed) predictors of work engagement are really precursors of work engagement – it cannot be ruled out that they are a consequence of work engagement or that work engagement and its (assumed) predictors are influenced by one joint third variable. Thus, ideally, work engagement and it predictors and consequences should be assessed at different points in time during each day; and when analyzing such data, the work engagement level of the previous measurement occasion should be used as a control variable. As such multiple measures are rather difficult to obtain, studies often use less frequent measures, making the conclusion not always non-equivocal.

One important issue when analyzing within-person processes refers to the statistical treatment of data. Basically, having repeated measures at hand, two approaches might be used. One approach is based on longitudinal regression analyses and related techniques (e.g., structural equation modeling), and the other approach employs hierarchical linear models and the like (e.g., variance component models). In almost all instances, researchers chose the latter approach and they analyzed the data with software programs such as HLM or MLWin. In this approach, multiple measures of independent (IV) and dependent variables (DV) obtained for each person are used to estimate the relation between IV and DV for each person as well as for the entire sample. Within this group of statistical analyses, an important question is how to center the predictor variables (Ilies et al., 2007). Basically, researchers follow one of two approaches: they center the predictor variables around the grand mean (Hofmann & Gavin, 1998; i.e., subtract each observation of the predictor variable from the sample mean of this variable), mainly in order to reduce problems associated with multicollinearity, or they center the predictor variables around the respective person mean (i.e., subtract each observation of the predictor variable from each participant's person-specific mean of this variable). This approach eliminates all between-variance in the predictor variables and "strictly reflects intraindividual processes" (Ilies et al., 2007, p. 335).

The centering decision is not just a "technical issue", but refers to substantially different research questions. Whereas one method of centering the data (grand-mean centering) basically allows for conclusions about differences between persons, another method (person-mean centering) allows for conclusions about fluctuations within persons. Thus, the first method is appropriate when one is interested in a research question such as "how is day-specific social support provided by one's peers related to day-specific work engagement?" (i.e., one will analyze the extent to which people receiving more day-specific social support will experience higher levels of day-specific work engagement). The second method is needed when one is interested in a research question such as "do persons on days when they received more social support than they normally receive experience higher levels of work engagement?" (i.e., one will analyze the extent to which the relative level of social support within the person matters for work engagement, irrespective of this person's average level of work engagement).

Predictors of state engagement

In the previous section, we summarized research showing that work engagement fluctuates within individuals, with more than one third of the overall variance of work engagement being attributable to within-person variation. Studies have demonstrated that this within-person variation is not just random, but can be partially explained by variations of within-person predictors. In this section, we summarize empirical findings on predictors of day-level or week-level engagement.

Most of the studies that examined day-level predictors of work engagement concentrated on day-specific states of the person, such as day-level recovery, day-level self-efficacy and other states. In some studies, also variations in job situation variables have been considered as predictors of within-person variability of SWE. In her study of public service employees, Sonnentag (2003) addressed day-level recovery as a potential predictor of day-level SWE. Day-level recovery refers

to a person's experience that he or she has unwound from yesterday's job stress and now feels refreshed. In this study, day-level recovery was assessed in the morning before the start of the working day, and SWE was assessed in the afternoon at the end of the working day. Multi-level modeling using person-mean centered scores of day-level recovery showed that day-level SWE was significantly higher on days when employees felt recovered in the morning, compared to days when they did not feel well recovered. This finding reflects our conceptual definition of SWE, according to which some form of energy is required to experience vigor, dedication, and absorption.

Bakker, van Emmerik, Geurts, & Demerouti, (2008) started from a similar research question and examined day-level recovery (assessed in the morning before work) as a predictor of day-level SWE (assessed in the evening after work) in a sample of assembly line workers. Multi-level analysis showed that day-level recovery in the morning predicted SWE during the day. Moreover, Bakker et al. identified an interesting interaction effect with job demands. Employees who faced high job demands and who were at the same time highly recovered in the morning experienced the highest level of SWE during the day. The authors concluded from this finding that recovery turns high job demands into challenges, which further enhances the experience of SWE on a specific day.

These findings can be interpreted within the conservation of resources (COR) framework (Hobfoll, 1998). Recovery during leisure time builds up resources that in turn facilitate SWE (Bakker & Demerouti, 2007). Studies have found evidence for a relation between resources and work engagement when following a between-person approach (Hakanen, Perhoniemi, & Toppinen-Tammer, 2008). Xanthopoulou and her co-workers, however, addressed this question at the within-person level. In two studies they examined if day-level personal resources predict day-level SWE.

In the above-mentioned study with flight attendants, Xanthopoulou et al. (2008) examined state self-efficacy before the flight as a predictor of SWE during the flight. Multi-level analyses showed that state self-efficacy before the flight predicted SWE during the flight. In the second study among employees from a fast-food restaurant, Xanthopoulou et al. (2009) extended the scope of the personal-resource variables included in the study. In addition to day-level self-efficacy, they also assessed day-level organizational-based self-esteem and optimism in the evenings of the working days and centered these variables around each participant's individual mean. All three personal resources were significant positive predictors of day-level SWE. Thus, the more self-efficacious a person felt, the more organization-based self-esteem he or she experienced, and the more optimistic he or she was on the specific day, the higher was the level of SWE during this specific day. This result reflects our conceptual definition of SWE, according to which the involvement of the self, such as feeling self-efficacious and esteemed helps to experience vigor, dedication, and absorption. Conversely, on a day when a job overtaxes one's resources or when it does not support one's self-esteem, it is unlikely that an individual experiences SWE.

Although, strictly speaking, a strong conclusion about causality cannot be drawn from these findings, these studies as a whole suggest that personal resources most probably foster day-level SWE. The degree to which a person feels recovered may be seen as a more distal predictor of SWE. It is plausible to assume that recovery increases day-level resources such as day-level self-efficacy. Day-level self-efficacy and related resources in turn may help one to fully concentrate on one's work, thus to be dedicated and get absorbed in what one is doing at the moment. In addition to the personal resources addressed in these studies (Xanthopoulou et al., 2008, 2009), there might be also other personal resources such as physical (stamina), cognitive (ability to concentrate), and emotional energy (Shirom, 2007; Chapter 6, this volume) or positive emotions in general (Fredrickson, 1998) that increase SWE, particularly the vigor component. Support for this interpretation that positive emotions are important for work engagement comes from an experience sampling study with 55 software

developers (Bledow et al., 2008). Study participants completed a web-based survey twice a day over a period of nine working days. State positive emotions, but not state negative emotions predicted SWE.

In their study with employees in the fast-food restaurants, Xanthoupoulou and her co-workers (2009) looked not only at personal resources but also at job resources. More specifically, they examined day-specific autonomy, coaching and team climate as predictors of day-level SWE. Analyses showed that all three job resources predicted day-level SWE. Interestingly, the effects of autonomy and coaching were fully mediated by day-specific levels of personal resources. This finding might imply that availability of job resources at the day level stimulates small changes in day-level self-efficacy, self-esteem, and optimism – or at least the awareness of these personal resources – which in turn stimulates SWE.

Bakker and Bal (in press) examined predictors of week-level SWE in teachers and also focused on job resources. They found that week-level autonomy, week-level exchange with the supervisor, and week-level opportunities for development, but not week-level social support predicted week-level SWE.

Thus, the studies that addressed within-individual variation in SWE (Bakker & Bal, in press; Xanthopoulou et al., 2009) consistently suggest that autonomy plays an important role. With respect to the more social resources (coaching, team climate, social support, exchange with supervisor), the results are less clear. It might be that the type of job is a moderator here. For example, in line with the matching hypotheses (de Jonge & Dormann, 2006), it can be assumed that social resources play a more important role in relatively low-skilled jobs where close cooperation between the employees is needed (fast-food company), whereas social resources are less important for teachers who often work in a setting where they are relatively isolated from their co-workers and supervisors. Maybe other factors (e.g., factors related to the pupils) are more important for work engagement in teachers. Moreover, it could be that in low-status jobs, self-esteem needs are more apparent, and thus, esteem support is important to experience a sense of self-involvement, which, according to our conceptual definition, is an essential ingredient of SWE. In high-status jobs, however, organization-based self-esteem does not fluctuate on a daily or weekly basis and therefore, is less relevant for explaining variability on SWE. Another explanation of the diverse findings refers to the differences in time frame (day-level versus week-level).

Surprisingly, job stressors have rarely been addressed as potential predictors of SWE. One reason might be seen in the predictions of the job demands-resources model that posits that job demands (i.e., job stressors) are less important direct predictors of work engagement (Bakker & Demerouti, 2007). One study, however, also included a measure of day-level job demands (i.e., workload) when predicting day-level SWE (Bakker, et al., 2008). Interestingly, day-level job demands were *positively* related to day-level SWE. This effect was qualified by an interaction effect. Thus, the explanation for the positive relationship between daily job demands and SWE is that job demands are challenging if employees have recovered from previous effort and strain. Thus, it seems that on the day level, high job demands are not irrelevant for SWE or even detrimental for SWE, but may foster vigor, dedication, and absorption at the day level, particularly when employees have high energy reserves, i.e., are recovered from the previous day's fatigue. Most probably, when there is much to do on a specific day, people get activated and mobilize resources in order to meet the high demands. However, with respect to the finding that situational day-specific demands seem to stimulate state engagement, it is important to note that these demands must not last too long, otherwise they "burn" all energy resources and as a consequence also state engagement cannot be maintained.

To sum up, day-level recovery seems to be an important predictor of day-level SWE. Moreover, day-level personal resources (i.e., self-efficacy, optimism, and organization-based self-esteem) also predicted SWE at the day level. With respect to situation-specific factors, day-level (or week-level) autonomy seems to be particularly important for experiencing SWE. Other factors in the

work environment such as social support might be important in some jobs, but not in all. These findings about SWE parallel but do not fully overlap with findings about trait work engagement, supporting the distinctive status of SWE experience which we put forward of this chapter.

Outcomes of state work engagement

Work engagement is a desirable experience for employees. In some of the studies, researchers went one step further and examined if work engagement predicts other positive outcomes such as proactive behavior (e.g., personal initiative) or job performance. For example, Sonnentag (2003) analyzed if day-level SWE was related to day-level proactive behavior. Multi-level analyses showed that during days employees experienced a high level of SWE they also reported high levels of personal initiative and learning behavior. Results are similar when looking at in-role performance instead of proactive behavior: Bakker et al. (2008) found that day-level SWE predicted day-level job performance. The study by Bakker and Bal (in press) demonstrated that week-level SWE also predicts week-level job performance. It seems that the experience of SWE enables employees to perform well at their jobs because work engagement enables them to put all their energy and attention into the (in-role and proactive) tasks they have decided to work on (cf. Beal et al., 2005).

Probably the most impressive data on the potential outcomes of SWE at the day level have been presented by Xanthopoulou and her co-workers (2009). Among other things, these authors investigated how daily fluctuations in job resources (autonomy, coaching, and team climate) are related to daily work engagement and daily financial returns. Forty-two employees working in three branches of a fast-food company completed a questionnaire and a diary booklet over five consecutive workdays. Consistent with the hypotheses, multi-level analyses revealed that day-level job resources had an effect on SWE through day-level personal resources. This finding held even after controlling for general levels of personal resources and prior engagement. Day-level coaching, a type of daily resource, also had a direct positive relationship with SWE. Finally, this study showed that workers' day-level SWE predicted day-level financial returns of the fast-food restaurant.

It has to be noted that in most studies that examined the relationship between SWE and performance or proactive behavior, most variables have been assessed simultaneously. Therefore, conclusions about causality are speculative. It is very plausible to assume that SWE fosters performance and proactive behavior; however, based on the studies conducted so far, it cannot be ruled out that the experience of performing well and being particularly proactive during a specific day increases SWE during this day. Maybe, SWE on the one hand and performance and proactive behavior on the other hand are linked by more complex gain spirals (Hobfoll, 1998).

Interestingly, research has not yet paid much attention to other potential outcomes of day-level SWE. For example, it would be particularly interesting and important to assess affective and particularly strain-related consequences of SWE. On the one hand, one may assume that experiencing high levels of SWE during the day increases positive affect and day-level job satisfaction of employees because high levels of engagement make work a meaningful and fulfilling experience. On the other hand, however, one may argue that being absorbed in one's work and spending high levels of energy at work may drain resources and may increase fatigue. Here, future work is needed.

Moreover, it is largely an open question how day-level SWE is related to day-level non-work state engagement. Rothbard (2001) examined engagement in the work and family domain with a between-person approach. She found that absorption at work was positively correlated to absorption in the family. Thus, individuals who are engaged in their work are also engaged in activities outside their working life (Schaufeli, Taris, Le Blanc, Peeters, Bakker, & De Jonge, 2001). Until now, it is largely unclear how these engagement processes work on the day-level. Day-level research has shown that job stress is related to subsequent affect and behavior in the family (Ilies et al., 2007; Repetti, 1989). Therefore, one might assume that day-level SWE also plays a role in experiences and behaviors in the family.

Developing a comprehensive model of state work engagement

Figure 3.1 displays our model of SWE. The model proposes that proximal day-level personal resources play a core role in state work engagement. These proximal day-level personal resources include resources such as state self-efficacy, self-esteem, optimism, positive affect, and energy. These resources increase work engagement as they increase the employee's belief about being able to adequately address his or her tasks and to achieve the desired outcomes. This belief is helpful in immersing oneself fully in one's work, to become absorbed and to dedicate oneself to the task at hand. As Fredrickson (2001) described, positive emotions motivate individuals to develop themselves further, enhance their outward focus and broaden their behavioral repertoires. When, however, state self-efficacy, self-esteem, and optimism are low, it is much more difficult for employees to dedicate themselves to the task and to become absorbed because the self-related doubts associated with low self-efficacy and low self-esteem will interfere with the engagement process and will make employees more susceptible to distraction from the environment. In addition, positive affect as a proximal day-level personal resource will foster excitement and interest that in turn will increase feelings of vigor. Taken together, we suggest resources and experiences that provide energy are necessary, but not sufficient prerequisites for SWE. It seems that states activating positive aspects of the self (e.g., self-efficacy, state self-esteem) are of particular importance for the experience of SWE to occur.

In addition to these proximal day-level personal resources, we suggest that day-level demands will also increase day-level work engagement. High demands present on the day itself make it a necessity to focus one's attention on the task at hand and to mobilize a high level of energy. High demands reduce the likelihood of getting distracted by irrelevant cues and, therefore, foster absorption in one's work. Moreover, we suggest that day-level demands interact with day-level

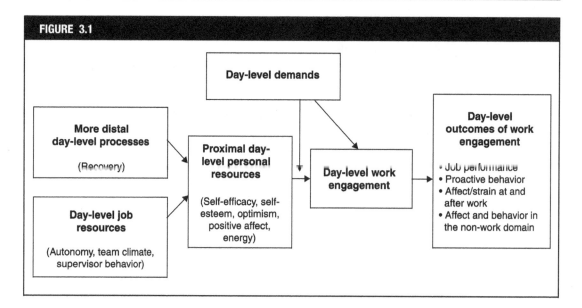

FIGURE 3.1

Model of state work engagement.

personal resources in predicting SWE. SWE will be at a particularly high level when day-level demands meet a high level of personal resources available at the specific moment. However, constant high demands on a daily level and the accumulation of fatigue over the course of time will exhaust the person and therefore will undermine work engagement in the long run.

We propose that the proximal day-level personal resources as immediate predictors of state work engagement will benefit from more distal day-level processes (particularly recovery) and from day-level job resources. Recovery restores personal resources that might have been threatened by previous demands. The restoration process is reflected in an increase in self-efficacy, self-esteem, optimism, or positive affect. Day-level job resources refer to day-level autonomy, team-related variables, and supervisor behavior, namely aspects that help individuals to fulfill their tasks and minimize the unfavorable impact of job demands on a specific day (Demerouti, Bakker, Nachreiner, & Schaufeli, 2001). Therefore, day-level job resources will enhance individuals' positive self-evaluations (i.e., personal resources) and positive affect on that day and consequently their enthusiasm and energy in their work. Most

probably, objective job autonomy does not fluctuate substantially from day to day in many jobs. However, the perception of job autonomy and the possibility to use autonomy may largely differ from day to day. Team-related variables and supervisor behavior refer to social support, positive feedback, and other factors that have the potential to increase self-efficacy, self-esteem, optimism and positive affect. These job resources are more likely to fluctuate on a daily basis particularly in dynamic work environments where cooperation is necessary for task execution. With respect to supervisor behavior, actions and statements reflecting transformational leadership might be particularly important for the enhancement of SWE.

Figure 3.1 is most likely a simple representation of the processes involved in SWE. More complex relationships including reciprocal feedback loops and interactions might better describe the daily dynamics in the constructs involved. For instance, the experience of vigor and dedication on a specific day might motivate employees to take over more tasks (i.e., increase job demands) or might increase the attention that the employee receives from the supervisor (increase in job resources). This is an illustration of how SWE might be involved in individual job design, where individuals create their own working conditions on a daily basis. Next to such reciprocal relationships, interactions between job demands and job resources have been found to predict trait work engagement (e.g., Bakker et al., 2007) and might be relevant for predicting SWE as well. In their study among Finnish teachers, Bakker et al. (2007) found that job resources become more salient when job demands are high and diminish the negative relationship between pupil misbehavior and trait work engagement. In addition, they found that job resources particularly influence trait work engagement when teachers are confronted with high levels of pupil misconduct.

Suggestions for future research

Research on state engagement has just started. Thus, existing studies suffer from some conceptual and methodological shortcomings – and many important and interesting research questions have not been addressed yet. First, we suggest intensifying conceptual work on day-specific (or even momentary) work engagement in order to arrive at a better understanding of how day-specific engagement corresponds to trait engagement in experienced quality and configuration. Second, it is necessary to improve the research

methodology in order to disentangle causality between work engagement and its assumed predictors and outcomes. Here, it is particularly important to temporarily separate measures of resources from measures of work engagement and to temporarily separate measures of work engagement from measures of its outcomes. When addressing questions of causality, reverse causality also should be tested. Third, although the construct validity of scales measuring trait work engagement such as the UWES has been established (see Schaufeli & Bakker, Chapter 2, this volume), it is an open question whether these scales are valid for the measurement of SWE. For instance, usually a low day-level frequency of particular feelings and thoughts can be expected to reduce the respective inter-item correlations (which would normally lead to more extracted factors in factor analysis). Therefore, it could well be that the three factors of vigor, dedication, and absorption might be insufficient to fully represent SWE. In a related vein, it is possible that the modification of trait measures to capture SWE might be insufficient and that new instruments measuring states (of work engagement) as they can be experienced on a daily basis are necessary.

Most of the existing studies on work engage-

Practical implications

Research on state work engagement has implications for practice. It can inform individuals and organizations about how to foster work engagement in specific situations or during specific times when it is particularly important that work engagement is high. Such specific situations and times include new and very difficult tasks, situations characterized by high adversity, meetings with highly relevant customers or other stakeholders, and other situations where it is necessary that employees (and also self-employed workers) go beyond their average level of engagement.

First of all, attention should be paid to factors that are proximal predictors of state work engagement such as state self-efficacy, state self-esteem, state positive affect, and energy. For example, state self-efficacy can be increased by deliberately entering situations that provide mastery experiences, by remembering past successes, or by envisioning role models that succeeded in similar tasks. Supervisors may foster state self-esteem by focusing on positive feedback (and avoiding negative feedback) when they want their employees to be highly work engaged in a specific situation. Moreover, individuals may want to engage in deliberately regulating their affect regulation in order to increase positive affect and energy. In addition, it is equally important to avoid situations and events that may drain energy.

Moreover, more distal predictors can be addressed. Here, adequate recovery is particularly relevant. In practical terms, it is crucial that employees unwind and recuperate well from previous strains, for example by mentally detaching themselves from their job, by engaging in activities that provide new resources (e.g., sport and exercise), and by sleeping well. Thus, when high work engagement is needed on a specific day, it is crucial that individuals refill their "resource reservoir" beforehand.

Finally, more distal predictors in the work situation also contribute to high state work engagement. Because high autonomy is of highest relevance, supervisors should grant a high degree of autonomy, particularly on days when they expect high work engagement. In addition, supervisors can increase state work engagement more directly by coaching their subordinates and by putting emphasis on their strengths. In addition, state work engagement can increase when the team climate is good. Thus, teams should try to find solutions to still unresolved social conflicts before time periods during which team members need to have high work engagement. More short-term improvements in team climate may be achieved by providing opportunities for informal exchange among team members.

ment tested for main effects of resources on work engagement. We think that it would be a particularly fruitful avenue for future research also to examine interaction effects between the various predictors of work engagement (for a study that addressed such interaction effects, see Bakker et al., 2008). In addition, we suggest that researchers should address mutual effects between work engagement and performance, as well as between work engagement and job resources. One can assume that work engagement improves job performance and the experience of job performance and positive feedback associated with performance in turn will increase subsequent work engagement and probably will also enhance resources (see also Salanova et al., Chapter 9, this volume).

Until now, personality variables have been largely neglected in research on work engagement. Personality might have an effect on the variability of work engagement within a person and it might show interaction effects between resources and actual state work engagement (for a first study that included personality as a moderator when predicting state engagement, see Bledow et al., 2008).

We assume that state engagement is not just "happening" to employees, but rather that employees can actively create engagement experiences. Therefore, it will be particularly interesting to examine strategies that employees use on a daily basis to increase their work engagement. Here, one might think of active search for feedback, focusing on positive events, and other volitional processes and self-regulatory processes. In our view, it would be particularly interesting to examine SWE in the context of ego depletion theory (e.g., Muraven & Baumeister, 2000) or within the episodic-performance framework (Beal et al., 2005), which allows some further predictions to be made. For example, on the one hand, one can assume that work activities that are not fully in line with individuals' selves (i.e., work activities that do not allow for SWE) will deplete self-regulatory resources. On the other hand, however, the more self-regulatory resources are available, the easier it becomes to fulfill the demands at work and the more likely it is to experience SWE even if the tasks are not entirely intrinsically motivating.

Overall, the concept SWE has several theoretically and empirically interesting properties that augment existing theory and research on work engagement. We suggest that future studies should also investigate the relationship between trait and state engagement in greater detail. For example, does an increase of the average level of state engagement over a certain time period lead to an increase in trait engagement? If not, what are the antecedents of trait engagement? On a more general level, it is important to integrate models of state and trait engagement. One of the most challenging questions here is whether the predictors and outcomes of work engagement are identical at the state and at the trait level. Overall, we are convinced that studying the processes related to state work engagement will help to develop a better understanding of the work engagement phenomenon. Building on this knowledge, organizations can support and facilitate the processes that enhance state work engagement because this was found to be beneficial for daily well-being and performance at work.

References

Bakker, A. B., & Bal, P. M. (in press). Weekly work engagement and performance: A study among starting teachers. *Journal of Occupational and Organizational Psychology*.

Bakker, A. B., & Demerouti, E. (2007). The job demands-resources model: State of the art. *Journal of Managerial Psychology*, *22*, 309–328.

Bakker, A. B., Hakanen, J. J., Demerouti, E., & Xanthopoulou, D. (2007). Job resources boost work engagement, particularly when job demands are high. *Journal of Educational Psychology*, *99*, 274–284.

Bakker, A. B., van Emmerik, I. H., Geurts, S. A. E., & Demerouti, E. (2008). *Recovery turns job demands into challenges: A diary study on work engagement and performance*. Working paper. Erasmus University Rotterdam.

Beal, D. J., Weiss, H. M., Barros, E., & MacDermid, S. M. (2005). An episodic process model of affective influences on performance. *Journal of Applied Psychology*, *90*, 1054–1068.

Bledow, R., Schmitt, A., & Frese, M. (2008). *Work engagement as a dynamic process: The interplay of events, emotions and resources.* Poster presented at the 2008 Conference of the Society of Industrial and Organizational Psychology, San Francisco, CA.

Bolger, N., Davis, A., & Rafaeli, E. (2003). Diary methods: Capturing life as it is lived. *Annual Review of Psychology, 54,* 597–616.

Bolger, N., DeLongis, A., Kessler, R. C., & Schilling, E. A. (1989). Effects of daily stress on negative mood. *Journal of Personality and Social Psychology, 57,* 808–818.

Chen, G., Gully, S. M., & Eden, D. (2001). Validation of a new general self-efficacy scale. *Organizational Research Methods, 4,* 62–83.

Dalal, R. S., Brummel, B. J., Wee, S., & Thomas, L. L. (2008). Defining employee engagement for productive research and practice. *Industrial and Organizational Psychology: Perspectives on Science and Practice, 1,* 52–55.

de Jonge, J., & Dormann, C. (2006). Job demands, job resources and psychological well-being: A longitudinal test of the triple match principle. *Journal of Applied Psychology, 91,* 1359–1374.

Demerouti E., Bakker, A. B., Nachreiner, F., & Schaufeli, W. B. (2001). The Job Demands-Resources model of burnout. *Journal of Applied Psychology, 86,* 499–512.

Fredrickson, B. L. (1998). What good are positive emotions? *Journal of General Psychology, 2,* 300–319.

Fredrickson, B. L. (2001). The role of positive emotions in positive psychology: The broaden-and-build theory of positive emotions. *American Psychologist, 56,* 218–226.

Hakanen, J. J., Perhoniemi, R., & Toppinen-Tammer, S. (2008). Positive gain spirals at work: From job resources to work engagement, personal initiative and work-unit innovativeness. *Journal of Vocational Behavior, 73,* 78–91.

Hobfoll, S. E. (1998). *Stress, culture, and community: The psychology and physiology of stress.* New York: Plenum.

Hofmann, D. A., & Gavin, M. B. (1998). Centering decisions in hierarchical linear models: Implications for research in organizations. *Journal of Management, 24,* 623–641.

Hormuth, S. E. (1986). The sampling of experiences in situ. *Journal of Personality, 54,* 262–293.

Ilies, R., Schwind, K. M., & Heller, D. (2007). Employee well-being: A multilevel model linking work and nonwork domains. *European Journal of Work and Organizational Psychology, 16,* 326–341.

Kahn, W. A. (1990). The psychological conditions of personal engagement and disengagement at work. *Academy of Management Journal, 33,* 692–724.

Luthans, F., Avolio, B. J., Avey, J. B., & Norman, S. M. (2007). Positive psychological capital: Measurement and relationship with performance and satisfaction. *Personnel Psychology, 60,* 541–572.

Macey, W. H., & Schneider, B. (2008). The meaning of employee engagement. *Industrial and Organizational Psychology: Perspectives on Science and Practice, 1,* 3–30.

Mauno, S., Kinnunen, U., & Ruokolainen, M. (2007). Job demands and resources as antecedents of work engagement: A longitudinal study. *Journal of Vocational Behavior, 70,* 149–171.

Muraven, M., & Baumeister, R. F. (2000). Self regulation and depletion of limited resources: Does self control resemble a muscle? *Psychological Bulletin, 126,* 247–259.

Niklas, C., & Dormann, C. (2005). The impact of state affect on job satisfaction. *European Journal of Work and Organizational Psychology, 14,* 367–388.

Repetti, R. L. (1989). Effects of daily workload on subsequent behavior during marital interaction: The roles of social withdrawal and spouse support. *Journal of Personality and Social Psychology, 57,* 651–659.

Rothbard, N. P. (2001). Enriching or depleting? The dynamics of engagement in work and family roles. *Administrative Science Quarterly, 46,* 655–684.

Schaufeli, W. B., & Bakker, A. B. (2004). Job demands, job resources, and their relationship with burnout and engagement: a multi-sample study. *Journal of Organizational Behavior, 25,* 293–315.

Schaufeli, W. B., Salanova, M., González-Romá, V., & Bakker, A. B. (2002). The measurement of engagement and burnout: A two sample confirmatory factor analytic approach. *Journal of Happiness Studies, 3,* 71–92.

Schaufeli, W. B., & Salanova, M. (2007). Work engagement: An emerging psychological concept and its implication for organizations. In S. W. Gilliland, D. D. Steiner & D. P. Skarlicki (Eds.), *Research in social issues in management (Volume 5): Managing social and ethical issues in organizations* (pp. 135–177). Greenwich: CT: Information Age Publishers.

Schaufeli, W., Taris, T., Le Blanc, P., Peeters, M., Bakker, A. B., & De Jonge, J. (2001). Maakt arbeid gezond? Op zoek naar de bevlogen werknemer. [Does work make healthy? The quest for the engaged worker]. *De Psycholoog, 36,* 422–428.

Shirom, A. (2007). Explaining vigor: On the antecedents and consequences of vigor as a positive affect at work. In D. L. Nelson & C. L. Cooper

(Eds.), *Positive organizational behavior* (pp. 86–100). London: Sage.

Sonnentag, S. (2003). Recovery, work engagement, and proactive behavior: A new look at the interface between non-work and work. *Journal of Applied Psychology, 88*, 518–528.

Weiss, H. M., & Cropanzano, R. (1996). Affective events theory: A theoretical discussion of the structure, causes and consequences of affective experiences at work. In B. M. Staw & L. L. Cummings (Eds.), *Research in organizational behavior* (Vol. 18, pp. 1–74). Stamford, CT: JAI Press.

Xanthopoulou, D., Bakker, A. B., Demerouti, E., & Schaufeli, W. B. (2009). Work engagement and financial returns: A diary study on the role of job and personal resources. *Journal of Occupational and Organizational Psychology, 82*, 183–200.

Xanthopoulou, D., Bakker, A. B., Heuven, E., Demerouti, E., & Schaufeli, W. B. (2008). Working in the sky: A diary study on work engagement among flight attendants. *Journal of Occupational Health Psychology, 13*, 345–356.

The push and pull of work: The differences between workaholism and work engagement

Toon W. Taris, Wilmar B. Schaufeli, and Akihito Shimazu

The term workaholism has been part of our everyday vocabulary for almost four decades now. Given the widespread use of this term among lay people, it is quite remarkable that our scientific understanding of workaholism is as yet quite limited: even the correct conceptualization of this concept is still heavily debated (Burke, 2006). Is workaholism more than just devoting too much time to work? Should workaholics be considered with compassion as they suffer from a serious disorder that requires treatment, or is workaholism a desirable state that has positive consequences, for both the individual workers and their employers?

And, most importantly in the present context, how does workaholism relate to the concept of work engagement, which also involves notions of hard work, high work involvement, and superior performance? The current chapter first discusses the origins and conceptualization of workaholism. After addressing the conceptual distinctions and similarities between workaholism and work engagement, we explore the empirical evidence on the differentiation between the two concepts – are they really different? Finally, we draw conclusions regarding the distinction between work engagement and work addiction, and provide a short inventory of issues to be addressed in future research.

What is workaholism?

The idea that work can be addictive and may have adverse consequences for employee well-being and his or her social environment is not new. For example, on 24 April 1852, the French novelist Gustave Flaubert (1821–1880) writes in a letter to his mistress Louise Colet that "I love my work with a frenetic and perverted love" (cited in Unwin, 2004, p. 10). Writing was all for Flaubert: "I am a man of the quill. I feel through it, because of it, in relation to it, and much more with it." One of the consequences of his approach to writing was that he left several thousands of pages of jottings, drafts, and notebooks with plans and scenarios, most of which were never used. Meanwhile, normal life was postponed. The many letters to Colet show that Flaubert was in the habit of putting off proposed meetings with his mistress, usually because he wanted to finish a section or a chapter of *Madame Bovary*. His tendency to consider everything that occurred as potential writing material led Flaubert's mother to tell him that "your obsession with sentences has dried up your heart" (Unwin, 2004, p. 11). Clearly, working was tremendously important for Flaubert, evidently at the cost of his relationships with other people – he never married or led anything like a normal family life; a workaholic *avant la lettre*. Similarly, in his treatise "Das Recht auf Faulheit" ("The right to be lazy"), the German anarchist Paul Lafargue (1883) speaks of "Arbeitssucht" (work addiction) as the cause of the "Erschöpfung der Lebensenergie des Einzelnen und seiner Nachkommen" ("Exhaustion of vital energy of the individual and his offspring", translation ours). As a third example of the early awareness that work may be addictive and may have undesirable consequences, the Hungarian psychiatrist Sándor Ferenczi, a follower of Sigmund Freud, described in 1919 the "Sunday neurosis", i.e., the phenomenon that healthy people experienced recurring anxiety, headaches, stomach aches, depression, and nausea during their respite on Sunday (for Jews, on Saturday), out of fear that the lack of their day-to-day work routines would unleash repressed impulses.

In its current meaning, the term workaholism has been coined by the Baptist clergyman, professor of the psychology of religion, and author of over 50 books reverend Wayne E. Oates, who told of his personal awakening to the realization of his own compulsion to overwork after his 5-year old son asked for an appointment at his office to talk about something that bothered him (Killinger, 2006). Oates realized that his way of dealing with his work strongly resembled one of his clients' addiction to alcohol – hence the term work*ahol*ism, "a semihumorous word for the addiction to work" (1971, p. 13). Oates described his "uncontrollable need to work incessantly" in 1968 in an article in *Pastoral Psychology*. The term attracted worldwide attention after Oates published *Confessions of a workaholic* (1971), a book written for a broad audience of lay people, defining a workaholic as "a person whose need to work has become so excessive that it creates noticeable disturbances in his health, happiness or relationships". Since then, the term workaholism has been used widely in the popular press, and entering the key word "workaholic" yields over 2.7 million hits on the internet (July 2008). Interestingly, scientific attention to this concept has lagged behind this popular interest. Taris and Schaufeli (2007) searched the scientific *PsycINFO* database for publications including the key words *workaholic*, *workaholics* or *workaholism*, and found that during the 1970–1980 time window only three publications included at least one of these key words in their titles and/or abstracts. However, after 1980 the number of publications on this subject roughly doubled every five years; during the 2001–2006 time frame, no less than 88 papers on workaholism were published. Although this figure is still modest relative to the attention given to phenomena such as work satisfaction, commitment and burnout, the scientific interest in workaholism is clearly on the rise.

Conceptualization and definition of workaholism

In spite of the growing interest in workaholism, our understanding of this phenomenon is still quite limited (McMillan, O'Driscoll, & Burke, 2003). According to Burke (2001a), "much of the writing [on workaholism] has not been guided by a clear definition of the concept or by well-developed measures" (p. 65) – indeed, researchers tend to disagree fundamentally regarding the true nature of workaholism. For example, in a recent review McMillan and O'Driscoll (2006) discussed no less than nine "major" workaholism definitions, not mentioning the "minor" definitions that are around as well. Many scholars agree with Oates' (1971) view that workaholism is by definition bad because it is an addiction that is similar to alcoholism (e.g., Cherrington, 1980; Killinger, 2006; Robinson, 1989). As Porter (1996) put it, "Whereas an alcoholic neglects other aspects of life for the indulgence in alcohol, the workaholic behaves the same for excessive indulgence in work" (pp. 70–71). Conversely, others view workaholism as a state with *positive* consequences for both workaholics and the organizations they work for (Korn, Pratt, & Lambrou, 1987; Machlowitz, 1980; Peiperl & Jones, 2001). Cantarow (1979) considers the workaholic personality as positive, because its hallmark is the joy of creativity; according to her, workaholics seek passionate involvement and gratification through their work. Similarly, Peiperl and Jones (2001) consider workaholics to be "hard workers who enjoy and get a lot out of their work" (p. 388).

Yet others view workaholism both positively and negatively, distinguishing between different types of workaholism, some of which are good whereas others are bad. For example, Keichel (1989) distinguished between happy and dysfunctional workaholics, whereas Naughton (1987) compares "good" job-involved workaholics (who are high in commitment and low in compulsion) with "bad" workaholics (who are high in commitment as well as compulsion). Scott, Moore, and Miceli (1997) identified compulsive-dependent workaholics, perfectionist workaholics, and achievement-oriented workaholics; the latter group is very similar to Korn et al.'s (1987) "hyper-performers". The currently most widely used approach to measuring workaholism distinguishes three supposedly underlying dimensions – the so-called "workaholism-triad" (Spence & Robbins, 1992): work involvement (being highly committed to work and devoting a good deal of time to it), drive (feeling compelled to work hard because of inner pressures), and work enjoyment (experiencing work to be pleasant and fulfilling). Crossing these three dimensions leads to six different types of workers, including three types of workaholics; (i) *non-enthusiastic workaholics*, who are high in commitment and drive, and low in enjoyment; (ii) *enthusiastic workaholics*, who are high in pleasure, commitment, and drive; and (iii) *work enthusiasts*, who are high in commitment and enjoyment, but who are lacking the drive to work hard. Buelens and Poelmans (2004) refer to the latter group as the "happy and hard workers", who are "enthusiastic, meet interesting people, love their jobs, and avoid conflict at home and in the workplace, possibly owing to their resulting positive attitude and a high level of social intelligence" (p. 454).

Workaholism versus engagement

As Schaufeli, Taris, and Bakker (2006b) note, the above description of work enthusiasts strongly resembles the recently introduced concept of work engagement, the positive opposite of job burnout (e.g., Maslach, Leiter, & Schaufeli, 2001). Engaged employees have a sense of energetic and effective connection with their work activities and they see themselves as able to deal well with the demands of their jobs. More specifically, job engagement refers to a positive, fulfilling, work-related state of mind that is characterized by vigor, dedication and absorption (Schaufeli, Salanova, Gonzalez-Roma, & Bakker, 2002b). *Vigor* is characterized by high levels of energy and mental resilience while working, the willingness to invest effort in one's work, and persistence, also in the face of difficulties. *Dedication* refers to being strongly involved in one's work, and experiencing a sense of significance, enthusiasm, inspiration, pride and challenge. Finally, *absorption* is characterized by being fully concentrated on and happily engrossed in one's work, whereby time passes quickly and one has difficulties with detaching oneself from work.

Engaged employees thus work hard (vigor), are involved (dedicated) and feel happily engrossed (involved) in their work. In this sense they are similar to workaholics. However, contrary to workaholics, engaged workers lack the typical compulsive drive that is characteristic of any addiction, including an addiction to work. For engaged workers work is fun and not a compulsion, as was concluded from a qualitative study of 15 engaged workers (Schaufeli, Taris, LeBlanc, Peeters, Bakker, & De Jonge, 2001). These workers worked hard because they liked it and not because they were driven by a strong inner urge they could not resist. Thus, for the sake of conceptual clarity, instead of distinguishing between "good" and "bad" forms of workaholism, it seems appropriate to discriminate between workaholism (being intrinsically bad) and work engagement (being intrinsically good). This agrees with the recommendation of Porter (1996) to "return to the origin of the term as a starting point for future research", i.e., Oates' initial definition of workaholism. This view of workaholism as a "bad" phenomenon thus excludes perspectives that consider workaholism as "good" (e.g., Cantarow, 1979; Korn et al., 1987; Machlowitz, 1980; Peiperl & Jones, 2001).

What, then, are the core characteristics of workaholism? The early definition of Oates (1971) of workaholism as "the compulsion or the uncontrollable need to work incessantly" includes two features that return in most later definitions of workaholism: (i) working excessively hard; and (ii) the existence of a strong, compulsive, inner drive. The former points to the fact that workaholics tend to allocate an exceptional amount of time to work and that they work beyond what is reasonably expected to meet organizational or economic requirements. The latter recognizes that workaholics persistently and frequently think about work, even when not working, suggesting that workaholics are "obsessed" with their work. In our view, workaholics work harder than their job prescriptions require and they invest much more effort in their jobs than is expected by the people with whom or for whom they work, and in doing so they neglect their life outside their job. Typically, they work so hard out of an inner compulsion, need, or drive, and not because of external factors such as financial rewards, career perspectives, organizational culture, or even poor marriage. This reasoning is consistent with that of McMillan and O'Driscoll (2006), who proposed that "workaholism is generally understood to involve an unwillingness to disengage from work. Workaholics' most notable characteristics are tendencies to (a) work with a passion that is obvious to the outside observer; (b) think about work [. . .] more frequently, compared to non-workaholics, after most other people have 'mentally switched off'; (c) focus their conversation on work, even in social situations; (d) strive for tangible achievements in the workplace; (e) work slightly more hours than others" (p. 89). Characteristics b and c refer to the compulsive element of workaholism (i.e., difficulties in distancing themselves from the job), whereas characteristics a, d, and e refer to effort expenditure in the workplace. According to McMillan and O'Driscoll (2006), the compulsive element of workaholism may be an antecedent of excessive effort expenditure at work, similar to enjoyment in work (cf. Spence & Robbins, 1992); as the latter is not part of Oates' (1971) original conceptualization of workaholism, it seems best not to include it in any measure of workaholism. Thus, workaholism is best defined in terms of (i) a strong inner drive to work hard, in combination with (ii) high effort expenditure. It can be distinguished from engagement in that engaged employees also work hard and show high levels of dedication, but they lack the compulsive inner drive to do so; engaged workers work hard simply because they like their job so much and not because they cannot resist a strong inner urge to work. In other words, engaged workers are pulled to work because they enjoy it for its own sake, whereas workaholics are pushed to work because they have to obey their obsession.

Workaholism versus engagement: The empirical evidence

As shown above, it is not particularly difficult to distinguish conceptually between workaholism and engagement. However, any conceptual distinction should be warranted empirically to be valid. Thus, this section examines the evidence for our position that engagement and workaholism are related, yet distinct concepts. We present evidence on two types of questions, namely

(i) factor-analytic evidence on the relationships between the dimensions of engagement and workaholism, and (ii) correlational evidence on the relationships between engagement and workaholism on the one hand, and theoretically related concepts (such as job characteristics, work outcomes and health) on the other.

The relationships between the dimensions of engagement and workaholism

As indicated above, research on workaholism is relatively scarce. Moreover, the concept of engagement has not been around very long. It is therefore not surprising that very few studies deal with the relationships between workaholism and engagement. Two exceptions to this rule are Schaufeli et al. (2006b) and Schaufeli, Taris, & Van Rhenen (2008). These studies are described in more detail below.

Study 1

Schaufeli et al. (2006b) drew on data from a convenience sample of 2164 workers who responded to a survey that was published on the website of a popular Dutch psychology magazine. Visitors to its home page were invited to learn more about their work-related well-being, and could complete a 60-item questionnaire. After filling out the survey, participants were instantly (i.e., online) informed about their levels of engagement and workaholism, and received computer-customized feedback concerning their scores. Comparison of the demographic characteristics of the sample to those of the Dutch workforce revealed that males, young workers (< 24 years old), and more highly educated people were overrepresented in the sample, which is not uncommon in internet-based research (Taris, Schreurs, & Sepmeijer, 2005b). *Workaholism* was measured with two scales. The first was a nine-item Dutch version (Taris, Schaufeli, & Verhoeven 2005a) of the Compulsive Tendencies scale proposed by Flowers and Robinson (2002), which was relabeled Working Excessively (WE, α = .84, sample items are "I seem to be in a hurry and racing against the clock" and "I find myself continuing to work after my co-workers have called it quits"). The second scale is the eight-item Drive scale of Spence and Robbins' (1992) WorkBat, which was relabeled Working Compulsively (WC, α = .86, sample items are "I feel obliged to work hard, even when it is not enjoyable" and "I feel guilty when I take time off work"). *Work engagement* was measured with the nine-item shortened version of the Utrecht Work Engagement Scale (UWES, Schaufeli, Bakker, & Salanova, 2006a, α = .93; see Chapter 2 for all items of the UWES).

Study 2

The sample used in Schaufeli et al. (2008; Study 2) included 587 middle managers and executives of a Dutch telecom company (response rate 69%). The majority were men, lived with a partner, and held at least a college degree. Workaholism was measured with virtually the same instrument as used in Study 1. Work engagement was measured with the 17-item version of the Utrecht Work Engagement Scale (Schaufeli et al., 2002b; see also Schaufeli & Bakker, Chapter 2, this volume). Six items tapped Vigor (α = .88), five items measured Dedication (α = .93), and six items measured Absorption (α = .80).

Results

Figure 4.1 summarizes the findings for Study 1 regarding the relationships between the dimensions of workaholism and engagement. In Study 1, confirmatory factor analysis was used to compare two models: a one-factor model in which all 17 workaholism items and all 9 engagement items loaded on the same latent factor, and a three-factor model in which all engagement items loaded on one factor, the items measuring WE loaded on a second factor, and the items tapping WC loaded on the third factor. The three latent factors were allowed to correlate. Results indicated that the three-factor model fitted the data significantly better than the one-factor model. Figure 4.1 presents the correlations between the three latent factors. The subscales of workaholism are strongly associated, but the correlations between engagement and the two workaholism indicators are non-significant (for WC) or modest (for WE). Thus, it appears that engagement and workaholism are empirically different concepts, the main findings being that

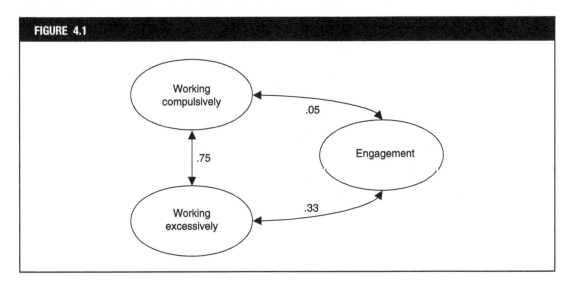

FIGURE 4.1

Relationships between the dimensions of engagement and workaholism (Study 1).

(i) engaged employees have a tendency to work hard, and (ii) engagement is unrelated to working compulsively.

The value of the findings obtained in Study 1 is somewhat limited, in that no distinction was made between the subscales of engagement. Study 2 was designed to overcome this limitation, testing a similar series of models as in Study 1, but now involving five distinct subscales: three for engagement and two for workaholism. Again, a one-factor model in which all five scales loaded on a single factor was compared to a two-factor model, with the three engagement indicators loading on the first factor and the two workaholism scales loading on the second factor. Although the two-factor model fit the data considerably better than the single-factor model, model modification was necessary to obtain an acceptable fit to the data. Specifically, a factor loading relating absorption to workaholism had to be added (cf. Figure 4.2). As the figure shows, the loadings of vigor, dedication, and absorption on engagement are high and statistically significant; additionally, working excessively and working compulsively have substantial loadings on the workaholism factor. What was unexpected, though, is that absorption also loads substantially (standardized loading = .35, $p < .001$) on workaholism. This confirms the idea that workaholics are fully immersed

in their work and are reluctant to disengage from work (McMillan & O'Driscoll, 2006). However, theoretically it is assumed that the underlying motivation for being absorbed in one's work differs; where engaged workers are absorbed in their work because it is so much fun, workaholics feel driven to work – their absorption is a matter of compulsion, not of enjoyment. In other words, engaged workers are intrinsically motivated or pulled towards work, whereas workaholics are intrapersonally motivated or pushed to work. Further, it is interesting to see that the factor-level association between engagement and workaholism is low (–.07, *ns*); thus, after accounting for the fact that both workaholics and engaged workers are absorbed in their jobs, there is no reason to assume that there is a relationship of substantive interest between the two concepts.

Summary

All in all, the factor-analytic evidence discussed here supports the conceptual distinction between engagement and workaholism. The available evidence clearly shows that it is empirically warranted to distinguish between these concepts, in that WC and WE were in both studies only moderately (estimate = .33, for the relationship between WE and engagement in Study 1) or not at all (all other relationships) related to engagement. The

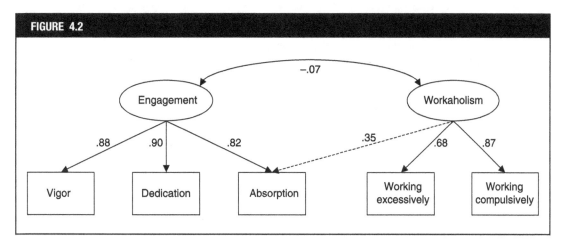

FIGURE 4.2

Relationships between the dimensions of engagement and workaholism (Study 2).

Absorption subscale of engagement (that is, forgetting about time) might be construed as a workaholism indicator, reflecting the theoretical notion that both workaholics and engaged workers have difficulties in disengaging from work – although the underlying reasons for being unable to disengage may well be different for the two groups.

Although this evidence suffices to show that engagement and workaholism can be measured separately and independently, it cannot be concluded that these measures really tap different constructs. That is, if engagement and workaholism are truly different, one would expect them to retain different patterns of relationships with other variables, such as work characteristics, work outcomes, and health. This issue is discussed in the next section, drawing on data from the same two studies.

The relationships between engagement, workaholism, and other variables

In order to assess the differential validity of workaholism vis-à-vis engagement, Schaufeli and colleagues (2006b, 2008) investigated their relationships with several sets of variables. For the present chapter these clusters of variables were regrouped into four broad clusters, covering (i) working time-related variables, (ii) work characteristics, (iii) health and well-being, and (iv) organizational behaviors.

Working time

The most obvious characteristic of workaholics is that they work beyond what is required, devoting much more time to their work than others do (Buelens & Poelmans, 2004; Scott et al., 1997). Brett and Stroh (2003) reported that North American workaholics work on average 50–60 hours per week, with those with high scores on the drive/working compulsively component working the longest hours (Spence & Robbins, 1992; Taris et al., 2005a). Not surprisingly, positive correlations have been found between the time committed to the job (such as working overtime, working during weekends and taking work home) and workaholism (Taris et al., 2005a). A large representative sample of the Dutch workforce revealed that work engagement is also related to working overtime (Beckers, Van der Linden, Smulders, Kompier, Van Veldhoven, & Van Yperen, 2004). Thus, both workaholics and engaged workers are expected to devote much time to their work.

Schaufeli et al.'s (2006b, 2008) findings confirm this expectation. Table 4.1 shows that the workaholism indicators as well as engagement are positively related to spending more hours at work. These associations are strongest and most systematic for working excessively; employees obtaining high scores on this concept work more hours than others, and spend more time overworking. Although similar tendencies are

TABLE 4.1

Correlates of indicators of workaholism and engagement

	Working excessively	Working compulsively	Work engagement
Working time			
Overwork[a, c, d]	.40	.29	.27
Overwork[b, e]	.24	ns	ns
Percentage of overtime[b]	.15	.15	ns
Working hours[a, c]	.47	.29	.24
Work characteristics			
Job demands[b]	.46	.23	.13
Job control[b]	ns	−.17	.18
Co-worker support[b]	ns	ns	.12
Supervisor support[b]	ns	−.10	ns
Health and well-being			
Self-perceived health[a]	−.08	−.24	.35
Distress[b]	ns	.17	−.23
Depression[b]	ns	ns	ns
Anxiety[b]	ns	ns	ns
Psychosomatic complaints[b]	.09	.15	.11
Absenteeism[a]	ns	ns	−.09
Life satisfaction[a]	ns	−.26	.31
Job satisfaction[b]	ns	ns	.24
Organizational commitment[b]	.10	.11	.14
Organizational performance			
In-role performance[a]	ns	ns	.37
Extra-role performance[a]	.10	.11	.32
Innovativeness[a]	.23	ns	.37

Note. All associations are significant at $p < .05$ (*ns*, $p > .05$).

a Estimate derived from Study 1, $N = 2156$. Effects are standardized regression estimates, except[c].

b Estimate derived from Study 2, $N = 587$. Effects are standardized maximum likelihood estimates. The correlations with engagement were obtained by averaging the correlations with vigor, dedication and absorption reported by Schaufeli et al. (2008).

c This is a raw correlation coefficient.

d Overwork was computed as a combination of "works at weekends", "takes work home", and the percentage of overtime relative to the total number of hours worked.

e Overwork was computed as a combination of "works at weekends" and "takes work home".

observed for work engagement and especially working compulsively, here the associations are considerably weaker.

Work characteristics

In their attempts to continue working, work-aholics may go as far as to actively create more work for themselves, e.g., by making projects more complicated than necessary, by self-imposed dead-lines, or by refusing to delegate work (Machlow-itz, 1980; Porter, 1996). This may also lead to a low quality of social relationships at work (Porter, 2001). Further, strong correlations were found between workaholism and job demands (Taris et al., 2005a). Conversely, Schaufeli and Bakker (2004) reported that engagement was positively related to job resources such as social support from colleagues, but *not* to job demands. The evidence collected by Schaufeli et al. (2006b, 2008) corroborates these impressions. Both workaholics and engaged workers experience relatively high job demands; again, this association is strongest for Working Excessively. Working Compulsively is associated with low levels of job control and low levels of supervisor support; conversely, engaged workers experience high levels of control and high co-worker support. Thus, although both workaholics *and* engaged workers report high job demands, the workaholics judge other characteristics of their work negatively, whereas the engaged workers evaluate their work positively.

Health and well-being

Workaholics report relatively high levels of job strain and (mental) health complaints, particularly as far as the drive/compulsion component is concerned (Buelens & Poelmans, 2004; McMillan & O'Driscoll, 2004; Spence & Robbins, 1992; Taris et al., 2005a). Similarly, life satisfaction of workaholics is low (Bonebright, Clay, & Ankenmann, 2000). The latter study also showed that work enthusiasts (the "good" workaholics, or engaged workers, in our terminology) reported high life satisfaction. Comparable findings were obtained by Buelens and Poelmans (2004), showing that work enthusiasts were satisfied with their salary and relationships at work, whereas "bad" workaholics were dissatisfied in these respects. Other evidence revealed that work engagement is negatively related to psychosomatic health complaints (Schaufeli & Bakker, 2004) and positively to mental health (see Bakker & Leiter, Chapter 13, this volume).

The findings reported by Schaufeli et al. (2006b, 2008) are in line with these notions. Whereas workaholics tend to report low levels of self-perceived health and satisfaction and high levels of distress, the engaged workers report the opposite pattern of effects; they are happy workers, enjoy relatively good health, are relatively less often absent, are satisfied with their lives, and show low levels of distress. Interestingly – and in line with our expectations – both workaholics and engaged workers are committed to their work. Furthermore, in these two studies both workaholics and engaged workers report slightly more psychosomatic complaints than others. The finding that workaholism is positively related to

mental health complaints has been confirmed elsewhere. For example, a recent study among Dutch and Japanese employees – using shortened versions of the WE and WC scales – showed that workaholics reported higher levels of burnout than non-workaholics (with correlations of .53 and .64 in the Dutch and Japanese samples, respectively; Schaufeli, Shimazu & Taris, in press). However, Schaufeli et al.'s (2006b, 2008) finding that engaged workers also report higher levels of psychosomatic complaints has not been replicated. Schaufeli et al. (in press) showed that engagement was negatively related to burnout (with correlations of −.75 and −.50 in the Dutch and Japanese samples, respectively), whereas Shimazu et al. (2008) found that engaged workers reported better health and well-being than unengaged workers. Clearly, additional research is needed to clarify the relationship between engagement and psychosomatic complaints.

Organizational behavior

Whereas some authors maintain that workaholics are extremely productive workers (e.g., Korn et al., 1987; Machlowitz, 1980; Peiperl & Jones, 2001), others claim the opposite (Oates, 1971; Porter, 2001). The latter argue that workaholics may work hard, rather than smart, creating difficulties for themselves and their co-workers; they suffer from perfectionism, are rigid and inflexible, and cannot delegate tasks to others. Burke (2001b) reported some circumstantial evidence that workaholics perform not particularly well; for instance, workaholic behaviors were *not* associated with salary increases. Thus, it appears that workaholics are not necessarily good (and perhaps even poor) performers. As regards engagement, there is preliminary evidence that engaged employees perform better than others. For instance, Salanova et al. (2005a) recently showed that levels of work engagement of contract employees in hotels and restaurants were positively related to service quality, as perceived by customers. Similarly, engaged students passed more exams during subsequent semesters (Schaufeli, Martinez, Marques-Pinto, Salanova, & Bakker, 2002a) and obtained a higher point grade average during next year's grade point average (Salanova, Bresó, & Schaufeli,

2005b). Demerouti and Cropanzano (Chapter 11, this volume) discuss further evidence for the work engagement–work performance relationship. All in all, it appears that engagement is positively related to organizational performance, whereas the association between workaholism and performance is still unclear.

The findings reported by Schaufeli et al. (2006b) support these notions. Indeed, the differences between workaholics and engaged workers were perhaps most visible for variables tapping organizational performance. Whereas engaged workers reported higher levels of in- and extra-role behavior and innovativeness than unengaged workers, workaholics were considerably less convinced of their performance in these respects. There were no significant relationships between both workaholism indicators and in-role performance, and although both Working Excessively and Working Compulsively are positively related to extra-role performance, these associations were considerably weaker than for engagement.

Summary

As for the factor-analytic evidence discussed above, the pattern of relationships with various clusters of correlates presented in this section suggests that engagement and workaholism are empirically distinct constructs. There are some similarities, e.g., both engaged workers and workaholics tend to spend much time working, report high job demands, are committed to their jobs, and report relatively high levels of extra-role performance. However, it appears that high levels of engagement are usually associated with good health and well-being and with desirable job characteristics (in terms of support and control); conversely, such relationships are absent or negative for workaholic workers. Generally, it appears that whereas engaged workers work hard, they are quite happy with their jobs and feel that they perform well; workaholics work hard as well, but tend to evaluate their work and well-being negatively. These findings are largely in line with our expectations and with previous research that compared work enthusiasts and "good" workaholics with "bad" workaholics.

Concluding remarks

The present chapter was designed to provide a short overview of the similarities and differences between workaholism and engagement. We first discussed the concept of workaholism. Historically, many different forms of workaholism have been distinguished, some of which are considered "positive" (e.g., "work enthusiasts", Spence & Robbins, 1992; cf. Buelens & Poelmans, 2004), whereas other forms are considered "negative" (e.g., Flowers & Robinson, 2002; Porter, 2001). This did not contribute to the conceptual clarity of the concept. Moreover, it is quite possible that divergent findings on the antecedents, correlates, and consequences of workaholism are due to differences in the conceptualization and measurement of workaholism. Therefore, in defining workaholism we returned to the origins of the concept, drawing on the classic notion of Oates (1971) of a workaholic as "a person whose need to work has become so excessive that it creates noticeable disturbances in his health, happiness or relationships" – i.e., as a concept that has distinctly *negative* consequences for the person and his or her environment. Conversely, the "positive" forms of workaholism bear more than a slight resemblance to the concept of work engagement. Both workaholics and engaged workers work hard and are highly involved in their work. However, whereas workaholics work hard due to a strong, compulsive inner drive they cannot resist (intrapersonal motivation – they are pushed to work), engaged workers do so because they enjoy their work so much (intrinsic motivation – they are pulled towards work). It can be speculated that the underlying motivation to work hard differs fundamentally between engaged workers and workaholics, for instance in terms of reinforcement sensitivity (cf. Van der Linden, Beckers, & Taris, 2007). Perhaps engaged workers are more likely to be sensitive to rewards and are reinforced by positive incentives (e.g., social approval, challenge, and resourceful jobs), whereas workaholics are more likely to be sensitive to punishments and are reinforced by negative incentives (e.g., social disapproval, fear of failure, or feelings of guilt when not working).

Thus, theoretically work engagement and work

addiction are two different concepts – but is this distinction warranted empirically as well? Evidence from two independent Dutch studies revealed that workaholism (as measured in terms of working excessively and working compulsively) could clearly be distinguished from work engagement (involving the notions of vigor, dedication, and absorption). One remarkable finding here was that the third indicator of engagement (absorption) showed a substantial loading on workaholism as well. This led Schaufeli et al. (2008) to conclude that absorption "is perhaps not a unique feature of work engagement" (p. 196). Theoretically, it seems plausible that absorption overlaps with workaholism as well; the latter concept clearly includes the notion of being immersed in one's work. Apart from this overlap, it appeared that workaholism and engagement are only weakly related.

The conceptual distinction between engagement and workaholism was confirmed by inspection of the pattern of relationships between both states on the one hand, and various clusters of other concepts on the other. Whereas both engagement and workaholism are characterized by high effort expenditure at work (in terms of the time spent working and high job demands), high scores on workaholism are generally accompanied with adverse work characteristics (control and social support), lack of well-being (especially mental health), and only moderate trust in one's own work performance. Conversely, engaged workers are generally quite satisfied with their jobs and their lives, report good health, and state that they perform well. In sum, our findings underline the distinction between "good" and "bad" workaholism; good workaholics (i.e., engaged workers) tend to experience their work and health positively, whereas bad workaholics are indeed the unhappy individuals portrayed in early accounts of workaholism. These results agree with a recent, comprehensive review of research with the widely used workaholism triad (Burke, 2006). Although "work enthusiasts" or good workaholics work the same number of hours per week as "non-enthusiastic" or bad workaholics, the former have higher self-esteem, feel more personally secure, show less Type A behavior

(impatience and irritability), and experience more job, life, family, and community satisfaction than the "real" workaholics. Moreover, "work enthusiasts" have better career prospects, have a lower intention to quit, exhibit better physical and psychosomatic health, and show better well-being (Burke, 2006).

Future research

The findings discussed above suggest that work engagement can (and even must) be distinguished from workaholism. However, it should be acknowledged that the evidence presented here draws on only a limited amount of research. To our knowledge, only two studies (Schaufeli et al., 2006b, 2008) directly compared engagement and workaholism to each other. Although the findings of these two studies are quite consistent, and seem to agree with research on the workaholism triad as reviewed by Burke (2006), it would seem desirable to replicate and extend their findings using independent databases, preferably involving non-Dutch workers. The only study in which a non-Dutch – Japanese – sample was included is rather limited in scope and focused exclusively on the differential relationship of engagement and workaholism with burnout (Schaufeli et al., in press).

Moreover, the evidence so far has been collected using cross-sectional designs. Although such designs may provide a first indication of the differences and similarities between workaholism and engagement, they cannot provide any reliable indication of the possible causal direction of the associations between these two concepts, their temporal stability, and the causal order of their relationships with other variables. For example, theoretically the main distinction between these two types of workers is that workaholics work hard because they feel this strong inner drive, whereas engaged workers work hard because they like their job so much. Is it possible that these motivations for working hard change over time, e.g., could an engaged worker who is disappointed in the job maintain the same behavioral pattern (working hard) but for different reasons? Similarly, qualitative evidence (Schaufeli et al., 2001) revealed that engaged workers may have

Practical implications

The present chapter compared the concepts of workaholism and engagement with each other. Whereas it is clear that engagement (i.e., "good" workaholism) has generally positive consequences for both the individual worker and the organization they work for, the consequences of workaholism (defined as working excessively and compulsively) are generally negative. Yet, conceptually both concepts overlap to a substantial degree; both imply a (very) high level of commitment and effort expenditure; the main difference being that workaholics' high effort expenditure is due to an inner compulsion, whereas engaged workers work hard because they enjoy their work so much. There are indications that both states may alternate (Schaufeli et al., 2001), such that engaged workers may have been workaholics and vice versa. Thus, it seems important for organizations to cherish their engaged workers as well as to monitor them closely – cherish them because they are valuable to the organization; monitor them, because organizations presumably want to keep these workers happy and productive. In doing so, organizations are well-advised to provide their employees with the necessary job resources because resourceful jobs drive work engagement (see Halbesleben, Chapter 8, and Salanova, et al., Chapter 9, this volume).

There are no clear indications that workaholism involves any advantages to the organization or the individual worker. In contrast, it seems that workaholics negatively affect organizational performance, for instance by refusing to delegate tasks and making tasks unnecessarily complicated (Machlowitz, 1980; Porter, 2001). For organizations this means that they should be concerned about individuals who appear to be their most conscientious and hard-working employees. This can be done, amongst others, by:

- counteracting the typical workaholic culture of glorifying excessive long work hours, for example by role modeling of supervisors;
- training supervisors; they should make clear to their subordinates what the meaning, purpose, and importance of their work is. This could lead to a decrease in workaholism (especially working compulsively) and an increase in work engagement (especially dedication);
- avoiding hiring workaholics, for instance by including personality tests that tap typical workaholic traits such as need for dominance, obstinacy, orderliness, and rigidity (Mudrack, 2006);
- Offering Employee Assistance Programs for workaholic employees (Porter & Herring, 2006).

Unfortunately, person-directed interventions specifically aimed at reducing workaholism are scarce. Robinson (2007) has devised a guidebook for workaholics, their families, and the professionals treating them. Other person-directed interventions may include:

- improving coping skills using cognitive-behavioral techniques, for instance, time management and problem-solving training (to decrease the need to work excessively hard), and rational emotive therapy (to decrease the need to work compulsively);
- joining self-help groups like Workaholics Anonymous (www.workaholics-anonymous.org).

Hence the bottom line is that engagement – or the pull to work – is likely to be increased by organizational-level interventions, whereas workaholism – or the push to work – is likely to be decreased by individual-level interventions, albeit that organizations might facilitate the latter type of interventions for their workaholic employees.

experienced spells of burnout in the past; as burnout may be a consequence of workaholism (Taris et al., 2005a), it appears possible that workaholics may become engaged workers under the right circumstances. Thus, it seems important to study the temporal stability of workaholism and engagement as well as possible changes in these concepts, as well as the factors that facilitate these changes. For example, increases in family obligations could mean that for some engaged workers their work suddenly interferes with their family life, which is an indicator of workaholism. Similarly, positive changes at work may lead workaholic workers to reinterpret the reasons why they work excessively hard – now they work for fun rather than because they feel they must,

meaning that they are classified as engaged workers rather than workaholics.

Finally, on a more fundamental level, an attempt could be made to link engagement and workaholism to different underlying motivational systems. Based on our conceptual analyses and on the empirical findings that we have reviewed above, it could be speculated that engagement is related to an appetitive motivational system, whereas workaholism is related to an avoidant motivational system. Relevant theoretical approaches would be: reinforcement sensitivity theory (Gray & McNaughton, 2000) with reward versus punishment sensitivity; regulatory focus theory (Higgins, 2006) with promotion versus prevention focus; and goal orientation with mastery versus performance goals (Dweck, 1999). It could be hypothesized that the underlying motivation of engaged workers is reinforced by rewards (e.g., job resources), promotion focused (e.g., learning new things), and directed towards achieving mastery goals (e.g., self-enhancement). This is consistent with the notion of being pulled towards work. In contrast, the motivation of workaholics would be reinforced by punishments (e.g., disapproval from others), prevention focused (e.g., not making mistakes and errors), and directed towards achieving performance goals (e.g., outperforming colleagues). This is consistent with the notion of being pushed to work.

All in all, whereas the available evidence suggests that engagement and workaholism may be distinguished both theoretically and empirically, the relationships between these concepts and their possible correlates are as yet far from clear. Future (preferably longitudinal) research should examine more comprehensive models for the relationships between these concepts as well as their antecedents and consequences, and motivational underpinnings. We expect that in this vein more insight will be obtained in the similarities and distinctions between these two concepts, as well as in their interrelationships. For the time being, it seems that employees can be both pulled and pushed to work.

References

Beckers, D. G. J., Van der Linden, D., Smulders, P. G. W., Kompier, M. A. J., Van Veldhoven, J. P. M., & Van Yperen, N. W. (2004). Working overtime hours: Relations with fatigue, work motivation, and quality of work. *Journal of Occupational and Environmental Medicine, 46*, 1282–1289.

Bonebright, C. A., Clay, D. L., & Ankenmann, R. D. (2000). The relationship of workaholism with work-life conflict, life satisfaction, and purpose in life. *Journal of Counseling Psychology, 47*, 469–477.

Brett, J. M., & Stroh, L. K. (2003). Working 61-plus hours per week: Why do managers do it? *Journal of Applied Psychology, 88*, 67–78.

Buelens, M., & Poelmans, S. A. Y. (2004). Enriching the Spence and Robbins typology of workaholism: Demographic, motivational and organizational correlates. *Organizational Change Management, 17*, 459–470.

Burke, R. J. (2001a). Editorial: Workaholism in organizations. *International Journal of Stress Management, 8*, 65–68.

Burke, R. J. (2001b). Workaholism components, job satisfaction, and career progress. *Journal of Applied Social Psychology, 31*, 2339–2356.

Burke, R. J. (2006). Workaholic types: It is not how hard you work but why and how you work hard. In R. J. Burke (Ed.), *Research companion to working time and work addiction* (pp. 173–192). Cheltenham, UK: Edward Elgar.

Cantarow, E. (1979). Women workaholics. *Mother Jones, 6*, 56.

Cherrington, D. J. (1980). *The work ethic*. New York: American Management Association.

Dweck, C. (1999). *Self theories: Their role in motivation, personality and development*. Philadelphia: Psychology Press.

Ferenczi, S. (1919/1950). Sunday neuroses. In J. Rickman (Ed.), *Further contributions to psychoanalysis* (2nd ed., pp. 174–177). London: Hogarth Press.

Flowers, C., & Robinson, B. E. (2002). A structural and discriminant analysis of the Work Addiction Risk Test. *Educational and Psychological Measurement, 62*, 517–526.

Gray, J. A., & McNaughton, N. (2000). *The neuropsychology of anxiety* (2nd ed.). New York: Oxford University Press.

Higgins, E. T. (2006). Value for hedonic experience and engagement. *Psychological Review, 113*, 439–460.

Keichel, W. (1989). The workaholic generation. *Fortune, 119*, 50–62.

Killinger, B. (2006). The workaholic breakdown syndrome. In R. J. Burke (Ed.), *Research companion to working time and work addiction* (pp. 61–88). Cheltenham, UK: Edward Elgar.

Korn, E. R., Pratt, G. J., & Lambrou, P. T. (1987). *Hyper-performance: The A.I.M. strategy for releasing your business potential*. New York: John Wiley.

Lafargue, P. (1883). *Das Recht auf Faulheit: Widerlegung des "Recht auf Arbeit" von 1848*. Retrieved from http://www.wildcat-www.de/material/m003lafa.htm on 23 June, 2008.

Machlowitz, M. (1980). *Workaholics: Living with them, working with them*. New York: Simon & Schuster.

Maslach, C., Leiter, M. P., & Schaufeli, W. B. (2001). Job burnout. *Annual Review of Psychology, 52*, 397–422.

McMillan, L. H. W., & O'Driscoll, M. P. (2004). Workaholism and health: Implications for organizations. *Organizational Change Management, 17*, 509–519.

McMillan, L. H. W., & O'Driscoll, M. P. (2006).

Exploring new frontiers to generate an integrated definition of workaholism. In R. J. Burke (Ed.), *Research companion to working time and work addiction* (pp. 89–107). Cheltenham, UK: Edward Elgar.

McMillan, L. H. W., O'Driscoll, M. P., & Burke, R. J. (2003). Workaholism: A review of theory, research, and future directions. In C. L. Cooper & I. T. Robertson (Eds), *International review of industrial and organizational psychology* (Vol. 18, pp. 167–189). New York: Wiley.

Mudrack, P. E. (2006). Understanding workaholism: The case for behavioral tendencies. In R. J. Burke (Ed.), *Research companion to working time and work addiction* (pp. 108–128). Northampton, MA: Edward Elgar.

Naughton, T. J. (1987). A conceptual view of workaholism and implications for career counseling and research. *Career Development Quarterly, 35*, 180–187.

Oates, W. E. (1968). On being a "workaholic" (a serious jest). *Pastoral Psychology, 19*, 16–20.

Oates, W. E. (1971). *Confessions of a workaholic.* Nashville: Abingdon.

Peiperl, M., & Jones, B. (2001). Workaholics and overworkers: Productivity or pathology? *Group and Organization Management, 26*, 269–393.

Porter, G. (1996). Organizational impact of workaholism: Suggestions for research the negative outcomes of excessive work. *Journal of Occupational Health Psychology, 1*, 70–84.

Porter, G. (2001). Workaholic tendencies and the high potential for stress among co-workers. *International Journal of Stress Management, 8*, 147–164.

Porter, G., & Herring, R. A. (2006). The unlikely referral of workaholics to an employee assistance program. In R. J. Burke (Ed.), *Research companion to working time and work addiction* (pp. 242–269). Northampton, MA: Edward Elgar.

Robinson, B. E. (1989). *Work addiction.* Dearfield Beach, FL: Health Communications.

Robinson, B. E. (2007). *Chained to the desk: A guidebook for workaholics, their partners and children, and the clinicians who treat them* (2nd ed.). New York: New York University Press.

Salanova, M., Agut, S., & Peiro, J. M. (2005a). Linking organizational resources and work engagement to employee performance and customer loyalty: The mediation of service climate. *Journal of Applied Psychology, 90*, 1217–1227.

Salanova, M., Bresó, E., & Schaufeli, W. B. (2005b). Hacia un modelo espiral de la autoeficacia en el estudio del burnout y Engagement [Towards a spiral model of self-efficacy in burnout and engagement research] *Ansiedad y Estrés, 11*, 215–231.

Schaufeli, W. B., & Bakker, A. B. (2004). Job demands, job resources and their relationship with burnout and engagement: A multi-sample study. *Journal of Organizational Behaviour, 25*, 293–315.

Schaufeli, W. B., Bakker, A. B., & Salanova, M. (2006a). The measurement of work engagement with a short questionnaire: A cross-national study. *Educational and Psychological Measurement, 66*, 701–716.

Schaufeli, W. B., Martinez, I., Marques Pinto, A., Salanova, M., & Bakker, A. B. (2002a). Burnout and engagement in university students: A cross-national study. *Journal of Cross-Cultural Psychology, 33*, 464–481.

Schaufeli, W. B., Salanova, M., Gonzalez-Roma. V., & Bakker, A. B. (2002b). The measurement of engagement and burnout: A confirmative factor analytic approach. *Journal of Happiness Studies, 3*, 71–92.

Schaufeli, W. B., Shimazu, A, & Taris, T. (in press). Being driven to work exceptionally hard. The evaluation of a two-factor measure of workaholism in the Netherlands and Japan. *Cross-Cultural Research.*

Schaufeli, W. B., Taris, T. W., & Bakker, A. B. (2006b). Dr Jekyll or Mr Hyde? On the differences between work engagement and workaholism. In R. J. Burke (Ed.), *Research companion to working time and work addiction* (pp. 193–217). Cheltenham, UK: Edward Elgar.

Schaufeli, W., Taris, T., LeBlanc, P., Peeters, M., Bakker, A. B., & De Jonge, J. (2001). Maakt arbeid gezond? Op zoek naar de bevlogen werknemer (Can work produce health? The quest for the engaged worker). *De Psycholoog, 36*, 422–428.

Schaufeli, W. B., Taris, T. W., & Van Rhenen, W. (2008). Workaholism, burnout, and work engagement: Three of a kind or three different kinds of employee well-being? *Applied Psychology: An International Review, 57*, 173–203.

Scott, K. S., Moore, K. S., & Miceli, M. P. (1997). An exploration of the meaning and consequences of workaholism. *Human Relations, 50*, 287–314.

Shimazu, A., Schaufeli, W. B., Kosugi, S., Suzuki, A., Nashiwa, A., et al. (2008). Work engagement in Japan: Validation of the Japanese version of the Utrecht Work Engagement Scale. *Applied Psychology: An International Review, 57*, 510–523.

Spence, J. T., & Robbins, A. S. (1992). Workaholism: Definition, measurement, and preliminary results. *Journal of Personality Assessment, 58*, 160–178.

Taris, T., & Schaufeli, W. (2007). Workaholisme [workaholism]. In W. Schaufeli and A. Bakker (Eds), *De psychologie van arbeid en gezondheid* (2nd ed., pp. 359–372). Houten, The Netherlands: Bohn Stafleu van Loghum.

Taris, T. W., Schaufeli, W. B., & Verhoeven, L. C. (2005a). Workaholism in the Netherlands: Measurement and implications for job strain and work-nonwork conflict. *Applied Psychology: An International Review, 54,* 37–60.

Taris, T., Schreurs, P., & Sepmeijer, K. J. (2005b). Web-based data collection in occupational health psychology. In J. Houdmont and S. McIntyre (Eds), *Occupational Health Psychology: Key papers of the European Academy of Occupational Health Psychology* (pp. 398–406). Oporto: Publishmai.

Unwin, T. (2004). Gustave Flaubert, the hermit of Croisset. In T. Unwin (Ed.), *The Cambridge companion to Flaubert* (pp. 1–24). Cambridge: Cambridge University Press.

Van der Linden, D., Beckers, D. G. J., & Taris, T. W. (2007). Reinforcement sensitivity theory at work: Punishment sensitivity as dispositional source of job-related stress. *European Journal of Personality, 21,* 889–909.

The power of positive psychology: Psychological capital and work engagement

David Sweetman and Fred Luthans

Similar to the role of positivity in the workplace, the importance of engaged employees has long been recognized and assumed to have an impact on performance. However, also like positivity in general, only in recent times, with the advent of evidence-based management, has focused scientific attention (i.e., theory building and empirical analysis) been given to the better understanding of engagement and its impact. Yet, despite the now recognized importance, Gallup surveys consistently find that most employees in all types of organizations across the world are not fully engaged in their work (e.g., Avolio & Luthans, 2006; Harter, Schmidt, & Hayes, 2002).

In the face of today's turbulent environment characterized by organizational downsizing and rapidly escalating technological advancement and innovation, employees are expected to adapt to new environments with greater demands and fewer resources. As indicated in the Gallup data, employee engagement is being severely challenged in contemporary organizations. The chapters of this book offer better understanding and alternative ways to meet these challenges of work engagement. In this chapter, the purpose is to apply our recent work on positive organizational behavior (POB) and particularly psychological capital (PsyCap) to understanding the process and meeting the challenge of employee engagement in today's organizations. Specifically, after first briefly summarizing what we mean by psychological capital (PsyCap) and work engagement, we propose a conceptual model that relates these two constructs and also the role that positive emotions may play. Particular attention is given to the role that each of the four recognized psychological resources (i.e., efficacy, optimism, hope, and resiliency) making up PsyCap, as well as overall PsyCap and positive emotions, play in employee engagement. The chapter then concludes with the practical implications that PsyCap and positive emotions may have for meeting the challenges of work engagement.

Positive approach to organizational behavior

An analysis of the popular business press found that in recent times the use of negatively based words (e.g., beat, stress) increased four times more than the use of positively based words (e.g., compassion, virtue) (Walsh, Weber, & Margolis, 2003). At the same time, positively-oriented personal development books in the business professional literature have been very successful. In the academic world, psychology has been clearly dominated by the negative (Seligman & Csikszentmihalyi, 2000), but as was recently noted by Luthans and Avolio (2009), over the years probably more attention in organizational behavior has been given to the positive than the negative. Nevertheless, there is still a "need to address underrepresented positive constructs in the OB field such as hope, optimism, and resiliency [and] it is important to aggressively pursue research on positive constructs, because like it or not, the practitioners are doing so and too often are advocating concepts, methods and interventions with no proven validity" (Luthans & Avolio, 2009).

While industrial-era organizations relied heavily on control by mechanistic management and efficiency principles exemplified by the pioneering work of Frederick W. Taylor, modern organizations are focusing more on managing human capital. Most are beginning to recognize the need for employees who are confident in their abilities, optimistic about success, focused on the willpower and means to achieve goals, and are able to bounce back when faced with adversity and setback. In other words, in today's context, there is becoming a recognized need to go beyond managing for deficits only, beyond just managing to avoid employee burnout, and move to the opposite, positive end of the spectrum,

developing psychological capital and enabling engagement in the workplace.

Specifically, we define POB as "the study and application of positively oriented human resource strengths and psychological capacities that can be measured, developed, and effectively managed for performance improvement in today's workplace" (Luthans, 2002b, p. 59). As noted above, this POB approach does not claim to have discovered the importance of positivity in the workplace, but rather is simply calling for focused attention on positive, state-like psychological resources that have performance impact (see Luthans, 2002a, 2002b). To differentiate from the positive-oriented popular-press personal development literature, or the relatively fixed, trait-like positively oriented organizational behavior literature, the specific inclusion criteria that we use for POB include: (1) having a basis in theory and research, (2) possessing validly measurable qualities, (3) being "state-like" and thus developable, and (4) having workplace performance impact (Luthans, 2002b, p. 59; see also, Luthans, 2002a; Luthans, Youssef, & Avolio, 2007b).

While this conception of POB could be considered a utilitarian management-driven view which does not consider employee well-being (Wright, 2003), it is not. On the contrary, as argued by Zwetsloot and Pot (2004), there is strategic value in employee health and well-being, with investment in employee wellness and development producing substantial workplace performance impact, and leading to an engaged workforce. As Bakker and Schaufeli (2008) have noted, this can be accomplished through different forms of capital possessed by the organization and employees. This includes economic capital, the material assets of the organization; human capital, the knowledge, experience, and expertise of employees; social capital, the network of relationships; and what we have identified as psychological capital (Luthans & Youssef, 2004; Luthans et al., 2007b), the focus of this chapter as related to work engagement.

Psychological capital

Psychological capital or simply PsyCap is an outgrowth of POB and is defined as:

an individual's positive psychological state of development characterized by: (1) having confidence (self efficacy) to take on and put in the necessary effort to succeed at challenging tasks; (2) making a positive attribution (optimism) about succeeding now and in the future; (3) persevering toward goals, and when necessary, redirecting paths to goals (hope) in order to succeed; and (4) when beset by problems and adversity, sustaining and bouncing back and even beyond (resilience) to attain success.

(Luthans et al., 2007b, p. 3)

The positive agentic resources individuals possess across situations, and which enable one to move towards flourishing and success, are the common theme underlying each of the four positive psychological resource capacities (i.e., efficacy, optimism, hope, and resiliency). Although these four psychological resources are commonly used in everyday language, we use very precise meanings of them based on theory, measurement, and research support from positive psychology (Seligman & Csikszentmihalyi, 2000; Snyder & Lopez, 2002) and positive organizational behavior (Luthans et al., 2007b). In combination, these four positive resources represent a second-order, core factor called psychological capital (Luthans, Avolio, Avey, & Norman, 2007a; Luthans et al., 2007b). A widening stream of research on the PsyCap construct has found support for the validity of the core construct itself, as well as its relation to a number of desired outcomes such as performance and satisfaction (see Luthans et al., 2007a).

Research has demonstrated that the core construct of PsyCap is more strongly related to desired outcomes than the individual constructs of which it is comprised (Luthans et al., 2007a). Conceptually this can be explained by the combined motivational effects being broader and more impactful than any one of the constructs individually. For example, if employees are resiliently able to bounce back from a setback, while also being efficacious, optimistic, and hopeful, they will be more motivated to persist and be successful even beyond the level at which they were

before the adverse event. Empirically, Luthans et al. (2007a), compared measurement models testing various factor loadings. In each of the model comparisons, the strongest fit was the second-order factor model indicating that while each of the four components shares distinct properties, they are best understood as representing the common underlying psychological resource termed psychological capital (Luthans et al., 2007a)

Psychological capital is measured by the Psy-Cap Questionnaire (PCQ; see Luthans et al., 2007b for the entire instrument and Luthans et al., 2007a for the validity analysis). The PCQ includes six items for each of the four components: efficacy, optimism, hope, and resiliency. Items are measured on a six-point Likert scale, and items include: "I feel confident helping to set targets/goals in my work area" (efficacy); "When things are uncertain for me at work, I usually expect the best" (optimism); "If I should find myself in a jam at work, I could think of many ways to get out of it" (hope); and "I usually take stressful things at work in my stride" (resiliency). While each of these four constructs is commonly recognized in positive psychology, the conceptualization and empirical support of the core construct of psychological capital or PsyCap is still emerging (see Luthans & Avolio, 2009; Luthans et al., 2007a, 2007b; Luthans & Youssef, 2007) and has not yet been conceptually related to work engagement. We propose in this chapter that PsyCap can contribute to better understanding and support of the importance of work engagement in general, and specifically be related to the elements of vigor, dedication, and absorption that are recognized to comprise work engagement (Schaufeli, Bakker, & Salanova, 2006).

Work engagement

As defined by Kahn (1990, p. 3), work engagement of employees relates to "how the psychological experiences of work and work contexts shape the process of people presenting and absenting themselves during task performance." The individual accomplishes this through expression and employment of the "preferred self" in connecting with the task and others, and being personally present and fully active in performance of the role (Kahn, 1990). Using this definition as our point of departure, we now turn to the current state of research on work engagement. As this book is dedicated to the topic, we will only provide here a brief overview in order to provide some background for our proposed relationship of PsyCap to work engagement. For a more comprehensive discussion of work engagement, please refer to the other chapters in this volume.

For our purposes, we draw from the job demands-resources (JD-R) model (Bakker & Demerouti, 2007; Schaufeli & Bakker, 2004). The JD-R model integrates previous lines of research on work engagement, as well as burnout, by positioning work engagement as the antipode of burnout (Maslach, Schaufeli, & Leiter, 2001). This approach to work engagement tends to use the Utrecht Work Engagement Scale to measure engagement (Schaufeli & Bakker, Chapter 2, this volume; Schaufeli, Salanova, Gonzalez-Roma, & Bakker, 2002). Similar to PsyCap, importantly engagement is viewed as a "state-like" phenomenon, not as a fleeting, temporary state such as mood, nor as relatively non-malleable, fixed characteristics such as the Big Five personality traits. Specifically, engagement is portrayed as an affective-cognitive state-like condition not focused on a specific individual, object, event, or behavior (Schaufeli, Bakker, & Salanova, 2006). Empirical investigations of the JD-R model have provided evidence to support the idea that job resources have the greatest impact on work engagement when demands of the job (e.g., workload, poor physical environment) are high (Bakker & Demerouti, 2007). In another important way similar to PsyCap, this form of engagement is theorized to be a higher-order core factor comprising three interrelated constructs: vigor, dedication, and absorption (Schaufeli et al., 2006).

Vigor is defined as consisting of high levels of willingness to invest energy into the work at hand, coupled with the mental resilience to persevere even in the case of difficulties (Schaufeli et al., 2006). Energy is the underlying bipolar dimension with vigor at one end, and emotional exhaustion at the other (Gonzalez-Roma,

Schaufeli, Bakker, & Lloret, 2006). We would suggest that this vigor directly relates to the PsyCap capacities of efficacy in motivating the effort, hope in providing the willpower and developing alternate pathways to achievement, optimism in expecting future success, and resiliency in the continued pursuit of goals.

Dedication in the context of the JD-R model is described as "being strongly involved in one's work and experiencing a sense of significance, enthusiasm, inspiration, pride, and challenge" (Schaufeli et al., 2006, p. 3). Identification is the underlying bipolar dimension, with opposite ends of dedication and cynicism (Gonzalez-Roma et al., 2006). Once again we believe that there are direct linkages to all four of the individual components of PsyCap: the efficacy related to involvement in one's work, optimism in attributions of significance and pride, hope in dedicated waypower and pathways, and resiliency in continuing in the face of challenging obstacles and adversity.

Absorption is the third and final aspect of engagement. Individuals absorbed in their work can be thought of as being fully engrossed in, and in a mindset enabling full concentration in that work (Schaufeli et al., 2006). At the positively deviant end of the absorption spectrum, individuals experience a state called flow, whereby time passes quickly and one has difficulties with detaching oneself from work (Csikszentmihalyi, 1990). We would argue that this component of work engagement directly relates to individual efficacy through having the confidence to be absorbed, optimism through the individual expecting positive outcomes will occur, and the resiliency to be persistently absorbed in the task.

The JD-R model posits these three facets are impacted by two factors: (1) job resources and (2) job demands (Bakker & Demerouti, 2007; Schaufeli & Bakker, 2004). Job resources are the psychological, social, organizational, and physical resources that (a) enable goal achievement, (b) reduce or buffer against job demands, and (c) enable growth and development. Job demands, on the other hand, consume psychological and physical energy. Examples include high workload and poor working conditions. Within this framework, the higher-order PsyCap construct, as well as the individual component positive capacities, can be thought of as job resources, enabling goal achievement, reducing the impact of job demands, and enabling the individual to develop and grow.

To gain insight and understanding into the four capacities that comprise PsyCap, and how they relate to the three components of work engagement, we now turn our attention to independently examining each component of PsyCap and its proposed relation to work engagement. Figure 5.1 provides a graphical depiction of these relationships, and also includes the role PsyCap plays in impacting work engagement indirectly through positive emotions. We will then conclude with our proposition of the greater predictive power of PsyCap for work engagement versus the four components individually.

Efficacy and work engagement

Perhaps best fitting the criteria for PsyCap inclusion is efficacy (Luthans et al., 2007b). Based on the extensive theory and research of Albert Bandura (1997), efficacy, simply stated, is confidence, or the belief in one's ability to succeed at a particular task in a specific context. Applied to the workplace by Stajkovic and Luthans (1998b, p. 66), efficacy is defined as "the employee's conviction or confidence about his or her abilities to mobilize the motivation, cognitive resources, and courses of action needed to successfully execute a specific task within a given context."

Efficacy is widely recognized to come from four primary sources (Bandura, 1997) that we would propose are all relevant to work engagement. First, task-mastery (i.e., the ability to successfully accomplish specific tasks) is a primary source of efficacy, and leads to the belief that success can be replicated in the future (Bandura, 1997). When considering the JD-R model of work engagement, mastery would seem to be an important ingredient in absorption. That is, an individual competently able to accomplish a particular task can become absorbed in the overall achievement of the task, rather than being distracted by trying

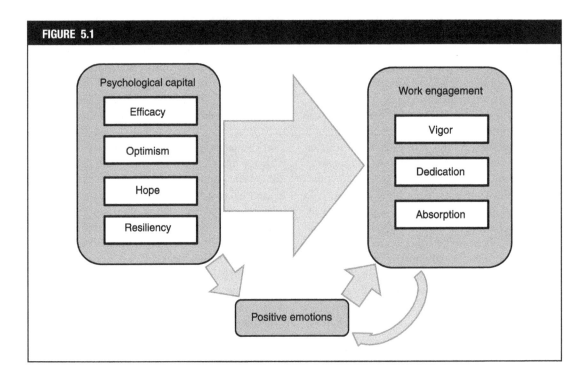

FIGURE 5.1

Proposed conceptual model relating psychological capital to work engagement through positive emotions.

to comprehend all the detailed steps necessary to complete the task. Mastery should also increase vigor, as more energy becomes available to devote to the task.

Other major sources of efficacy identified by Bandura (1997) include vicarious learning or modeling from someone considered similar and relevant to oneself. The basic idea here is "if they can do it, I can too." A third is the social persuasion, positive feedback or encouragement from a coach, mentor, or other respected role model. Both vicarious learning and encouragement behaviors would seem to impact one's engagement through dedication. In other words, someone whose confidence is increased through modeling or through encouragement will be able to identify with personally being able to accomplish the task, while also reducing their cynicism (e.g., see Avey, Wernsing, & Luthans, 2008b). Fourth and finally, Bandura (1997) found that efficacy can be increased through the motivation of emotional or physical arousal. In terms of work engagement, this would seem to lead to increased vigor and energy.

Those high in efficacy are often characterized by their tenacity and persistence, driven by their belief in future success. Conversely, low efficacy has been found to predict burnout, the antipode of work engagement (Gonzalez-Roma et al., 2006). Furthermore, burnout has been found to reduce efficacy, creating a downward spiral of disengagement (Schaufeli & Bakker, 2004). Bandura (1997) has been able to clearly demonstrate that greater efficacy is related to becoming absorbed in the task as well as to expending higher levels of energy and effort to complete a task. It can be argued that efficacy is the most important psychological mechanism for producing positive work-related outcomes (e.g., see the meta-analysis by Stajkovic & Luthans, 1998a). Overall, we propose that the efficacy component of PsyCap relates directly to each of the three components of work engagement: vigor, dedication, and absorption.

Optimism and work engagement

Another key positive resource meeting the inclusion criteria of PsyCap is optimism. Simply stated, "optimists are people who expect good

things to happen to them; pessimists are people who expect bad things to happen to them" (Carver & Scheier, 2002, p. 231). Utilizing an expectancy framework, optimism plays an influential role in one's approach to job duties, with those high in optimism expecting success when presented with a challenge. However, it should be noted that optimism is an individual-level attribution, that is, individuals who are high in optimism are high in their belief in their individual success, but not necessarily group-level or organizational-level outcomes (Avey et al., 2008b).

Although there are similarities, there is both conceptual (Luthans et al., 2007b) and empirical (Luthans et al., 2007a) evidence that optimism is distinct from efficacy. For example, those high in optimism believe they will succeed regardless of their abilities (Avey et al., 2008b). Therefore, in order to be effective, optimism must be realistic (Seligman & Csikszentmihalyi, 2000).

In addition to expecting future success, Seligman (1998) has also found that an individual's explanatory (or attribution) style relates to their level of optimism. In other words, those high in optimism tend to attribute success to the self and to global attributes, while attributing failures to external, uncontrollable, or specific to the situation attributes. Thus, optimists conclude success is something they can replicate and control. In contrast, pessimists tend to attribute failures to themselves and global attributes while attributing success to external factors over which they have little or no control. Moreover, pessimists further conclude that future attempts at a task would likely result in unfamiliar and stressful events marked by failure.

While efficacy and optimism are distinct, a positive explanatory style increases efficacy beliefs regarding future tasks. Optimism is also related to other PsyCap constructs in that it helps people to "see adversity as a challenge, transform problems into opportunities [hope], put in hours to refine skills, persevere in finding solutions to obstacles or difficult problems [resiliency], maintain confidence [efficacy], rebound quickly after setbacks and persist [resiliency]" (Schulman, 1999, p. 32). In sum, those employees possessing high levels of optimism will continue to believe in their positive potential regardless of previous experiences (Avey et al., 2008b).

While high job demands can limit engagement through a decreased feeling of control and increased cynicism, this can be counteracted through the impact of the resource of optimism in reducing cynicism and increasing dedication by a sense of personal control over the demands at hand (Karasek, 1979). In this regard, the optimism associated with feeling in control is a buffer of sorts against stressful job demands (Kahn & Byosiere, 1992). The optimistic explanatory style may also lower the adverse impact of stressors and make them feel more understandable (Bakker & Demerouti, 2007). For example, this may occur by optimistically making external attributions for a stressful condition and thus not feeling the stressor was caused by a personal inadequacy, a systemic internal factor. In addition, optimism enables one to be more psychologically available through the expectation of a positive outcome. That is, the optimist may be more likely to choose to be available to the task at hand, given the expectation of a positive outcome. This greater psychological availability leads to higher levels of proposed engagement through absorption (Kahn, 1990). In sum, we propose that the optimism component of PsyCap relates directly to the dedication and absorption components of work engagement.

Hope and work engagement

The third identified facet of PsyCap is hope, defined by Snyder, Irving, and Anderson (1991, p. 287) as a "positive motivational state that is based on an interactively derived sense of successful (1) agency (goal-directed energy) and (2) pathways (planning to meet goals)." As explained by a social cognitive framework, the construct of hope may help explain how appropriate intentionality is derived from greater cognitive complexity. Those high in hope have the ability to not only determine a pathway to achieve their goal, but also to generate multiple pathways and adapt their plans as needed. They continue to provide hope for goal achievement, even in the face of new challenges.

Hope should not be confused with optimism.

Whereas optimism involves a vision and expectation of positive outcomes, hope involves the pragmatic execution of reaching a specific desired goal or outcome. Additionally, those high in hope are able to frame tasks in such a way as to provide the internal motivation necessary to complete the task (Avey et al., 2008b).

In relation to efficacy, hope is people's belief in their abilities to (a) generate possible pathways to a goal, (b) take actions toward achieving the goal, and (c) be successful in goal attainment. With high willpower (i.e., motivation) and high waypower (i.e., capacity to determine many alternate methods to achieving a goal), individuals would be expected to incorporate more pathways into the mental strategy and therefore increase their capacity to take proper perspective. These willpower and waypower components of hope can create a positive upward spiral where one component builds on the other (Luthans et al., 2007b), similar to a spiral of resources directly impacting work engagement (Salanova, Schaufeli, Xanthopoulou, & Bakker, Chapter 9, this volume). Moreover, while building the capacity for agency and pathways for achieving goals, hope also builds capacities for resilience, optimism, and efficacy.

Hope, the motivated, persistent pursuit of goals and proactively determined pathways to the goals, is proposed here to be a psychological antecedent to the vigor component of work engagement. Specifically, we suggest hope can lead to enabling the energy to be vigorously dedicated to a goal. This is in contrast to the feeling of exhaustion and depletion of energy associated with burnout. As noted by Snyder (2002, p. 258), hope "takes on special significance when people encounter impediments. During such instances of blockage, agency helps the person to apply the requisite motivation to the best alternative pathway." In this way, by being hopeful, one is showing persistent dedication toward achieving one's goals.

Hope would not only seem to be a positive contributor to work engagement, it may even be a requirement. Lack of hope is associated with burnout. Without hope, the willpower is not present for one to accept new challenges, nor the waypower to successfully determine pathways to achievement (Maslach et al., 2001). Overall, we propose that the hope component of PsyCap relates directly to the vigor and dedication components of work engagement.

Resiliency and work engagement

The fourth and final primary component of PsyCap is resiliency, defined as a "positive psychological capacity to rebound, to 'bounce back' from adversity, uncertainty, conflict, failure, or even positive change, progress and increased responsibility" (Luthans, 2002a, p. 702). Central to this resiliency is the capacity to positively adapt to, and move beyond, significant changes. As described by Masten and Reed (2002), the individual possessing resilience not only survives, but also thrives through positive adjustment to current adversities. Resilient individuals may also find they are at ease outside of their normal comfort zone. This enables individuals to challenge their personal assumptions and build further resilient capacities through positive adaptation to challenging situations (Luthans et al., 2007b). As with optimism, a positive explanatory style may also increase resiliency, because an external attribution of negative events enables successful coping with, and moving beyond, unexpected events.

It should be noted that although the JD-R model and PsyCap both incorporate resiliency, the construct is conceptualized in somewhat different ways. Whereas both articulate the same outcome of resiliency – that is, continuing toward pursuit of a goal – a difference lies in the mechanisms to achieve that resiliency. In terms of engagement, especially in the vigor dimension of the JD-R model, resiliency is equated with persistence. However, under PsyCap, resiliency is conceptualized to a larger extent as a psychological capacity to "bounce back" from adversity and readily face future uncertainty. However, rather than a potential disjoint in the relationship between PsyCap and work engagement, or even a simple issue of tautology, this difference provides theoretical support for the proposed relationship between PsyCap and work engagement. In particular, PsyCap can be thought of as a general

pool or "bank" of psychological resources from which one can draw when faced with any of a large number of difficult situations (Avolio & Luthans, 2006). This relationship is supported in the work engagement literature by Xanthopoulou, Bakker, Demerouti, & Schaufeli's (2007) study involving efficacy and optimism. In contrast, work engagement is an outcome of leveraging such a bank of positive psychological resources.

In the case of resiliency, the individuals draw from their psychological resource pool in order to exert resilient behaviors through the motivation of engagement in the work at hand, thus exhibiting the vigor of persistence. The enacting of these psychological resources can lead to individual differences in handling potentially stressful aspects of the work environment. This is consistent with findings demonstrating that individual differences in reactions are not caused by some inborn or dispositional relatively fixed trait, but by the developable capability to handle such situations and return to, never leave, or even increase the level of well-being experienced (Bakker, Van Der Zee, Lewig, & Dollard, 2006a).

Resiliency resources can produce a buffering effect, whereby work engagement is maintained despite burnout-inducing job demands (Bakker, Demerouti, & Euwema, 2005). Consistent with Kahn's (1992) view, this buffering hypothesis claims that the individual with resiliency can buffer the effect of potentially stressing job demands. While the ability to be resilient is developable, as informed by research on resource drain (Edwards & Rothbard, 2000), the "buffer of resiliency" itself can be seen as even more state-like, needing to be "re-charged" following especially demanding aspects of the job. This buffering can reduce the likelihood that activities will be stress-inducing, alter perceptions and cognitions of such potential stressors, and even reduce the health-damaging consequences of such responses or, simply put, reduce disengagement (Kahn & Byosiere, 1992, p. 622). However, if an individual's buffer of resiliency is low and other job resources are few, these same activities can invoke greater levels of stress, leading to deeper disengagement (Bakker et al., 2005).

The resiliency buffer can fluctuate rapidly. The

day-to-day level of recovery of one's buffer of resiliency can positively relate to the day-to-day level of work engagement the following work day (Sonnentag, 2003). The recovery and development of this resiliency then has a direct, positive effect on energy, increasing engagement through greater vigor (Marks, 1977; Sonnentag, 2003). Masten and colleagues suggest that one way to develop such resiliency is through personal assets or resources (e.g., cognitive abilities, positive self-perception and self-regulation, and especially relationship-based assets, see Masten & Reed, 2002). Thus, building such personal resources leading to resiliency may result in heightened work engagement. Hobfoll and Shirom (2001) also argue that employees not guarding scarce personal resources will dedicate them to the task at hand. Rather than guarding these resources, individuals will be able to bring their personal selves to their work and therefore become engaged (Maslach et al., 2001).

Not only can resiliency serve as a buffer against stress-inducing job demands, it can also serve to undo the negative effects of past stress. According to the broaden-and-build model, positive psychological states, such as resiliency, are able to reverse the effects of job demands while building long-lasting capacity for the future (Fredrickson, 2003). These effects are reversed through a broadening of one's cognitive strategies and thought–action repertoire for understanding and interacting in the present environment. This in turn leads to building of the enduring resources to continue to do so into the future. Thus, resiliency is related to work engagement through increasing personal resources to handle job demands as well as through resources to undo the negative effects of past job demands. In total, we propose that the resiliency component of PsyCap relates directly to all three components of work engagement: vigor, dedication, and absorption.

Psychological capital and work engagement

While the four psychological resources comprising an individual's PsyCap – efficacy, hope, optimism, and resiliency – have direct relations to the three components of work engagement – vigor, dedication, and absorption – we propose even

greater predictive power may come from considering the higher-order relationship of these factors. For example, with regard to the overall core construct of PsyCap and employee dedication, recent research has found a direct impact linking increased levels of PsyCap with decreased levels of cynicism, with an additional indirect effect through positive emotions (Avey et al., 2008). Regarding overall PsyCap and absorption, many theoretical links have been drawn to PsyCap capacities creating the conditions necessary for flow, where individuals become absorbed in their work (Luthans et al., 2007b). As noted earlier, research has shown that PsyCap overall provides a greater resource than the four psychological resources taken individually (Luthans et al., 2007a). This finding supports the notion that PsyCap may be a resource that is a greater buffer to burnout than the individual components, and also may be above and beyond simply reducing job demands (Bakker et al., 2005).

The four PsyCap resources have been shown to have discriminant validity (Luthans et al., 2007a), but they are still somewhat interrelated (i.e., convergent validity, Luthans et al., 2007a). We propose that they build upon each other in order to create an upward spiral of resources which can lead to employee engagement. This upward spiral may subsequently broaden an individual's mindset (Fredrickson, 2003; also see Dweck's, 2006 concept of "growth mindset" that people can change and develop their behavior over time). This broadened, growing mindset from enhanced PsyCap may provide greater energy and engagement than is possible with lower levels of PsyCap. That is, not only do cognitive and metacognitive processes broaden and grow, but in addition greater behavioral repertoires are built (Fredrickson, 2003; Dweck, 2006). Furthermore, high levels of positive psychological resources produce a greater likelihood of individuals risking these resources for the potential of leveraging them into additional increased resources, leading to a further gain spiral.

We would argue that our proposed relationship between PsyCap and work engagement would also be supported by other extant theories. For example, the relationship between PsyCap and work engagement would be supported by Hobfoll's (2001) conservation of resources (COR) theory whereby PsyCap enables the accumulation of resources valued and protected by individuals, and necessary for engagement to occur. Taken together, the synergistic potential of efficacy, hope, optimism, and resiliency making up PsyCap would seem to be a powerful predictor of the interrelated components of vigor, dedication, and absorption associated with work engagement. Given this potentially powerful relationship, we would propose that a key component in developing work engagement can be found in developing PsyCap.

Psychological capital: A developable resource

Given the state-like, developable nature of PsyCap (Luthans, Avey, & Patera, 2008; Luthans et al., 2007b), the also state-like nature of work engagement (Sonnentag, Dormann, & Demerouti, Chapter 3, this volume), and the relationships proposed between the two in this chapter, it follows that work engagement can be both positively influenced and developed through the development of PsyCap. The development of PsyCap has been demonstrated through the use of PsyCap Micro-Interventions (PMI): short, 1–3 hour training workshops which leverage developmental mechanisms including task-mastery experiences, positive role modeling, goal setting, contingency planning, and social support activities (Luthans, Avey, Avolio, Norman, & Combs, 2006; Luthans et al., 2007b; 2008). These PMI training modules are aimed at developing all four resources and are integrated to develop overall PsyCap. Not only does the PMI develop PsyCap and its components, it also serves to generate greater awareness and sensitivity of the individual's strengths, which we propose in turn would lead to increased engagement through the individual's realization of the availability of these resources (Kahn, 1990). Further, PMI may enable individuals to be authentically present (i.e., engaged) in their roles, which in turn creates an effective response to change and growth in a variety of settings. This authentic presence may occur through greater self-awareness of one's own personal strengths and confidence (i.e., efficacy) to successfully contribute in a given situation; set goals and pathways to accomplishing these goals (i.e., hope); have a positive expectation and explanatory style of success (i.e., optimism); and the resources to bounce back and beyond from a setback (i.e., resiliency). Importantly, this PsyCap development has been demonstrated in PMI workshops (Luthans et al., 2006) and online (Luthans et al., 2008).

These developmental possibilities become especially relevant when the notable intra-individual differences in work engagement are considered (Fisher, 2000; Kahn, 1990). In addition to the potential to increase work engagement through developing PsyCap, it would also be possible to focus on building work engagement directly (Leiter & Maslach, Chapter 12, this volume). Thus, given the state-like qualities of both PsyCap and work engagement, the development of these resources seems both viable and desirable. Also relevant to developing PsyCap and work engagement are other resources that can be influenced by PsyCap and may then in turn influence work engagement. As shown in Figure 5.1, this is why we propose a partially mediating effect of positive emotions in the PsyCap–work engagement relationship.

The role of positive emotions

In addition to the proposed direct impact PsyCap may have upon work engagement, there is also preliminary research indicating that PsyCap may have a mediated effect on engagement through positive emotions (Avey et al., 2008b). Specifically, higher levels of PsyCap were found to predict higher positive emotions which, in turn, led to more engaged employees. This empirically derived relationship is theoretically supported through cognitive mediation theory of emotions in the workplace (see Lazarus, 1993, for overview; also see Weiss & Cropanzano, 1996). This theory posits that employee psychological beliefs, expectancies, and appraisals (e.g., efficacy, optimism, hope, and resilience; and overall PsyCap) may be a source of positive emotions and subsequent employee attitudes and behaviors (e.g., work engagement).

One explanation for the empirically supported relationship may be that PsyCap leads to higher levels of positive emotions through the ways in which events are interpreted. For example, the same event can cause stressful emotions for one individual but not another. In other words, employees may automatically interpret organizational events in such ways that the events cause them to experience disengaging attitudes such as cynicism and burnout. This often occurs without the individual being consciously aware of the connection between these thoughts and emotions (Lazarus, 1993). Alternatively, employees can interpret events in a positive way, though in this case the mechanisms of efficacy, optimism, hope, and resiliency (i.e., PsyCap). For example, Tugade and Fredrickson (2004) have found support for the notion that cognitive states and abilities, such as resilience, are antecedents to positive emotions, with "high-resilient individuals tend[ing] to experience positive emotions even amidst stress" (p. 331). Individuals with such psychological capacities are more likely to experience positive emotions, even during events that may be interpreted as stressful by co-workers (Avey et al., 2008b). This theory and research support our proposal that PsyCap may be a source of positive emotions.

The literature suggests several possible mechanisms through which positive emotions may impact desirable outcomes. These include better decision making (Chuang, 2007), as well as a number of indicators of success and well-being (Lyubomirsky, King, & Diener, 2005). Additionally, Fredrickson's (2003) broaden-and-build theory posits that positive emotions *broaden* people's momentary thought–action repertoires and *build* their enduring personal resources. This suggests that somewhat momentary emotional states can produce conditions leading not only to work engagement through the broadening of one's thought–action repertoire, but may also contribute to the building of psychological capacities such as efficacy, optimism, hope, and resiliency – capacities which are relatively more enduring (i.e., "state-like") than the fleeting, momentary emotional state that helped to create them. For example, Fredrickson and Losada (2005) found

positive emotions can spark dynamic processes with downstream repercussions for growth and resilience. In this regard, in conjunction with PsyCap, we suggest these positive emotions can create a self-reinforcing upward spiral of outcomes leading to greater levels of work engagement (see also Salanova et al., Chapter 9, this volume).

Higher levels of positive emotion have been found to frequently lead to more social integration and higher levels of engagement (Wright & Staw, 1999; Salanova, Agut, & Pieró, 2005; Giardini & Frese, 2008). Positive emotions also may lead to increased levels of energy and vigor (Marks, 1977), and being more available to engage in a role (Rothbard, 2001). Additionally, with regard to decreasing disengagement, positive emotions may be able to "undo" the dysfunctional effects of the negative emotions (Fredrickson, 2003). These negative emotions are associated with burnout and job demands (for a meta-analysis, see Lee & Ashforth, 1996). Conversely, preliminary research has demonstrated that those individuals low in PsyCap experience lower levels of positive emotions, which in turn leads to lower levels of work engagement (Avey et al., 2008b). However, too much of anything may become a problem, and positive emotions are no exception.

Just as there would be no conception of the benefits of daytime without a conception of nighttime, so too the benefits of positive emotions are predicated on the existence of negative emotions. Fredrickson and colleagues' (Fredrickson & Losada, 2005; Losada, 1999; Losada & Heaphy, 2004) research regarding the "balance" of positive and negative emotions for healthy, productive relationships in the workplace has shown a ratio of about 3:1 positive to negative as ideal. This ideal 3:1 blend generally leads to the most positively deviant levels of engaged functioning and well-being, often referred to as flourishing or thriving (Keyes, 2002; for more on flourishing/thriving, see Spreitzer, Lam, & Fritz, Chapter 10, this volume). This notion of balancing positive and negative emotions could be thought to complicate the idea of enabling the development of engagement in employees.

However, on the contrary, it also seems to underscore the importance of developing employee PsyCap, which not only has a direct positive impact on work engagement, but also is an important personal resource for effectively managing both positive and negative emotions.

Conclusion

In this chapter, to help meet the challenges of work engagement we have proposed and supported psychological capital as a potential valuable positive psychological resource which relates to, and when developed, may lead to increased employee engagement in today's workplace. In the process, we have discussed the relationship of this higher-order, core construct directly, the component resources individually, and the additional impact PsyCap may have on work engagement through positive emotions. Today's organizations need members who are what Van Maanen and Schein (1979) called many years ago "engaged role innovators" as opposed to "static custodians". The engagement process may benefit through a number of mechanisms related to PsyCap, including confidence in one's abilities, expectation of positive outcomes, willpower and pathways to achieve goals, and the ability to bounce back and beyond in the face of job demands and obstacles.

The "Practical implications" box indicates some specific ways that PsyCap positively impacting work engagement may have beneficial effects in meeting today's challenges concerning the human side of organizations. The needed next step will be to use the conceptual model presented in this chapter to stimulate future research and provide the empirical tests of the proposed relationships. Given the state-like nature of both PsyCap and work engagement, future studies should be longitudinal in order to better inform our understanding of the relationship between PsyCap and work engagement across time (see Avey et al., 2008a). Such longitudinal designs could contribute to answering research questions such as is there a simple linear relationship, a point at which an optimal relationship is achieved (i.e., an inverted U relationship), or perhaps something different altogether. Further research could also use the relationship between the higher-order constructs of PsyCap and work engagement in order to inform our understanding of the component constructs that comprise them, and whether additional dimensions should be included in either core construct. Finally, future research needs to more fully examine the nature of causation between PsyCap, positive emotions, and work engagement.

Practical implications

Today's organizations need employees who are vigorously energetic, identify with the work with dedication, and absorb themselves in their work. In other words, for organizations to thrive, or even survive in these turbulent times, they need employees who are engaged at all levels (Bakker & Schaufeli, 2008). Some demonstrated direct and indirect benefits of work engagement include: the positivity of the experience itself (Schaufeli et al., 2002); good health (Rothbard, 2001); reduced turnover intentions (Schaufeli & Bakker, 2004); improved individual performance (Kahn, 1990); greater business-unit performance (Harter et al., 2002); and improved managerial effectiveness (Luthans & Peterson, 2002). In this chapter we have presented the case that developing employees' PsyCap (made up of their efficacy, hope, optimism, and resiliency) will increase valuable positive psychological resources that will lead to greater engagement. Practically speaking, since both PsyCap and engagement are state-like constructs, they can be developed. Thus, developing PsyCap may enhance work engagement.

While this chapter has provided insights and better understanding of the intra-individual impact of PsyCap and positive emotions on work engagement, there are also important interpersonal implications. Besides the obvious implications of developing PsyCap in order to enhance work engagement, a more subtle but still very important implication can be found in the contagion effect. Specifically, through the positive emotions of being engaged, the motivation and emotions of those up, down and across (i.e., 360-degree impact) can occur with resulting increased work engagement for the entire organization. Support for such a practical contagion effect was found in a multi-level analysis showing that team-level engagement was predictive of individual member engagement (Bakker, Van Emmerik, & Euwema, 2006b).

Besides the positive spiral effect, there should also be the practical benefit of reducing and replacing (i.e. "undoing") the negative. Burnout occurs through social contexts; through the processes individuals use to interpret the behaviors of others. Given the negative emotional demands experienced in many aspects of contemporary work, a positive contagion effect may be valuable in reducing levels of burnout across the organization. Specifically, developing individuals at all levels of the organization to be able to provide effective social support can create a buffer against job demands and thus burnout (Bakker et al., 2005).

Ongoing research provides a window into the seeming mutually-reinforcing spiral between PsyCap and work engagement, with a compound effect that those individuals with greater pools of positive resources may experience a reduced chance of resource loss (Hobfoll & Shirom, 2001). As articulated by Kahn (1992), being engaged involves the bringing of oneself into the role through one's psychological resources in reaching an authentic wholeness with the organization. Hopefully this chapter has made a contribution toward making such engagement in one's work possible, with a win for both the individual employee and the organization, and ultimately society as a whole.

References

Avey, J. B., Luthans, F. & Mhatre, K. H. (2008a). A call for longitudinal designs in positive organizational behaviour. *Journal of Organizational Behaviour*, *29*, 705–711.

Avey, J. B., Wernsing, T. S., & Luthans, F. (2008b). Can positive employees help positive organizational change? Impact of psychological capital and emotions on relevant attitudes and behaviors. *Journal of Applied Behavioral Science*, *44*, 48–70.

Avolio, B. J., & Luthans, F. (2006). *The high impact leader*. New York: McGraw-Hill.

Bakker, A. B., & Demerouti, E. (2007). The job demands-resources model: State of the art. *Journal of Managerial Psychology*, *22*, 309–328.

Bakker, A. B., Demerouti, E., & Euwema, M. C. (2005). Job resources buffer the impact of job demands on burnout. *Journal of Occupational Health Psychology*, *10*, 170–180.

Bakker, A. B., & Schaufeli, W. B. (2008). Positive organizational behavior: Engaged employees in flourishing organizations. *Journal of Organizational Behavior*, *29*, 147–154.

Bakker, A. B., Van Der Zee, K. I., Lewig, K. A., & Dollard, M. F. (2006a). The relationship between the Big Five personality factors and burnout: A study among volunteer counselors. *Journal of Social Psychology*, *146*, 31–50.

Bakker, A. B., Van Emmerik, I. J. H., & Euwema, M. C. (2006b). Crossover of burnout and engagement in work teams. *Work and Occupations*, *33*, 464–489.

Bandura, A. (1997). *Self-efficacy: The exercise of control*. New York: Freeman.

Carver, C. S., & Scheier, M. S. (2002). Optimism. In C. R. Snyder & S. J. Lopez (Eds.), *Handbook of positive psychology* (pp. 231–243). Oxford: Oxford University Press.

Chuang, S. C. (2007). Sadder but wiser or happier and smarter? A demonstration of judgment and decision-making. *Journal of Psychology*, *141*, 63–76.

Csikszentmihalyi, M. (1990). *Flow: The psychology of optimal experience*. New York: Harper.

Dweck, C. S. (2006). *Mindset: The new psychology of success*. New York: Random House.

Edwards, J. R., & Rothbard, N. P. (2000). Mechanisms linking work and family: Clarifying the relationship between work and family constructs. *Academy of Management Review*, *25*, 178–199.

Fisher, C. D. (2000). Mood and emotions while working: Missing pieces of job satisfaction? *Journal of Organizational Behavior*, *21*, 185–202.

Fredrickson, B. L. (2003). Positive emotions and upward spirals in organizations. In K. S. Cameron, J. Dutton, & R. Quinn (Eds.), *Positive organizational scholarship* (pp. 164–175). San Francisco: Berrett-Koehler.

Fredrickson, B. L., & Losada, M. F. (2005). Positive affect and the complex dynamics of human flourishing. *American Psychologist*, *60*, 678–686.

Giardini, A., & Frese, M. (2008). Linking service employees' emotional competence to customer satisfaction: A multilevel approach. *Journal of Organizational Behavior*, *29*, 155–170.

Gonzalez-Roma, V., Schaufeli, W. B., Bakker, A. B., & Lloret, S. (2006). Burnout and work engagement: Independent factors or opposite poles? *Journal of Vocational Behavior*, *68*, 165–174.

Harter, J. K., Schmidt, F. L., & Hayes, T. L. (2002). Business-unit-level relationship between employee satisfaction, employee engagement, and business outcomes: A meta-analysis. *Journal of Applied Psychology*, *87*, 268–279.

Hobfoll, S. E. (2001). The influence of culture, community, and the nested-self in the stress process: Advancing conservation of resources theory. *Applied Psychology: An International Review*, *50*, 337–370.

Hobfoll, S. E., & Shirom, A. (2001). Conservation of resources theory: Applications to stress and management in the workplace. In R. T. Golembiewski (Ed.), *Handbook of organizational behavior* (pp. 57–81). New York: Dekker.

Kahn, W. A. (1990). The psychological conditions of personal engagement and disengagement at work. *Academy of Management Journal*, *33*, 692–724.

Kahn, W. A. (1992). To be fully there: Psychological presence at work. *Human Relations*, *45*, 321–349.

Kahn, R. L., & Byosiere, P. (1992). Stress in organizations. In M. D. Dunnette & L. M. Hough (Eds.), *Handbook of industrial and organizational psychology* (Vol. 3, 2nd ed., pp. 571–650). Palo Alto, CA: Consulting Psychologists Press.

Karasek, R. A. (1979). Job demands, job decision latitude, and mental strain: Implications for job redesign. *Administrative Science Quarterly, 24,* 285–308.

Keyes, C. L. M. (2002). The mental health continuum: From languishing to flourishing in life. *Journal of Health and Social Behavior, 43,* 207–222.

Lazarus, R. S. (1993). From psychological stress to the emotions: A history of changing outlooks. *Annual Review of Psychology, 44,* 1–21.

Lee, R. T., & Ashforth, B. E. (1996). A meta-analytic examination of the three dimensions of burnout. *Journal of Applied Psychology, 81,* 123–133.

Losada, M. (1999). The complex dynamics of high performance teams. *Mathematical and Computer Modeling, 30,* 179–192.

Losada, M., & Heaphy, E. (2004). The role of positivity and connectivity in the performance of business teams. *American Behavioral Scientist, 47,* 740–765.

Luthans, F. (2002a). The need for and meaning of positive organizational behavior. *Journal of Organizational Behavior, 23,* 695–706.

Luthans, F. (2002b). Positive organizational behavior: Developing and managing psychological strengths. *Academy of Management Executive, 16,* 57–72.

Luthans, F., Avey, J. B., Avolio, B. J., Norman, S. M., & Combs, G. M. (2006). Psychological capital development: Toward a micro-intervention. *Journal of Organizational Behavior, 27,* 387–393.

Luthans, F., Avey, J. B., & Patera, J. L. (2008). Experimental analysis of a web-based intervention to develop positive psychological capital. *Academy of Management Learning and Education, 7,* 209–221.

Luthans, F., & Avolio, B. J. (2009). The "point" of positive organizational behavior. *Journal of Organizational Behavior, 30,* 291–307.

Luthans, F., Avolio, B. J., Avey, J. B., & Norman, S. M. (2007a). Psychological capital: Measurement and relationship with performance and job satisfaction. *Personnel Psychology, 60,* 541–572.

Luthans, F., & Peterson, S. (2002). Employee engagement and manager self-efficacy. *Journal of Management Development, 21,* 376–387.

Luthans, F., & Youssef, C. M. (2004). Human, social, and now positive psychological capital management. *Organizational Dynamics, 33,* 143–160.

Luthans, F., & Youssef, C. M. (2007). Emerging positive organizational behavior. *Journal of Management, 33,* 321–349.

Luthans, F., Youssef, C. M., & Avolio, B. J. (2007b). *Psychological capital: Developing the human competitive edge.* Oxford: Oxford University Press.

Lyubomirsky, S., King, L., & Diener, E. (2005). The benefits of frequent positive affect: Does happiness lead to success. *Psychological Bulletin, 131,* 803–855.

Marks, S. R. (1977). Multiple roles and role strain: Some notes on human energy, time, and commitment. *American Sociological Review, 42,* 921–936.

Maslach, C., Schaufeli, W. B., & Leiter, M. P. (2001). Job burnout. *Annual Review of Psychology, 52,* 397–422.

Masten, A. S., & Reed, M. G. J. (2002). Resilience in development. In C. R. Snyder & S. Lopez (Eds.), *Handbook of positive psychology* (pp. 74–88). Oxford: Oxford University Press.

Rothbard, N. P. (2001). Enriching or depleting? The dynamics of engagement in work and family roles. *Administrative Science Quarterly, 46,* 655–684.

Salanova, M., Agut, S., & Pieró, J. M. (2005). Linking organizational resources and work engagement to employee performance and customer loyalty: The mediation of service climate. *Journal of Applied Psychology, 90,* 1217–1227.

Schaufeli, W. B., & Bakker, A. B. (2004). Job demands, job resources, and their relationship with burnout and engagement: A multi-sample study. *Journal of Organizational Behavior, 25,* 293–315.

Schaufeli, W. B., & Bakker, A. B. (2009). Defining and measuring work engagement: Bringing clarity to the concept. In A. B. Bakker & M. P. Leiter (Eds.), *Work engagement: A handbook of essential theory and research.* New York: Psychology Press.

Schaufeli, W. B., Bakker, A. B., & Salanova, M. (2006). The measurement of work engagement with a short questionnaire: A cross-national study. *Educational and Psychological Measurement, 66,* 701–716.

Schaufeli, W. B., Salanova, M., Gonzalez-Roma, V., & Bakker, A. B. (2002). The measurement of engagement and burnout: A two sample confirmatory factor analytic approach. *Journal of Happiness Studies, 3,* 71–92.

Schulman, P. (1999). Applying learned optimism to increase sales productivity. *Journal of Personal Selling and Sales Management, 19,* 31–37.

Seligman, M. E. P. (1998). *Learned optimism.* New York: Pocket Books.

Seligman, M. E. P., & Csikszentmihalyi, M. (2000). Positive psychology. *American Psychologist, 55,* 5–14.

Snyder, C. R. (2002). Hope theory: Rainbows in the mind. *Psychological Inquiry, 13,* 249–276.

Snyder, C. R., Irving, L. M., & Anderson, J. R. (1991). Hope and health. In C. R. Snyder (Ed.), *Handbook of social and clinical psychology* (pp. 295–305). Oxford: Oxford University Press.

Snyder, S. R., & Lopez, S. J. (Eds.). (2002). *Handbook of positive psychology*. New York: Oxford University Press.

Sonnentag, S. (2003). Recovery, work engagement, and proactive behavior: A new look at the interface between non-work and work. *Journal of Applied Psychology, 88,* 518–528.

Stajkovic, A. D., & Luthans F. (1998a). Self-efficacy and work-related performance: A meta-analysis. *Psychological Bulletin, 124,* 240–261.

Stajkovic, A. D., & Luthans F. (1998b). Social cognitive theory and self-efficacy: Going beyond traditional motivational and behavioral approaches. *Organizational Dynamics,* Spring, 62–74.

Tugade, M. M., & Fredrickson, B. L. (2004). Resilient individuals use positive emotions to bounce back from negative emotional experiences. *Journal of Personality and Social Psychology, 86,* 320–333.

Van Maanen, J., & Schein, E. H. (1979). Toward a theory of organizational socialization. In B. Shaw (Ed.), *Research in organizational behavior* (Vol. 1, pp. 209–264). Greenwich, CT: JAI Press.

Walsh, J. P., Weber, K., & Margolis, J. D. (2003). Social issues in management: Our lost case found. *Journal of Management, 29,* 859–881.

Weiss, H. M., & Cropanzano, R. (1996). An affective events approach to job satisfaction. *Research in Organizational Behavior, 18,* 1–74.

Wright, T. A. (2003). Positive organizational behavior: An idea whose time has truly come. *Journal of Organizational Behavior, 24,* 437–442.

Wright, T. A., & Staw, B. M. (1999). Affect and favorable work outcomes: Two longitudinal tests of the happy-productive worker thesis. *Journal of Organizational Behavior, 20,* 1–23.

Xanthopoulou, D., Bakker, A. B., Demerouti, E., Schaufeli, W. B. (2007). The role of personal resources in the job demands-resources model. *International Journal of Stress Management, 14,* 121–141.

Zwetsloot, G., & Pot, F. (2004). The business value of health management. *Journal of Business Ethics, 55,* 115–124.

6

Feeling energetic at work: On vigor's antecedents[1,2]

Arie Shirom

Vigor refers to individuals' feelings that they possess physical strength, emotional energy, and cognitive liveliness, a set of interrelated affective states experienced at work. This chapter focuses on vigor's antecedents and enabling organizational processes because vigor was found to positively predict employees' good health and proactive behaviors. Following a description of the conceptual framework of vigor and a review of past studies of vigor, I present a theoretical model, based on the conservation of resources theory, which presents hypothesized work-related potential predictors of vigor. In the discussion section, I describe a dynamic perspective to theorizing on vigor. I conclude by suggesting several open research questions that concern the study of the antecedents of vigor at work

Feeling invigorated connotes the combined feeling of a positive energy balance and pleasantness or contentment. Someone who feels tense, angry, or anxiously aroused may feel energized but this feeling is coupled with unpleasantness and displeasure, unlike feeling vigorous. The focus on vigor is congruent with recent calls that researchers study human strengths and positive psychological capacities (Peterson & Seligman, 2004; Seligman, Steen, Park, & Peterson, 2005). This focus is also in tune with the emergence of positive organizational behavior, which emphasizes positive traits, states, and behaviors of employees in organizations (Bakker & Schaufeli, 2008). Vigor has not yet been theoretically modeled in terms of its antecedents and consequences (for an exception, see Shirom, 2004).

The construct of vigor, referred to by other names but basically representing one's affective experience of being energetic physically (having physical strength), mentally (feeling cognitive liveliness), and interpersonally (possessing emotional energy relative to significant others), is quite ancient. Theories of traditional Chinese medicine view the human body as having natural patterns of energy flows, or qi (in Japan, ki), that circulate in the body in energy channels called meridians. Energy flow in the body, according to Chinese philosophy, represents the interaction of yin and yang (or earth and heaven) as two opposing and, at the same time, complementary aspects of any one phenomenon. Furthermore, the ancient Japanese cultural traditions used the concept of ki as representing one's feelings of being able to mobilize mental and physical energy (Peterson & Seligman, 2004, pp. 274–277). Psychoanalytic thought, including the contributions of Freud, Jung, and Perls, emphasized the construct of psychic energy, mostly arguing that it could be lost (e.g., by investing it in defense or conflicts) or gained depending on how one invests it. In contrast with Eastern philosophies and psychoanalytic thought, I view vigor, following positivism as a scientific approach, as an inherently measurable construct.

Why is vigor considered as an affective state? Following past research (e.g., Elfenbein, 2007; Fisher, 2000), I use the term affect to refer to both emotions and moods – two relatively distinct types of affect. The concept of mood tends to be fuzzy because in most definitions neither the duration of the mood nor its degree of stability is clearly defined (Russell, 2003). Some authors (e.g., Reisenzein & Schimmack, 1999) define "affect" as a term covering emotional experiences and related feelings covered by typical mood questionnaires; as described below, many mood questionnaires included vigor as a component, focusing on physical strength and sometimes on cognitive liveliness also. I consider vigor as closer to a mood state in that it lasts longer than momentary emotions; however, because it is contextualized in the work situation, and because it was found to be associated with specific work-related enablers (see below), I refer to it as an affect. The practice of investigating moods and mood-like feeling states as affects is common in the literature (e.g., Fisher & Ashkanasy, 2000; Tsenkova, Dienberg Love, Singer, & Ryff, 2008).

The chapter is organized in four sections. The first section explains the reason for studying vigor, and it is followed by a section which provides a brief summary of past conceptual approaches to it and measures constructed to assess it. The next section depicts a theoretical model, based on the conservation of resources (COR) theory, which specifies vigor's work-related enablers. I conclude by suggesting avenues for further developing the theoretical model and by pointing out a few open research questions in the study of vigor.

Why study vigor? Vigor, individuals' health, and organizational effectiveness

Why is the scientific study of vigor important? Most people want to feel energetic and view it as a significant dimension of their affective experiences. For example, it was found that a major reason people engage in physical activity is to experience vigor (Hansen, Stevens, & Coast, 2001; Reed & Ones, 2006). Additionally, because vigor constitutes a positive affect, reasons discussed in the literature for studying positive affective states (e.g., Lyubomirsky, King, & Diener, 2005) apply to vigor as well. As indicated below, vigor was found to be associated with highly important individual health outcomes and it is expected to be linked to organizational effectiveness. The following sections present evidence that supports these arguments, starting with the relationship between vigor and any motivational processes in organizations.

Vigor and motivation

Vigor, which reflects individuals' feelings concerning the energy reservoirs that they possess at work, is expected to predict job performance and organizational effectiveness because vigor is closely related to motivational processes at work. Work motivation is often viewed as a set of energetic forces that originate within individuals, energetic forces that determine the form, direction, and intensity of work-related behavior (Latham & Pinder, 2005). Thus motivational processes in organizations represent in part individuals' decisions to allocate energy over time from their energetic resources among different activities. Consequently, vigor could be regarded as a precursor of motivation at work (Forgas &

George, 2001; George & Brief, 1996). It follows that one could consider a certain threshold vigor as a prerequisite to any motivational processes in organization. Supporting this argument, it was found that when the mental representation of a behavioral goal is associated with positive affects, it automatically signals to the person that the goal is desired and worth pursuing and therefore promotes motivational activity designed to accomplish the goal (Custers & Aarts, 2005). Vigor, like most other positive affects, facilitates goal-directed behavior (Carver & Scheier, 1990) or approach behavior (Fredrickson & Joiner, 2002; Watson, 2002) and therefore could be expected to prompt individuals to engage with their job and work environment. Both qualitative and quantitative studies found that engaged employees, variously defined, have high energy (cf. Bakker & Demerouti, 2008).

Vigor, job performance, and organizational effectiveness

Why do I expect vigor to be positively related to organizational effectiveness and individual job performance? Several emotion theorists have argued that certain affective states are associated with specific action tendencies (e.g., Frijda, Kuipers, & Ter Schure, 1989; Lazarus & Cohen-Charash, 2001), and vigor is expected to be associated with a positive action tendency. Fredrickson (2002), in her broaden-and-build model of positive emotions, has argued that positive emotions are accompanied by augmented thought–action repertoires, or an urge to think or act in a certain direction. It follows that feeling vigorous may generate a particular thought–action repertoire that expands activity, broaden the range of options, and promote creative solutions for work-related problems (cf. Fredrickson & Losada, 2005). Additionally, based on the above arguments, linking experienced vigor with motivation, vigor is expected to be positively related to job performance and organizational effectiveness. Another reason is related to the arguments, provided below, that vigor is positively associated with improved state of physical health, and to the evidence supporting this linkage. Better physical health could be

expected to increase the likelihood of vigor being associated with elevated levels of job performance (Côté, 1999).

While the theoretical arguments supporting the positive effects of vigor on performance and organizational effectiveness appear robust, there is a paucity of research investigating this proposition at work. There is, however, a wealth of research, recently reviewed (Boehm & Lyubomirsky, 2008; Tsai, Chen, & Liu, 2007), which suggests that happy people, or generally employees with high positive affect, display superior performance, perform more prosocial behaviors at work such as helping others, and generally are better organizational citizens. Also, there is evidence indicating that successful transfer of positive moods among team members led to greater cooperation among them and to augmented team performance (Barsade, 2002). Boehm and Lyubomirsky (2008) reviewed longitudinal evidence indicating that happiness often precedes enhanced levels of career success and elevated levels of job performance, and also experimental evidence suggesting that the induction of positive affect led to improved workplace outcomes. Also, a recent meta-analytic study found that job satisfaction is more likely to predict subsequent performance rather than the reverse (Riketta, 2008), providing support, albeit indirect, to the hypothesis that vigor is a precursor of high levels of job performance or effectiveness.

I assume that the body of findings on the relations between positive affect and performance is relevant to the case of vigor. This assumption is supported by the body of studies that found vigor, as assessed by the Profile of Mood States (POMS) vigor subscale or by vigor subscales of mood inventories based on the POMS, to predict sports performance (Beedie, Terry, & Lane, 2000) and academic performance (Lane, Whyte, Terry, & Nevill, 2005; Thelwell, Lane, & Weston, 2007). In a recent study (Salanova, Agut, & Peiro, 2005), relative to the other subscales of the Utrecht Work Engagement Scale (UWES) only the subscale of vigor was found to be positively and significantly associated with customer-rated performance in 114 service units, with $r = .15$;

however, this effect-size represents data aggregated across the work units and not individual level data. Expanding the domain of job performance to include contextual performance – defined to include prosocial and organizational citizenship behaviors – then several studies found positive affect coupled with energetic arousal to be associated with helping co-workers, spreading goodwill, and creative and innovative behaviors at work (for a review of these studies, see George & Brief, 1992). For example, a study of 221 salespeople (George, 1991) found a measure of high positive mood, largely based on items corresponding to above definition of the physical strength facet of vigor (e.g, feeling active, strong, peppy, elated), to significantly and positively predict both extra-role and role-prescribed prosocial organizational behaviors. The effects of vigor on performance could be mediated by variables such as one's self-efficacy and coping resources. A recent study found that positive mood states that included vigor predicted task performance indirectly through social support, self-efficacy, and task persistence (Tsai, Chen, & Liu, 2007). It could also be that the unidirectional effects flow from behavior to the experienced affect of vigor, as when a certain behavior is chosen because it breeds feelings of vigor.

Physical and mental health
The broaden-and-build model of positive emotions, frequently used in the area of positive affect and health, proposes that positive emotions, like happiness, joy, pride, and love, have health-protecting physiological effects (Fredrickson, 2002; Tugade, Fredrickson, & Feldman Barrett, 2004). The enhancing effects of positive feelings on physical health and longevity are supported by an accumulating body of evidence (Pressman & Cohen, 2005; Rozanski, Blumenthal, Davidson, Saab, & Kubzansky, 2005).

Individuals' level of vigor may be considered as an indicator of their optimal psychological functioning. Indeed, many investigators defined the conceptual domain of health-related quality of life as including vigor. A salient example is the construct of work engagement, defined as a positive, fulfilling, work-related state of mind that is characterized by vigor, dedication, and absorption (Bakker & Demerouti, 2008). Vigor, as one of the three components of the UWES, was defined to include items such as: "At my work, I feel bursting with energy", and "At my job, I feel strong and vigorous". As demonstrated by other chapters in this volume, the UWES is used in several countries. Yet another salient example is the operational definition of well-being by the World Health Organization (WHOQOL Group, 1994); as used in their questionnaire, it includes items like "I feel energetic", "I feel active", I feel vigorous", and "I wake up feeling fresh", items used in part in the measure of vigor described elsewhere (Shirom, 2004). In the same vein, one of the domains in the measure of the Health-Related Quality of Life (Stewart & Ware, 1992), a measure often used (e.g., Stewart, King, Killen, & Ritter, 1995) is vitality, represented by four items: feel tired (reverse-coded), have enough energy to do the things you want, feel worn-out (reverse-coded), and feel full of pep. Note that the most-often cited and used model of well-being is Ryff's six-factor model (cf. Ryff & Singer, 2006) which does not include vigor as a component. While vigor's likely effects on mental well-being are straightforward, its effects on physical well-being are more complex (cf. Edwards & Cooper, 1988).

Several studies found vigor to predict subsequently assessed indicators of physical health. Thus feeling vigorous and objective physical fitness (gauged based on functional capacity) were found to interact in predicting the change over time in self-rated health (SRH) among apparently healthy male and female employees – the higher the physical fitness, the more pronounced the effects of the initial levels of vigor on these changes in SRH (Shirom, Toker, Berliner, Shapira, & Melamed, 2008a). Another study (Shirom, Vinokur, & Vaananen, 2008b), which used structural equation modeling to analyze data of two sizeable samples of employees in Finland and Sweden ($N = 6188$ and $N = 3345$, respectively), found that feeling vigorous was positively associated with both self-rated health and subjective work capacity, controlling for socio-demographic predictors. Emotional exhaustion, the negative antipode of vigor, was found in the same model to negatively influence the same indicators. This finding, cross-validated across two countries, provides strong support to the view that vigor and emotional exhaustion (representing the core component of burnout as assessed by the Maslach Burnout Inventory: see Taris, Le Blanc, Schaufeli, & Schreurs, 2005) have each unique and independent effects on indicators of subjective health (cf. Bakker & Schaufeli, 2008).

The above two studies (Shirom et al., 2008a; 2008b) used self-rated health because it was shown in several large meta-analytic studies to be a robust predictor of subsequent survival and mortality even after adjusting for a variety of risk factors (cf. Shirom et al., 2008a). What are the biological mechanisms that transmit the effects of vigor on self-rated health? While these mechanisms are unknown, they are likely to include the effects of vigor, as a positive affect, on enhancing the immune system's capacity to mount an effective response to challenges and the adoption of healthy life-style habits (cf. Rozanski & Kubzansky, 2005; Ryff, Singer, & Dienberg Love, 2004). Two recent studies provide empirical support to these pathways linking vigor with one's state of health. Vigor was found to be negatively correlated with several inflammation biomarkers (Shirom, Toker, Berliner, Shapira, & Melamed, 2006), thus suggesting that they could represent possible pathways linking vigor with improved physical health. In another study, Toker (2008) found that vigor predicted subsequent elevations of the intensity of exercise behavior among males and females.

This discussion of the reasons for focusing on vigor emphasized its unidirectional effects on organization- and individual-relevant outcomes. These reasons were provided in response to the question: why study vigor? The current chapter focuses on the antecedents rather than the consequences of vigor, and therefore the potential consequences of vigor were only briefly described without due attention given to possible mediators and/or moderators of the unidirectional effects

discussed above. Suffice to indicate that these unidirectional effects could be mediated and/or moderated by other variables, including cognitive reappraisal and self-regulatory processes (Elfenbein, 2007), coping strategies (Folkman, 2008), and physiological processes accompanying experienced vigor.

Conceptualizing vigor as an affect

Following past research (e.g., Elfenbein, 2007; Fisher, 2000), we use the term affect to refer to both emotions and moods as two relatively distinct phenomena. Moods tend to be longer lasting, often mild and relatively enduring affective states of uncertain origin, while emotions are more intense, short-lived, and have a clear object or cause (Brief & Weiss, 2002; Kelly & Barsade, 2001; Scherer, 2000). Vigor is closer to a mood state in that it was conceptualized as lasting considerably longer than momentary emotions, but because it is contextualized in the work situation I refer to it as an affect.

Based on Lazarus and Folkman's appraisal theory (1984, pp. 273–274, 284–285), I consider individuals' appraisals of their energetic resources as theoretically distinct from the feeling of vigor. In nature, these appraisals and the feeling of vigor probably appear conjointly, mutually affecting each other over time. The focus on vigor as an affect follows the cognitive-motivational-relational theory developed by Lazarus and his colleagues (Lazarus, 2001; Smith & Lazarus, 1993). This theory implies a discrete-category approach to affects, each having its own core relational themes and coping implications. Furthermore, it posits that conceptualizing the distinctive characteristics, antecedents, and consequences of each affective state enriches and extends our understanding of employees' attempts to survive and flourish in their work environment (Lazarus & Cohen-Charash, 2001).

COR theory (Hobfoll, 1989, 2002) categorizes individual resources into four kinds: objects (e.g., a house); conditions (e.g., seniority, tenure, marital relationship); personal characteristics (e.g., self-efficacy, optimism); and energies (e.g., money, expert knowledge). Why the focus, in the conceptualization of vigor, on one's feelings concerning the three facets of energetic resources?

There were several theoretical reasons for the focus on the affective experiences of physical strength, cognitive liveliness, and emotional energy as the three facets constituting vigor. First, these three facets are individually possessed. Other energetic resources at work, like authority or autonomy, are clearly other-dependent. Second, COR theory, based on past empirical evidence (Hobfoll, 1989, 2002), posits that the more proximal a resource is to the self, the higher its saliency relative to resources distal from the self. Following this COR theory tenet, I argue that the three facets of vigor probably represent the three most salient domains of energy that humans possess, physical, emotional, and cognitive, relative to other types of energetic resources such as having a credit in the bank. Third, again based on COR theory, I hypothesize that the three facets of vigor facilitate the development and enable the gain of other resources. For example, emotional energy probably facilitates obtaining social support, and physical strength is probably instrumental in maintaining an improved state of health (Hobfoll, 2002). Fourth, the three facets of vigor represent types of affective states that are intrinsically valuable in their own right to most people, as documented below. In comparison, having money, as an energetic resource, is valued primarily as a means to obtain centrally valued ends (Hobfoll, 1998, 2002). Fifth, the three facets of vigor represent a coherent set that does not overlap any other established behavioral science concept, such as resilience, engagement, commitment, or potency, or any aspect of the self-concept, such as self-esteem and self-efficacy. Furthermore, this conceptualization of vigor clearly differentiates it from its likely consequences such as organizational commitment or job involvement. Additionally, there is empirical support for the tri-facet definition of vigor (Shirom et al., 2008a). For example, in a qualitative study (Shraga & Shirom, 2009) it was found that employees actually describe the three facets of vigor as components of their experience of vigor.

Other conceptualizations of vigor and its relations with other affective states

In contrast to burnout and anxiety, vigor is a component of the approach-oriented behavior facilitation system. This system, according to Watson (2002), directs organisms toward situations and experiences that potentially may yield pleasure and reward and facilitates the procuring of resources like food, shelter, and sexual partners – resources that are essential for the survival of both the individual and the species.

As an affect term, feeling vigorous has been included in many mood inventories, often in a cluster referred to as positive energy or energetic arousal (Burke, George, Brief, Roberson, & Webster, 1989; Thayer, 1989; Yik, Russell, & Barrett, 1999). In a study using multidimensional scaling analysis to categorize 48 descriptions of emotional states, vigor was found to represent a cluster distinct from neighboring clusters that loaded high only on either the dimension of pleasure or on the dimension of arousal (Russell & Steiger, 1982). It was identified as a distinct factor and therefore was measured by a distinct scale in the POMS (McNair, Lorr, & Droppleman, 1971). This POMS factor was subsequently re-validated (Cranford, Shrout, Iida, Rafaeli, Yip, & Bolger, 2006). I did not follow the conceptualization of the POMS' vigor scale for two major reasons. First, the items used in it (e.g., lively, energetic, full of pep, vigorous) do not reflect the aforementioned cognitive (cognitive liveliness) and interpersonal-emotional (emotional energy) facets of our conceptualization of vigor. Second, as empirically constructed, it includes adjectives that reflect other positive affective states, including happiness (e.g., feeling cheerful) and pleasantness (e.g., feeling carefree), found in past research (cf. Russell & Steiger, 1982) to load high only on the dimension of pleasure; therefore, there is some doubt regarding its construct validity.

In the studies using the POMS, results that concern the vigor scale have often been reported. In the area of sports psychology, a recent meta-analysis of studies that have used the POMS in association with either athletic achievement or athletic performance (Beedie, Terry, & Lane,

2000) found a moderate effect size between the POMS vigor subscale and performance outcomes. Studies that have used the POMS and its vigor subscale to predict physiological outcomes abound in the literature. For example, the vigor subscale was found to positively predict sleep quality (Bardwell, Berry, Ancoli-Israel, & Dimsdale, 1999), as well as shorter duration of recovery from injury (Quinn & Fallon, 1999). As Payne (2001) noted, different aspects of the construct validity of this scale have been extensively studied, but primarily with clinical samples such as cancer patients, drug abusers, and brief psychotherapy patients, with hardly any past use in work organizations.

A construct that, to a certain extent, overlaps with vigor is that of *vitality*, conceptualized as combining the subjective experience of being full of energy and of feeling alive or vital (for the original scale, see Ryan & Frederick, 1997). Vigor differs from vitality in that the latter construct includes also the components of feeling alive and vital and of feeling awake and alert. Yet another related construct, thriving at work (Spreitzer, Sutcliffe, Dutton, Sonenshein, & Grant, 2005; see also, Spreitzer, Lam, & Fritz, Chapter 10, this volume), was defined as a subjective experience that combines learning (i.e., greater understanding) and a sense of vitality (aliveness). Therefore, it hardly includes the core content of vigor, as defined above.

A frequently-used alternative conceptualization of vigor views it as a component of engagement and defines it as comprising a high level of energy, motivation to invest effort at work, and resilience (e.g., Hakanen, Bakker, & Schaufeli, 2006; Schaufeli, Salanova, Gonzalez-Roma, & Bakker, 2002b). I argue that this conceptualization of vigor confounds high level of energy with its possible consequences, motivation and resilience, and therefore it was not adopted (cf. Shirom, 2004). In the instrument designed to assess vigor as part of the UWES (e.g., Schaufeli, Martinez, Marques Pinto, Salanova, & Bakker, 2002a; see also Schaufeli & Bakker, Chapter 2, this volume), out of six items, two refer to resiliency and one to an aspect of motivation. It should be noted that the short version of the UWES, which comprises nine items, does not include the above three items tapping resiliency and motivation (Schaufeli, Bakker, & Salanova, 2006). Based on the above conceptualization of vigor, I argue that this specific affect can be experienced regardless of individuals' behaviors following encounters with adverse events – namely resilience (Jackson, Firtko, & Edenborough, 2007; Luthar & Brown, 2007). Furthermore, while vigor could be a prerequisite of motivation to invest effort at work, vigor as an affect and motivation belong to different conceptual domains.

The nature of the relationships between vigor, as conceptualized above, and the two constitutive components of the work engagement construct dubbed dedication and absorption represents an open research question. Kahn (1992) proposed that employees must feel that they have physical and emotional energies in order to be able to dedicate themselves to their work. It follows that feeling vigorous is a necessary precursor to dedication, as operationalized by the UWES. It is also possible that these relationships depend upon certain contextual factors. For example, it could be expected that vigorous employees would fully immerse themselves in their work and become absorbed by it only if they experience psychological safety, trust their superiors and enjoy procedural justice, as suggested by Kahn (1990).

Some measures of vigor as a mood state were based on the theoretical position that the pair of vigor on the one hand and fatigue, burnout or tiredness on the other hand represents bipolar affective states on the same dimension that cannot be experienced simultaneously. This theoretical position is reflected in the practice of reverse-scoring tiredness or fatigue items in the vigor scales to arrive at a total score representing the positive mood of vigor. This practice has been followed by several researchers who have assessed vigor either as a component of job-related affective well-being (Payne, 2001; Daniels, 2000), as a stress reaction (William & Cooper, 1998), or as representing energy, the polar opposite of exhaustion on the same dimension (Maslach & Leiter, 2008). In contrast, I argue for the theoretical position that vigor and burnout are obliquely related and do not represent the extreme poles of the same dimensional continuum, perhaps with the exception of situations characterized by very high levels of stress (Reich & Zautra, 2002). This theoretical position rests first on the fact that the biological systems underlying approach and avoidance activations have been shown to be basically independent (Cacioppo, Gardner, & Berniston, 1999). Second, positive and negative affective states are physiologically represented in different systems (Davidson, 2000). Third, positive and negative affective states are known to have different antecedents (Baumeister, Bratslavsky, Finkenauer, & Vohs, 2001), may function relatively independently (Davis, Zautra, & Smith, 2004), and are differentially represented in people's behaviors (Gendolla, 2000). Therefore, on theoretical grounds, it could be concluded that the relationships between positive and negative affective states is not bipolar but bivariate. Considerable support for this position has been provided by studies that found different across-time fluctuations of positive and negative affect (cf. Yasuda, Lawrenz, Whitlock, Lubin, & Lei, 2004), that the relationship between tension and energy self-ratings was not bipolar (Vautier, Steyer, Jmel, & Raufaste, 2005), and that suggested that the practice of reversed-polarity items to represent unidimensional constructs was associated with substantive methodological and interpretational problems (Herche & Engelland, 1996).

A theoretical model of vigor's antecedents

In the following model proposing vigor's antecedents, I follow COR theory (Hobfoll, 1989, 2002) in identifying potential enablers of vigor. COR theory's central tenets are that people have a basic motivation to obtain, retain and protect that which they value. The things that people value are called resources, of which there are several types, including material, social, and energetic resources. Hobfoll (1989, 2002) maintained that resources are those personal energies and characteristics, objects and conditions that are valued by individuals or that serve as the means for the attainment of other objects,

personal characteristics, conditions, or energies (Hobfoll, 2002). Examples of internal personality factors that are considered resources are optimism, self-esteem, and self-efficacy. Examples of external resources are employment, social support, and economic status.

Key assumptions

The proposed model is based on several key assumptions. First, I consider vigor as predicted primarily by work-based proximal energetic resources. This assumption is based on the fact that vigor is conceptually defined and measured as contextualized in the work domain. It does not preclude the possibility that genetic predispositions, socio-demographic variables, and personality traits could influence the levels of vigor. However, I argue that these influences are probably partially mediated by work-based proximal enablers of vigor. In the same vein, certain individual traits may predispose some individuals to feel vigorous more than others. The literature on dispositional influences on affective states may lead to the expectation that those high on the personality trait of extraversion (or positive affectivity) are more likely to experience vigor relative to those high on the trait of neuroticism (cf. Brief & Weiss, 2002). The proposed model, however, is based on the postulate that most people have the capacity to experience the feeling of vigor given the enabling work contexts.

The second assumption is related to the tri-faceted conceptualization of vigor. I argue that people feel ongoing changes in the physical, cognitive, and emotional energy levels that they possess and that these changes are related to specific positive features of their work environment and specific characteristics of their jobs. I assume that changes in physical, emotional, and cognitive energies are interrelated, because personal resources affect each other and exist as a resource pool – an expansion of one is often associated with the other being augmented (Hobfoll, 1999, 2002). Therefore, in the following discussion of vigor's antecedents, the focus will be on global vigor as the criterion.

The third assumption follows directly from the above discussion of the relationships between vigor and its negative counterpart, burnout. As noted above, vigor and exhaustion (burnout) are considered as only obliquely related, represented by two dimensions of the multidimensional domain of affective states. Therefore, reducing the job-related predictors of burnout, such as work overload (Shirom, 2003), would not necessarily augment felt vigor among the employees concerned.

Work-related predictors of vigor

Employees' work-related affective states tend to reflect their appraisals of their on-the-job experiences. Organizations do not have a direct way of eliciting specific affective responses in their employees; this could be accomplished only via vigor enablers to become operative. In the following, I will discuss work features likely to increase the likelihood of employees feeling invigorated.

Job characteristics

In a qualitative study on the antecedents of vigor (Shraga & Shirom, 2009) we examined the fit of 107 situations and events described by 36 respondents as enablers of experienced vigor with one of the components of the job characteristics model (the JCM; Hackman & Oldham, 1974, 1980). The JCM components are job significance, job identity, skill variety, task autonomy/perceived control, and feedback from one's supervisor (Hackman & Oldham, 1974, 1980). Job significance describes the degree to which the job has an impact on other people, both inside and outside the work organization, or on the employing organization itself. The majority of the enablers (46%) belonged to this category. This major finding of our qualitative study is strongly supported by quantitative research. For example, the most potent predictor of vigor as assessed by the UWES was found to be organization-based self-esteem, most of whose items reflect high task significance (Mauno, Kinnunen, & Ruokolainen, 2007), and task significance was found (Saavedra & Kwun, 2000) to be the strongest predictor of activated pleasant affect as gauged by the Job Affect Scale (Brief, Burke, George, Robinson, & Webster, 1988).

Feedback from supervisors measures the extent to which one receives information about the effectiveness of one's efforts from one's supervisor; 27% of the enablers belonged to this category. Achieved success on a job task was found in other studies to be associated with employees feeling energetic (Brown & Ryan, 2003; Ryan & Frederick, 1997). Task identity refers to the extent to which the job is an identifiable piece of work, possible to accomplish from beginning to end, and we found that 23% of the vigor enablers belonged to this category. Our respondents did not mention any enablers in the categories of skill variety (the degree to which the job requires the use of a number of different skills and talents on the part of the employee), task autonomy (the level of discretion the employee has in regard to the work process), and perceived control (the ability to influence the work environment). Task autonomy is a form of control limited to the employee's own job tasks, whereas perceived control is a broader term that includes aspects of the organization that may not be directly related to one's job (cf. Spector, 1997, pp. 43–44). The findings of our qualitative study suggest the job characteristics that directly enable employees to focus on a significant task having an identifiable core, characteristics likely to lead to positive feedback when a task at hand is successfully completed, are those most likely to enable the experience of vigor. Supporting our findings, in a series of experimental studies, experienced success simulating common work situations was manipulated and resulted in positive affective states, including vigor (Nummenmaa & Niemi, 2004). Additional support to the findings of the above qualitative study was provided by a diary study that found that daily attainment of goals at work was associated with activated pleasurable affect at the end of the working day (Harris, Daniels, & Briner, 2003). This set of findings, if confirmed by quantitative studies, indicate that different combinations of work characteristics predict vigor relative to other affective, attitudinal, and behavioral outcomes.

Job-related interactions with others

The strand of research on the ways people influence each other's mood states, which includes the study of conceptually overlapping processes such as mood linkage (Totterdell, Wall, Holman, Diamond, & Epitropaki, 2004), emotional contagion (Neumann & Strack, 2000), and emotional crossover and spillover (Song, Foo, & Uy, 2008), indicates that employees influence each other's mood. This influence was found in the above studies to be independent of shared work events and circumstances but to be dependent on the extent to which employees interact with each other at work. Therefore, interpersonal processes which operate over a period of time at work may lead to employees' moods becoming linked. For example, a study that focused on the link between team-level and individual-level vigor found the former to impact the latter (vigor in this study was assessed as part of the engagement construct; see Bakker, Van Emmerik, & Euwema, 2006).

Leadership style
There are indications in the literature that leaders who feel energetic are likely to energize their followers (cf. Brief & Weiss, 2002). Displaying vigor is probably expected from employees in managerial roles (Church & Waclawski, 1998). In a similar vein, the leadership literature argues that transformational leaders often exhibit energizing emotions in order to arouse similar emotional states among their followers (Avolio, 1999). This literature suggests that intellectual stimulation, a component of transformational leadership which consists of encouraging followers to think creatively (Avolio, 1999), is likely to have a direct positive effect on cognitive liveliness, a component of vigor.

Group-level resources
Work groups tend to share emotions because of common socialization experiences and common organizational features, norms and regulations that govern the expression of emotions, task interdependence, and the phenomenon of emotional contagion (Brief & Weiss, 2002). Work teams characterized by mutual trust and high social support tend to be more cohesive and goal-directed, and these qualities, in turn, lead to favorable employee morale and job-related well-being (Karasek & Theorell, 1990). Specifically,

work group cohesion was found to predict vigor, measured as a mood state (Terry et al., 2000).

Organizational resources
Employee participation in decision making has the potential to increase one's exposure to many sources of information, enhancing one's ability to adjust more flexibly to the demands of diverse role partners, and enabling one's capability to develop cognitive skills like finding creative solutions that integrate diverse viewpoints (Spector, 1986).

Directions for future research
The suggested focus on vigor is in tune with the new development of the field of positive psychology (Seligman et al., 2005) and the emergence of positive organizational behavior (Luthans, 2002; Luthans & Youssef, 2007). Vigorous feelings at work possibly allow employees to effectively cope with work-related demands, and more importantly are likely to have a positive impact on their well-being. There are several promising paths of research which could increase our understanding of the antecedents and etiology of vigor at work.

A dynamic perspective on vigor's possible antecedents
A major limitation of the proposed model of the antecedents of vigor is its static nature. I propose that transforming the model to one that is based on a dynamic perspective is perhaps the most promising path for future research. Like other affects, vigor should be considered as an ongoing process which begins with a focal employee, who perceives a situation or a condition, finds it meaningful, experiences a feeling state and possibly also physiological changes accompanying it, and then changes his/her attitudes, cognitions, or behaviors following the experienced vigor. For each stage of the process, the focal employee could exercise self-regulation processes. For each stage of the process, it is possible to envision feedback-loops operating at the intra-individual, inter-individual, individual-group and individual-organization levels of analysis. Thus the model presented above is but a first approximation of

considerably more complex dynamics (for an attempt to construct this model for affective states, see Elfenbein, 2007).

Several theoretical threads could help in this task of recasting the model proposed above in a dynamic mold. COR theory (Hobfoll, 2002) posits also that those with greater resources (e.g., higher levels of vigor or life satisfaction) are more capable of further resource gain. Conversely, those who lack resources (e.g., report high levels of burnout) are more vulnerable to further losses and less capable of resource gain. These loss and gain cycles occur over time (cf. Hobfoll, 2001). Fredrickson's (2001) broaden-and-build theory of positive affect posits that when they recur over time, they improve people's coping resources by broadening their thought–action repertoire – leading them to build a range of personal resources, including physical resources (e.g., good health and longevity), social resources, and psychological resources (e.g., resilience). There is some evidence supporting the theoretical proposition of an upward resource spiral triggered by positive affect (Fredrickson & Losada, 2005). Fredrickson and Joiner (2002) found that positive emotions broaden the scopes of attention and cognition and, by consequence, initiate upward spirals toward increasing emotional well-being. The augmented personal resources can be drawn on to cope with any work-related demand that may arise in one's job. In work organizations, little is known about this possible spiral of augmented personal resources.

Vigor and goal-directed behaviors

The study of vigor at work may offer new insights in the process of goal-directed behaviors, or the process by which employees initiate, regulate and maintain their task-related behaviors over time and over changing circumstances. DeShon and Gillepsie (2005) proposed that goal-directed behaviors be viewed as specific manifestations of self-regulation efforts. Individuals self-regulate their behaviors to a considerable extent based on their feeling states, as documented above. One way of assessing the validity of the proposition that vigor is a prerequisite of goal-directed behavior is to examine these relationships over

time. Such a longitudinal study may also test the propositions that elevations in vigor lead to more effective coping with work-related demands.

There are several open questions awaiting empirical clarification with regard to using vigor in actual research. Are there individual differences in the ability to "intelligently" use vigor as a means of guiding and maintaining one's behavior? Feelings provide meaning to work-related employee experiences. In line with recent thinking on emotional intelligence, the ability to identify and regulate feelings and use the information provided by feelings is considered important for adaptive social behavior (Salovey, Mayer, Goldman, Turvey, & Palfai 1995). If such differences are found to exist, do they reflect differences in the above skills, and can these skills be learnt (Salovey, Bedell, Detweiler, & Mayer, 2000 & Mayer, 2000)? Emotional intelligence represents just one, albeit important, possible modulator of vigor's relationship with behavioral responses.

Another open question has to do with the effects of vigorous feelings at work on organizations. In this chapter, the emphasis has been on job and work characteristics conducive to employee vigor, and on the influence of employee vigor on job performance. However, how does employee vigor affect the organization as a whole? Are there vigorous organizations, and if so, what are their inherent characteristics? Vigorous organizations could be regarded as organizations whose managerial apex effectively created the conditions that generate, foster and maintain employee vigor throughout the organization and mobilized these energetic resources in the pursuit of organizational effectiveness. Based on emotional and cognitive contagion processes (Barsade, 2002), organizational vigor probably reflects the synergistic accumulation of individual employees' level of vigor. Vigorous organizations could be expected to be highly innovative, proactively adjust to environmental changes, and otherwise distinguish themselves in their product and labor markets (Bruch & Ghoshal, 2003; Cross, Baker, & Parker, 2003).

Vigor may be experienced as an affective response to events and situations that individuals encounter outside of work. It is possible that vigor felt at work spills over to the family and other life domains and vice versa. These are open questions that need to be addressed in future research. The same is true regarding the possible reciprocal relations between vigor and job performance or proactive behavior in organizations.

Vigor represents an affect experienced at work. While available research on vigor at work is in its infancy, existing research on vigor as a mood state would suggest that it is strongly related to individuals' well-being and health. The link proposed above between vigor and physical health, indirectly supported by the body of studies that have examined positive affect–physical health relationships, indicate that additional research on vigor at work may provide an understanding of possible pathways by which organizations can reduce absenteeism and healthcare costs. Therefore, there exists a need for future research on vigor at work.

Notes

1. I would like to acknowledge the financial support of the Israel Science Foundation.
2. The scale constructed to gauge vigor is available for downloading in Word format in several languages, including English: www.shirom.org or: www.tau.ac.il/~ashirom.

References

Avolio, B. J. (1999). *Full leadership development.* London: Sage.

Bakker, A. B., & Demerouti, E. (2008). Towards a model of work engagement. *Career Development International, 13*, 209–223.

Bakker, A. B., & Schaufeli, W. B. (2008). Positive organizational behavior: Engaged employees in flourishing organizations. *Journal of Organizational Behavior, 29*, 147–154.

Bakker, A. B., Van Emmerik, H., & Euwema, M. C. (2006). Crossover of burnout and engagement in work teams. *Work and Occupations, 33*, 464–489.

Bardwell, W. A., Berry, C. C., Ancoli-Israel, S., & Dimsdale, J. E. (1999). Psychological correlates of sleep apnea. *Journal of Psychosomatic Research, 47*, 583–596.

Barsade, S. G. (2002). The ripple effect: Emotional contagion and its influence on group behavior. *Administrative Science Quarterly, 47*, 644–677.

Baumeister, R. F., Bratslavsky, E., Finkenauer, C., & Vohs, K. D. (2001). Bad is stronger than good. *Review of General Psychology, 5*, 323–370.

Beedie, C. J., Terry, P. C., & Lane, A. M. (2000). The profile of mood states and athletic performance: Two meta-analyses. *Journal of Applied Sport Psychology, 12*, 49–68.

Boehm, J. K., & Lyubomirsky, S. (2008). Does happiness promote career success? *Journal of Career Assessment, 16*, 101–116.

Brief, A. P., Burke, M. J., George, J. M., Robinson, B. S., & Webster, J. (1988). Should negative affectivity remain an unmeasured variable in the study of job stress? *Journal of Applied Psychology, 73*, 193–198.

Brief, A. P., & Weiss, H. M. (2002). Organizational behavior: Affect in the workplace. *Annual Review of Psychology, 53*, 279–307.

Brown, K. W., & Ryan, R. M. (2003). The benefits of being present: Mindfulness and its role in psychological well-being. *Journal of Personality and Social Psychology, 84*, 822–848.

Bruch, H., & Ghoshal, S. (2003). Unleashing organizational energy. *MIT Sloan Management Review, 44*, 45–51.

Burke, M. J., George, J. M., Brief, A. P., Roberson, L., & Webster, J. (1989). Measuring affect at work: Confirmatory factor analysis of competing mood structure with conceptual linkage to cortical regulatory systems. *Journal of Personality and Social Psychology, 57*, 1091–1102.

Cacioppo, J. T., Gardner, W. L., & Brenston, G. G. (1999). The affect system has parallel and integrative components: Form follows function. *Journal of Personality and Social Psychology, 76*, 839–854.

Carver, C. S., & Scheier, M. F. (1990). Origins and functions of positive and negative affect: A control-process view. *Psychological Review, 97*, 19–35.

Church, A., & Waclawski, J. (1998). The relationship between individual orientation and executive leadership behavior. *Journal of Occupational and Organizational Psychology, 71*, 99–127.

Côté, S. (1999). Affect and performance in organizational settings. *Current Directions in Psychological Science, 8*, 65–68.

Cranford, J. A., Shrout, P. E., Iida, M., Rafaeli, E., Yip, T., & Bolger, N. (2006). A procedure for evaluating sensitivity to within-person change: Can mood measures in diary studies detect change reliably? *Personality and Social Psychology Bulletin, 32*, 917–929.

Cross, R., Baker, W., & Parker, A. (2003). What creates energy in organizations? *MIT Sloan Management Review, 44*, 51–56.

Custers, R., & Aarts, H. (2005). Positive affect as implicit motivator: On the nonconscious operation of behavioral goals. *Journal of Personality and Social Psychology*, *89*, 129–142.

Daniels, K. (2000). Measures of five-aspects of affective well-being at work. *Human Relations*, *53*, 275–294.

Davidson, R. J. (2000). Affective style, psychopathology, and resilience: Brain mechanisms and plasticity. *American Psychologist*, *55*, 1196–1214.

Davis, M. C., Zautra, A. J., & Smith, B. W. (2004). Chronic pain, stress, and the dynamics of affective differentiation. *Journal of Personality*, *72*, 1133–1160.

DeShon, R. P., & Gillespie, J. Z. (2005). A motivated action theory account of goal orientation. *Journal of Applied Psychology*, *90*, 1096–1127.

Edwards, J. R., & Cooper, C. L. (1988). The impact of positive psychological states on physical health: A review and theoretical framework. *Social Science and Medicine*, *27*, 1447–1459.

Elfenbein, H. A. (2007). Emotions in organizations. *The Academy of Management Annals*, *1*, 315–386.

Fisher, C. D. (2000). Mood and emotions while working: Missing pieces of job satisfaction? *Journal of Organizational Behavior*, *21*, 185–202.

Fisher, C. D., & Ashkanasy, N. M. (2000). The emerging role of emotions in work life: An introduction. *Journal of Organizational Behavior*, *21*, 123–129.

Folkman, S. (2008). The case for positive emotions in the stress process. *Anxiety, Stress and Coping*, *21*, 3–14.

Forgas, J. P., & George, J. M. (2001). Affective influences on judgments and behavior in organizations: An information processing perspective. *Organizational Behavior and Human Decision Processes*, *86*, 3–34.

Fredrickson, B. L. (2001). The role of positive emotions in positive psychology: The broaden-and-build theory of positive emotions. *American Psychologist*, *56*, 218–226.

Fredrickson, B. L. (2002). Positive emotions. In C. R. Snyder & S. J. Lopez (Eds.), *Handbook of positive psychology* (pp. 120–134). New York: Oxford University Press.

Fredrickson, B. L., & Joiner, T. (2002). Positive emotions trigger upward spirals toward emotional well-being. *Psychological Science*, *13*, 172–175.

Fredrickson, B. L., & Losada, M. F. (2005). Positive affect and the complex dynamics of human flourishing. *American Psychologist*, *60*, 678–686.

Frijda, N. H., Kuipers, P., & Ter Schure, E. (1989). Relations among emotion, appraisal, and emotional action readiness. *Journal of Personality and Social Psychology*, *57*, 212–228.

Gendolla, G. H. E. (2000). On the impact of mood on behavior: An integrative theory and a review. *Review of General Psychology*, *4*, 378–408.

George, J. M. (1991). State or trait: Effects of positive mood on prosocial behaviors at work. *Journal of Applied Psychology*, *76*, 299–307.

George, J. M., & Brief, A. P. (1992). Feeling good-doing good: A conceptual analysis of the mood at work-organizational spontaneity relationship. *Psychological Bulletin*, *112*, 310–329.

George, J. M., & Brief, A. P. (1996). Motivational agendas in the workplace: The effects of feelings on focus of attention and work motivation. In B. M. Staw & L. L. Cummings (Eds.), *Research in organizational behavior* (Vol. 18, pp. 75–109). Greenwich, CT: JAI Press.

Hackman, J. R., & Oldham, G. R. (1974). *The job diagnostic survey: An instrument for the diagnosis of jobs and evaluation of job redesign projects*. New Haven, CN: Department of Administrative Sciences, Yale University.

Hackman, J. R., & Oldham, G. R. (1980). *Work redesign*. Reading, MA: Addison-Wesley.

Hakanen, J. J., Bakker, A. B., & Schaufeli, W. B. (2006). Burnout and work engagement among teachers. *Journal of School Psychology*, *43*, 495–513.

Hansen, C. J., Stevens, L. C., & Coast, J. R. (2001). Exercise duration and mood state: How much is enough to feel better? *Health Psychology*, *20*, 267–275.

Harris, C., Daniels, K., & Briner, R. B. (2003). A daily diary study of goals and affective well-being at work. *Journal of Occupational and Organizational Psychology*, *76*, 401–410.

Herche, J., & Engelland, B. (1996). Reversed-polarity items and scale unidimensionality. *Journal of the Academy of Marketing Science*, *24*, 366–374.

Hobfoll, S. E. (1989). Conservation of resources: A new attempt at conceptualizing stress. *American Psychologist*, *44*, 513–524.

Hobfoll, S. E. (1998). *The psychology and philosophy of stress, culture, and community*. New York: Plenum.

Hobfoll, S. E. (2002). Social and psychological resources and adaptation. *Review of General Psychology*, *6*, 307–324.

Jackson, D., Firtko, A., & Edenborough, M. (2007). Personal resilience as a strategy for surviving and thriving in the face of workplace adversity: A literature review. *Journal of Advanced Nursing*, *60*, 1–9.

Kahn, W. A. (1990). Psychological conditions of personal engagement and disengagement at work. *Academy of Management Journal, 33*, 692–724.

Kahn, W. A. (1992). To be fully there: Psychological presence at work. *Human Relations, 45*, 321–349.

Karasek, R. A., & Theorell, T. (1990). *Healthy work.* New York: Basic Books.

Kelly, J. R., & Barsade, S. G. (2001). Moods and emotions in small groups and work teams. *Organizational Behavior and Human Decision Processes, 86*, 99–130.

Lane, A. M., Whyte, G. P., Terry, P. C., & Nevill, A. M. (2005). Mood, self-set goals and examination performance: The moderating effect of depressed mood. *Personality and Individual Differences, 39*, 143–153.

Latham, G. P., & Pinder, C. C. (2005). Work motivation theory and research at the dawn of the twenty-first century. *Annual Review of Psychology, 56*, 485–516.

Lazarus, R. S. (2001). Relational meaning and discrete emotions. In K. R. Scherer, A. A. Schorr, & T. Johnston (Eds.), *Appraisal processes in emotions: Theory, Research, Methods* (pp. 37–67). New York: Oxford University Press.

Lazarus, R. S., & Cohen-Charash, Y. (2001). Discrete emotions in organizational life. In R. L. Payne & C. L. Cooper (Eds.), *Emotions at work* (pp. 21–45). Chichester, UK: Wiley.

Lazarus, R. S., & Folkman, S. (1984). *Stress, appraisal, and coping.* New York: Springer.

Luthans, F. (2002). Positive organizational behavior: Developing and managing psychological strengths. *Academy of Management Executive, 16*, 57–72.

Luthans, F., & Youssef, C. M. (2007). Emerging positive organizational behavior. *Journal of Management, 33*, 321–349.

Luthar, S. S., & Brown, P. J. (2007). Maximizing resilience through diverse levels of inquiry: Prevailing paradigms, possibilities, and priorities for the future. *Development and Psychopathology, 19*, 931–955.

Lyubomirsky, S., King, L., & Diener, E. (2005). The benefits of frequent positive affect: Does happiness lead to success? *Psychological Bulletin, 131*, 803–855.

McNair, D. M., Lorr, M., & Droppleman, L. F. (1971). *Manual: Profile of Mood States.* San Diego, CA: Educational and Industrial Testing Service.

Maslach, C., & Leiter, M. P. (2008). Early predictors of job burnout and engagement. *Journal of Applied Psychology, 93*, 498–512.

Mauno, S., Kinnunen, U., & Ruokolainen, M. (2007). Job demands and resources as antecedents of work engagement: A longitudinal study. *Journal of Vocational Behavior, 70*, 149–171.

Neumann, R., & Strack, F. (2000). "Mood contagion": The automatic transfer of mood between persons. *Journal of Personality and Social Psychology, 79*, 211–223.

Nummenmaa, L., & Niemi, P. (2004). Inducing affective states with success-failure manipulations: A meta-analysis. *Emotion, 4*, 207–214.

Payne, R. L. (2001). Measuring emotions at work. In R. L. Payne & C. L. Cooper (Eds.), *Emotions at work* (pp. 107–133). Chichester, UK: Wiley & Sons.

Peterson, C., & Seligman, M. E. P. (2004). *Character strengths and virtues. A handbook and classification.* Washington, DC: Oxford University Press.

Pressman, S. D., & Cohen, S. (2005). Does positive affect influence health? *Psychological Bulletin, 131*, 925–971.

Quinn, A. M., & Fallon, B. J. (1999). The changes in psychological characteristics and reactions of elite athletes. *Journal of Applied Sport Psychology, 11*, 210–229.

Reed, J., & Ones, D. S. (2006). The effect of acute aerobic exercise on positive activated affect: A meta-analysis. *Psychology of Sport and Exercise, 7*, 477–514.

Reich, J. W., & Zautra, A. J. (2002). Arousal and relationship between positive and negative affect: An analysis of the data of Ito, Caccioppo, and Lang (1998). *Motivation and Emotion, 26*, 209–222.

Reisenzein, R., & Schimmack, U. (1999). Similarity judgments and covariations of affects: Findings and implications for affect structure research. *Personality and Social Psychology Bulletin, 25*, 539–556.

Riketta, M. (2008). The causal relations between job attitudes and performance: A meta-analysis of panel studies. *Journal of Applied Psychology, 93*, 472–481.

Rozanski, A., Blumenthal, J. A., Davidson, K. W., Saab, P., & Kubzansky, L. D. (2005). The epidemiology, pathophysiology, and management of psychosocial risk factors in cardiac practice: The emerging field of behavioral cardiology. *Journal of the American College of Cardiology, 45*, 637–651.

Rozanski, A., & Kubzansky, L. D. (2005). Psychologic functioning and physical health: A paradigm of flexibility. *Psychosomatic Medicine, 67*(Supp. 1), S47–S53.

Russell, J. A. (2003). Core affect and the psychological construction of emotion. *Psychological Review, 110*, 145–172.

Russell J. A., & Steiger J. H. (1982). The structure in person's implicit taxonomy of emotions. *Journal of Research in Personality, 16*, 447–469.

Ryan, R. M., & Frederick, C. (1997). On energy, personality, and health: Subjective vitality as a dynamic reflection of well-being. *Journal of Personality*, *65*, 529–565.

Ryff, C. D., & Singer, B. (2002). From social structure to biology: Integrative science in the pursuit of human health and well-being. In C. R. Snyder & E. J. Lopez (Eds.), *Handbook of positive pyschology* (pp. 541–556). New York: Oxford University Press.

Ryff, C. D., Singer, B. H., & Dienberg Love, G. (2004). Positive health: Connecting well-being with biology. *Philosophical Transactions of the Royal Society of London Part B: Biological Science*, *359*, 1383–1394.

Saavedra, R., & Kwun, S. K. (2000). Affective states in job characteristics theory. *Journal of Organizational Behavior*, *21*, 131–146.

Salanova, M., Agut, S., & Peiro, J. M. (2005). Linking organizational resources and work engagement to employee performance and customer loyalty: The mediation of service climate. *Journal of Applied Psychology*, *90*, 1217–1227.

Salovey, P., Bedell, B. T., Detweiler, J. B., & Mayer, J. D. (2000). Current directions in emotional intelligence research. In M. Lewis & J. M. Haviland-Jones (Eds.), *Handbook of emotions* (2nd ed., pp. 504–520). New York: Guilford.

Salovey, P., Mayer, J. D., Goldman, S., Turvey, C., & Palfai, T. (1995). Emotional attention, clarity and repair: exploring emotional intelligence using the Trait Meta-Mood scale. In J. W. Pennebaker (Ed.), *Emotion, disclosure and health* (pp. 125–154). Washington, DC: American Psychological Association.

Schaufeli, W. B., Bakker, A. B., & Salanova, M. (2006). The measurement of work engagement with a short questionnaire: A cross-national study. *Educational and Psychological Measurement*, *66*, 701–716.

Schaufeli, W. B., Martinez, I. M., Marques Pinto, A., Salanova, M., & Bakker, A. B. (2002a). Burnout and engagement in university students: A cross-national study. *Journal of Cross-Cultural Psychology*, *33*, 464–481.

Schaufeli, W. B., Salanova, M., Gonzalez-Roma, V., & Bakker, A. B. (2002b). The measurement of engagement and burnout: A two sample confirmatory factor analytic approach. *Journal of Happiness Studies*, *3*, 71–92.

Scherer, K. R. (2000). Emotion. In M. Hewstone & W. Stroebe (Eds.), *Introduction to social psychology: A European perspective* (3rd ed., pp. 151–191). Oxford: Blackwell.

Seligman, M. E. P., Steen, T. A., Park, N., & Peterson, C. (2005). Positive psychology progress: Empirical validation of intervention. *American Psychologist*, *60*, 410–421.

Shirom, A. (2003). Job-related burnout: A review. In J. C. Quick & L. E. Tetrick (Eds.), *Handbook of Occupational Health Psychology* (pp. 245–265). Washington, DC: American Psychological Association.

Shirom, A. (2004). Feeling vigorous at work? The construct of vigor and the study of positive affect in organizations. In D. Ganster & P. L. Perrewe (Eds.), *Research in organizational stress and well-being* (Vol. 3, pp. 135–165). Greenwich, CT: JAI Press.

Shirom, A., Toker, S., Berliner, S., Shapira, I., & Melamed, S. (2006). Work-related vigor and job satisfaction relationships with inflammation biomarkers among employed adults. In A. Delle Fave (Ed.), *Dimensions of well-being: Research and intervention* (pp. 254–274). Milan: Franco Angeli.

Shirom, A., Toker, S., Berliner, S., Shapira, I., & Melamed, S. (2008). The effects of physical fitness and feeling vigorous on self-rated health. *Health Psychology*, *27*, 567–575.

Shirom, A., Vinokur, A. D., & Vaananen, A. (2008b). *Vigor and emotional exhaustion are independently associated with self-rated health and work capacity: A cross-country comparison*. Manuscript in preparation. Faculty of Management, Tel Aviv University, Tel Aviv, Israel.

Shraga, O., & Shirom, A. (2009). The construct validity of vigor and its antecedents: A qualitative study. *Human Relations*, *62*, 271–291.

Smith, C. A., & Lazarus, R. S. (1993). Appraisal components, core relational themes and the emotions. *Cognition and Emotion*, *7*, 233–269.

Song, Z. L., Foo, M. D., & Uy, M. A. (2008). Mood spillover and crossover among dual-earner couples: A cell phone event sampling study. *Journal of Applied Psychology*, *93*, 443–452.

Spector, P. E. (1986). Perceived control by employees: A meta-analysis of studies concerning autonomy and participation at work. *Human Relations*, *39*, 1005–1016.

Spector, P. E. (1997). *Job satisfaction: Applications, assessment, causes and consequences*. Thousand Oaks, CA: Sage.

Spreitzer, G., Sutcliffe, K., Dutton, J., Sonenshein, S., & Grant, A. M. (2005). A socially embedded model of thriving at work. *Organization Science*, *16*, 537–549.

Stewart, A. L., King, A. C., Killen, J. D., & Ritter, P. L. (1995). Does smoking cessation improve health-related quality-of-life? *Annals of Behavioral Medicine*, *17*, 331–338.

Stewart, A. L., & Ware, J. E. (1992). *Measuring*

functioning in well-being: The Medical Outcomes Study approach. Durham, NC: Duke University Press.

Taris, T. W., Le Blanc, P. M., Schaufeli, W. B., & Schreurs, P. J. G. (2005). Are there causal relationships between the dimensions of the Maslach Burnout Inventory? A review and two longitudinal tests. Work & Stress, 19, 238–256.

Terry, P. C., Carron, A. V., Pink, M. J., Lane, A. M., Jones, G. J. W., & Hall, M. P. (2000). Perceptions of group cohesion and mood in sport teams. Group Dynamics: Theory, Research, and Practice, 4, 244–253.

Thayer, R. E. (1989). The biopsychology of mood and arousal. New York: Oxford University Press.

Thelwell, R. C., Lane, A. M., & Weston, N. J. V. (2007). Mood states, self-set goals, self-efficacy and performance in academic examinations. Personality and Individual Differences, 42, 573–583.

Toker, S. (2008). Vigor predicts subsequent elevations in the intensity of exercise behavior. Manuscript in preparation. Stanford Research Institute, Stanford University, California.

Totterdell, P., Wall, T., Holman, D., Diamond, H., & Epitropaki, O. (2004). Affect networks: A structural analysis of the relationship between work ties and job-related affect. Journal of Applied Psychology, 89, 854–867.

Tsai, W. C., Chen, C. C., & Liu, H. L. (2007). Test of a model linking employee positive moods and task performance. Journal of Applied Psychology, 92, 1570–1583.

Tsenkova, V. K., Dienberg Love, G., Singer, B. H., & Ryff, C. D. (2008). Coping and positive affect predict longitudinal change in glycosylated hemoglobin. Health Psychology, 27(2, Suppl), S163–S171.

Tugade, M. M., Fredrickson, B. L., & Feldman Barrett, L. F. (2004). Psychological resilience and positive emotional granularity: Examining the benefits of positive emotions on coping and health. Journal of Personality, 72, 1161–1190.

Vautier, S., Steyer, R., Jmel, S., & Raufaste, E. (2005). Imperfect or perfect dynamic bipolarity? The case of antonymous affective judgments. Structural Equation Modeling, 12, 391–410.

Watson, D. (2002). Positive affectivity: The disposition to experience pleasurable emotional states. In C. R. Snyder & S. J. Lopez (Eds.), Handbook of positive psychology (pp. 106–120). New York: Oxford University Press.

WHOQOL Group (1994). Development of the WHOQOL: Rationale and current status. International Journal of Mental Health, 23, 24–56.

Williams, S., & Cooper, C. L. (1998). Measuring occupational stress: Development of the Pressure Management Indicator. Journal of Occupational Health Psychology, 3, 306–321.

Yasuda, T., Lawrenz, C., Whitlock, R. V., Lubin, B., & Lei, P. W. (2004). Assessment of intraindividual variability in positive and negative affect using latent state-trait analyses. Educational and Psychological Measurement, 64, 514–530.

Yik, M. S. M., Russell, J. A., & Barrett, L. F. (1999). Structure of self-reported current affect: Integration and beyond. Journal of Personality and Social Psychology, 77, 600–619.

Using the job demands-resources model to predict engagement: Analysing a conceptual model

Jari J. Hakanen and Gert Roodt

To illustrate the basic premise of the job demands-resources model, we first ask you to focus on all the aspects in your work that cause feelings of stress and exhaustion. Next, we ask you to examine the aspects that help you to succeed in work tasks, even in stressful circumstances: things that make you feel energetic, provide a sense of pride and purpose, and enable you to enjoy what you are accomplishing – i.e., all that contributes to a sense of engagement. These aspects are likely to cover a wide variety of items, most of which can be termed either job demands (answers to the first question) or job resources

(answers to the second question). In addition, some of the stressful aspects of work may also consist of a lack of resources necessary to accomplish required tasks.

In this chapter, we present theoretical underpinnings and empirical evidence for the job demands-resources (JD-R) model emphasizing engagement. The JD-R model was first introduced by Demerouti and her colleagues in 2001. One year later the first study on engagement that employed the Utrecht Work Engagement Scale (UWES) was published (Schaufeli, Salanova, González-Romá, & Bakker, 2002). To date, studies on engagement have used the JD-R model as the theoretical framework more often than any other theory or model. We start the present chapter by outlining a general theoretical overview of the JD-R model. We then present empirical findings on the following topics: (1) the dual processes assumed by the model, especially the main effects of job resources on engagement and through engagement on organizational commitment (the motivational process), (2) studies with a specific focus on the motivational process and its relationship with job performance; (3) findings based on different ways of conceptualizing and measuring job resources; (4) the role of non-work resources, such as personal and home resources in the model and in engagement; and (5) the interactions of job resources with job demands regarding engagement. Finally, we end our chapter with a brief assessment of future prospects for our proposed modified JD-R model for predicting engagement.

Theoretical overview of the JD-R model and engagement

The origin of the JD-R model can be traced back to several balance models of job stress, such as the demands-control model (DCM) of Karasek (1979). According to these balance models, job stress is caused by high job demands (work overload) and low job control, i.e., the imbalance between job demands and control. Hakanen, Bakker, and Schaufeli (2006) argue that several models in the stress literature are based on the viewpoint that stress is the result of the disturbance of the equilibrium between the demands that employees are exposed to, and the resources they have at their disposal. The appeal of the DCM thus rests in its simplicity in that it focuses on only one type of job demand (psychological workload) and one type of job resource (job control). The theory predicts that a balance of job demands with job control results in low job stress.

According to Bakker and Demerouti (2007) the strength of the DCM may also be its most important weakness, in the sense that the complex reality of working organizations is reduced to only two variables. Second, a related critique is the static nature of the DCM. Third, they

argued that a variety of demands and resources prevail across work contexts. In other words, job resources and demands may vary in content and in nature from one work setting to another. The job demands-resources (JD-R) model (Demerouti, Bakker, Nachreiner, & Schaufeli, 2001) takes this argument one step further. It is a heuristic model that includes two specific sets of working conditions, job demands and job resources, in its prediction of employee well-being, regardless of occupational group.

Job demands "represent characteristics of the job that potentially evoke strain, in case they exceed the employee's adaptive capability" (Bakker, Hakanen, Demerouti, & Xanthopoulou, 2007, p. 275). More precisely defined, job demands refer to: "those physical, social, or organizational aspects of the job that require sustained physical and/or psychological (i.e., cognitive and emotional) effort on the part of the employee, and are therefore associated with certain physiological and/or psychological costs" (Demerouti et al., 2001, p. 501). Although job demands are not necessarily negative, they may become job stressors when meeting the required demands entails great effort to sustain an expected performance level, thereby eliciting negative responses such as chronic fatigue and burnout (Schaufeli & Bakker, 2004). Examples of job demands are time and work pressure, the emotional demands of client work, an adverse physical work environment, role ambiguity, role conflicts, and role overload.

Job resources, on the other hand, refer to working conditions that provide resources for individual employees. More specifically, job resources refer to "those physical, psychological, social, or organizational aspects of the job that may (a) reduce job demands and the associated physiological and psychological costs, (b) are functional in achieving work goals, and (c) stimulate personal growth, learning and development" (Demerouti et al., 2001, p. 501). Job resources may be located on the following levels: *organization* (e.g., salary, career opportunities, job security); *interpersonal and social relations* (e.g., supervisor and co-worker support); *organization of work* (e.g., role clarity, participation in decision-making); and *task* (e.g., performance feedback, skill variety, autonomy) (Bakker, Demerouti, & Verbeke, 2004).

In general, job demands and resources are negatively correlated, because high job demands may prevent the mobilization of job resources (Bakker & Demerouti, 2007). The JD-R model thus proposes that high job demands and a lack of resources may create a fertile breeding ground for burnout and reduced work engagement respectively (Schaufeli & Bakker, 2004). On the other hand, high job resources combined with either a high or low level of job demands may result in high motivation and engagement (Bakker & Demerouti, 2007).

The dual process

An important assumption of the JD-R model is that the two sets of working conditions referred to above may evoke two psychologically different, although related processes (Bakker & Demerouti, 2007; Schaufeli & Bakker, 2004): (1) an energy-sapping, health impairment process in which high job demands exhaust employees' mental and physical resources leading to burnout, and eventually to ill-health; and (2) a positive motivational process in which job resources foster engagement and organizational commitment.

The original complete JD-R model (Schaufeli & Bakker, 2004), consisting of the mediated main effects predicting positive and negative outcomes, is graphically displayed in Figure 7.1.

In the first so-called *health impairment process*, the demanding aspects of work (qualitative and quantitative demands) may lead to constant overload and eventually to exhaustion and ill-health. Hockey's (1997) compensatory regulatory-control model best illustrates this process through the concepts of *benefits* and *costs*. According to this model, employees under stress face a trade-off between the protection of their primary performance goals (benefits) and the mental effort required to sustain the job (costs). Regulatory problems occur when demands increase, that is, when compensatory effort has to be mobilized in order to deal with increased demands and to maintain performance levels. This, in turn, is associated with increased physiological and psychological costs. Continuous mobilization of compensatory effort drains the employee's energy and might therefore lead to burnout and, in the long run, to ill-health (Schaufeli & Bakker, 2004).

The second so-called *motivational process* links job resources with, for example, organizational commitment through engagement. Job resources

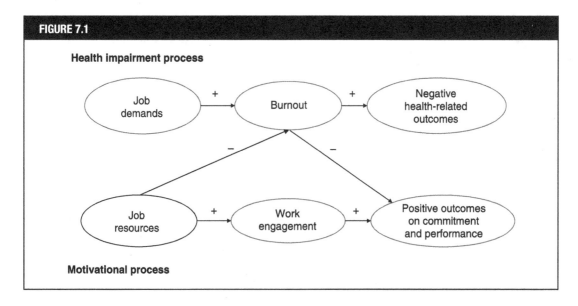

FIGURE 7.1

Health impairment process

Job demands → (+) → Burnout → (+) → Negative health-related outcomes

Job resources → (−) → Burnout

Job resources → (+) → Work engagement → (+) → Positive outcomes on commitment and performance

Burnout → (−) → Positive outcomes on commitment and performance

Motivational process

The complete dual process of the job demands-resources model (adapted from Demerouti et al., 2001; Schaufeli & Bakker, 2004).

may foster extrinsic motivation at work because they are necessary for dealing with job demands and for achieving work goals. In addition, by satisfying the basic human needs of autonomy, belongingness, and competence, job resources are also intrinsically motivating for employees (Van den Broeck, De Witte, Lens, & Vansteenkiste, 2008). Irrespective of whether intrinsic or extrinsic needs are satisfied, the outcome for the employee is positive, leading to engagement a fulfilling, positive work-related state of mind. It is therefore plausible that engaged employees are committed to the organization that provides them with job resources that enable their work goals, presenting them with opportunities for learning, growth, and development (Demerouti et al., 2001). In addition, the complete JD-R model includes the negative associations between job resources and burnout, and between burnout and organizational commitment.

A central theme of the JD-R model is the link between job resources and employee well-being, for example: motivation, engagement, and positive work attitudes. Thus, the JD-R model is not only an extension of the DCM (Karasek, 1979), but also has similarities with earlier motivational theories, using resources at work as a starting point for positive motivational outcomes. For example, the job characteristic theory (Hackman & Oldham, 1980) highlighted the underlying motivational and wellness-promoting potential of job-related task resources in an occupational context. In addition, bearing a resemblance to the JD-R model, Herzberg (1959), as early as 50 years ago, introduced a two-factor model of job satisfaction and motivation. According to this model, on the one hand, resources intrinsic to the job (e.g., achievement, responsibility, professional growth, and "work itself" referring to task variety) are "motivators" that will enhance job satisfaction and other positive work attitudes. On the other hand, resources extrinsic to the job (e.g., supervision, salary, interpersonal relations, and job security) are "hygiene factors" that may at best prevent motivational problems, and when lacking, lead to dissatisfaction. Thus, both the job characteristics theory and the motivation-hygiene theory underline the importance of resources

at work, but in contrast to the JD-R model, do not make specific assumptions concerning job demands. Moreover, unlike the job characteristics theory, the JD-R model assumes that task-level resources are only one, albeit important, category of job resources. Also, in contrast to Herzberg's theory, the JD-R model proposes that both intrinsic resources as well as those surrounding the employee may foster engagement, or if lacking, lead to disengagement.

On a more general level, it is noteworthy that not only stress and motivational models but also more general approaches that have bridged research and practice, such as quality of working life (e.g., Levine, Taylor, & Davis; 1984) and healthy organizations (e.g., Cooper & Cartwright, 1994), have emphasized the role of resources in organizations. In addition, several theories support the impact of resources on psychological well-being, as resources are valued because of the satisfaction of needs they may provide. Hobfoll's (1998, 2002) conservation of resources (COR) theory is based on the assumption that various resources are salient factors in gaining new resources and in enhancing well-being. The capacity of resources to facilitate acquiring additional resources leads to the concepts of *resource caravans* and *loss* and *gain spirals*. According to the COR theory, resources are things that people value and therefore strive to obtain, retain, and protect. Hobfoll and Shirom (2001) have argued that: (a) individuals must bring in additional resources to prevent the loss of existing resources; (b) individuals with a greater pool of resources are less susceptible to resource loss; (c) individuals who do not have access to strong resource pools are more likely to experience increased loss (*loss spiral*); and (d) strong resource pools lead to a greater likelihood that individuals will seek opportunities to risk resources to increase resource gains (*gain spiral*). Assuming that there are gain spirals between job resources and engagement implies that they reciprocally strengthen each other. When employees are provided with necessary job resources, they may become more engaged over time, and engaged employees are likely to be more energized to take better advantage of existing job resources, and more motivated to create new ones. Hobfoll (2002) further argued that resource gain only has a modest effect, but instead acquires its saliency in the context of resource loss.

Another theory that may provide some perspective to the role of resources in work engagement is Fredrickson's (2000) broaden-and-build (BAB) theory of positive emotions. This theory claims that positive emotions broaden people's momentary thought-action repertoires, and build their enduring personal resources. These positive emotions spark the willingness to play, try things out, and experiment. This kind of initiative and creativity fosters new ideas and novel solutions which can be directly linked to *personal initiative* (PI), a concept coined by Frese, Fay, Hilburger, Leng, and Tag (1997), which refers to active and initiative-taking behaviour that goes beyond any formal requirements at work, and is positively associated with performing well in formal and informal tasks. Hakanen, Perhoniemi, and Toppinen-Tanner (2008a) further deduce that the path from job resources to work engagement and from work engagement to PI can also be inferred from Hobfoll's COR and Fredrickson's BAB theory. One of the sub-principles of Hobfoll's COR theory is that those with greater resources are less vulnerable to resource loss and more capable of resource gain, so that resource reservoirs tend to develop in resource caravans (Hobfoll, 2002). PI can also be linked to Fredrickson's BAB theory in that initiative and creativity fosters new ideas and solutions. Positive emotions may lead individuals towards optimal functioning, creativity, and achievement motivation in the long run (Fredrickson, 2000).

Thus, although here we have particularly focused on job resources and the motivational processes they may trigger, the remarkable innovation of the JD-R model is the proposition that ill-being (burnout) and true well-being (engagement) coexist with related health impairment and motivational processes. This dual process assumption enables a balance between the traditional ill-health orientated ("negative") psychology focusing on psychopathologies, and positive psychology highlighting human resources, strengths, and potentials.

JD-R interactions and the salience of resources

In addition to the main effects comprising the dual process, the JD-R model also asserts that job resources and demands may have interaction effects on employee well-being. First, the buffering hypothesis explains interactions between job demands and job resources by suggesting that the relationship between job demands and engagement is weaker for employees who have many job resources at their disposal. Second, on the basis of the COR theory (Hobfoll & Shirom, 2001), the JD-R model takes this hypothesis a step further by not only assuming buffering effects but also positing a so-called coping or motivational hypothesis, i.e., job resources are expected to gain their salience particularly when employees meet high levels of job demands. In other words, the positive association between job resources and engagement is expected to be stronger when job demands are high. Thus, The JD-R model conceptually integrates and expands the demand-control model (Karasek, 1979) and the effort-reward imbalance model (Siegrist, 1996).

Empirical support for JD-R model and engagement

Empirical support for the dual process

Since the seminal study by Demerouti and her colleagues in 2001, nearly 20 studies have been published to date which test the assumption of the dual processes of motivation and health impairment. No doubt this number will grow considerably in the future. The first studies to investigate the main (and mediated) effects proposed in the JD-R model did not include engagement as an outcome or a mediator, but interchangeably measured some other motivational aspects of work-related well-being as outcomes: cynicism and the efficacy dimensions of burnout (Bakker, Demerouti, Taris, Schaufeli, & Schreurs, 2003c); the affective, continuance, and normative dimensions of commitment to predict absence frequency (Bakker, Demerouti, De Boer, & Schaufeli, 2003a); involvement as indicated by commitment and dedication to predict turnover intention (Bakker, Demerouti, & Schaufeli,

2003b); and connectedness to predict determination to continue in volunteer work (Lewig, Xanthopoulou, Bakker, Dollard, & Metzer, 2007). In addition, the model has been tested using the opposite of engagement, i.e., disengagement, as an outcome of job resources (Demerouti et al., 2001) and as a mediator between job resources and extra-role performance (Bakker et al., 2004).

More recently, several studies have aimed at testing the comprehensive JD-R model with engagement as a potential mediator between job resources and one specific outcome, namely organizational commitment (or turnover intentions). Of these, a study by Schaufeli and Bakker (2004) was the first to investigate the comprehensive JD-R model, including the antecedents and consequences of both engagement and burnout, i.e., the motivational and health impairment processes. The results confirmed that whereas burnout mediated the impact of job demands on health problems, engagement mediated the impact of job resources on turnover intentions. Moreover, job resources were negatively associated with burnout, which, in turn, was positively associated with turnover intentions. The findings indicated the robustness of the proposed model as it was tested simultaneously on four different samples of white-collar employees in four Dutch service organizations.

Further support for the dual process was found in a study of over 2000 Finnish teachers (Hakanen et al., 2006). In this study, the sample was randomized into two groups of equal size after which the JD-R model was tested in the first group of teachers and then cross-validated in the other. The results were the same in both groups, showing, for example, that engagement fully mediated the effects of job resources on organizational commitment. In addition, it was found that the final model fitted the following groups equally well: women and men; respondents under and over the age of 45; workers with both permanent and fixed-term contracts; and those with a job tenure of both under and over 10 years. Other studies have also been conducted in various professional and cultural settings with similar findings, supporting the JD-R model and the mediated process linking job resources to organizational commitment via

engagement. Fully or partially mediated dual processes have also been identified, for example, among South African educators (Jackson, Rothmann, & van de Vijver, 2006), Norwegian police officers (Richardsen, Burke, & Martinussen, 2006), and Spanish and Dutch employees (Llorens, Schaufeli, Bakker, & Salanova, 2007).

Although the findings have been supportive of the proposed model, it may be worthwhile considering some of the results in more detail. Schaufeli and Bakker (2004) noted in their study that the association between engagement and turnover intentions was the weakest association among the main processes of the JD-R model. In addition, the relationship between job resources and engagement was rather weak among Finnish teachers (Hakanen et al., 2006). This specific finding may have been due to the fact that in the study in question, most of the job resources measured were organizational and out-of-the-classroom (e.g., social climate and supervisor support) which may not be the *most* salient job resources for teachers. Later discussions with teachers suggested that daily positive interaction with pupils and both immediate and long-term feedback are even more important and engaging elements in teaching. In addition, both among Finnish and South African educators (Jackson et al., 2006) an exceptionally high negative association was found between burnout and engagement. Interestingly, in the Finnish research project it was also possible to test the same model among blue-collar workers (school cooks and cleaners, etc.) and other white-collar workers (principals, school psychologists, social workers, etc.) working in schools in Helsinki or holding administrative posts in the educational organization of the City of Helsinki (Hakanen, 2002a). Among those groups, the association between (organizational) job resources and engagement was clearly stronger than among teachers, supporting the proposition that the same job resources can be relevant to engagement in varying degrees in different professional groups, even for those employed by the same organization. Moreover, health impairment and motivational processes may be more strongly intertwined in some occupational groups than others. On the whole, these findings underline the importance of context sensitivity in the planning of studies (and measures) using the JD-R model.

All the above cited studies have used a cross-sectional design. However, similar results were gained in a recent study using a two-wave cross-lagged panel design among 2555 Finnish dentists (Hakanen, Schaufeli, & Ahola, 2008b). Accordingly, the results supported both the motivational and the health impairment processes over a 3-year follow-up period: job resources influenced future engagement, which in turn positively predicted organizational commitment, whereas job demands predicted burnout over time, which in turn predicted future depression. In addition, job resources had a weak negative impact on burnout. Here, support for the original model was even stronger because in this longitudinal dentist study it was possible to control for the effects of baseline variables and to examine potential reversed and reciprocal cross-lagged effects in the JD-R model.

Special focus on motivational process and job performance

It may be concluded that studies testing the comprehensive JD-R model have consistently supported the proposition of a dual process and the role of job resources as the major antecedent of engagement and further positive outcomes. However, a common feature of all these above-mentioned studies testing the comprehensive JD-R model is that various indicators of *organizational commitment* have been used as the final positive outcome of the motivational process. There exist, nevertheless, several other studies which have focused solely on the motivational process (job resources → engagement → positive outcome), and in many of these studies, different indicators of *job performance* have been used as the positive outcome which is hypothesized to follow from job resources and engagement. Most notably perhaps, Salanova and her colleagues (Salanova, Agut, & Peiró, 2005) found, in a study of 342 Spanish employees from hotels and restaurants, that engagement mediated the impact of job resources on service climate, which in turn influenced customer loyalty through customers' assessments of employee performance. Thus, the energizing and wellness-promoting impacts of

job resources and engagement may extend beyond employee attitudes towards the organization and customers. In addition, Salanova and Schaufeli (2008) conducted a study using two independent samples consisting of 385 Spanish technology employees and 338 Dutch telecom managers to investigate the antecedents of (self-reported) proactive behaviour. In their multinational study, engagement fully mediated the impact of job resources on proactive behaviour. Using a somewhat different operationalization of engagement, Saks (2006) showed, in a heterogeneous sample of 102 employees, that job and organization engagement partially mediated the effects of a variety of job resources on, for example, organizational citizenship behaviour.

In a similar vein, using a half-longitudinal design among dentists, Hakanen (2009) showed that engagement at Time 1 partially mediated the impact of Time 1 job resources on the latent job performance variable indicated by in-role and extra-role performance and personal initiative at Time 2 3 years later. Furthermore, adding job demands to the model did not diminish the motivational process linking job resources, via engagement, to performance. In addition, even though job demands were also related to performance both directly and indirectly via engagement, both these associations were significantly weaker than the corresponding associations with job resources. Similarly, previous studies have also found that engagement may be related to job demands, but these associations are typically weaker than associations between engagement and job resources (e.g., Mauno, Kinnunen, & Ruokolainen, 2007; see also Halbesleben, Chapter 8 in this book).

Finally, using a cross-lagged panel design in a large sample of Finnish dentists, it was found that job resources predicted engagement, which in turn predicted proactive and initiative-taking behaviour labelled as PI, which then positively influenced perceptions of work-unit innovativeness over a 3-year period (Hakanen et al., 2008a). Hence, according to this study, the motivational process triggered by job resources and engagement may lead to positive outcomes concerning both individual performance (PI) and organizational performance (innovativeness). In addition, the cross-lagged relationships between job resources and engagement, and engagement and PI were reciprocal, indicating positive gain spirals (see Salanova et al., Chapter 9 in this book).

Alternative ways of conceptualizing and measuring job resources

The above cited studies that have used the Utrecht Work Engagement Scale to either test the comprehensive JD-R model or explore motivational processes have included a variety of job resources. Among the most often included job resources are performance feedback/results (6 studies), job control/autonomy (5 studies), social support from colleagues (5 studies), task variety/growth opportunities (4 studies), and supervisory support/coaching (3 studies). To a lesser extent, job resources such as advancement, organizational training, and social climate have also been included. Often these resources have been chosen on the basis of prior qualitative interviews with the relevant employees of the involved organizations, so that an understanding of the most salient resources (and demands) in the specific occupational context can be reached, and tailor-made questionnaires constructed (see Bakker & Demerouti, 2007). It is likely that there are many other types of job resources that could be included in studies to predict engagement.

Due to a widely shared perception of an increased significance of the notion of psychological contract in understanding employment relationships, the number of studies on psychological contracts has grown extensively in the past 15 years (e.g., Zhao, Wayne, Glibkowski, & Bravo, 2007). However, most of these studies have focused on breach of contract, and only a few studies have investigated the implications of psychological contracts for employee well-being. Parzefall and Hakanen (in press) aimed to integrate the psychological contract approach and the JD-R model. They specifically focused on perceived contract fulfilment in order to investigate the motivational process among 178 Finnish employees of a research organization. The starting point was that the prerequisites for psychological contract fulfilment were viewed as the resources that employees expect the employer to provide. When provided, these resources influence the quality of the employment relationship, encouraging more than a mere obligation to reciprocate. Consistent with the JD-R model, it was hypothesized that different aspects of contract fulfilment, for example the training necessary to do the job well, participation in goal-setting, and autonomy regarding job content, help employees to achieve their work goals and stimulate their own personal growth. In addition, contract fulfilment were expected to promote engagement and positive attitudes towards the organization. The results supported the fully mediated model, in which engagement mediated the effect of psychological contract fulfilment on affective commitment, with the additional consequence of diminished turnover intentions.

Thus far, most conceptualizations of job resources have been positive by nature. This begs the question, do opposites to job resources exist, i.e., aspects of the job that are dysfunctional and may thus increase job demands, hinder the achievement of work goals, and at the same time demotivate and drain the energies of employees? Hakanen and Lindbohm (2008) conducted a study among 398 employed breast cancer survivors and 560 of their matched referents from a general working population to investigate the role of social and interpersonal job resources and optimism (and pessimism) in engagement, comparing these associations between the two study groups. In addition to "true" job resources – organizational climate and social support at work – measures for "lacking" job resources were developed especially for the study, namely avoidance behaviour by supervisor and avoidance behaviour by colleagues. These negative aspects of job resources were expected to be relevant to cancer survivors returning to work, because in some previous studies, cancer survivors have been found to experience discrimination due to their illness. In this study, we found that both "positive" and "negative" types of job resources were equally strongly (although in opposite directions) related to engagement. In addition, when comparing the two groups, no differences were detected in the level of different types of job resources or in the strength of their associations with engagement. On the whole, there are several ways to conceptualize and measure job resources or the lack of job resources, and it was found that these are conceptually distinct from job demands.

Incorporating non-work characteristics into the JD-R model

By definition, the JD-R model bases its premises of health impairment, employee well-being and motivation promotion on work characteristics. In one of the earliest studies on engagement, it was found that there might also be other, non-work-related factors that enhance engagement. This study by Sonnentag (2003) showed that psychological, day-level recovery during leisure time predicted higher engagement, which in turn, positively predicted proactive behaviour.

Several studies have also shown the relationship between engagement and personal variables. For example, engagement has associated positively with achievement-striving (Hallberg, Johansson, & Schaufeli, 2007), high extraversion and low neuroticism (Langelaan, Bakker, van Doornen, & Schaufeli, 2006), and adaptive perfectionism (Zhang, Gan, & Cham, 2007). Moreover, Mauno and her colleagues (2007) found that organization-based self-esteem – a context-specific personal resource – was longitudinally associated with every dimension of engagement. Interestingly, Xanthopoulou, Bakker, Demerouti, and Schaufeli (2007) incorporated the conception of personal resources into the JD-R model. In contrast to personality traits and temperament, personal resources can be described as states that can develop, and be developed and managed for improved work performance. Xanthopoulou and her colleagues argued that personal resources as positive self-evaluations that are closely linked to resilient coping strategies are related to positive work-related outcomes. Their study among Dutch employees supported these assumptions by showing that personal resources (self-efficacy, organizational-based self-esteem, and optimism) mediated the impact of job resources on engagement (as well as on exhaustion).

In the study among Finnish employed breast cancer survivors and their referents (Hakanen & Lindbohm, 2008), structural equation modelling was used to investigate and compare the strength of the associations of job resources and optimism (and pessimism) with engagement between the two groups and within the groups. It was found that compared to various job resources, optimism (and also pessimism) was consistently more strongly related to cancer survivors' engagement. Moreover, although job resources were equally strongly associated with engagement in both groups, optimism was more strongly related to engagement among cancer survivors compared to their referents, whereas pessimism did not even significantly predict engagement among the general population. Having a serious illness such as cancer can be regarded as a resource loss often accompanied by other losses and threats, and in dealing with these conditions, personal resources may become challenged and acquire special saliency (Hobfoll, 1989; Hobfoll & Shirom, 2001). Thus, these findings suggest that personal resources may be especially relevant for engagement in certain situations and occupational groups.

In addition to individual resources, it is possible that home characteristics could also have an impact on the processes in the JD-R model. For example, positive work–home interaction was found to partially mediate the impact of social resources on engagement among Dutch newspaper managers (Montgomery, Peeters, Schaufeli, & Den Ouden, 2003). Several studies have also established the negative association between family and non-work-related support and burnout (for a review, see Halbesleben, 2006). One of the numerous interesting findings in the study by Bakker, Demerouti, and Schaufeli (2005) was that home resources (although to a lesser extent than job resources) were positively associated with engagement in both men and women, and that emotional home demands were negatively associated with engagement among women. However, longitudinal research on the impact of home conditions on engagement and burnout has been lacking until now. In the study among Finnish dentists to longitudinally test the complete JD-R model (Hakanen et al., 2008b), we further investigated whether home resources and home demands would influence engagement and burnout over time, after controlling for the effects of job demands and resources. The findings showed that home characteristics did not have an impact on either engagement or burnout. Instead, only a reversed positive effect of burnout on future home demands was found, thus suggesting that the health impairment process may spill over into the home situation. These results are also of practical importance, since it is sometimes claimed that burnout is primarily caused by problems at home. Moreover, the starting point for interventions for preventing burnout and promoting engagement seems to lie in job resources and job demands, as proposed by the JD-R model.

On the basis of the few studies that have added non-work aspects to the JD-R model, the evidence of the additional value of non-work factors is still inconclusive. However, we expect future longitudinal studies to confirm the importance of personal resources and successful recovery to both health-related and motivational processes.

Salience of job resources in the context of resource threats

Thus far, most of the studies testing the JD-R model have focused on the main and mediated effects of job resources, engagement, and related variables. The empirical evidence and the theoretical model is consistent with COR theory's assumptions of cumulative resource gains (the motivational process) and losses (the health impairment process). In addition, the proposition that job resources may reduce the impact of job demands on job strain is rooted in the JD-R model (Bakker & Demerouti, 2007) and as a more restricted formulation (job control × workload) in the demand-control model (Karasek, 1979). Indeed, research has supported the assumption that different job resources may buffer the negative effects of various job demands on engagement (e.g., Hakanen, Bakker, & Demerouti, 2005) and on burnout (e.g., Bakker, Demerouti, & Euwema, 2005). One of the most challenging assumptions of the COR theory claims, however, that resources may not only act as buffers, but

also acquire their salience first and foremost in the context of resource loss and/or threat (Hobfoll, 1998). Thus, in addition to the buffer hypothesis, job resources may also motivate and influence engagement *particularly* under high job demands.

Two studies have tested the beneficial effects of different job resources on engagement in various demanding working conditions. Hakanen and his colleagues (2005) investigated five job resources (e.g., task variety and professional contacts) and four job demands (e.g., emotional dissonance and physical work environment) and their joint effects on engagement in a sample of 1919 Finnish dentists employed in the public sector. In total, 17 out of 40 possible interactions were found, and all five job resources had beneficial effects on engagement under at least one type of high demand. For example, positive professional contacts particularly boosted engagement when negative work changes that took place after major dental law reforms affected the dentists. In a similar vein, Bakker and his colleagues (2007) examined the interaction effects of six job resources (e.g., job control, appreciation, and supervisory support) with a major job demand in teaching, i.e., pupil misconduct, on dimensions of engagement among 805 Finnish teachers. In line with the previous study, 14 out of 18 possible interaction effects were found. Thus, these two studies conducted in different occupational contexts, and using different instruments to measure job demands and resources showed that, in addition to the unique main effects, job resources and job demands may also have joint effects on engagement. In line with the COR theory, job resources not only acted as buffers against the negative impact of job demands, but also boosted engagement, especially when job demands were high. These findings lend further support to the theoretical expansion of the DCM, and to a more comprehensive and context-sensitive JD-R model.

Towards a modified JD-R model of work engagement and possible future directions

On the basis of research evidence cited in this chapter and based on the reviews by Bakker and Demerouti (2007, 2008), it is possible to elaborate the dual process model of job demands and resources and propose a more focused JD-R model to predict engagement. This model (depicted in Figure 7.2) includes personal resources as predictors of engagement and reciprocal associations between personal and job resources, and engagement; defines the modifying role of job demands in the JD-R model; and proposes several potential positive outcomes. Figure 7.2 can also be used to illustrate gaps in present knowledge and to identify challenges and avenues for future research on the JD-R model, with a view to predicting engagement and other positive outcomes. We classify these challenges and future avenues into three categories: (1) the content (variables) of some of the boxes in Figure 7.2, (2) the overall model, and (3) work-based identity issues and the JD-R model.

Components in the JD-R model

A wide variety of job resources and job demands has been covered in studies on the JD-R model. However, surprisingly, little attention has been paid to the effects of job resources such as leadership issues on engagement. Leadership styles, such as transformational and servant leadership, which emphasize the importance of inter-personal relationships, are most likely to act as "energizers" in building engagement. Because engagement is contagious, the interaction between the leader and the employee could also provide new insight into how to keep employees engaged even in highly stressful conditions. In addition, job resources can be located on the levels of task, organization of work, interpersonal and social relations, and organization. Hence, some studies have included scales to represent different levels of job resources (e.g., Schaufeli & Bakker, 2004), whereas others have focused on one level of job resources, e.g., the task level, which is expected to be most relevant to the participants (e.g., Hakanen et al., 2008a). Investigating the relative relevance of the different levels of job resources would provide a challenging topic for research. Empirically, differentiation between various levels of job resources may prove difficult, but it would be useful for identifying the most energizing types of job resources in different situations and contexts.

As regards job demands, it is important to distinguish between the demands/stressors which, similarly to job resources, may promote personal growth and achievement, i.e., *challenge stressors*

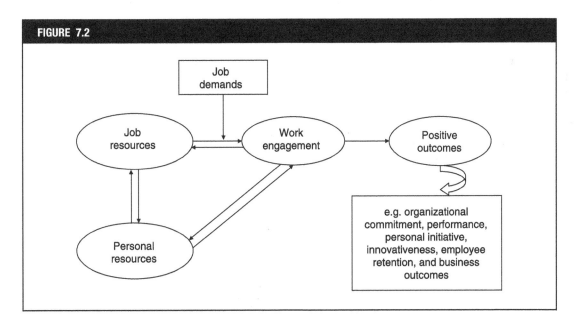

FIGURE 7.2

The modified JD-R model of work engagement (based on Bakker & Demerouti, 2007).

(e.g., time urgency), and the demands/stressors that constrain growth and achievement, i.e., *hindrance stressors* (e.g., role conflicts and role ambiguity). A recent meta-analysis by LePine, Podsakoff, and LePine (2005) showed that although challenge and hindrance stressors were both positively related to strain variables, they were differently related to motivation and performance. In addition, studies using the JD-R model have sometimes found that challenge and hindrance demands are differently related to engagement (Mauno et al., 2007; Van den Broeck et al., 2008). It might be worthwhile investigating the mediating role of engagement between (a) challenge and hindrance stressors and (b) positive motivational outcomes. As regards interaction effects, it would be interesting to systematically examine whether hindrance and challenge stressors in different occupations would differently interact with various job resources. Perhaps in highly challenging work situations, job resources could facilitate success in work tasks and provide rewarding experiences for employees, and thereby further increase engagement. However, under the influence of hindrance stressors, employees may at best maintain their level of engagement with the help of job resources.

Thus far, most of the studies on the JD-R model have employed organizational commitment and performance as the final outcomes of the motivational process although there are several other interesting options. For example, Salanova et al. (2005) experimented with an approach that is interesting from the viewpoint of future research, by investigating the motivational process of predicting customer satisfaction. Moreover, although in the studies on the JD-R model, (ill-)health has been mostly related to job demands and burnout, it should be noted that job resources also seem to play a role in the health-related process (Hakanen et al., 2008b; Schaufeli & Bakker, 2004). In addition, some studies have found positive associations between engagement and health (Hakanen et al., 2006; Hallberg & Schaufeli, 2006; Schaufeli, Taris, & van Rhenen, 2008). Thus, the motivational process might even extend to positive health outcomes. Indeed, Parzefall and Hakanen (in press) found support not only for the motiv-

ational process, but also for a health-enhancing process in which engagement fully mediated the impact of psychological contract fulfilment on mental health. Examining how the JD-R model predicts other business outcomes (e.g., innovations) and also objective health outcomes would be valuable. We can expect job resources and engagement to strengthen many individual, interpersonal, and organizational resources and outcomes (see also Fredrikson, 2000), and research on these processes has only just begun.

Finally, the concept of engagement itself: Several studies have shown that engagement is empirically distinct from many close constructs. However, as noted earlier, studies using the JD-R model have sometimes interchangeably used the concept of engagement with some other motivational construct, which raises the question whether engagement has a unique contribution to the predictions of the JD-R model. In addition to conceptual clarification, one solution could be to more closely investigate the mechanisms (e.g., efficacy beliefs, need satisfaction, and proactive behaviour) linking job resources, engagement, and positive outcomes.

Testing the overall model

A second avenue for future research relates to further testing and developing the overall model with heterogeneous samples and different methods. For example, only a few studies testing the model have accounted for the diversity of employees and organizations. Although the study among Finnish teachers (Hakanen et al., 2006) supported the dual processes regardless of age, gender, job tenure, or type of contract, this may not necessarily be the case in other occupational groups. For example, it is noteworthy that two studies have found the level of engagement to be higher among those with fixed-term contracts than among those with permanent contracts (Hakanen, 2002b; Mauno, Kinnunen, Mäkikangas, & Nätti, 2005). Moreover, in an interesting study by De Lange, De Witte, and Notelaers (2008) the longitudinal relationships between job resources and engagement showed different patterns among stayers, promotion makers, and external job movers. Investigating engagement and its specific antecedents and consequences in different occupational and contract groups, using the JD-R model, might shed new light on diversity issues in worklife.

Furthermore, studies on the JD-R model thus far have supported COR theory's assumptions of cumulative resource loss (health impairment) and gain (motivational) processes and also showed the salience of job resources in the context of high job demands. However, COR theory also hypothesizes gain and loss spirals (Hobfoll, 1998). The few existing longitudinal studies on the JD-R model have found only partial support for the reciprocal effects suggestive of the spirals. We agree with Bakker, Schaufeli, Demerouti, and Euwema (2006) that future studies on the JD-R model could benefit from focusing more on the concepts of loss and gain spirals. Furthermore, when using longitudinal designs, being able to estimate the optimal time-lags of the effects between the variables in the model would be important from a theoretical and practical point of view. According to a review by Zapf, Dormann, and Frese (1996), excessively short time lags may lead to the conclusion that no causal effects exist, whereas excessively long time lags will lead to an underestimation of the true causal relationships. For example, the 3-year follow-up period in the study on Finnish dentists was perhaps optimal to investigate cross-lagged associations between job demands and burnout, and between burnout and depression. However, shorter time lags would perhaps have been more optimal to identify a stronger impact of job resources on work engagement. We call for both short-term and long-term follow-up studies (preferably also including interventions) on the model to further elaborate on the optimal effects and long-term duration of the impacts.

Finally, it would be worthwhile examining change and developmental trajectories in engagement across time. Latent growth modelling (see e.g., Bentein, Vandenberg, Vandenberghe, & Stinglhamber, 2005) with at least three time-waves would enable researchers to examine, for example, whether intra-individual changes in job resources would predict changes in engagement and commitment, aside from the individual's

baseline situation in these constructs. Another relatively new technique called factor mixture modelling (see e.g. Hakanen, Feldt, & Leskinen, 2007) could be used to examine whether it is possible to identify natural groups of individuals in the data, on the basis of the level of engagement they showed over time. If such latent groups can be identified, the next question could again be whether there are differences in the predictors and consequences of engagement between these groups. Another less employed approach would be to investigate engagement and the JD-R model both at the individual and organizational level of analysis which could have high practical utility, since for managers and leaders, the focus is typically on unit characteristics and unit outcomes, not on individuals (Pugh & Dietz, 2008).

Work identity formation and the JD-R model

A third future research avenue rests on the assumption that the work identity formation process precedes work engagement. Earlier, Kahn (1990, p. 694) conceptualized engagement at work as "the harnessing of organizational *members' selves* to their work roles". It would be informative to investigate the nature and development of the identification (continuum between dedication and cynicism) and work identity formation processes and outcomes. Possible research questions that can be raised are, for example: if work engagement is a state of mind, what other processes than those assumed in the JD-R model precede the formation of this predisposition? Does the identification process already start at the pre-employment decision stage? Does identification deepen and does it transform into involvement at the post-employment decision stage? If so, what strategies and practices do individuals and organizations engage in at this stage, in creating an optimal engagement and commitment context? Research on the formation of work identity could also shed light on the differences between high engagement and workaholism, and differences in the processes leading up to them (see Roodt, 1991, 1997; Roodt, Bester, & Boshoff, 1994; Schaufeli, Taris, Le Blanc, Peeters, Bakker,

Practical implications

Using the lessons from the studies on the JD-R model, practitioners should take note of the following in order to build a highly engaged and committed workforce:

- The first necessary step in increasing job resources is *to identify* the key job resources the individual employee or the workplace needs in order to achieve their work goals and to flourish. For example, in Finland we have developed an intervention programme for workplaces in which the principles of positive psychology, the JD-R model, and COR theory are applied. As part of the intervention workshops, one aim is to identify the already *available* job resources in the workplace ("strengths"), the *potential* job resources (resources that for some reason are not currently used in the organization), and the job resources that are *lacking*.
- The JD-R model suggests that employees' level of work engagement is directly related to the qualitative nature and extent of the resources (interpersonal relations, task, work-role, and organizational) at their disposal. After identifying the key job resources, increasing the nature and extent of these resources would enhance engagement and consequently improve proactive behaviour and organizational commitment.
- Another option with which organizations can build engagement is to focus on increasing personal resources, for example efficacy beliefs, optimism, hope, gratitude, and empathy.
- Efforts to improve job resources would be especially beneficial when the job demands are high, for example during organizational changes. Under such conditions, job resources may not only mitigate the negative impact of job demands on engagement, but the positive relationship between job resources and engagement is actually likely to be strongest when employees are exposed to high demands.
- Several existing human resources management (HRM) strategies focusing on the development of job and personal resources may play an important role in fostering engagement. For example, employee development agreements, wellness audits, workshops, job (re)design and work changes, leadership practices, and career planning and development (Schaufeli & Salanova, 2008) are all examples of means to identify and increase resources and to build engagement.
- The dual challenge of preventing ill-health and building engagement as illustrated by the JD-R model links the interests of occupational health and HRM professionals. Health is no longer only associated with medical problems. Instead, employee health and vitality are seen as a significant condition of company success. Therefore business activities (e.g., leadership), the company as a whole, and related stakeholders (e.g. unions) all need to be involved in building employee well-being and engagement (Zwetsloot & Pot, 2004).

& De Jonge, 2001). In addition, work identity is a personal resource that may develop over time, and result in even deeper engagement and commitment over the work career.

Conclusion

We have noticed in our studies that the level of engagement is not determined as such on the basis of employee status or position at work, and that regardless of job or profession, it is possible to feel vigorous, be dedicated, and become absorbed at work. Several worklife surveys and overviews have suggested that worklife may be polarizing into workplaces that are thriving and others that are deteriorating, for example through a decreased level of employee well-being. By the same token, in many cases it seems impossible to characterize the exact professional sectors or groups belonging to either the former or latter end. By emphasizing the role of different job demands and resources, the JD-R model helps us to understand the salience of immediate working conditions for both the positive processes leading to resource caravans and the loss processes trig-

gered by lack of job resources and excessively high job demands. According to the studies on the JD-R model and engagement, the resources may lead to many different gains on individual, work-unit, and organizational levels, regardless of the demands and threats in the external environment. Organizations are well-advised to focus on improving job resources which, by definition, help workers achieve work goals and stimulate personal growth, learning and development. As a result of fostering extrinsic and intrinsic motivation, employees will be both *able* and *willing* to give their best performance at work.

References

Bakker, A. B., & Demerouti, E. (2007). The Job Demands-Resources model: state of the art. *Journal of Managerial Psychology, 22*, 309–328.

Bakker, A. B., & Demerouti, E. (2008). Towards a model in work engagement. *Career Developmental International, 13*, 209–223.

Bakker, A. B., Demerouti, E., De Boer, E., & Schaufeli, W. B. (2003a). Job demands and resources as predictors of absence duration and frequency. *Journal of Vocational Behavior, 62*, 341–356.

Bakker, A. B., Demerouti, E., & Euwema, M. C. (2005). Job resources buffer the impact of job demands on burnout. *Journal of Occupational Health Psychology*, *10*, 170–180.

Bakker, A. B., Demerouti, E., & Schaufeli, W. B. (2003b). Dual processes at work in a call centre: An application of the Job Demands-Resources model. *European Journal of Work and Organizational Psychology*, *12*, 393–417.

Bakker, A. B., Demerouti, E., & Schaufeli, W. B. (2005). The crossover of burnout and work engagement among working couples. *Human Relations*, *58*, 661–689.

Bakker, A. B., Demerouti, E., Taris, T., Schaufeli, W. B., & Schreurs, P. (2003c). A multi-group analysis of the Job Demands-Resources model in four home care organizations. *International Journal of Stress Management*, *10*, 16–38.

Bakker, A. B., Demerouti, E., & Verbeke, W. (2004). Using the Job Demands-Resources model to predict burnout and performance, *Human Resource Management*, *43*, 83–104

Bakker, A. B., Hakanen, J. J., Demerouti, E., & Xanthopoulou, D. (2007). Job resources boost work engagement, particularly when job demands are high. *Journal of Educational Psychology*, *99*, 274–284.

Bakker, A. B., Schaufeli, W. B., Demerouti, E., & Euwema, M. C. (2006). An organizational and social psychological perspective on burnout and work engagement. In M. Hewstone, H. Schut, J. de Wit, K. van den Bos & M. Stroebe (Eds.), *The scope of social psychology: Theory and applications* (pp. 229–252). Andover, UK: Psychology Press.

Bentein, K., Vandenberg, R., Vandenberghe, C., & Stinglhamber, F. (2005). The role of change in the relationship between commitment and turnover: A latent growth modeling approach. *Journal of Applied Psychology*, *90*, 468–482.

Cooper, C. L., & Cartwright, S. (1994). Healthy mind; healthy organization – A proactive approach to occupational stress. *Human Relations*, *47*, 455–471.

De Lange, A. H., De Witte, H., & Notelaers, G. (2008). Should I stay or should I go? Examining the longitudinal relation between job resources and work engagement for stayers versus movers. *Work & Stress*, *22*, 201–223.

Demerouti, E., Bakker, A. B., Nachreiner, F., & Schaufeli, W. B. (2001). The job demands-resources model of burnout. *Journal of Applied Psychology*, *86*, 499–512.

Fredrickson, B. (2000). Why positive emotions matter in organizations. Lessons from the broaden-and-build model. *The Psychologist-Manager Journal*, *4*, 131–142.

Frese, M., Fay, D., Hilburger, T., Leng, K., & Tag, A. (1997). The concept of personal initiative: Operationalization, reliability, and validity in two German samples. *Journal of Occupational and Organizational Psychology*, *70*, 139–161.

Hackman, J. R., & Oldham, G. R. (1980). *Work redesign.* Reading, MA: Addison-Wesley.

Hakanen, J. J. (2002a, July). Testing a model of engagement and burnout. In W.B. Schaufeli (Chair), *Job engagement.* Symposium conducted at the meeting of The 25th International Congress of Applied Psychology ICAP, Singapore.

Hakanen, J. J. (2002b). Työuupumuksesta työn imuun – positiivisen työhyvinvointikäsitteen ja – menetelmän suomalaisen version validointi opetusalan organisaatiossa [From burnout to job engagement – validation of the Finnish version of an instrument for measuring job engagement (UWES) in an educational organization]. *Työ ja ihminen, 16*, 42–58.

Hakanen, J. J. (2009). Do engaged employees perform better at work? The motivating power of job resources and work engagement on future job performance. In M. Christensen (Ed.), *Validation and test of central concepts in positive work and organizational psychology – The second report of the Nordic Project.* (TemaNord 2009: 564, pp. 65–71). Copenhagen: Nordic Council of Ministers.

Hakanen, J. J., Bakker, A. B., & Demerouti, E. (2005). How dentists cope with their job demands and stay engaged: The moderating role of job resources. *European Journal of Oral Sciences, 113*, 479–487.

Hakanen, J. J., Bakker, A. B., & Schaufeli, W. B. (2006). Burnout and work engagement among teachers. *Journal of School Psychology, 43*, 495–513.

Hakanen, J., Feldt, T., & Leskinen, E. (2007). Changes and stability of sense of coherence in adulthood: Longitudinal evidence from the healthy child study. *Journal of Research in Personality, 41*, 602–617.

Hakanen, J. J., & Lindbohm, M. L. (2008). Work engagement among breast cancer survivors and their referents: The importance of optimism and social resources at work. *Journal of Cancer Survivorship, 2*, 283–295.

Hakanen, J. J., Perhoniemi, R., & Toppinen-Tanner, S. (2008a). Positive gain spirals at work: From job resources to work engagement, personal initiative, and work-unit innovativeness. *Journal of Vocational Behavior, 73*, 78–91.

Hakanen, J. J., Schaufeli, W. B., & Ahola, K. (2008b).

The job demands-resources model: A three-year cross-lagged study of burnout, depression, commitment, and work engagement. *Work & Stress, 22*, 224–241.

Halbesleben, J. R. (2006). Sources of social support and burnout: A meta-analytic test of the conservation of resources model. *Journal of Applied Psychology, 91*, 1134–1145.

Hallberg, U. E., Johansson, G., & Schaufeli, W. B. (2007). Type A behavior and work situation: Associations with burnout and work engagement. *Scandinavian Journal of Psychology, 48*, 135–142.

Hallberg, U., & Schaufeli, W. B. (2006). "Same same" but different? Can work engagement be discriminated from job involvement and organizational commitment? *European Psychologist, 11*, 119–127.

Herzberg, F. (1959). *The motivation to work*. New York: John Wiley.

Hobfoll, S. E. (1989). Conservation of resources: A new attempt at conceptualizing stress. *American Psychologist, 44*, 513–524.

Hobfoll, S. E. (1998). *Stress, culture and community: The psychology and philosophy of stress*. New York: Plenum Press.

Hobfoll, S. E. (2002). Social and psychological resources and adaptation. *Review of General Psychology, 6*, 307–324.

Hobfoll, S. E., & Shirom, A. (2001). Conservation of resources theory: Applications to stress and management in the workplace. In R. T. Golembiewski (Ed.), *Handbook of Organizational Behavior* (pp. 57–81). New York: Dekker.

Hockey, G. R. J. (1997). Compensatory control in the regulation of human performance under stress and high workload: A cognitive-energetic framework. *Biological Psychology, 45*, 73–93.

Jackson, L. T. B., Rothmann, S., & Van de Vijver, F. J. R. (2006). A model of work-related well-being for educators in South Africa. *Stress and Health, 22*, 263–274.

Kahn, W. A. (1990). Psychological conditions of personal engagement and disengagement at work. *Academy of Management Journal, 33*, 692–724.

Karasek, R. A. (1979). Job demands, job decision latitude, and mental strain: implications for job design, *Administrative Science Quarterly, 24*, 285–308.

Langelaan, S., Bakker A. B., Van Doornen, L. J. P., & Schaufeli W. B. (2006). Burnout and work engagement: Do individual differences make a difference? *Personality and Individual Differences, 40*, 521–532.

LePine, J. A., Podsakoff, N. P., & LePine, M. A. (2005). A meta-analytic test of the challenge stressor-hindrance stressor framework: An explanation for inconsistent relationships among stressors and performance. *Academy of Management Journal, 48*, 764–775.

Levine, M. F., Taylor, J. C., & Davis, L. E. (1984). Defining quality of working life. *Human Relations, 37*, 81–104.

Lewig, K. A., Xanthopoulou, D., Bakker, A. B., Dollard, M. F., & Metzer, J. C. (2007). Burnout and connectedness among Australian volunteers: A test of the Job Demands–Resources model. *Journal of Vocational Behavior, 71*, 429–445.

Llorens, S., Schaufeli, W. B., Bakker, A. B., & Salanova, M. (2007). Testing the robustness of the Job Demands-Resources Model. *International Journal of Stress Management, 13*, 378–391.

Mauno, S., Kinnunen, U., Mäkikangas, A., & Nätti, J. (2005). Psychological consequences of fixed-term employment and perceived job insecurity among health care staff. *European Journal of Work and Organizational Psychology, 14*, 209–237.

Mauno, S., Kinnunen, U., & Ruokolainen, M. (2007). Job demands and resources as antecedents of work engagement: A longitudinal study. *Journal of Vocational Behavior, 70*, 149–171.

Montgomery, A. J., Peeters, M., Schaufeli, W. B., & Den Ouden, M. (2003). Work-home interference among newspaper managers: Its relationship with burnout and engagement. *Anxiety, Stress, and Coping, 16*, 195–211.

Parzefall, M., & Hakanen, J. J. (in press). Psychological contract and its motivational and health-enhancing outcomes. *Journal of Managerial Psychology*.

Pugh, S. D., & Dietz, J. (2008). Employee engagement at the organizational level of analysis. *Industrial and Organizational Psychology, 1*, 44–47.

Richardsen, A. M., Burke, R. J., & Martinussen, M. (2006). Work and health outcomes among police officers: The mediating role of police cynicism and engagement. *International Journal of Stress Management, 13*, 555–574.

Roodt, G. (1991). *Die graad van werkbetrokkenheid as voorspeller van persoonlike welsyn: 'n Studie by bestuurders* (The degree of job involvement as predictor of personal well-being: A study on managers). Unpublished D Admin thesis. Bloemfontein, South Africa: University of the Orange Free State.

Roodt, G. (1997). Theoretical and empirical linkages between work-related commitment foci. *Journal of Industrial Psychology, 23*, 6–13.

Roodt, G., Bester, C. L., & Boshoff, A. B. (1994). Die graad van werkbetrokkenheid: 'n bipolêre kontinuum? (The degree of work involvement: A bipolar continuum?). *Tydskrif vir Bedryfsielkunde, 20,* 21–30.

Saks, A. M. (2006). Antecedents and consequences of employee engagement. *Journal of Managerial Psychology, 21,* 600–619.

Salanova, M., Agut, S., & Peiró, J. M. (2005). Linking organizational facilitators and work engagement to employee performance and customer loyalty: The mediation of service climate. *Journal of Applied Psychology, 90,* 1217–1227.

Salanova, M., & Schaufeli, W. B. (2008). A cross-national study of work engagement as a mediator between job resources and proactive behaviour. *International Journal of Human Resource Management, 19,* 116–131.

Schaufeli, W. B., & Bakker, A. B. (2004). Job demands, job resources, and their relationship with burnout and engagement: a multi-sample study. *Journal of Organizational Behavior, 25,* 293–315.

Schaufeli, W. B., & Salanova, M. (2008). Enhancing work engagement through the management of human resources. In K. Näswall, M. Sverke & J. Hellgren (Eds.), *The individual in the changing working life* (pp. 380–404). Cambridge: Cambridge University Press.

Schaufeli, W. B., Salanova, M., González-Romá, V., & Bakker, A. B. (2002). The measurement of engagement and burnout: A two sample confirmatory factor analytic approach. *Journal of Happiness Studies, 3,* 71–92.

Schaufeli, W. B., Taris, T., LeBlanc, P., Peeters, M., Bakker, A. B., & de Jonge, J. (2001). Maakt arbeid gezond? Op soek naar de bevlogen werknemer. (Work and health: The quest for the engaged worker). *Psycholoog, 36,* 422–428.

Schaufeli, W. B., Taris, T. W., and van Rhenen, W. (2008). Workaholism, burnout and work engagement: Three of a kind or three different kinds of employee well-being? *Applied Psychology: An International Review, 57,* 173–203.

Siegrist, J. (1996). Adverse health effects of high effort–low reward conditions. *Journal of Occupational Health Psychology, 1,* 27–41.

Sonnentag, S. (2003). Recovery, work engagement, and proactive behavior: A new look at the interface between non-work and work. *Journal of Applied Psychology, 88,* 518–528.

Van den Broeck, A., De Witte, H., Lens, W., & Vansteenkiste, M. (2008). The role of basic need satisfaction in explaining the relationships between job demands, job resources, burnout and engagement. *Work & Stress, 22,* 277–294.

Xanthopoulou, D., Bakker, A. B., Demerouti, E., & Schaufeli, W. B. (2007). The role of personal resources in the job demands-resources model. *International Journal of Stress Management, 14,* 121–141.

Zapf, D., Dormann, C., & Frese, M. (1996). Longitudinal studies in organizational stress research: A review of the literature with reference to methodological issues. *Journal of Occupational Health Psychology, 1,* 145–169.

Zhang, Y., Gan, Y., & Cham, H. (2007). Perfectionism, academic burnout and engagement among Chinese college students: A structural equation modeling analysis. *Personality and Individual Differences, 43,* 1529–1540.

Zhao, H., Wayne, S. J., Glibkowsky, B. C., & Bravo, J. (2007). The impact of psychological contract breach on work-related outcomes: A meta-analysis. *Personnel Psychology, 60,* 647–680.

Zwetsloot, G., & Pot, F. (2004). The business value of health management. *Journal of Business Ethics, 55,* 115–124.

8

A meta-analysis of work engagement: Relationships with burnout, demands, resources, and consequences

Jonathon R. B. Halbesleben

This book highlights the vastness and diversity of the engagement literature. Researchers have examined a seemingly endless variety of variables in their attempt to better understand the conceptualization of engagement relative to other variables (especially burnout) as well as relationships with engagement's antecedents and consequences. As research on engagement has expanded very quickly, a need has emerged for a synthesis of existing empirical studies. Thus, the purpose of this chapter is to provide a meta-analysis of the correlates of engagement. To that end, I offer a very brief summary of the expected relationships from the literature. I emphasize the brief nature of the review in light of space limitations and to avoid redundancy; readers will be well-served to examine other chapters in the present volume for more detail on the theories underlying the relationships between engagement and its correlates. I then discuss the manner in which the meta-analysis was carried out along with its primary findings. This will lead to a discussion of the current state of the empirical engagement literature and suggestions for future research.

Relationships with burnout dimensions

Much of the early work concerning engagement was centered on examining its relationship with burnout. Indeed, as the engagement construct was being developed, particularly among empirical scholars, it was considered the positive antithesis to burnout, building on the emerging trend toward the study of positive psychology (Schaufeli & Salanova, 2007a). This research has typically suggested that the dimensions of vigor and exhaustion are most strongly related (on opposite ends of a continuum labeled "energy"; see González-Romá, Schaufeli, Bakker, & Lloret, 2006; Schaufeli & Bakker, 2001), that dedication and cynicism are strongly associated (via a continuum labeled "identification"), and that the dimension absorption does not necessarily have a corresponding burnout dimension. Similarly, the reduced personal efficacy dimension of burnout does not have a specific engagement counterpart; this reflects a growing literature examining this dimension and finding it may not be as core to burnout as originally thought (cf. Halbesleben & Buckley, 2004; Lee & Ashforth, 1996; Maslach, Schaufeli, & Leiter, 2001). In fact, studies of burnout and engagement find that it frequently loads onto an engagement latent factor rather than the predicted burnout factor (cf. Demerouti, Bakker, de Jonge, Janssen, & Schaufeli, 2001; Schaufeli & Bakker, 2004; Schaufeli, Taris, & Van Rhenen, 2008). Moreover, as Schaufeli and Salanova (2007a) describe, the notion of efficacy does not seem to capture the experience of engagement. Instead, based on their work, they argue that the experience of absorption (similar to the notion of "flow") is more reflective of the broader construct of engagement.

Given the numerous attempts to examine the relationship between engagement and burnout constructs, I felt this was an important starting point for a meta-analysis of the engagement literature. Based on the previous literature, I hypothesize the following:

Hypothesis 1: Dimensions of engagement should be negatively associated with dimensions of burnout. Specifically, it is expected that vigor will be most strongly and negatively associated with exhaustion and dedication will be most strongly and negatively associated with cynicism.

Antecedents

Researchers have explored an extraordinary variety of potential causes of engagement. Much of this work has focused on the role of work-related resources in predicting engagement, consistent with a variety of theoretical approaches including job characteristics theory (Hackman & Oldham, 1980), self-determination theory (Ryan & Deci, 2000), social cognitive theory (Bandura, 1997); job demands-resources theory (Bakker & Demerouti, 2008; Hakanen, Schaufeli, & Ahola, 2008; see also Hakanen & Roodt, Chapter 7, this volume), conservation of resources theory (Gorgievski & Hobfoll, 2008; Hobfoll & Shirom, 2000), and broaden-and-build theory (Fredrickson, 2001). In effect, all of these theories suggest that resources should increase engagement.

In the engagement literature, resources have been very broadly defined. As such, I take both a general and specific approach in examining the relationships between resources and engagement. In addition to exploring the aggregate effect of resources on engagement, I examine specific resources that have been commonly studied in the engagement literature.

Hypothesis 2: Resources will be positively associated with engagement. Specifically, social support, autonomy, feedback, positive organizational climate, and self-efficacy will be positively associated with engagement.

However, in addition to resources, a number of theories have suggested that job demands play a role in engagement, typically by reducing available resources and thus reducing engagement. However, theory and research on the topic of demands typically suggests that demands are of secondary importance in predicting engagement, with resources serving as the more important and direct factor (Bakker, Hakanen, Demerouti, & Xanthopoulou, 2007; Schaufeli & Salanova, 2007a). As such, I predict that demands will be negatively associated with engagement; however, the relationship between demands and engagement will be weaker than the relationship between resources and engagement. In a manner similar to resources, I will examine both aggregate demands and specific (commonly studied) demands.

Hypothesis 3a: Demands will be negatively associated with work engagement. Specifically, work overload, work–family conflict, and family–work conflict will be negatively associated with engagement.

Hypothesis 3b: The relationship between job demands and engagement will be weaker than the relationship between resources and engagement.

Consequences

Within the engagement literature, the study of engagement's consequences is the area that has seen the least attention. Perhaps this is not surprising, as it is often assumed that engagement *is* the outcome. In this sense, the engagement literature might be following a pattern similar to the burnout literature, where much of the earlier work was dedicated to understanding its causes (cf. Halbesleben & Buckley, 2004). That said, there is reason to believe that engagement leads to important outcomes and researchers have begun to explore those relationships.

One mechanism for linking engagement and its consequences is the notion of resource investment from conservation of resources (COR) theory. COR theory argues that individuals strategically invest their resources to gain additional resources (Halbesleben & Bowler, 2007; Siegall & McDonald, 2004). If one considers that engagement is a result of high availability of job resources (see Hypothesis 1), then one might expect that engagement is associated with a number of positive outcomes in the workplace as individuals invest their extra resources in positive endeavors (see Salanova, Schaufeli, Xanthopoulou, & Bakker, Chapter 9, this volume). For example, the high-identification nature of engagement should result in high levels of association with outcomes such as organizational commitment and turnover intentions, constructs that are related to one's identification with one's job.

Moreover, given that engagement is indicative of very high energy at work, one might expect it to be associated with higher levels of performance and health (especially the vigor component of engagement; Shirom, 2003; Shirom, Toker, Berliner, Shapira, & Melamed, 2006, 2008; see also Shirom, Chapter 6, this volume).

Hypothesis 4: Work engagement will be positively associated with positive outcomes at work. Specifically, engagement will be positively associated with organizational commitment, performance, and health. Engagement will be negatively associated with turnover intentions.

Method

Literature search

An extensive literature search was conducted to collect studies that had investigated correlates, predictors, and outcomes of engagement. The first step in the search involved the utilization of databases that abstract sources relevant to engagement (*PsycINFO*, *Business Source Elite*, *JStor*, *MEDLine*, and *Google Scholar*). The following key words were utilized: engagement, vigor (and vigour), dedication, absorption, flow, and self-engagement. The abstracts of those articles that came up as hits were checked for indications that their content would be appropriate for the meta-analysis (e.g., they had conducted an empirical study where engagement was measured in some form).

Because some studies have included engagement (or its components) in their data collection without it serving as the primary focus of the study, I conducted a number of manual searches to supplement the computer search above. First, I reviewed the reference section of a previous meta-analysis relevant to the topic (Christian & Slaughter, 2007). Second, I reviewed a bibliography of engagement hosted online by a leading engagement scholar (available at www.schaufeli.com). Third, I conducted manual searches of journals that might include relevant articles, including the *Journal of Applied Psychology*, *Academy of Management Journal*,

Personnel Psychology, Journal of Organizational Behavior, Journal of Occupational and Organizational Psychology, and *Journal of Occupational Health Psychology, Work & Stress,* and *Anxiety, Stress, & Coping.* Finally, I sent correspondence to prominent researchers of engagement (including authors within the present book) to solicit missed, in press, or unpublished manuscripts and datasets.

Inclusion and exclusion criteria

I utilized a number of criteria to determine which studies would be included in the meta-analysis. First, the study had to provide correlations between engagement and another variable (or information that would allow us to calculate correlations, e.g., regression coefficients). In the cases where this information was not clearly provided, but appeared to have been available, I attempted to contact authors for the necessary information.

In terms of engagement measures, I did not limit the studies to those that had utilized the Utrecht Work Engagement Scale (UWES), as had been done in a previous meta-analysis of engagement correlates (Christian & Slaughter, 2007). While the UWES is the most common operationalization of engagement in the literature, a number of alternative measures have been developed (e.g., the Shirom–Melamed Vigor Measure). In some cases, traditional burnout measures were used (e.g., the Maslach Burnout Inventory), but reversed. These cases were treated as measures of engagement if the authors specifically conceptualized the construct as engagement (e.g., studies about burnout were not included). Alternative measures, whether of engagement or of one of its theoretical components, were included in the analysis in order to broaden the perspective. If these measures truly measure engagement, the inclusion of measures other than the UWES should only strengthen a meta-analysis. Moreover, it helps to circumvent arguments that a construct is equivalent to a single group of questions on one measure. We coded each article for the measure utilized and conducted a moderator analysis to test for differences in population estimates across engagement measures.

Since a common criticism of meta-analysis has been that it may overestimate effect sizes due to the inclusion of published studies that have a bias toward statistically significant results (Rosenthal, 1991), the present analysis included unpublished data obtained directly from researchers. However, to account for the counter argument that such other sources may not have been subject to the rigors of peer-review, I treated publication status as a moderator variable and tested for differences in population estimates among publication sources.

I excluded articles that were not published in the English language for which I was unable to obtain a translation. Despite this exclusion, samples from a very wide variety of countries were represented in the meta-analyzed studies. Moreover, file-drawer analysis (discussed below) suggests a very large number of non-English articles would have to report findings contrary to the rest of the literature (e.g., positive correlations with burnout dimensions) to actually impact the findings of this study.

I also excluded articles that studied populations (e.g., students) that did not necessarily involve work (e.g., Schaufeli, Martínez, Pinto, Salanova, & Bakker, 2002), as the focus of this study was on engagement in work contexts. In cases where the identical sample was studied in multiple published works, I included only one of the group of articles, the most recently published, in order to maintain independence of the data points. I only included studies that examined individual work engagement, excluding those that examined group (collective) engagement (e.g., Salanova, Llorens, Cifre, Martinez, & Schaufeli, 2003).

After removing those publications that did not fit the above inclusion criteria, a total of 53 papers that represented 74 unique samples were obtained. The publications yielded a total sample size of 45,683 participants.

Data analysis

The articles were initially coded by two different coders; a graduate student research assistant and the chapter author. To assist in consistency, the coders were provided with a training manual that discussed the general nature of the project (without providing the hypotheses) and instructions for coding articles. The manual included one example article with associated coding information and one practice article that each coder was asked to complete. Next, a training session was held where the practice article was discussed and discrepancies in coding were discussed and resolved. Finally, the coders independently coded the same set of 15 articles (about 25% of the total number of articles) to determine interrater reliability. In general, the percentage agreement between the coders was very high, ranging from 95% (for reliability estimates of engagement measures) to 100% (for a number of characteristics, including published/not published, sample size, and engagement measure). The coders then independently coded approximately one-half of the remaining articles.

In general, there was a mix of cross-sectional and longitudinal studies represented in the literature (with a promising trend toward a greater number of longitudinal studies). When longitudinal studies were encountered, we considered whether the non-engagement variable was an antecedent (e.g., social support) or an outcome (e.g., performance). This determination was made by examining how the variables had been positioned in the article, whether through hypotheses or, occasionally, via figures displaying the predicted model. For antecedents, we used the correlation between the Time 1 antecedent and Time 2 engagement. For outcomes, we used Time 1 engagement and Time 2 outcome. This allowed us to preserve the longitudinal nature of these studies. When examining the relationship between engagement and burnout factors, we used data from the same time (e.g., both Time 1). We coded studies as cross-sectional or longitudinal for purposes of a moderator analysis.

With regard to the measurement of engagement, we coded the dimensions of work engagement (vigor, absorption, and dedication) separately. However, a number of studies use aggregated measures of engagement (e.g., taking a mean of all of the UWES items rather than analyzing each dimension separately). Those cases were analyzed separately under the category of "overall work engagement". Therefore, in the analyses reported below, samples measuring overall work engagement do not overlap with those that analyzed each dimension separately.

In order to examine differences in engagement as a result of differences in demands and resources, we coded antecedent variables as demands, resources, or other. Other was used in cases where it was not clear if the variable was a demand or resource (e.g., demographics like age and gender). Two coders (the author and a research assistant) coded all of the articles and then compared coding. Often, the article stated whether the variable was to be considered a resource or demand (e.g., in the description of the measures). The percentage agreement among the coders was very high, ranging from 94% for demands to 97% for resources. Discrepancies were addressed through discussion between the two coders and additional examination of the article in question.

With regard to demands, resources, and outcomes, I analyzed these two ways. First, I examined the overall effect of demands and resources, including all studies that examined a demand, resource, or outcome. These effects are reported in the bolded lines in Tables 8.2–8.5. Additionally, I examined specific demands, resources, and outcomes that have been most commonly studied in the literature; these are reported below the overall results. For example, studies reported as a specific demand (e.g., work–family conflict) were also included in the overall analysis of demands. I took this approach in order to assess the overall hypotheses regarding demands, resources, and outcomes while also allowing for a deeper analysis of relationships that have commonly appeared in the literature.

The data were analyzed using procedures described by Arthur, Bennett, and Huffcutt (2001) for the SAS statistical package. Their procedures follow the meta-analytic procedures described by Hunter and Schmidt (2004). As part of the meta-analysis, I made corrections to the data for unreliability of both the predictor and criterion variables when they were reported by the authors of included studies. Two of the coded articles did not report scale reliabilities; in those cases, the correction for unreliability was not employed. While the Hunter and Schmidt method of meta-analysis recommends corrections for range restrictions, information to make such corrections was reported by so few researchers that I did not correct for this artifact.

Results

The meta-analysis of engagement and burnout dimensions appears in Table 8.1. In instances where there were too few studies to conduct a reliable meta-analysis, dashes are entered into the tables. While there has been no clear determination of the number of studies needed for reliable estimates from meta-analysis, Brannick and Hall (2001) argued that when there are very small numbers of studies in a meta-analysis, population estimates become extremely unreliable. As such, I took a somewhat conservative approach of including a variable if there were at least five samples that appeared in at least two different papers. This was meant to eliminate the possibility of drawing conclusions based on a small number of samples or from one article, which could lead to making conclusions about the literature based on a spurious finding.

In Hypothesis 1, I predicted that dimensions of engagement would be negatively associated with dimensions of burnout; specifically predicting that vigor and exhaustion and dedication and cynicism would be most strongly related. As indicated in Table 8.1, I found support for the first part of Hypothesis 1; with one exception (the relationship between cynicism and overall engagement, $\rho = .00$), the estimated population correlations were negative. The prediction that vigor would be most highly associated with exhaustion was partially supported. When one examines the estimated population correlations of exhaustion and the three engagement dimensions, the strongest relationship is with vigor ($\rho = -.37$). However, examination of the estimated population correlations between vigor and the three burnout dimensions reveals that vigor is actually more highly correlated with the other two dimensions of burnout than with exhaustion.

The hypothesis that dedication would be most strongly associated with cynicism was also partially supported. While dedication is most strongly related to cynicism (compared to the other two burnout dimensions), it is only slightly more strongly related to cynicism than reduced personal efficacy. However, the estimated population correlation between cynicism and dedication ($\rho = -.65$) is much higher than the estimated population correlations between cynicism and other engagement dimensions.

The meta-analysis results for antecedents and consequences of overall engagement, vigor, dedication, and absorption are presented in Tables 8.2–8.5, respectively. With Hypothesis 2, I predicted a positive relationship between resources and engagement. Inspection of Tables 8.2–8.5 yields consistent support for this prediction when examining overall resources ($\rho = .35$ for overall engagement, $\rho = .30$ for vigor, $\rho = .34$ for dedication, and $\rho = .25$ for absorption). The pattern holds true when looking at specific resources; autonomy/job control and self-efficacy seem to have particularly high estimated population correlations with engagement.

Hypothesis 3a predicted that demands would be negatively associated with engagement. This prediction was supported, when looking at general demands ($\rho = -.09$ for overall engagement, $\rho = -.07$ for vigor, $\rho = -.24$ for dedication, and $\rho = -.07$ for absorption). Generally speaking, specific demands (work–family conflict, family–work conflict, and work overload) were also negatively associated with engagement, with two exceptions. When examining studies that used a composite score of work engagement, work–family conflict and family–work conflict were highly *positively* associated with engagement. Hypothesis 3b, the prediction that the relationship between job demands and engagement will be lower than the relationship between resources and engagement, appears to be consistently reported. In nearly all cases, the estimated population correlations with resources are stronger than those with demands.

Finally, in Hypothesis 4, I predicted that engagement would be positively associated with positive outcomes at work. While the number of samples available to test this hypothesis was a bit lower, the hypothesis was supported, both in terms of aggregated outcomes and more specific outcomes. Interestingly, while the "identification

TABLE 8.1

Meta-analytic results: Burnout dimensions

	r	SD_r	ρ	SD_ρ	$\%V_{art}$	95% Con Int	95% Cred Int	k	N	χ^2
Criterion: Overall engagement										
Exhaustion	−.38	.06	−.44	.06	40.31	−.39:−.37	−.48:−.26	32	22096	79.38*
Depersonalization/ Disengagement	.00	.55	.00	.64	0.54	−.02:.01	−1.26:1.23	28	1808	4284.71***
Reduced personal efficacy/accomplishment	–	–	–	–	–	–	–	0	–	–
Criterion: Vigor										
Exhaustion	−.29	.15	−.37	.18	6.36	−.31:−.29	−.66:.06	34	23585	535.11
Depersonalization/ Disengagement	−.38	.01	−.47	.16	9.17	−.39:−.37	−.70:−.07	32	19974	349.08
Reduced personal efficacy/accomplishment	−.50	.30	−.62	.37	2.10	−.52:−.49	−1.22:.21	21	12275	999.62
Criterion: Dedication										
Exhaustion	−.20	.19	−.24	.22	3.99	−.21:−.19	−.63:.24	34	23585	851.94
Depersonalization/ Disengagement	−.54	.12	−.65	.13	12.37	−.55:−.53	−.80:−.28	32	19974	258.59
Reduced personal efficacy/accomplishment	−.53	.29	−.63	.34	2.18	−.54:−.52	−1.19:.14	21	12275	963.26
Criterion: Absorption										
Exhaustion	−.13	.12	−.17	.15	9.90	−.15:−.12	−.42:.15	32	23585	343.50
Depersonalization/ Disengagement	−.32	.16	−.41	.20	6.39	−.34:−.32	−.72:.06	32	19974	501.05
Reduced Personal efficacy/accomplishment	−.33	.37	−.41	.46	1.31	−.34:−.31	−1.23:.58	21	12275	1604.81

Note: r = sample-weighted mean correlation, SD_r = standard deviation of sample-weighted correlations, ρ = estimated population correlation (corrected for artifacts), SD_ρ = standard deviation of estimated population correlation, $\%V_{art}$ = percentage of the variance in ρ accounted for by study artifacts, 95% Con Int = 95% confidence interval around ρ, 95% Cred Int = 95% credibility interval around *r*, *k* = number of unique samples, *N* = total sample size. * indicates $p < .05$, ** indicates $p < .01$, *** indicates $p < .001$, $df = k − 1$.

outcomes" of commitment and turnover intention seem to be more strongly correlated with dedication, the "energy outcomes" of performance and health are only slightly more strongly correlated with vigor than with dedication.

Moderator analysis

I inspected two common indicators of moderators (confounds) in the relationships between engagement and its correlates. One test involves inspection of the percentage of variance attribut-

able to artifacts ($\%V_{art}$ in Table 8.1); when that number is below 25%, it is generally assumed that moderators are not acting upon the data (Arthur et al., 2001). A second test of the existence of moderators is the inspection of credibility intervals; a credibility interval that includes zero or is very large suggests that moderators may be impacting the data (Arthur et al., 2001). As one will note in Tables 8.1–8.5, there are a number of instances where the percent variability attributable to artifacts exceeds 25% and/or a

TABLE 8.2

Relationships between demands, resources, and outcomes and overall engagement

	r	SD_r	ρ	SD_ρ	$\%V_{art}$	95% Con Int	95% Cred Int	k	N	χ^2
Demands	**−.07**	**.20**	**−.09**	**.23**	**2.94**	**−.09:−.07**	**−.54:.37**	**111**	**94678**	**3763.29***
Work–family conflict	.36	.20	.43	.32	5.24	.34:.39	−.09:.82	9	4131	171.82**
Family–work conflict	.21	.12	.25	.13	8.46	.18:.24	−.05:.47	6	5517	70.90**
Work overload	.16	.05	.19	.02	83.33	.13:.19	.11:.21	10	3784	11.57*
Resources	**.29**	**.18**	**.35**	**.21**	**4.20**	**.29:.30**	**−.12:.71**	**180**	**136620**	**4284.71***
Social support	.32	.04	.37	.02	73.34	.31:.33	.27:.36	32	35243	43.63*
Autonomy/Control	.23	.26	.27	.31	2.54	.37:.83	.21:.24	26	14985	1025.10***
Feedback	–	–	–	–	–	–	–	–	–	–
Organizational climate	–	–	–	–	–	–	–	–	–	–
Self-efficacy	.50	.16	.59	.18	10.77	.48:.52	.15:.85	17	5163	157.90**
Optimism	.37	.12	.44	.13	18.37	.33:.41	.13:.62	5	1799	27.21*
Outcomes	**.11**	**.30**	**.13**	**.35**	**1.54**	**.11:.12**	**−.58:.81**	**81**	**57738**	**5246.37***
Commitment	.32	.13	.38	.14	10.09	.30:.34	.04:.60	14	8623	138.81**
Performance	.30	.06	.36	.05	40.41	.27:.33	.21:.39	7	4433	13.88*
Health	.17	.19	.20	.23	3.92	.15:.19	−.27:.61	17	11593	433.34***
Turnover intention	−.22	.10	−.26	.11	19.61	−.26:−.18	−.43:.00	4	1893	20.40*

Note: r = sample-weighted mean correlation, SD_r = standard deviation of sample-weighted correlations, ρ = estimated population correlation (corrected for artifacts), SD_ρ = standard deviation of estimated population correlation, $\%V_{art}$ = percentage of the variance in ρ accounted for by study artifacts, 95% Con Int = 95% confidence interval around ρ, 95% Cred Int = 95% credibility interval around r, k = number of unique samples, N = total sample size. * indicates $p < .05$, ** indicates $p < .01$, *** indicates $p < .001$, $df = k − 1$.

very large credibility interval exists. For those variables, I explored a variety of moderators that I believed, *a priori*, could be influencing the data. These included publication status (published journal articles versus non-published/peer reviewed works), study design (cross-sectional versus longitudinal) and engagement measure utilized in the study (Utrecht Work Engagement Survey versus other measures of engagement).

I conducted a subgroup meta-analysis, where the moderating variable is analyzed by breaking it into each level of the categorical moderator variable and differences between the parameter estimates are tested for differences. Cortina (2003) has suggested that this is a useful strategy for analyzing categorical moderator variables. In nearly all cases, the correlations between engagement and correlates were highly similar across the levels of the moderator variables. Given the general pattern of findings from the moderator analysis,

it was determined that these moderator variables were not significant influences on the results of the analysis. In light of the very large number of variables examined in the study and in consideration of space, these findings are not included, but are readily available from the author.

File drawer analysis

Rosenthal (1991) has argued that, due to a bias toward statistically significant results in published literature, studies included in meta-analyses may not be representative of the population of studies available about a topic. To test the possibility of such a bias, I computed the number of samples that would be required to bring the estimated population correlation to a level that would no longer be considered significant (.05). In all cases, significantly more unpublished/unavailable samples with zero correlations would need to exist in order to change the results. This offers increased

TABLE 8.3

Relationships between demands, resources, and outcomes and vigor

	r	SD_r	ρ	SD_ρ	$\%V_{art}$	95% Con Int	95% Cred Int	k	N	χ^2
Demands	−.06	.14	−.07	.17	5.93	−.06:−.05	−.39:.27	111	94678	1873.10
Work–family conflict	−.18	.03	−.22	.00	15.99	−.21:−.15	−.18:−.18	9	4131	4.17
Family–work conflict	−.16	.07	−.19	.08	20.30	−.18:−.13	−.31:.05	6	5517	29.55
Work overload	.03	.00	.04	.00	35.76	.00:.06	.13:.20	10	3784	27.95*
Resources	.24	.15	.30	.18	6.24	.24:.25	−.11:.60	187	137522	2996.08***
Social support	.21	.10	.25	.12	9.93	.20:.22	−.03:.44	34	35447	342.54
Autonomy/Control	.32	.14	.40	.16	9.29	.31:.34	.00:.64	26	14985	279.75
Feedback	.33	.17	.41	.20	4.93	.31:.35	−.06:.72	8	6495	162.38
Organizational climate	.19	.01	.23	.00	10.25	.17:.22	.19:.19	10	6843	.97
Self-efficacy	.41	.10	.50	.10	28.91	.38:.43	.20:.61	17	5163	58.80
Optimism	–	–	–	–	–	–	–	–	–	–
Outcomes	.09	.29	.12	.35	1.76	.09:.10	−.60:.78	90	61834	5109.91***
Commitment	.25	.29	.31	.35	2.09	.23:.27	−.44:.94	15	8725	717.16
Performance	.24	.07	.29	.07	35.65	.21:.26	.10:.37	10	6131	28.05*
Health	.11	.24	.13	.29	2.49	.09:.12	−.45:.67	22	15860	881.51***
Turnover intention	−.20	.06	−.25	.05	45.77	−.23:−.17	−.30:−.10	6	3693	11.95*

Note: r = sample-weighted mean correlation, SD_r = standard deviation of sample-weighted correlations, ρ = estimated population correlation (corrected for artifacts), SD_ρ = standard deviation of estimated population correlation, $\%V_{art}$ = percentage of the variance in ρ accounted for by study artifacts, 95% Con Int = 95% confidence interval around ρ, 95% Cred Int = 95% credibility interval around r, k = number of unique samples, N = total sample size. * indicates $p < .05$, ** indicates $p < .01$, *** indicates $p < .001$, $df = k − 1$.

confidence in the nature and interpretation of the findings presented above. In light of the very large number of variables examined in the study and in consideration of space, these findings are not included, but are readily available from the author.

Discussion

To summarize, I found, with a few exceptions, that work engagement constructs were negatively associated with burnout as predicted by the literature. Also as predicted, resources were positively related and demands were negatively related to engagement, but resources were much more strongly related. Finally, engagement was positively associated with positive outcomes at work, including a stronger relationship between dedication – an identification-based component of engagement – and commitment and turnover intention.

The findings of the present study were consistent with a previous meta-analysis of engagement (Christian & Slaughter, 2007) in that resources and demands were both related to engagement, but resources held a much stronger relationship. Moreover, the pattern of relationships between engagement and burnout dimensions were quite consistent. However, it is worthwhile to note the key differences in the present analysis and Christian and Slaughter's work. First, this study includes a much wider base of studies and much large number of observations, and as a result, is likely to provide more reliable findings. For example, I did not limit the study to only those that had used the UWES in order to separate the construct from its measure. A number of studies measured vigor, dedication, and absorption independently and using measures other than the UWES, since they purport to measure constructs that are, at least somewhat, similar to the work engagement construct, I felt that their inclusion would be justified. As the moderator

TABLE 8.4

Relationships between demands, resources, and outcomes and dedication

	r	SD_r	ρ	SD_ρ	$\%V_{art}$	95% Con Int	95% Cred Int	k	N	χ^2
Demands	**−.02**	**.16**	**−.24**	**.22**	**3.99**	**−.21:−.19**	**−.63:.29**	**111**	**94678**	**851.94**
Work–family conflict	–	–	–	–	–	–	–	–	–	–
Family–work conflict	–	–	–	–	–	–	–	–	–	–
Work overload	.04	.10	.05	.10	28.79	.01:.07	−.14:.23	10	3784	34.73
Resources	**.28**	**.15**	**.34**	**.18**	**6.07**	**.28:.29**	**−.06:.64**	**187**	**137522**	**3081.33**
Social support	.23	.10	.27	.11	10.69	.22:.24	.01:.44	34	35447	318.08
Autonomy/Control	.38	.19	.45	.22	4.83	.39:.39	−.05:.81	26	14985	537.50
Feedback	.38	.13	.46	.22	3.97	.36:.40	−.04:.81	8	6495	201.46
Organizational climate	.25	.04	.30	.01	82.76	.23:.27	.23:.27	10	6843	10.47
Self-efficacy	.39	.09	.47	.08	31.97	.37:.41	.23:.55	17	5163	44.08
Optimism	–	–	–	–	–	–	–	–	–	–
Outcomes	**.17**	**.28**	**.20**	**.33**	**1.91**	**.16:.17**	**−.47:.81**	**90**	**61834**	**4713.67**
Commitment	.44	.09	.52	.10	19.81	.42:.45	.24:.63	15	8725	75.71
Performance	.23	.13	.27	.15	9.36	.21:.26	−.06:.53	10	6131	106.88
Health	.12	.18	.14	.21	4.25	.10:.13	−.29:.53	22	15860	517.26
Turnover intention	−.37	.02	−.45	.0	4.90	−.40:−.35	−.38:−.38	6	3693	1.22

Note: r = sample-weighted mean correlation, *SD_r* = standard deviation of sample-weighted correlations, ρ = estimated population correlation (corrected for artifacts), *SD_ρ* = standard deviation of estimated population correlation, $\%V_{art}$ = percentage of the variance in ρ accounted for by study artifacts, 95% Con Int = 95% confidence interval around ρ, 95% Cred Int = 95% credibility interval around *r*, *k* = number of unique samples, *N* = total sample size. * indicates $p < .05$, ** indicates $p < .01$, *** indicates $p < .001$, $df = k − 1$.

analysis demonstrated, this decision was justified in that there were no significant differences as a result of which measure was used. Second, this study included more in press and unpublished work that had been considered previously. This allows for more current results (the in press work) as well as some protection against publication bias.

One unexpected finding was the relationship between work–family conflict, family–work conflict, and engagement in studies that used an overall indicator of engagement. While these are typically seen as demands and thus one would predict they would be negatively associated with engagement (and were in studies where individual dimensions were reported), they held a positive correlation in studies that used an overall indicator of engagement. Of course, it is possible that this is a spurious result that is isolated to

the small number of samples included in the analysis. However, it may also suggest careful consideration of the strategy of aggregating work engagement dimensions into an overall measure of work engagement.

Another potential explanation, suggested by Halbesleben, Harvey, and Bolino (2009), is that too much engagement can actually exacerbate work–family and family–work conflicts, beyond the effects of workaholism. Their work concludes that if an employee is too engrossed in work, whether physically or psychologically, he or she may experience higher conflict between work and family roles. Certainly, more work is needed to examine this issue, especially in light of studies breaking out the engagement dimensions that are not supporting this thinking. See also Chapter 4 (Taris, Schaufeli, & Shimazu) on the differences between work engagement and workaholism.

TABLE 8.5

Relationships between demands, resources, and outcomes and absorption

	r	SD_r	ρ	SD_ρ	%V_{art}	95% Con Int	95% Cred Int	k	N	χ^2
Demands	−.06	.17	−.07	.21	4.16	−.06:−.05	−.35:.46	111	94678	2667.36
Work–family conflict	–	–	–	–	–	–	–	–	–	–
Family–work conflict	–	–	–	–	–	–	–	–	–	–
Work overload	–	–	–	–	–	–	–	–	–	–
Resources	.20	.11	.25	.13	11.62	.19:.21	−.05:.46	187	137522	1609.44
Social support	.20	.09	.25	.10	13.55	.19:.21	−.01:.40	34	35447	250.85
Autonomy/Control	.29	.11	.37	.13	14.89	.27:.30	.04:.54	26	14985	174.63
Feedback	–	–	–	–	–	–	–	–	–	–
Organizational climate	–	–	–	–	–	–	–	–	–	–
Self-efficacy	.24	.06	.31	.03	81.26	.22:.27	.17:.31	17	5163	20.92
Optimism	–	–	–	–	–	–	–	–	–	–
Outcomes	.07	.20	.08	.24	3.75	.06:.07	−.41:.55	90	61834	2399.43
Commitment	.35	.08	.44	.09	26.47	.33:.37	.17:.52	15	8725	56.66
Performance	–	–	–	–	–	–	–	–	–	–
Health	.04	.15	.05	.18	6.26	.02:.05	−.32:.34	22	15860	351.20
Turnover intention	−.24	.05	−.30	.04	51.85	−.27:−.21	−.32:−.15	6	3693	9.95

Note: r = sample-weighted mean correlation, SD_r = standard deviation of sample-weighted correlations, ρ = estimated population correlation (corrected for artifacts), SD_ρ = standard deviation of estimated population correlation, %V_{art} = percentage of the variance in ρ accounted for by study artifacts, 95% Con Int = 95% confidence interval around ρ, 95% Cred Int = 95% credibility interval around r, k = number of unique samples, N = total sample size. * indicates $p < .05$, ** indicates $p < .01$, *** indicates $p < .001$, $df = k − 1$.

Practical implications

In addition to suggesting directions for future research, the present study holds potentially valuable implications for practice. Organizations have become increasingly interested in how to develop engagement in employees. This interest is reinforced in the present analysis, with significant associations with critical outcomes such as commitment, performance, health, and turnover intention. While employee engagement may be in-and-of-itself a worthwhile objective, certainly clear association with important outcomes should spark a need to address this issue in the workforce.

This present study reinforces the long-held notion that development of employee resources is the best mechanism for organizations to consider as they focus on engagement-development interventions. One resource with particularly strong associations with engagement was self-efficacy.

One can argue that employees must feel self-efficacious before they will invest the resources in work associated with high engagement. In his review of self-efficacy in the context of employee development, Maurer (2001) suggested a number of mechanisms for developing self-efficacy. While his suggestions were primarily targeted at developing self-efficacy among older employees, they apply in a more general sense to all workers. They included such steps as making sure employees have challenging tasks; recognizing and making visible stories about successful employees; providing support and encouragement to employees; and reducing emphasis on competition (see p. 136 of Maurer, 2001 for additional details).

However, the present analysis also suggests that more general work and environment resources play an important role in engagement. Developing social support, changing work systems to enhance control or autonomy, and making positive changes to organizational climate require a system-wide effort. In the burnout literature, action research approaches have been advocated to reduce burnout (e.g., Halbesleben, Osburn, & Mumford, 2006; Le Blanc, Hox, Schaufeli, Taris, & Peeters, 2007; LeBlanc & Schaufeli, 2008). Given the strong relationships between burnout and engagement, both empirically and theoretically, one might consider action research approaches to develop engagement as well. In fact, action research might have a doubly positive impact on engagement by both addressing precursors to engagement (e.g., Halbesleben et al.'s, 2006, attempts to develop social support) but also actively involving employees in efforts to improve the organization. Such active involvement in the organization may itself stimulate engagement in work as it emphasizes a personal connection between the employee and his or her work.

Limitations

I recognize that this study has a number of limitations. First, as with any meta-analysis of correlations, I certainly cannot infer causality between engagement and the variables studied. Moreover, simple correlations may miss some of the important intervening variables to help explain the underlying dynamics regarding engagement and its antecedents or consequences. The goal of the present work was to summarize important variables that are associated with engagement in order to assess the state of the field and offer observations about future research opportunities. Future research is needed to expand on the present study through creative research designs that might allow causal conclusions.

Related to this limitation is the treatment of cross-lagged panel designs in the present study. Such designs posed an interesting challenge, as they were testing a spiral relationship (e.g., self-efficacy leads to higher engagement, which leads to even higher self-efficacy), making it unclear which variable is cause and which is effect (see also Salanova et al., Chapter 9, this volume). These articles were coded as studying antecedents to engagement, with the correlation between the Time 1 variable (e.g., self-efficacy) and Time 2

engagement entered. As these designs evolve and become more popular, a trend that already seems to have started based on the "in press" articles, it may be worthwhile to revisit the effects that these specific designs are revealing using a more powerful analysis strategy than was employed here.

Future research

One goal of this paper was to stimulate thinking about where the field stands in order to generate ideas for future research. Clearly, the relationships between engagement and the work–family interface, as briefly discussed above, stands out as an opportunity for additional exploration. Given the correlations between engagement and burnout dimensions, the notion of energy and identification poles may need to be further evaluated.

This study may also have a more direct impact on future research. Many researchers have begun taking the approach of testing theory by using meta-analytic correlations as their inputs to structural equation modeling (e.g., Bhaskar-Shrinivas, Harrison, Shaffer, & Luk, 2005), based in part on suggestions by leading methodologists (Hunter & Schmidt, 2004; Viswesvaran, & Ones, 1995). I encourage authors to consider the present study as a springboard to such research endeavors, of course, after carefully considering the limitations posed above and the specific approach I have taken in selecting and coding articles.

Another need to be considered concerns engagement interventions. While it is natural to explore the underlying causes and consequences of a construct first, very few of the studies included in the present analysis were evaluations of interventions designed to increase engagement. Given the finding that engagement is heavily related to resources, resource-based interventions, especially those focusing on social support, autonomy, and self-efficacy, may be worthwhile starting points for intervention studies.

References
(Articles that were analyzed as part of the meta-analysis are indicated by an asterisk.)

Arthur, W., Bennett, W., & Huffcutt, A. I. (2001).

Conducting meta-analysis using SAS. Mahwah, NJ: Lawrence Erlbaum.

Bakker, A. B., & Demerouti, E. (2008). Towards a model of work engagement. *Career Development International, 13*, 209–223.

*Bakker, A. B., Demerouti, E., & Schaufeli, W. B. (2005). The crossover of burnout and work engagement among working couples. *Human Relations, 58*, 661–689.

*Bakker, A. B., Hakanen, J. J. Demerouti, E., & Xanthopoulou, D. (2007). Job resources boost work engagement, particularly when job demands are high. *Journal of Educational Psychology, 99*, 274–284.

*Bakker, A. B., Van Emmerik, H., & Euwema, M. C. (2006). Crossover of burnout and engagement in work teams. *Work and Occupations, 33*, 464–489.

Bandura, A. (1997). *Self-efficacy: The exercise of control*. New York: Freeman.

Bhaskar-Shrinivas, P., Harrison, D. A., Shaffer, M. A., & Luk, D. M. (2005). Input-based and time-based models of international adjustment: Meta-analytic evidence and theoretical extensions. *Academy of Management Journal, 48*, 257–281.

Brannick, M. T., & Hall, S. M. (2001, April). *Reducing bias in the Schmidt-Hunter meta-analysis*. Poster presented at the 16th annual conference of the Society for Industrial and Organizational Psychology, San Diego, CA.

*Bresó, E., Schaufeli, W. B., & Salanova, M. (2008). *Can a self-efficacy-based intervention decrease burnout, increase engagement, and enhance performance? A quasi-experimental study*. Working paper, Universitat Jaume I, Spain.

*Britt, T. W. (2003). Aspects of identity predict engagement in work under adverse conditions. *Self and Identity, 2*, 31–45.

*Britt, T. W., Adler, A. B., & Bartone, P. T. (2001). Deriving benefits from stressful events: The role of engagement in meaningful work and hardiness. *Journal of Occupational Health Psychology, 6*, 53–63.

*Britt, T. W., & Bliese, P. D. (2003). Testing the stress-buffering effects of self engagement among soldiers on a military operation. *Journal of Personality, 71*, 246–265.

*Britt, T. W., Castro, C. A., & Adler, A. B. (2005). Self-engagement, stressors, and health: A longitudinal study. *Personality and Social Psychology Bulletin, 31*, 1475–1486.

*Cho, J., Spence Laschinger, H. K., & Wong, C. (2006). Workplace empowerment, work engagement, and organizational commitment of new graduate nurses. *Nursing Leadership, 19*, 43–60.

Christian, M. S., & Slaughter, J. E. (2007, August). *Work engagement: A meta-analytic review and directions for research in an emerging area*. Paper presented at the 66th annual meeting of the Academy of Management, Philadelphia, PA.

Cortina, J. M. (2003). Apples and oranges (and pears, oh my!): The search for moderators in meta-analysis. *Organizational Research Methods, 6*, 415–439.

*Demerouti, E., Bakker, A. B., de Jonge, J., Janssen, P. P. M., & Schaufeli, W. B. (2001). Burnout and engagement at work as a function of demands and control. *Scandinavian Journal of Work, Environment and Health, 27*, 279–286.

*Durán, A., Extremera, N., & Rey, L. (2004). Engagement and burnout: Analyzing their association patterns. *Psychological Reports, 94*, 1048–1050.

Fredrickson, B. L. (2001). The role of positive emotions in positive psychology: The broaden-and-build theory of positive emotions. *American Psychologist, 56*, 218–226.

González-Romá, V., Schaufeli, W. B., Bakker, A. B, & Lloret, S. (2006). Burnout and engagement: Independent factors or opposite poles? *Journal of Vocational Behavior, 68*, 165–174.

Gorgievski, M. J., & Hobfoll, S. E. (2008). Work can burn us out or fire us up: Conservation of resources in burnout and engagement. In J. R. B. Halbesleben (Ed.), *Handbook of stress and burnout in health care* (pp. 7–22). Hauppauge, NY: Nova Science Publishers.

Hackman, J. R., & Oldham, G. R. (1980). *Work redesign*. Reading, MA: Addison-Wesley.

*Hakanen, J. J, Bakker, A. B, & Demerouti, E. (2005). How dentists cope with their job demands and stay engaged the moderating role of job resources. *European Journal of Oral Science, 113*, 479–487.

*Hakanen, J. J, Bakker, A. B., & Schaufeli, W. B. (2005). Burnout and work engagement among teachers. *Journal of School Psychology, 43*, 495–513.

*Hakanen, J. J, Peeters, M., & Perhonimei, R. (2008). *Positive spillover processes between work and family – A three-year cross-lagged panel study*. Working paper, Finnish Institute of Occupational Health, Centre of Expertise for Work Organizations, Finland.

*Hakanen, J. J., Perhoniemi, R., & Toppinen-Tanner, S. (2008). Positive gain spirals at work: From job resources to work engagement, personal initiative, and work-unit innovativeness. *Journal of Vocational Behavior, 73*, 78–91.

*Hakanen, J. J., Schaufeli, W. B., & Ahola, K. (2008). The Job Demands–Resources model: A three-year cross-lagged study of burnout, depression, commitment, and work engagement. *Work & Stress, 22,* 224–241.

Halbesleben, J. R. B., & Bowler, W. M. (2007). Emotional exhaustion and job performance: The mediating role of motivation. *Journal of Applied Psychology, 91,* 93–106.

Halbesleben, J. R. B., & Buckley, M. R. (2004). Burnout in organizational life. *Journal of Management, 30,* 859–879.

*Halbesleben, J. R. B., Harvey, J., & Bolino, M. C. (2009). Too engaged? A conservation of resources view of the relationship between work engagement and work interference with family. *Journal of Applied Psychology, 94,* 1452–1465.

Halbesleben, J. R. B., Osburn, H. K., & Mumford, M. D. (2006). Action research as a burnout Intervention: Reducing burnout in the Federal Fire Service. *Journal of Applied Behavioral Science, 42,* 244–266.

*Halbesleben, J. R. B., & Wheeler, A. R. (2008). The relative role of engagement and embeddedness in predicting job performance and turnover intention. *Work & Sress, 22,* 242–256.

*Hallberg, U. E., Johansson, G., & Schaufeli, W. B. (2007). Type A behavior and work situation: Associations with burnout and work engagement. *Scandinavian Journal of Work, Environment and Health, 48,* 135–142.

*Hallberg, U. E., & Schaufeli, W. B. (2006). "Same same" but different? Can work engagement be discriminated from job involvement and organizational commitment? *European Psychologist, 11,* 119–127.

*Heuven, E., Bakker, A. B., Schaufeli, W. B., & Huisman, N. (2006). The role of self-efficacy in performing emotion work. *Journal of Vocational Behavior, 69,* 222–235.

Hobfoll, S. E., & Shirom, A. (2000). Conservation of resources: Applications to stress and management in the workplace. In R. T. Golembiewski (Ed.), *Handbook of organizational behavior* (2nd ed., pp. 57–81). New York: Dekker.

Hunter, J. E., & Schmidt, F. L. (2004). *Methods of meta-analysis* (2nd ed.). Thousand Oaks, CA: Sage.

*Korunka, C., Kubicek, B., Schaufeli, W. B., & Hoonakker, P. (2009). Work engagement and burnout: Testing the robustness of the Job Demands-Resources model. *Journal of Positive Psychology, 4,* 243–255.

*Langelaan, S., Bakker, A. B., Schaufeli, W. B., van Rhenen, W., & van Doornen, L. J. (2006). Do burned-out and work-engaged employees differ in the functioning of the hypothalamic-pituitary-adrenal axis? *Scandinavian Journal of Work, Environment and Health, 32,* 339–348.

*Langelaan, S., Bakker, A. B., Van Doornen, L. J. P., & Schaufeli, W. B. (2005). Burnout and work engagement: Do individual differences make a difference? *Personality and Individual Differences, 40,* 521–532.

LeBlanc, P. M., Hox, J. J., Schaufeli, W. B., Taris, T. W., & Peeters, M. C. W. (2007). Take care! The evaluation of a team-based burnout intervention program for oncology care providers. *Journal of Applied Psychology, 92,* 213–227.

LeBlanc, P. M., & Schaufeli, W. B. (2008). Burnout interventions: An overview and illustration. In J. R. B. Halbesleben (Ed.), *Handbook of stress and burnout in health care* (pp. 201–215). Hauppauge, NY: Nova Science Publishers.

Lee, R. T., & Ashforth, B. E. (1996). A meta-analytic examination of the correlates of the three dimensions of job burnout. *Journal of Applied Psychology, 81,* 123–133.

*Little, L. M., Simmons, B. L., & Nelson, D. L. (2007). Health among leaders: Positive and negative affect, engagement and burnout, forgiveness and revenge. *Journal of Managerial Studies, 44,* 243–260.

*Llorens, S., Bakker, A. B., Schaufeli, W. B., & Salanova, M. (2006). Testing the robustness of the Job Demands–Resources model. *International Journal of Stress Management, 13,* 378–391.

*Llorens, S., Schaufeli, W. B., Bakker, A. B., & Salanova, M. (2007). Does a positive gain spiral of resources, efficacy beliefs and engagement exist? *Computers in Human Behavior, 23,* 825–841.

Maslach, C., Schaufeli, W. B., & Leiter, M. P. (2001). Job burnout. *Annual Review of Psychology, 52,* 397–422.

*Mauno, S., Kinnunen, U., & Ruokolainen, M. (2007). Job demands and resources as antecedents of work engagement: A longitudinal study. *Journal of Vocational Behavior, 70,* 149–171.

Maurer, T. J. (2001). Career-relevant learning and development, worker age, and beliefs about self-efficacy for development. *Journal of Management, 27,* 123–140.

*May, D. R., Gilson, R. L., & Harter, L. M. (2004). The psychological conditions of meaningfulness, safety and availability and the engagement of the human spirit at work. *Journal of Occupational and Organizational Psychology, 77,* 11–37.

*Montgomery, A. J., Peeters, M. C. W., Schaufeli, W. B., & Den Ouden, M. (2003). Work-home interference among newspaper managers: Its relationship with burnout and engagement, *Anxiety, Stress and Coping, 16,* 195–211.

*Richardsen, A. M., Burke, R. J., & Martinussen, M. (2006). Work and health outcomes among police officers: The mediating role of police cynicism and engagement. *International Journal of Stress Management*, *13*, 555–574.

*Rodríguez-Sánchez, A. M., Schaufeli, W. B., Salanova, M., & Cifre, E. (2008). Flow experience among information and communication technology users. *Psychological Reports*, *102*, 29–39.

Rosenthal, R. (1991). *Meta-analytic procedures for social research*. Newbury Park, CA: Sage.

*Rothbard, N. P. (2001). Enriching or depleting? The dynamics of engagement in work and family roles. *Administrative Science Quarterly*, *46*, 655–684.

Ryan, R. M., & Deci, E. L. (2000). Self-determination theory and the facilitation of intrinsic motivation, social development, and well-being. *American Psychologist*, *55*, 68–78.

*Salanova, M., Agut, S., & Peiro, J. (2005). Linking organizational resources and work engagement to employee performance and customer loyalty: The mediation of service climate. *Journal of Applied Psychology*, *90*, 1217–1227.

*Salanova, M., Bakker, A. B., & Llorens, S. (2006). Flow at work: Evidence for an upward spiral of personal and organizational resources. *Journal of Happiness Studies*, *7*, 1–22.

*Salanova, M., Llorens, S., & Schaufeli, W. B. (2007, July). *Upward spirals of efficacy beliefs: A longitudinal and multi-sample study*. (working paper #SEJ2004-02755/PSIC).

Salanova, M., Llorens, S., Cifre, E., Martínez, I. M. & Schaufeli, W. B. (2003). Perceived collective efficacy, subjective well-being and task performance among electronic work groups: An experimental study. *Small Group Research*, *34*, 43–73.

*Salanova, M., & Schaufeli, W. B. (2008). A cross-national study of work engagement as a mediator between job resources and proactive behavior. *International Journal of Human Resource Management*, *19*, 116–131.

Schaufeli, W. B., & Bakker, A. B. (2001). Werk en welbevinden: Naar een positieve neandering in de Arbeits- en Gezondheidspsychologie [Work and well-being: Towards a positive approach in occupational health psychology]. *Gedrag & Organisatie*, *14*, 229–253.

*Schaufeli, W. B., & Bakker, A. B. (2004). Job demands, job resources, and their relationship with burnout and engagement: A multi-sample study. *Journal of Organizational Behavior*, *25*, 293–315.

Schaufeli, W. B., Martínez, I. M., Pinto, A. M.,

Salanova, M., & Bakker, A. B. (2002). Burnout and engagement in university students: A cross-national study work addiction to working time and work addiction. *Journal of Cross-Cultural Psychology*, *33*, 464–481.

Schaufeli, W. B., & Salanova, M. (2007a). Work engagement: An emerging psychological concept and its implications for organizations. In S. W. Gilliland, D. D. Steiner, & D. P. Skarlicki (Eds.), *Managing social and ethical issues in organizations* (pp. 135–177). Charlotte, NC: Information Age Publishing.

*Schaufeli, W. B., & Salanova, M. (2007b). Efficacy or inefficacy, that's the question: Burnout and work engagement, and their relationships with efficacy beliefs. *Anxiety, Stress, and Coping*, *20*, 177–196.

*Schaufeli, W. B., Salanova, M., González-Romá, V., & Bakker, A. B. (2002). The measurement of engagement and burnout: A two-sample confirmatory factor analytic approach. *Journal of Happiness Studies*, *3*, 71–92.

*Schaufeli, W. B., Taris T. W., & Van Rhenen W. (2008). Workaholism, burnout, and work engagement: Three of a kind or three different kinds of employee well-being? *Applied Psychology: An International Review*, *57*, 173–203.

*Shimazu, A., Schaufeli, W. B., Kosugi, S, Suzuki, A., Nashiwa, H., Kato, A., et al. (2008). Work engagement in Japan: Validation of the Japanese version of Utrecht Work Engagement Scale. *Applied Psychology: An International Review*, *57*, 510–523.

Shirom, A. (2003). Feeling vigorous at work? The construct of vigor and the study of positive affect in organizations. In D. Ganster & P. L. Perrewe (Eds.), *Research in organizational stress and well-being* (Vol. 3, pp. 135–165). Greenwich, CN: JAI Press.

*Shirom, A., Toker, S., Berliner, S., Shapira, I., & Melamed, S. (2006). Work-related vigor and job satisfaction relationships with inflammation biomarkers among employed adults. In A. Delle Fave (Ed.), *Dimensions of well-being: Research and intervention* (pp. 254–274). Milano, Italy: Franco Angeli.

*Shirom, A., Toker, S., Berliner, S., Shapira, I., & Melamed, S. (2008). The effects of physcial fitness and feeling vigorous on self-rated health. *Health Psychology*, *27*, 567–575.

Siegall, M., & McDonald, T. (2004). Person-organization congruence, burnout, and diversion of resources. *Personnel Review*, *33*, 291–301.

*Sonnentag, S. L. (2003). Recovery, work engagement, and proactive behavior: A new look at the interface between nonwork and work. *Journal of Applied Psychology*, *88*, 518–528.

*Sonnentag, S., Mojza, E. J. Binnewies, C., & Scholl, A. (2007). *Being engaged at work and detached at home: A week-level study on work engagement, psychological detachment and affect.* Working paper, University of Konstanz.

*Spence Laschinger, H. K., & Finegan, J. (2005). Empowering nurses for work engagement and health in hospital settings. *Journal of Nursing Administration, 35,* 439–449.

*Spence Laschinger, H. K., & Leiter, M. P. (2006). The impact of nursing work environments on patient safety outcomes: The mediating role of burnout engagement. *Journal of Nursing Administration, 36,* 259–267.

*Spence Laschinger, H. K., Wong, C. A., & Greco, P. (2006). The impact of staff nurse empowerment on person-job fit and work engagement/burnout. *Nursing Administration Quarterly, 30,* 358–367.

*Te Brake, H., Bourman, A-M., Corter R., Hoogstraten, J. J., & Eijkman, M. (2007). Professional burnout and work engagement among dentists. *European Journal of Oral Science, 115,* 180–185.

Viswesvaran, C., & Ones, D. S. (1995). Theory testing: Combining psychometric meta-analysis and structural equations modeling. *Personnel Psychology, 48,* 865–885.

*Xanthopoulou, D., Bakker, A. B., Demerouti, E., & Schaufeli, W. B. (2007). The role of personal resources in the job. *International Journal of Stress Management, 14,* 121–141.

*Xanthopoulou, D., Bakker, A. B., Demerouti, E., & Schaufeli, W. B. (2009). Reciprocal relationships between job resources, personal resources, and work engagement. *Journal of Vocational Behavior, 74,* 235–244.

*Xanthopoulou, D., Bakker, A. B., Heuven, E., Demerouti, E., & Schaufeli, W. B. (2008). Working in the sky: A diary study on work engagement among flight attendants. *Journal of Occupational Health Psychology, 13,* 345–356.

*Xanthopoulou, D., Bakker, A. B., Demerouti, E., & Schaufeli, W. B. (2009). Work engagement and financial returns: A diary study on the role of job and personal resources. *Journal of Occupational and Organizational Psychology, 82,* 183–200.

9

The gain spiral of resources and work engagement: Sustaining a positive worklife

Marisa Salanova, Wilmar B. Schaufeli, Despoina Xanthopoulou, and Arnold B. Bakker

People try to acquire resources at work which they value such as autonomy, social relationships, and feedback about their performance. These job resources are functional in achieving work goals and may stimulate personal growth, learning, and development. As such, job resources initiate a motivational process that may lead to work engagement and positive organizational outcomes, including enhanced performance (Bakker & Demerouti, 2008; Schaufeli & Bakker, 2004). This premise is consistent with traditional motivational approaches such as job characteristics theory (Hackman & Oldham, 1980) and self-determination theory (Ryan & Deci, 2000). According to the former approach, particular job characteristics such as skill variety, autonomy, and feedback have motivating potential and indirectly predict positive outcomes like intrinsic motivation (a concept closely related to work engagement), through the activation of positive psychological states. In a somewhat similar vein, self-determination theory posits that job resources are motivating because they fulfill basic human needs, such as the needs for autonomy, competence, and relatedness. Consequently, work contexts that provide resources such as job control (autonomy), feedback (competence), and social support (relatedness) would enhance well-being and increase intrinsic satisfaction at work (Ryan & Frederick, 1997).

Although these approaches are of great significance for understanding the psychological processes underlying work engagement, they are rather restrictive, because they are one-directional and do not take reciprocal causation into account. Reciprocal causation is plausible because we are dealing with dynamic processes that unfold over time. Therefore, it is important to understand sequences of psychosocial experiences and behaviors that explain work engagement, rather than isolated episodes. In other words, it would be an important step forward to identify the underlying dynamic motivational process that links various types of resources with engagement, and to comprehend how resources and engagement develop over time. This notion alludes to the concept of gain spirals.

Gain spirals are defined as amplifying loops in which cyclic relationships among constructs build on each other positively over time (Lindsley, Brass, & Thomas, 1995). In the present chapter, we will exclusively focus on gain spirals related to resources and engagement. For a gain spiral to exist, two conditions should be met: (1) normal *and* reversed causation (this is also called a reciprocal relationship); i.e., $A \rightarrow B$ *and* $B \rightarrow A$; and (2) an increase in levels over time; i.e., $A_{T2} > A_{T1}$ and $B_{T2} > B_{T1}$. Put differently, empirical evidence on reciprocal relationships and on changes over time are essential for the support of gain spirals. Two important notes have to be made here. First, statistically speaking, both conditions are independent. As we will see below, most empirical studies on gain spirals that involve work engagement comply with the first but rarely with the second condition. Consequently, this means that, strictly speaking, instead of gain "spirals" mainly "cycles" of positive, mutual reinforcement are demonstrated. Secondly, "real" causation can only be established when experimental designs are used with random assignment of subjects to conditions. Clearly, this is virtually never the case when engagement is studied in the natural work context. Nevertheless, theory-grounded longitudinal field studies that assess variables over time in proper sequence and intervals enhance confidence in (reciprocal) causal relationships (Mathieu & Taylor, 2006).

In this chapter we will discuss three psychological theories that are relevant for understanding potential gain spirals of resources and work engagement. Each approach has its own focus:

1. *Conservation of resources theory* (Hobfoll, 1989) may clarify the dynamic relationship between various types of resources (i.e., physical, social, and personal resources) and engagement.
2. *Social cognitive theory* (Bandura, 1986) may clarify the role of a specific personal resource (i.e., self-efficacy) in the dynamic relationship between engagement and performance.
3. *Broaden-and-build theory* (Fredrickson, 2001) may clarify the role of engagement in relation to the widening of the person's thought/action repertoire and the building of various types of resources.

The reason why we have chosen these specific theories is their motivational nature; all three theories try to understand what moves people by hypothesizing and examining complex reciprocal and upward spiraling relationships. However, these theories are rather general in nature and have only seldom been applied to occupational health psychology, let alone work engagement.

Conservation of resources theory and spirals of job and personal resources

About two decades ago, conservation of resources (COR) theory was offered as an alternative approach to stress and adaptation (Hobfoll, 1989). Meanwhile, COR theory has been adopted and received support in such various contexts as job burnout and encounters with traumatic events such as war and natural disasters. In this section, we will only briefly review COR theory and discuss its relevance for work engagement. For a detailed general discussion of the theory and its empirical support the reader is referred to Hobfoll (1989, 1998, 2001, 2002) and for the application to the workplace to Hobfoll and Shirom (2000) and Westman, Hobfoll, Chen, Davidson, and Laski (2005).

In essence, COR theory proposes a model of human motivation because the acquisition and accumulation of resources is considered to be a pivotal drive that initiates and maintains people's behavior. The basic tenet of COR theory is that people are seen as motivated to obtain, retain, foster and protect those things that they value. These things are called "resources" and are defined as "those entities that either are centrally valued in their own right, or act as means to obtain centrally valued ends" (Hobfoll, 2002, p. 307). COR theory distinguishes four types of resources that people have to acquire and maintain in order to adapt successfully to their environment:

- *Objects* (e.g., a home, food, tools).
- *Conditions* (e.g., tenure, social support, job control).
- *Personal characteristics* (e.g., professional skills, efficacy beliefs).
- *Energies* (e.g., time, money, knowledge).

Stress occurs when resources are threatened or lost, or when individuals invest resources and do not reap the anticipated level of benefits. Examples from the workplace are job insecurity and role ambiguity (resources are threatened), being fired at work and retirement (resources are lost), and the imbalance of efforts and rewards (the invested resources do not yield the expected benefits).

COR theory has two important assumptions. First, people have to invest their resources in order to deal with stressful conditions and prevent themselves from negative outcomes. For instance, employees may use social support from their colleagues in the form of hands-on assistance in order to deal with temporary work overload. Consequently, COR theory predicts that those with greater resources (e.g., more supportive colleagues) are less vulnerable to stress, whereas those with fewer resources (e.g., less supportive colleagues) are more vulnerable to stress.

Secondly, people must invest resources in order to protect against future resource loss, recover their resources, and gain new resources. For instance, Hobfoll, Johnson, Ennis, and Jackson (2003) showed that resource gain (mastery and social support) over a period of nine months predicted decreased emotional distress among inner city women. Moreover, individuals strive not only to protect their current resources, but also to *accumulate* them. For instance, employees learn new skills and competencies in order to increase their employability and reduce the risk of being laid off. COR theory predicts that those who possess more resources are also more capable of resource gain. In other words, initial resource gain begets future gain, thus constituting so-called "gain spirals". For example, increased employability not only reduces the risk of unemployment but also augments the possibility of landing a better job that offers additional opportunities for learning and development, which enhance engagement at work. Hence, gaining resources increases the resource pool, which makes it more likely that additional resources will be subsequently acquired.

According to COR theory, this accumulation and linking of resources creates "resource caravans". That is, resources tend not to exist in isolation, but rather they aggregate such that, for instance, employees working in a resourceful work environment (i.e., have task discretion, or receive high-quality coaching) are likely to reinforce their beliefs in their capabilities and resilience, to feel valued, and be optimistic about meeting their goals. COR theory predicts that in the long run such resource caravans result in positive personal outcomes like better coping, adaptation, and well-being.

In contrast to gain spirals, COR theory also assumes "loss spirals" implying that people who lack resources are susceptible to losing even more resources. A classic case is burnout, whereby the employees' personal and job resources are being progressively eroded leading to increased energy depletion and further diminishment of resources.

Gain spirals and work engagement

Is there empirical evidence that resources positively affect work engagement that, in its turn, positively affects resources? Or, is there evidence for the existence of "resources caravans" or gain processes? To date, six independent longitudinal and diary studies have been carried out that are suggestive of gain spirals.

First, Hakanen, Perhoniemi, and Toppinen-Tanner (2008) conducted a two-wave 3-year panel study among 2555 Finnish dentists to examine the energizing power of job resources and related gain spirals. Drawing on COR theory a reciprocal process was predicted: (1) job resources lead to work engagement and work engagement leads to personal initiative (PI), which, in turn, has a positive impact on work-unit innovativeness, and (2) work-unit innovativeness leads to PI, which has a positive impact on work engagement, which finally predicts future job resources. The results of structural equation modeling (SEM) generally confirmed these hypotheses. Positive and reciprocal cross-lagged associations were found between job resources and work engagement and between work engagement and PI. In addition, PI had a positive impact on work-unit innovativeness over time.

Second, Salanova, Bakker, and Llorens (2006) carried out a two-wave longitudinal study among 258 secondary school teachers to investigate the relationship between personal (i.e., self-efficacy) and job resources (i.e., social support climate and clear goals) on the one hand, and work-related flow – a psychological state akin to work engagement – on the other hand. Using SEM analyses, they found that the teachers' personal and job resources at the beginning of the academic year positively predicted their levels of flow at the end of the academic year, eight months later. Simultaneously, teachers' flow at the start of the academic year predicted both types of resources at the end of the academic year. Thus, a reciprocal relationship was observed between resources and teacher well-being, which is compatible with the notion of gain spirals as proposed by COR theory.

Third, Llorens, Schaufeli, Bakker, and Salanova (2007) conducted a two-wave longitudinal study with university students in a laboratory setting. This study examined the relation between personal (i.e., efficacy beliefs) and task resources (i.e., time control and method control) on the one hand, and task engagement on the other hand. Twenty-two groups of five members each were included, whereby each group performed an innovative task, as well as an intellective task.

Results showed that neither of the constructs included in the investigation can be considered as a single cause or consequence that perpetuates the spiral of resources, efficacy beliefs, and engagement. Instead, reciprocal causation seems to be the key. That is, task resources had a positive impact on efficacy beliefs, which, in turn, fostered task engagement. In addition, engagement boosted future efficacy beliefs, which, in turn, led to the perception of more task resources. Furthermore, reciprocal relationships existed between personal and task resources, suggesting that they reinforce each other, thus fostering resource accumulation.

Fourth, Xanthopoulou, Bakker, Demerouti, and Schaufeli (2009a) examined the role of personal resources (i.e. self-efficacy, self-esteem, and optimism) and job resources (i.e., job autonomy, supervisory coaching, performance feedback, and opportunities for professional development) in explaining work engagement. They carried out a two-wave longitudinal study among 163 employees with a 2-year time interval. It was hypothesized that job and personal resources, and work engagement are reciprocal over time. Indeed, results showed that not only resources and work engagement but also – as in the previous study – job and personal resources were mutually related. Most importantly, all effects (causal and reversed-causal) were equally strong. These findings support the assumption of COR theory that various types of resources and well-being evolve into a cycle that determines employees' successful adaptation to their work environments. The results also suggested that neither resources nor engagement may be considered as the most important initiator of this cyclical process.

Fifth, Xanthopoulou, Bakker, Demerouti, and Schaufeli (2009c) investigated how daily fluctuations in job resources (i.e., autonomy, coaching, and team climate) were related to employees' personal resources (i.e., self-efficacy, self-esteem, and optimism), work engagement, and the company's financial returns. Forty-two employees working in three branches of a fast food company completed a questionnaire and a diary booklet over five consecutive workdays. One of the most significant findings of this study was that previous day's coaching had a positive, lagged effect on next day's work engagement (through next day's optimism), and on next day's financial returns. Although the design of this study did not facilitate the examination of reciprocal effects, findings are in line with COR theory, which suggests that resources act in so-called caravans. Namely, existing resources bring more resources resulting in a gain process. For example, when supervisors communicate to their subordinates how well they perform on their assigned tasks, and suggest better ways for doing so, employees' optimism is boosted, and consequently they are likely to feel more engaged and be more productive.

Sixth, Xanthopoulou, Bakker, Heuven, Demerouti, and Schaufeli (2008) examined whether daily fluctuations in colleague support predicted day-levels of job performance through first self-efficacy and then work engagement. Forty-four flight attendants filled in a questionnaire and a diary booklet before and after consecutive flights to three intercontinental destinations. As in the previous study, the dynamic nature of the relationships between the study variables was investigated using a within-subjects design, in which a relatively small sample was followed on multiple occasions over a number of days. Results of multilevel analyses revealed that colleague support had unique positive lagged effects on work engagement and self-efficacy. This means that a supportive work environment not only determines flight attendants' work engagement, but also their personal resources (i.e., self-efficacy beliefs). The latter agrees with the COR notion of resource caravans: job resources breed personal resources.

To conclude, job resources breed personal resources, and vice versa. This underscores the notion of resource caravans as assumed by COR theory. Job and personal resources are reciprocal, because individuals, through learning experiences, may form stronger positive evaluations about themselves and in turn, they comprehend or create more resourceful work environments (Kohn & Schooler, 1982). Moreover, job resources and personal resources have a positive impact on work engagement, which, in its turn, seems to reinforce both types of resources. This dynamic, reciprocal relationship between resources and engagement as described by COR theory is compatible with and partly supports the notion of gain spirals.

Social cognitive theory and spirals of self-efficacy, engagement, and performance

Social cognitive theory (SCT) assumes that *agency*, or the capacity to exercise control over our lives, is the essence of humanness. Agency is characterized by a number of core features like intentionality and forethought, self-regulation, and self-reflection about one's capabilities (Bandura, 2001). According to SCT, among the mechanisms governing agency, a strong sense of efficacy to manage one's level of functioning and events that affect one's life plays a pivotal role. Self-efficacy is defined as: "beliefs in one's capabilities to organize and execute the courses of action required to produce given attainments" (Bandura, 1997, p. 3). Whatever other factors serve as motivators, they are rooted in the core belief that one has the power to produce desired effects by one's actions; otherwise, one has little incentive to act or to persevere in the face of difficulties. More recently, SCT has extended the conception of human agency to collective agency, which is defined as the people's shared belief in their collective power to produce desired outcomes (Bandura, 2001). Perceived collective efficacy is not simply the sum of the individual efficacy beliefs but an emergent group-level property that is governed by similar regulating properties as individual self-efficacy (Bandura, 2001).

While most research has focused on the moderating role of efficacy beliefs in the relationship between stressors and strain (Jex & Bliese, 1999; Jimmieson, 2000; Salanova, Peiró, & Schaufeli, 2002; Schaubroeck & Merrit, 1997; Stetz, Stetz, & Bliese, 2006), less attention has been given to its relationship with positive states like work engagement. An exception has to be made for studies on the relation between self-efficacy and job performance, which are more abundant (see the meta-analysis by Stajkovic & Luthans, 1998). Nevertheless, recent studies support the positive link between efficacy beliefs and work engagement, showing a causal as well as reciprocal relationship between the two constructs over time (Llorens et al., 2007; Xanthopoulou et al., 2008, 2009a). Moreover, Salanova, Llorens, and Schaufeli (2008) performed two-wave and three-wave longitudinal studies among secondary school and university students and found that efficacy beliefs (i.e., self- and collective efficacy) were related to positive emotions (i.e., enthusiasm, satisfaction, and comfort) which in their turn, predicted future work and task engagement. Finally, research has shown that groups with higher levels of collective efficacy show higher engagement and group performance (Salanova, Llorens, Cifre, Martínez, & Schaufeli, 2003). Thus, it is clear that self- and collective efficacy play a crucial role in explaining work engagement.

Spirals of efficacy beliefs, engagement, and performance

Past research has suggested that a positive gain spiral of self-efficacy and performance exists; self-efficacy enhances performance, which – in its turn – increases efficacy beliefs (Lindsley et al., 1995; Shea & Howell, 2000). It is quite plausible to include engagement in this spiraling process, as hypothesized by the so-called spiral model of efficacy beliefs (Salanova, Bresó, & Schaufeli, 2005; Salanova, Cifre, Llorens, & Martínez, 2007; Salanova, Llorens, & Schaufeli, 2008), which draws on the main assumptions of SCT and the job demands-resources model (Bakker & Demerouti, 2007).

The spiral model of efficacy beliefs proposes that efficacy beliefs (i.e., self- and collective efficacy) initiate gain spirals. The suggested psychological process operates as follows: before employees choose a goal and initiate their effort toward that goal, they tend to weigh, evaluate, and integrate information about their capabilities. According to SCT, expectations of personal efficacy will determine whether a behavior will be initiated, how much task-related effort will be spent, and how long that effort will be sustained despite disconfirming evidence. Moreover, levels of efficacy beliefs that employees and groups experience influence their perceptions of job demands and resources. Namely, when efficacy levels are high and individuals believe that they can control their environment effectively, job demands are more likely to be perceived as challenging and job resources as abundant. Consequently, individuals are more likely to be engaged in their tasks and perform well. This constitutes a process of mutual reinforcement that may result in upward spirals.

There is some evidence for the spiral model of efficacy beliefs. It has been shown that resources (i.e., efficacy beliefs and job resources) predict engagement in a positive way (see above and Chapters 7 and 8). However, the relationship between job demands and engagement is somewhat more complicated. Research has demonstrated that job demands are either very weakly or not at all related to engagement (Schaufeli & Bakker, 2004; Llorens, Bakker, Salanova, & Schaufeli, 2006). Nevertheless, job resources particularly impact engagement when demands are high (see Bakker, Hakanen, Demerouti, & Xanthopoulou, 2007). An explanation could be that there are different types of demands, such as challenge and hindrance demands, with different effects on engagement and motivation. For example, challenge demands may show a positive relationship with engagement while hindrance demands are unrelated to engagement (Cavanaugh, Boswell, Roehling, & Boudreau, 2000; LePine, Podsakoff, & LePine, 2005). Challenge demands (i.e., deadlines and time pressure, quantitative and mental overload) are related to goal attainment and work motivation, whereas hindrance demands (i.e., role conflict, situational obstacles) preclude goal attainment. In a sample of Spanish secondary teachers and users of information and communication technologies (Ventura, Salanova, & Llorens, 2008), multigroup SEM showed that high levels of efficacy beliefs were related with more challenge demands (i.e., mental overload), which in turn positively affected work engagement.

Sources of efficacy beliefs as drivers of spirals

As we have seen, according to SCT, self-efficacy initiates gain spirals. But it is also important to know the drivers of efficacy beliefs. SCT identifies four sources of efficacy beliefs: mastery experiences, vicarious experiences, verbal persuasion, and emotional states. Research has indicated that succeeding in a challenging task (i.e., *mastery experience*) is most effective in improving efficacy beliefs (Bandura, 2001). This is because enactive mastery is the only antecedent of self-efficacy that provides direct performance information for the formation of more stable and accurate efficacy judgments. However, changes in self-efficacy will not occur as a direct result of performance accomplishment. Rather, changes will depend on how employees process the information that the previous performance generated. This interpretation is supported by research showing that superior past performance of students (i.e., Grade Point Average) was positively related to high levels of self-efficacy and academic engagement, whereas inferior past performance was related to inefficacy and burnout (Salanova et al., 2005).

Given the amount of diagnostic information available in an organizational context, self- and collective efficacy appraisals are also influenced by *vicarious learning*, which occurs by observing efficacious individuals and groups perform a similar task. The greater the perceived similarity between the role model and the target person, the greater the influence of the model on the person's efficacy beliefs. *Verbal persuasion* by someone employees trust and see as expert serves as another means of strengthening self- and collective efficacy.

Finally, the fourth major sources of self-efficacy are *psychological and emotional states*. For example, when people feel content and satisfied, they are more likely to believe that they are competent. This relationship is illustrated by Salanova et al. (2006), who showed that flow at work was reciprocally related with teacher self-efficacy over the time. Also, results of a three-wave study among one hundred participants working in groups (Salanova et al., 2008) supported a positive gain spiral of collective efficacy beliefs, positive collective emotions (i.e., enthusiasm, satisfaction, and comfort), and collective task engagement. In this study, not only

was reciprocity confirmed but also levels of collective efficacy increased significantly over time (from T1 to T2 and from T2 to T3).

To conclude (self and collective) efficacy beliefs predict future engagement which, in turn, predicts performance in a reciprocal way. Research on efficacy beliefs and engagement suggests the existence of a gain spiral, where efficacy beliefs predict engagement and performance through perceptions of challenging job demands and job resources, which, in turn, foster efficacy beliefs over time.

Broaden-and-build theory: Positive emotions and engagement

Fredrickson's (1998, 2001) broaden-and-build (B&B) theory seeks to explain how positive emotions or pleasant affective states promote well-being. This recently formulated theory suggests that distinct positive emotions (e.g., joy, interest, enthusiasm, love, pride, contentment) share the ability to *broaden* people's momentary thought–action repertoires and *build* their enduring personal resources, including physical, intellectual, social, and psychological resources (Fredrickson, 2001). Positive affective states *broaden* by prompting momentary exploratory behaviors (e.g., flexibility, creativity), which in their turn create learning opportunities. Such opportunities *build* more accurate maps of what is good or threatening in the environment, which help individuals to successfully manage future challenges (Fredrickson, 2003). Accordingly, this acquired knowledge has a long-term adaptive value for individuals because it is translated into lasting resources. Consequently, the accumulating effects of the "building through broadening" may improve individuals' momentary and prospective health and well-being.

Empirical research has provided substantial support both for the broaden and the build hypotheses. Regarding the former, studies have shown that positive emotions broaden the scope of attention, cognition, and action (for a review see Fredrickson, 2001, 2003). For example, Fredrickson and Branigan (2005) found that individuals experiencing a higher activation state of amusement and/or a lower activation state of contentment exhibited broader scopes of attention and had more thought–action urges than those experiencing no particular emotion. In another experimental study, participants, after viewing videos eliciting joy, showed lower levels of own-race bias in face recognition (Johnson & Fredrickson, 2005).

To date, there are few studies supporting the build hypothesis. Results of a diary study revealed that daily job resources generate positive emotional experiences in employees, which in turn have an immediate effect on their personal resources (Xanthopoulou, Bakker, Demerouti, & Schaufeli, 2009b). Two longitudinal studies among insurance sales agents in Taiwan showed that positive moods (e.g., enthusiasm, excitement) predicted task performance through interpersonal (i.e., co-worker helping and support) and personal (i.e., self-efficacy and task persistence) resources (Tsai, Chen, & Liu, 2007). However, the strongest evidence comes from an experimental study by Fredrickson, Cohn, Coffey, Pek, and Finkel (2008), where a manipulation to increase positive emotional experiences was used. Employees of a company either attended a loving-kindness meditation workshop or had no intervention. Results indicated that meditation practices increased daily experiences of positive emotions, which in turn produced gains in personal resources (e.g., mastery, self-acceptance) 8 weeks later. Consequently, these increments in personal resources predicted increased life satisfaction and reduced depressive symptoms. This study is particularly crucial because it provides evidence for causal relationships and for actual increases (i.e., gains) over the course of time.

Upward spirals in the broaden-and-build theory

The research evidence concerning the broaden-and-build theory laid the ground for the hypothesis that positive emotions generate *upward* spirals. Positive emotions trigger upward spirals because the broadening of individuals' thought–action repertoires and the building of resources may, in their turn, promote well-being and adaptive functioning, as well as future experiences of positive emotions. Throughout this dynamic broaden-and-build process, individuals become more resilient and self-efficacious, and consequently create less threatening environments that facilitate the elicitation of positive emotions not only for themselves, but also for significant others (e.g., colleagues, partners). In other words, positive emotions not only make people feel good in the present, but by triggering positive gain spirals, increase the likelihood that people will function well and feel good in the future as well (Fredrickson, 2003).

In line with this assumption, Fredrickson and Joiner (2002) showed in a longitudinal study with a 5-week time interval that positive affect and broad-minded coping (i.e., taking a broad perspective on problems and generating multiple possible solutions) were reciprocal. When positive affect is experienced, individuals are more likely to have a broader view on their problems that helps them come up with multiple potential solutions and vice versa. When people can find multiple solutions for their problems, they are more likely to experience positive emotions. Additional analyses showed that positive affect and broad-minded coping serially enhanced one another. Thus, positive emotions initiated upward spirals toward emotional well-being. Recently, Burns et al. (2008) replicated this finding by showing that positive affect and broad-minded coping mutually build on one another over a 2-month period. Additionally, Burns and colleagues extended previous studies by demonstrating that upward spirals involve not only cognitive, but also interpersonal resources and benefits. Namely, they observed comparable upward spiral relations between positive affect and the social resource of interpersonal trust.

Work engagement in the broaden-and-build process

Empirical evidence regarding the B&B theory provides clear support for the existence of upward spirals, since there is evidence for both reciprocity and increase in levels. Having in mind the proposed psychological mechanisms, three possible functions of work engagement may be detected in relation to the upward spiral proposed by the B&B theory. Specifically, work engagement may serve the following functions:

1. A positive affective–motivational state.
2. The initiator of positive emotions.
3. The outcome of positive emotions.

First, work engagement, although more persistent and pervasive than momentary emotions (Schaufeli & Salanova, 2007; see also Chapter 2), is a distinct positive affective motivational state that may broaden employees' thought–action repertoires and build their enduring personal resources. In line with that, scholars have used the B&B framework to formulate the hypothesis that work engagement leads to cognitive broadening and resources building over time. For instance, Hakanen et al. (2008) in their two-wave study among a large sample of Finish dentists found that the experience of work engagement may broaden dentists' coping and action repertoires, including their levels of personal initiative (i.e., active and initiative-taking behavior that goes beyond formal work requirements). Results of crossed-lagged panel analyses not only supported the notion that work engagement predicted personal initiative 3 years later, but simultaneously supported the reversed-causal relationship.

Focusing on the build part of the theory, Xanthopoulou et al. (2009a) hypothesized that work engagement, by stimulating self-enhancement through learning and goal achievement (i.e., broadening), builds job resources (e.g., autonomy, and opportunities for professional development) and personal resources (self-efficacy, organizational-based self-esteem, and optimism) over time. The findings of this study among 163 employees of an electrical engineering and electronics company in The Netherlands showed that work engagement was indeed related to both job and personal resources 2 years later. Most importantly, the relationship between work engagement and resources was reciprocal over the course of time.

A second function of work engagement in relation to the B&B process is that of the *initiator* of positive emotions. Engaged employees are vigorous, enthusiastic, and absorbed in their work tasks because they derive fulfillment from

them. According to Fredrickson (2001), positive emotional states are elicited particularly when individuals are in pleasant situations. Engaged employees are considered to be in a pleasant situation, because although they may also have to deal with threats or demands in the work environment, they are more likely to perceive these as challenges. Moreover, the highest levels of work engagement are experienced in conditions combining high job resources *and* high job demands (Bakker et al., 2007). In this context, studies that examined work engagement as both an enduring quality, as well as an emotional state that may fluctuate from day to day, showed that the more engaged employees generally are, the more likely it is that they experience daily (momentary) states of enthusiasm and engagement (Xanthopoulou et al., 2008, 2009c). Put differently, "trait-like" engagement predicts "emotional-like" state engagement. These studies further supported the link between day-level engagement experiences and performance indicators like financial returns, thus substantiating the proposition of positive spirals.

Finally, work engagement, as an indicator of positive psychological well-being (Schaufeli & Salanova, 2007), may be a direct or indirect *outcome* of positive emotions. The view of work engagement as a *direct* outcome of positive emotions suggests that engagement may explain why positive emotions, by broadening cognitive functions, build resources. Frequent experiences of positive emotions in the workplace may lead to a more persistent, positive affective state, namely work engagement. Indeed, Salanova et al. (2008) showed that work and task engagement was predicted by positive emotions such as (individual and collective) enthusiasm, satisfaction, and comfort. Similarly, Schaufeli and Van Rhenen (2006) showed in their study among 815 Dutch managers that work-related positive affect partially mediated the relationship between job resources on the one hand, and work engagement and positive attitudes towards the organization on the other hand. In this context, employees who often feel enthusiasm, pride or joy while working are more likely to be interested in what they have to do and as a result may end up being in a more pervasive motivational state of energy, dedication, and total immersion in their work. Engaged employees, who are intrinsically motivated to fulfill their work goals, will look for or create resources in their environment, in order to achieve these goals, as assumed by COR theory (see above). Resourceful environments may improve the beliefs employees have regarding their capabilities to control and achieve their work goals successfully (i.e., personal resources). Consequently, this may lead to enhanced well-being and performance, which in their turn may elicit even more experiences of positive emotions.

The view of work engagement as an *indirect* outcome of positive emotions emphasizes the role of resources in explaining the link between the two. As we have seen, the main assumption of the B&B theory is that positive emotions broaden individuals' thought–action repertoires and build their resources (Fredrickson, 2001). Employees who experience positive emotions end up with more personal, but also more social or situational (i.e., job) resources. Also, this is in line with SCT, which suggest that positive emotional states are one of the main sources of efficacy beliefs (see above). There is convincing empirical evidence that job and personal resources, due to their extrinsic and intrinsic motivational potential, are the most important predictors of work engagement (for a review, see Bakker, 2009). Therefore, high levels of resources (as initiated by positive emotions) lead to engaged workforces. In turn, engaged employees not only report higher levels of well-being and exhibit better performance (for a review, see Bakker, 2009), but they are also likely to have more positive affective experiences and gain more resources over the course of time. This is in line with the study of Fredrickson et al. (2008), who showed that positive emotions lead to gains in personal resources, which in turn predicted gains in various well-being aspects.

To conclude, work engagement may be seen as: (1) the positive affective-motivational state, (2) as the initiator of positive emotions, and (3) as the outcome of positive emotions. It is important to make clear that these different functions (particularly 2 and 3) and the proposed underlying psychological processes are not independent of each other. Rather, they are complementary and explain all possible relationships between emotions, resources, and engagement in the development of upward spirals. Put differently, every single relationship described above is necessary in order to understand and explain the full spectrum of the B&B spirals.

Conclusion and outlook

In this chapter the notion of spiraling (personal and job) resources and work engagement was discussed. Despite the few studies on gain spirals in occupational health psychology, there is some empirical evidence that positive psychological constructs (like resources, positive emotions, and engagement) are mutually reinforcing each other. We used three theoretical perspectives for understanding the complex spiraling among job resources, personal resources, and engagement: (1) conservation of resources theory; (2) social cognitive theory; and (3) broaden-and-build theory. These three theories explain gain spirals of resources and engagement in a supplementary way, each of them dealing with a different facet. COR theory presents a general framework for different kinds of resources and for ways in which these resources accumulate over time in gain spirals. In the case of SCT, the main resource is a personal one – efficacy beliefs – that relates to engagement and performance in a reciprocal way. Finally, B&B theory focuses on upward spirals, where positive emotions play a central role in explaining resources and work engagement.

Most of the studies presented in this chapter were congruent with the predictions of these theories, suggesting reciprocal and positive relationships between resources and engagement. However, it is important to note that almost all studies that have been reviewed in this chapter meet only the first condition for demonstrating the existence of a gain spiral, namely reciprocal causation. Increases in levels over time – the second condition – were only rarely observed. Nevertheless, the reviewed studies propose a complex interplay of job and personal resources, positive emotions, work engagement, and positive organizational outcomes. It seems that these are all elements of a self-perpetuating, complex and dynamic motivational process. Self-perpetuating, because the elements are reciprocally related; complex, because all elements are directly, or indirectly related to each other; and dynamic, because the process unfolds across time, whereby feedback and feed-forward loops seem to exist. Therefore, it may be speculated that a positive cycle that includes job resources, personal resources, positive emotions, work engagement, and enhanced performance does exist. As in every cycle, the starting or ending point is not of main importance. Instead, it is crucial to understand how and why the factors shaping the cycle succeed and reinforce one another.

Critical remarks

There are certain methodological and theoretical issues concerning the concept of gain spirals that warrant discussion. As already mentioned, in order to fully support the hypothesized gain spirals, empirical evidence for reciprocal causation of each possible sequence of effects, although necessary, is not a sufficient condition. The idea of gain spirals also presupposes a real positive change (i.e., improvement in levels) over

time (see Lindsley et al., 1995) and our definition of gain spirals at the beginning of the chapter. Longitudinal studies described in this chapter provide convincing evidence for the assumption of reciprocity. However, few studies support actual gains in terms of increases in the levels of the variables of interest (Fredrickson et al., 2008). Finally, only the study by Salanova et al. (2008) provides evidence both for reciprocal and positive relationships between self-efficacy, positive emotions, and engagement, *and* for a monotonic and significant increase in self-efficacy levels over time. More studies focusing on changes are needed. In other words, it should be demonstrated that the pattern of relationships between resources and engagement over a series of waves or trials is characterized by monotonic increases, whereby changes in resources and engagement build on each other producing an amplifying loop over time.

COR theory and B&B theory explain two possible types of spirals, i.e., gain and loss spirals: the existence of resources or positive emotions may initiate gain spirals, whereas the absence or loss of resources and the existence of

Practical implications

Since work engagement is an essential, positive element of employee health and well-being, with relevant consequences for organizations, a crucial question is how to initiate and maintain gain spirals of engagement over the time. Gain spirals may be sparked by personal and job resources, as well as by positive emotions, and may result in various positive outcomes via work engagement. In turn, these positive outcomes increase resources and foster high levels of engagement, and so on. Following the logic of such gain spirals, work engagement may be increased by stimulating each link of the spiral.

Increasing job resources is likely to result in higher levels of work engagement. Hence, (re)designing jobs in order to promote engagement boils down to increasing job resources. Also, job rotation and changing jobs might result in higher engagement levels because they challenge employees, increase their motivation, and stimulate learning and professional development. Furthermore, since engagement seems to be contagious and may spread across members of work teams (Bakker, van Emmerik, & Euwema, 2006), leaders have a special role in fostering work engagement among their followers. It is to be expected that considerate leadership, and more particularly transformational leadership, is successful in accomplishing this. Indeed, research shows that transformational leaders are key social resources for the development of employee engagement (Tims, Bakker, & Xanthopoulou, 2009).

Further, training programs in organizations that aim at increasing work engagement could focus on building personal resources (e.g., efficacy beliefs, optimism, and resiliency). For example, training programs may cultivate the four sources of self-efficacy mentioned in this chapter as drivers of work engagement. Finally, cultivation of positive emotions in the work context may be beneficial for the initiation of gain spirals. Indeed, Fredrickson et al. (2008) showed that loving-kindness meditation techniques are successful in generating positive emotional experiences in the work context.

Several other studies included some of above proposed strategies in order to increase engagement over the time. Cifre, Salanova, and Rodríguez (2008) performed a stress management intervention in a Spanish tile company that focused on the improvement of job resources such as innovation climate and social relationships at work. Results showed that levels of personal resources (i.e., self-efficacy), job resources, and engagement did increase in the intervention group over the course of one year, but not in the control group. In addition, a stress management intervention program among students (Bresó, Schaufeli, & Salanova, 2008) that focused on the enhancement of positive emotional states (as a source of self-efficacy) was also successful in increasing engagement, self-efficacy, and academic performance in the intervention group (as compared to a control group).

negative emotions may initiate loss spirals. SCT proposes another way of development over time: the self-correcting cycle that may fluctuate upward or downward over relatively short periods of time, "wherein there is no discernible pattern of mutual causation" (Lindsley et al., 1995, p. 650). For example, in the case of resources and engagement, a self-correcting cycle would exist if there was a significant relationship between consecutive measures of resources and engagement, and at least one change in either resources or engagement was in the opposite direction of the usual pattern of changes (i.e., a negative change in either resources or engagement in an otherwise upward spiral, or a positive change in either resources or engagement in an otherwise downward spiral). In the future, not only gain and loss spirals but also self-corrective cycles of resources and engagement should be investigated.

Final remark

So far, although strictly speaking only limited empirical evidence exists for gain spirals as proposed by COR, SCT, and B&B theories, cycles in which resources and work engagement mutually influence each other have been convincingly demonstrated. This is an important finding which indicates that resources and engagement may activate and conserve positive conditions, beliefs, and affective states. This conclusion is significant theoretically because it identifies underlying psychological mechanisms, and practically because it implies that resourceful environments contribute to a flourishing workforce, and vice versa.

References

Bakker, A. B. (2009). Building engagement in the workplace. In R. J. Burke & C. L. Cooper (Eds.), *The peak performing organization* (pp. 50–72). Oxon, UK: Routledge.

Bakker, A. B., & Demerouti, E. (2007). The Job Demands-Resources Model: State of the art. *Journal of Managerial Psychology, 22*, 309–328.

Bakker, A. B., & Demerouti, E. (2008). Towards a model of work engagement. *Career Development International, 13*, 209–223.

Bakker, A. B., Hakanen, J. J., Demerouti, E., & Xanthopoulou, D. (2007). Job resources boost work engagement particularly when job demands are high. *Journal of Educational Psychology, 99*, 274–284.

Bakker, A. B., Van Emmerik, H., & Euwema, M. C. (2006). Crossover of burnout and engagement in teams. *Work and Occupations, 33*, 464–489.

Bandura, A. (1986). *Social foundations of thought and action: A social cognitive theory*. Englewood Cliffs, NJ: Prentice-Hall.

Bandura, A. (1997). *Self-efficacy: The exercise of control*. New York: Freeman.

Bandura, A. (2001). Social cognitive theory: An agentic perspective. *Annual Review of Psychology, 52*, 1–26.

Bresó, E., Schaufeli, W. B., & Salanova, M. (2008). *Can a self-efficacy-based intervention decrease burnout, increase engagement, and enhance performance? A quasi-experimental study*. Manuscript submitted for publication.

Burns, A. B., Brown, J. S., Sachs-Ericsson, N., Plant, E. A., Curtis, J. T., Fredrickson, B. L., et al. (2008). Upward spirals of positive emotions and coping: Replication, extension, and initial exploration of neurochemical substrates. *Personality and Individual Differences, 44*, 360–370.

Cavanaugh, M. A., Boswell, W. R., Roehling, M. V., & Boudreau, J. W. (2000). An empirical examination of self-reported work stress among U.S. managers. *Journal of Applied Psychology, 85*, 65–74.

Cifre, E., Salanova, M., & Rodríguez, A. (2008). *A stress management intervention based on the Job Demands–Resources model: A longitudinal study*. Manuscript submitted for publication.

Fredrickson, B. L. (1998). What good are positive emotions? *Review of General Psychology, 2*, 300–319.

Fredrickson, B. L. (2001). The role of positive emotions in positive psychology: The broaden-and-build theory of positive emotions. *American Psychologist, 56*, 218–226.

Fredrickson, B. L. (2003). Positive emotions and upward spirals in organization. In K. Cameron, J. Dutton, & R. Quinn (Eds.), *Positive organizational scholarship* (pp. 163–175). San Francisco: Berrett-Koehler.

Fredrickson, B. L., & Branigan, C. (2005). Positive emotions broaden the scope of attention and thought-action repertoires. *Cognition and Emotion, 19*, 313–332.

Fredrickson, B. L., Cohn, M. A., Coffey, K. A., Pek, J., & Finkel, S. M. (2008). Open hearts build lives: Positive emotions, induced through loving-kindness meditation, build consequential personal resources. *Journal of Personality and Social Psychology, 95*, 1045–1062.

Fredrickson, B. L., & Joiner, T. (2002). Positive emotions trigger upward spirals toward emotional well-being. *Psychological Science, 13*, 172–175.

Hackman, J. R., & Oldham, G. R. (1980). *Work redesign*. Reading, MA: Addison-Wesley.

Hakanen, J. J., Perhoniemi, R., & Toppinen-Tanner, S. (2008). Positive gain spirals at work: From job resources to work engagement, personal initiative, and work-unit innovativeness. *Journal of Vocational Behavior, 73*, 78–91.

Hobfoll, S. E. (1989). Conservation of resources: A new attempt at conceptualizing stress. *American Psychologist, 44*, 513–524.

Hobfoll, S. E. (1998). *Stress, culture and community. The psychology and philosophy of stress*. New York: Plenum.

Hobfoll, S. E. (2001). The influence of culture, community and the nested-self in the stress process: Advancing the Conservation of Resources theory. *Applied Psychology: An International Review, 50*, 337–421.

Hobfoll, S. E. (2002). Social and psychological resources and adaptation. *Review of General Psychology, 6*, 307–324.

Hobfoll, S. E., Johnson, R. J., Ennis, N., & Jackson, A. P. (2003). Resource loss, resource gain, and emotional outcomes among inner city women. *Journal of Personality and Social Psychology, 84*, 632–643.

Hobfoll, S. E., & Shirom, A. (2000). Conservation of resources theory: Applications to stress and management in the workplace. In R. Golembiewski (Ed.), *Handbook of organizational behaviour* (pp. 57–81). New York: Dekker.

Jex, S. M., & Bliese, P. D. (1999). Efficacy beliefs as a moderator of the impact of work-related stressors: A multilevel study. *Journal of Applied Psychology, 84*, 349–361.

Jimmieson, N. L. (2000). Employee reactions to behavioral control under conditions of stress: the moderating role of self-efficacy. *Work & Stress, 14*, 262–280.

Johnson, K. J., & Fredrickson, B. L. (2005). "We all look the same to me": Positive emotions eliminate the own-race bias in face recognitions. *Psychological Science, 16*, 875–881.

Kohn, M. L., & Schooler, C. (1982). Job conditions and personality: A longitudinal assessment of their reciprocal effects. *American Journal of Sociology, 87*, 1257–1286.

LePine, J. A., Podsakoff, N. P., & LePine, M. A. (2005). A meta-analytic test of the challenge stressor-hindrance stressor framework: An explanation for inconsistent relationships among stressors and performance. *Academy of Management Journal, 48*, 764–775.

Lindsley, D. H., Brass, D. J., & Thomas, J. B. (1995). Efficacy-performance spirals: A multilevel perspective. *Academy of Management Review, 20*, 645–678.

Llorens, S., Bakker, A., Schaufeli, W. B., & Salanova, M. (2006). Testing the robustness of Job Demands-Resources Model. *International Journal of Stress Management, 13*, 378–391.

Llorens, S., Schaufeli, W. B., Bakker, A. B., & Salanova, M. (2007). Does a positive gain spiral of resources, efficacy beliefs and engagement exist? *Computers in Human Behavior, 23*, 825–841.

Mathieu, J. E., & Taylor, S. R. (2006). Clarifying conditions and decision points for mediational type inferences in organizational behavior. *Journal of Organizational Behavior, 27*, 1031–1056.

Ryan, R. M., & Deci, E. L. (2000). Self-determination theory and the facilitation of intrinsic motivation, social development, and well-being. *American Psychologist, 55*, 68–78.

Ryan, R. M., & Frederick, C. M. (1997). On energy, personality, and health: Subjective vitality as a dynamic reflection of well-being. *Journal of Personality, 65*, 529–565.

Salanova, M., Bakker, A., & Llorens, S. (2006). Flow at work: Evidence for a gain spiral of personal and organizational resources. *Journal of Happiness Studies, 7*, 1–22.

Salanova, M., Bresó, E., & Schaufeli, W. B. (2005). Hacia un modelo espiral de las creencias de eficacia en el estudio del burnout y del engagement. [Towards a spiral model of efficacy beliefs, burnout and engagement]. *Ansiedad y Estrés, 11*, 215–231.

Salanova, M., Cifre, E., Llorens, S., & Martínez, I. M. (2007). *Caso a caso en la prevención de riesgos psicosociales. Metodología WONT para una organización saludable* [Case-to-case in the psychosocial risk prevention. WONT methodology to a healthy organization]. Bilbao: Lettera Publicaciones.

Salanova, M., Llorens, S., & Schaufeli, W. B. (2008). *Upward spirals of efficacy beliefs: A longitudinal and multi-sample study*. Manuscript submitted for publication.

Salanova, M., Llorens, S., Cifre, E., Martínez, I., & Schaufeli, W. B. (2003). Perceived collective efficacy, subjective well-being and task performance among electronic work groups: An experimental study. *Small Groups Research, 34*, 43–73.

Salanova, M., Peiró, J. M., & Schaufeli, W. B. (2002). Self-efficacy specificity and burnout among information technology workers: An extension of the Job Demands-Control Model. *European Journal of Work and Organizational Psychology*, *11*, 1–25.

Schaubroeck, J., & Merrit, D. (1997). Divergent effects of job control on coping with work stressors: The key role of self-efficacy. *Academy of Management Journal*, *40*, 738–754.

Schaufeli, W. B., & Bakker, A. B. (2004). Job demands, job resources and their relationship with burnout and engagement: A multi-sample study. *Journal of Organizational Behavior*, *25*, 293–315.

Schaufeli, W. B., & Salanova, M. (2007). Work engagement: An emerging psychological concept and its implications for organizations. In S. W. Gilliland, D. D. Steiner, & D. P. Skarlicki (Eds.), *Research in social issues in management (Volume 5): Managing social and ethical issues in organizations* (pp. 135–177). Greenwich, CT: Information Age Publishers.

Schaufeli, W. B., & Van Rhenen, W. (2006). Over de rol van positieve en negatieve emoties bij het welbevinden van managers: Een studie met de Job-related Affect-ive Well-being Scale (JAWS) [About the role of positive and negative emotions in managers' well-being: A study using the Job-related Affective Well-being Scale (JAWS)]. *Gedrag & Organisatie*, *19*, 323–244.

Shea, C. M., & Howell, J. M. (2000). Efficacy-performance spirals: An empirical test. *Journal of Management*, *26*, 791–812.

Stajkovic, A. D., & Luthans, F. (1998). Self-efficacy and work-related performance: A meta-analysis. *Psychological Bulletin*, *124*, 240–261.

Stetz, T. A., Stetz, M. C., & Bliese, P. D. (2006). The importance of self-efficacy in the moderating effects of social support on stressor-strain relationships. *Work & Stress*, *20*, 49–59.

Tims, M., Bakker, A. B., & Xanthopoulou, D. (2009). *Do transformational leaders enhance their followers' daily work engagement?* Manuscript submitted for publication.

Tsai, W. C., Chen, C. C., & Liu, H. L. (2007). Test of a model linking employee positive moods and task performance. *Journal of Applied Psychology*, *92*, 1570–1583.

Ventura, M., Salanova, M., & Llorens, S. (2008). *The predicting role of self-efficacy on burnout and engagement: the role of challenge and hindrance demands.* Manuscript submitted for publication.

Westman, M., Hobfoll, S. E., Chen, S., Davidson, O. B., & Laski, S. (2005). Organizational stress through the lens of conservation of resources (COR) theory. In P. L. Perrewé & D. L. Ganstyer (Eds.), *Research in occupational stress and well-being*, (Vol. 4, pp. 171–224). Oxford: Elsevier.

Xanthopoulou, D., Bakker, A. B., Demerouti, E., & Schaufeli, W. B. (2009a). Reciprocal relationships between job resources, personal resources, and work engagement. *Journal of Vocational Behavior*, *74*, 235–244.

Xanthopoulou, D., Bakker, A. B., Demerouti, E., & Schaufeli, W. B. (2009b). *A diary study on the happy worker: How job resources generate positive emotions and build personal resources.* Manuscript submitted for publication.

Xanthopoulou, D., Bakker, A. B., Demerouti, E., & Schaufeli, W. B. (2009c). Work engagement and financial returns: A diary study on the role of job and personal resources. *Journal of Occupational and Organizational Psychology*, *82*, 183–200.

Xanthopoulou, D., Bakker, A. B., Heuven, E., Demerouti, E., & Schaufeli, W. B. (2008). Working in the sky: A diary study on work engagement among flight attendants. *Journal of Occupational Health Psychology*, *13*, 345–356.

10

Engagement and human thriving: Complementary perspectives on energy and connections to work[1]

Gretchen M. Spreitzer, Chak Fu Lam, and Charlotte Fritz

In this chapter, we bring together literatures on two related constructs regarding employees' connection to work, which, to date, have been largely disparate: thriving and engagement. It is critical to examine the two constructs in relation to each other to determine their distinctiveness and uniqueness. To this end, we first define each construct and then demonstrate how the two constructs are distinct but have some conceptual overlap. We then examine key antecedents and outcomes of each construct. Finally, we discuss some of the leadership implications for how organizations can enable more engagement and thriving at work, and we will end with some directions for future research.

Defining the two constructs

What is engagement at work?
There are two main perspectives on studying engagement. The first is the more developed empirically and focuses on *work* engagement – more than 20 empirical articles have been published to date. Schaufeli, Bakker, and colleagues define work engagement as the positive opposite of burnout (e.g., Schaufeli & Bakker, Chapter 2,

this volume; Schaufeli, Bakker & Salanova, 2006a; Schaufeli, Martinez, Pinto, Salanova, & Bakker, 2002; Te Brake, Gort, Hoogstraten, & Eijkman, 2007). They have conceptualized engagement as a positive affective-motivational state of fulfillment as manifested in three dimensions:

- Vigor (exhaustion as the polar opposite dimension of burnout; Schaufeli & Bakker, 2004): high levels of energy and mental resilience while working; the willingness to invest effort in one's work; the ability to not be easily fatigued; persistence in the face of difficulties.
- Dedication (cynicism as the polar opposite dimension of burnout): strong involvement in one's work, accompanied by feelings of enthusiasm and significance; a sense of pride and inspiration (Bakker, Demerouti, & Schaufeli, 2005b).
- Absorption: being fully engrossed in one's work and having difficulties detaching oneself from it (Schaufeli et al., 2002).

Some of the more recent research on work engagement focuses exclusively on the first two dimensions of engagement – leaving absorption out of the analyses (e.g., Gonzalez-Roma, Schaufeli, Bakker, & Lloret, 2006; Rothmann & Jordaan, 2006). This development may be due to construct validity issues pertaining to the absorption construct as well as the fact that it is not the polar opposite of the third dimension of burnout – negative self-efficacy (Schaufeli & Salanova, 2007a).[2]

Empirical research finds that individual differences such as low neuroticism as well as high extraversion and mobility make some people more prone to engagement at work (Langelaan, Bakker, Van Doornen, & Schaufeli, 2006). Work engagement can also be discriminated from job involvement and organizational commitment (Hallberg & Schaufeli, 2006). Finally, work engagement can be found in teams, not just individuals (Bakker, Van Emmerik, & Euwema, 2006).

The second perspective on engagement is the more qualitative research by Kahn (1990) focusing on *role* engagement. He defines role engagement as "the harnessing of organizational members' selves to their work roles where employees express themselves physically, cognitively, and emotionally during role performances" (p. 694). In a sample of summer camp counselors and professionals in an architecture firm, he found that when people experience meaningfulness, psychological safety, and availability of critical resources in their work, they are more likely to fully engage their personal selves at work.

Additional empirical work by Rothbard (2001), in the context of work–family conflict, builds on Kahn's work and specifies two critical components of role engagement: attention (cognitive availability and the amount of time one spends thinking about a role) and absorption (being engrossed in a role and the intensity of one's focus on a role). In a large sample of university employees, she found that engagement in one role (i.e., work or family) can have both enriching and depleting effects on engagement in another role (i.e., work or family). Men tended to experience enrichment from work to family while women experience enrichment from family to work.

Both perspectives include an absorption dimension but differ in the mechanism regarding the connection to one's work – Schaufeli and colleagues refer to a more emotional and energetic connection to one's work role, while Kahn and Rothbard talk about a more cognitive and attentional connection to one's work role. Because this volume on engagement is focused primarily on the first perspective, we will focus most of our attention on it.

What is thriving?

Drawing on the theoretical work of Spreitzer, Sutcliffe, Dutton, Sonenshein, and Grant (2005), we define thriving as a psychological state focused on "a sense of progress or forward movement in one's self-development" (p. 538) captured in two dimensions of personal growth: learning and vitality. *Learning* refers to the sense that one is acquiring and can apply knowledge and skills to one's work (Dweck, 1986; Elliott & Dweck, 1988). Additionally, learning is about how individuals develop and continually improve. *Vitality* refers to the positive feeling of having energy (Ryan & Frederick, 1997; Nix, Ryan, Manly, &

Deci, 1999), involving a sense of spirit, feeling alert and awake, and looking forward to each new day. Vitality is similar to Shirom's (2004, 2006) construct of vigor and Thayer's (1978, 1987) calm energy, a state in which a person feels both energetic arousal and decreased tension. Both learning and vitality are theorized as essential components of thriving (Spreitzer et al., 2005). If a person is learning, but feels depleted and burned out, that person is not thriving. Conversely, if a person is energized, but finds his or her learning to be stagnant, that person is also not thriving. Thriving, then, is the joint experience of learning and vitality.

Why learning and vitality? First, the two dimensions encompass both the affective (vitality) and cognitive (learning) dimensions of the psychological experience of personal growth (e.g., Carver, 1998; Ryff, 1989). Ryff, for example, suggests that when individuals grow, they consider themselves to be expanding in ways that reflect enhanced self-knowledge and effectiveness (i.e., learning). Furthermore, she finds that personal growth is one important dimension of psychological well-being. Ryff's notion of personal growth in particular helps individuals cope with adverse life conditions. Likewise, Carver (1998) conceives of thriving as the psychological experience of a positive capacity, or a constructive and forward direction, that energizes and enlivens (i.e., vitality). Thus, prior research in psychology has already highlighted the affective and cognitive foundations of thriving.

Second, evidence from preliminary empirical research on narratives of growth (Sonenshein, Dutton, Grant, Spreitzer, & Sutcliffe, 2005) points to learning and vitality as pathways for human growth and development. In a sample of employees across three organizations (financial services, manufacturing, and a non-profit human services organization), Sonenshein and colleagues found that two key themes uncovered in interviews were energy and personal development when describing times in their life when employees experienced thriving at work.

We would like to highlight several other key definitional components of thriving. Thriving is theorized to be a continuum where people are

more or less thriving at any point in time (Spreitzer & Sutcliffe, 2007). Individuals can experience a range of thriving experiences rather than experiencing discrete states of either thriving or not thriving. Additionally, thriving is theorized as a psychological state capable of being shaped by the work context and not as an individual disposition. There may be personality traits that predispose individuals to experience more (or less) thriving at work – for example, someone with a learning orientation would be predisposed to opportunities for learning – but our conceptualization is that of thriving as a state. As the joint experience of learning and vitality, thriving reflects a continuum of the key cognitive and affective components of human growth.

Empirical research on thriving

Recent empirical work has provided preliminary support for the construct's validity including the two-dimensional conceptualization (Porath, Spreitzer, Gibson, Cobb, & Stevens, 2008b). Across three distinct samples (young professionals entering an MBA program, blue-collar trades people at a large university, and professionals in six industries), Porath and colleagues found that in each sample, the dimensions of learning and vitality contribute to a second-order construct of thriving. Specifically, a confirmatory factor analysis indicated a good fit of the theorized two-factor model to the data. In addition, reliabilities of the two dimensions of learning and vitality as well as the higher-order thriving construct are high (i.e., over .80). In addition, they empirically distinguished thriving from related constructs such as flourishing and core self-evaluations.

Further empirical research on the role of thriving at work has found that thriving contributes to positive adaptation amidst a changing work environment (Porath, Spreitzer, & Gibson, 2008a). More specifically, in a sample of young professionals entering an MBA program, respondents who reported more thriving prior to the start of the program were found to be more resilient in the face of difficulties experienced during their first semester and reported more high-quality connections with faculty and other students. Additionally, in a sample of professionals across six industries, respondents who reported more thriving were evaluated by their bosses as taking more initiative in their career development (i.e., they took more advantage of training opportunities and proactively sought out feedback about future directions).

Thriving has also been found to matter for in-role and extra-role job performance (Porath et al., 2008a) as well as for innovative behavior (Carmeli & Spreitzer, 2008). In a sample of blue-collar trades people, respondents who reported more thriving were described by their bosses as performing better in their jobs. The same seems to be true for white-collar employees: they were found to perform better in terms of in-role job performance as well as in terms of extra-role job performance (i.e., organizational citizenship behaviors). Both of these findings regarding job performance hold beyond traditional predictors of job performance including job satisfaction and organizational commitment. Finally, in a sample of Israeli professionals thriving was found to be related to higher levels of innovative behavior at work (Carmeli & Spreitzer, 2008).

What are the similarities and distinctions between thriving and engagement?

Clearly, thriving and engagement have important conceptual overlap (see Figure 10.1). Both are positive affective-motivational states. Neither is conceptualized as a more stable personality trait. Both have a dimension that is focused on energy

(vigor in engagement and vitality in thriving). However, the engagement definition of vigor is broader than vitality because vigor also includes notions of resilience and persistence amidst difficulties while vitality is strictly about energy at work.

Thriving and engagement also appear to have some distinctions. We use the word "appear" because to date no empirical research has examined the two constructs in tandem. Thus, our comments in this section are more speculative in nature. We suggest that work engagement may be focused on performance in the present state of one's work while thriving may be more improvement-focused. To be more specific, beyond vigor, the other two dimensions of engagement are dedication (pride and significance) and absorption (being deeply engrossed in work). These two dimensions capture the fulfillment and intensity of one's involvement in the work at hand. While engagement may fluctuate across days (Sonnentag, 2003), it seems more focused on being engaged in the job in its present state.

In contrast, thriving, given its second dimension of learning, may be more focused on improving or growing in one's job. Learning is about getting better, about developing into who we want to become. In this way, thriving represents progress or forward movement in one's development over time. Thriving is about one's trajectory of development or growth and forward progress. Rather than being focused primarily on one's

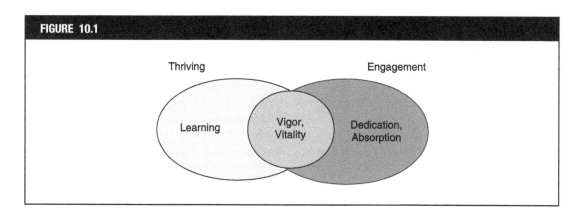

FIGURE 10.1

Thriving   Engagement

Learning   Vigor,   Dedication,
             Vitality   Absorption

The juxtaposition of thriving and engagement.

performance in the job in its current condition as may be true of the dedication and especially the absorption components of engagement, thriving has a learning component that is more improvement- or growth-oriented.

In summary, the conceptualizations of engagement and thriving are complementary but distinct. Each involves positive energy – vigor in engagement and vitality in thriving. As such, we believe that for the most part when individuals are engaged at work, they are also likely to be thriving. We assume that both are positively reinforcing to each other. Yet, because engagement focuses on dedication and absorption and thriving focuses on learning, it is possible for a person to be engaged at work and not thriving – or thriving and not engaged. For example, an employee can feel engaged at work – energized, dedicated to the purpose of their work, and highly absorbed (maybe even in flow) – but may not necessarily be learning and growing. This might be the case for individuals in a long-term job where they feel a real sense of purpose and involvement as well as experiencing a high level of competence and efficacy. They may still feel rather plateaued or stagnant in their opportunities for learning and personal growth. Conversely, one can be thriving – energized and learning/growing in new directions – but not necessarily engaged. Such individuals might be growing and developing in ways that reduce their dedication to their current job as they explore new avenues for their personal or career development, their work or even new positions. These may be those people seeking significant career changes (Ibarra, 2002).

In summary, while engagement and thriving are complementary in their common dimension of energy, they may also have differences as reflected in the additional dedication/absorption dimensions for engagement and learning for thriving. In the next section, we examine similar as well as different antecedents and consequences of engagement and thriving.

Antecedents and consequences of engagement and thriving

What predicts thriving and/or engagement?

Regarding work engagement, the most examined predictors in empirical research have been job demands and job resources. The majority of studies on job demands indicate that job demands such as time pressure (Demerouti, Bakker, de Jonge, Janssen, & Schaufeli, 2001a), job insecurity (Mauno, Kinnunen, & Ruokolainen, 2007), shift work (Demerouti et al., 2001a), and work overload (Llorens, Bakker, Schaufeli, & Salanova, 2006) as well as work–family conflict (Mauno et al., 2007) deplete energy, create stress, and contribute to burnout. They can reduce the dedication inherent in work engagement because job demands can be so cognitively and physically taxing. They can cause people to disengage from work rather than be absorbed.

However, empirical findings on effects of work engagement do not allow clear conclusions yet: job demands have been found to have a positive effect on the absorption and dedication dimensions of job engagement (Llorens et al., 2006) but no effect on the vigor dimension (Mauno et al., 2007). However, when looking at associations between job demands (i.e., task demands) and engagement over time (3 weeks later) no relationship was found (Llorens, Schaufeli, Bakker, & Salanova, 2007). Furthermore, in research on teachers, job demands are found to have a negative relationship with the vigor and dedication dimensions of engagement (Hakanan, Bakker, & Schaufeli, 2006). Thus, there have been mixed findings regarding associations between job demands and engagement.

Job resources like job control (Hakanen, Bakker, & Demerouti, 2005; Mauno et al., 2007), social support (Schaufeli & Bakker, 2004), supervisory coaching (Schaufeli & Bakker, 2004), climate (Hakanen et al., 2006), and performance feedback (Demerouti et al., 2001a; Llorens et al., 2006), in contrast, are found to consistently fuel engagement and provide fortifications against stress to manage job demands. They help build dedication to and identification with work (Demerouti, Bakker, Nachreiner, & Schaufeli,

2001b). In short, job resources contribute to more engagement at work (Llorens et al., 2006) while findings for job demands are mixed.

Little research to date has explicitly examined relationships between job demands, resources, and thriving, so this discussion is more speculative. Parallel to their positive effect on work engagement, job resources are expected to fuel the vitality inherent in thriving at work. Resources protect against the depleting effects of stress (Hobfoll, 1989). Accordingly, prior research has found that job resources such as trust and connectivity (Carmeli & Spreitzer, 2008), decision-making autonomy, broad information sharing, and a climate of trust and respect (Porath, Spreitzer, & Gibson, 2008a) contribute to thriving at work.

However, we suspect that job demands could have a more positive effect on thriving. Job demands like a new assignment or a picky customer may create opportunities for learning that are also manifested in thriving. Job demands that stimulate cognitive and emotional arousal create opportunities for people to try new things, take risks, and be challenged at work – all phenomena that may contribute to learning and growth at work. While there is no explicit research on the effects of job demands on thriving yet, we can draw from related ideas developed in Quinn's (2005b) notion of the fundamental state of leadership. He talks about how hardships like a major promotion opportunity, risks of a professional failure, serious illness, divorce, or death of a loved one can jolt us out of our comfort zone to increase the potential for learning. It is because these kinds of life jolts help us tap into our most fundamental values and most basic instincts. These ideas are also consistent with a fairly large literature on post-traumatic growth in psychology (Tedeschi, Park, & Calhoun, 1998).

One might hypothesize that there is a curvilinear relationship between job demands and thriving as well as engagement. Too few job demands may impede learning and limit dedication. But too many job demands (e.g., jobs with extreme time pressure or with extreme high levels of emotional labor) may deplete resources to a degree that the person does not feel energized

anymore and thus reduce thriving and engagement. Or too many job demands may lead to information overload and thus overwhelm rather than stimulate personal growth (Porath, et al., 2008a). In summary, job demands may have a curvilinear effect on thriving and on engagement.

It may be the interaction of job demands and job resources that is most interesting in predicting work engagement (Bakker, Demerouti, & Euwema, 2005a) and speculatively thriving. The influence of job demands on engagement becomes positive when job resources are high (Bakker, Hakanen, Demerouti, & Xanthopoulou, 2007; Hakanen et al., 2005). We suspect the same interaction between job demands and job resources is likely to hold for thriving as well.

We further suggest that resource endogeneity may be another important issue related to both engagement and thriving. Job demands and resources often are modeled as outside influences which affect employees (i.e., they are exogenous or externally produced). They are characteristics of the context in which the individual is embedded. It may be that work engagement and thriving specify a perspective on resources that is more endogenous (i.e., interdependent) with the employee. Such endogeneity suggests a reciprocal causal relationship consistent with Hobfoll's (1989) notion of a gain spiral in the conservation of resources theory. Some recent empirical work, on a group of Spanish university students, does begin to address the possibility of resource endogeneity: Findings indicate that engagement increases efficacy beliefs which in turn increase task resources over time (Llorens et al., 2007).

We believe this endogeneity will hold with regard to thriving as well. Spreitzer et al. (2005) hypothesize that thriving employees will actively work to co-create their work environment. Rather than just being influenced by their work environment, thriving employees shape and influence their work environment to meet their needs for energy creation and learning opportunities. This may take the form of job crafting (Wrzesniewski & Dutton, 2001) where employees make small or large changes in the way they do their work so that it is more attuned with their needs. This co-creation may also take the form of issue selling (Dutton, Ashford, O'Neill, & Lawrence, 2001) where individuals proactively persuade the organization to value initiatives that are of importance to them. The theoretical development on thriving sees the environment both influencing and being influenced by individuals at work. The same seems to be true for work engagement. In the next section we turn to the key outcomes of engagement and thriving.

How do engagement and thriving add value to employees and their organizations?

Key outcomes of the two constructs
Given the complementary but distinct aspects of engagement and thriving, we believe that the two constructs may predict some of the same, but also some different, outcomes. In terms of similarity, both constructs have been found to be related to high job performance. Because of their energetic roots, both constructs provide the motivation necessary to perform. More specifically, engagement has been found to be related to higher employee performance and customer loyalty (Salanova, Agut, & Peiro, 2005). Thriving has been found to be related to career initiative and to in-role and extra-role job performance (Porath et al., 2008a).

Prior empirical research has found support for the relationship between engagement and numerous outcomes including organizational commitment (Llorens et al., 2006), reduced intention to quit/turnover (Hallberg & Schaufeli, 2006; Schaufeli & Bakker, 2004), career satisfaction (Koyuncu, Burke, & Fiksenbaum, 2006), reduced burnout and health problems (Bakker et al., 2006; Hallberg & Schaufeli, 2006; Koyuncu et al., 2006; Schaufeli, Taris, & Bakker, 2006b), engagement of their spouses (Bakker et al., 2005b), and proactive behaviors (Sonnentag, 2003).

Prior empirical research has demonstrated that thriving is positively associated with adjustments to changing circumstances (Porath et al., 2008a), creative and innovative behavior (Carmeli & Spreitzer, 2008) as well as organizational citizenship behavior. Each of these outcomes includes behaviors that go beyond employees' current role requirements. This may be because engaging in positive adjustment, innovative behaviors, and organizational citizenship behaviors (OCBs) may themselves be rewarding from a learning perspective. In other words, employees learn something from these behaviors.

We also find that thriving is related to other outcomes such as resilience (Sutcliffe & Vogus, 2003) – the ability to bounce back and learn from problems and obstacles (Porath et al., 2008b). Since empirical research on thriving is more nascent, we also speculate on other outcomes that may relate to thriving drawing from conceptual ideas proposed by Spreitzer et al. (2005). We expect that thriving is related to proactive future-oriented outcomes like job crafting to create work which is more energizing and meaningful (Wrzesniewski & Dutton, 2001), exploration and experimentation with new endeavors, and transformational leadership focused on change toward a new vision (Bass, 2005). We further expect that the focus on learning and personal development will link thriving to these change-oriented forms of outcomes.

What are the mechanisms that enable thriving to have these kinds of proactive outcomes? One possible mechanism is sense-making (Weick, 1993). Sense-making is the process of creating *situational awareness* and *understanding* in situations of high complexity or uncertainty in order to make decisions. The learning and energy manifested in thriving may enable more sense-making of the work environment. The learning inherent in thriving may enable people to be more mindful (Langer, 1990) in their work about what is working and what could be improved. People may also be more mindful about their work context resulting in a clearer idea about threats and opportunities (Jackson & Dutton, 1988) for growth and development in the future. Through enhanced sense-making, employees monitor their moment-to-moment activities, anticipate problems in advance, and respond promptly to adverse events in a flexible rather than rigid way. By operating "mindfully" and making critical adjustments in a timely manner, employees are better able to manage the unexpected and keep a future orientation in a challenging, highly competitive environment. In short, they can better manage the unexpected as they move toward the future (Weick & Sutcliffe, 2007).

A second possible mechanism is the development of behavioral repertoires. As employees learn, they gain more job-specific knowledge. As a result, they "gain possession of a deep and broad range of possible actions that one can apply to resolve challenges" (Sutcliffe & Vogus, 2003, p. 107). Further, when one's behavioral repertoire is expanded, the person is able to recombine existing knowledge to solve novel challenges in the future – this is often referred to as bricolage (Weick, 1993). As a result, employees feel more self-efficacious about their work. Self-efficacy in turn facilitates resilience by reducing a sense of defense perception, or the experience that one becomes self-defensive when facing crises or failures. By reducing a sense of defense perception, individuals are more likely to decentralize control over decision making to those who are experts in solving the problem; reduced defense perception also encourages one to utilize slack resources (cognitive, emotional, and relational), all of which increases resilience (Sutcliffe & Vogus, 2003). Thus, thriving may enhance the creation of behavioral repertoires which enable people to be resilient in the face of adversity or unexpected events.

In the next and final section, we discuss issues for leaders as they seek to develop followers who are both engaged and thriving at work. We also seek to understand under what conditions leaders may want to focus on one or the other.

Key issues for leaders in developing engaged and/or thriving followers at work

In our discussion of the key outcomes of engagement and thriving, a key assumption is that both constructs are something desirable for leaders to pay attention to and aspire for in their employees. In this section of the chapter, we address some key issues for leaders to consider for developing their followers to be engaged and thriving. We also offer some cautions for leaders in creating optimal amounts of engagement and thriving at work.

Leaders must emulate what they expect from their followers

In order for followers to be engaged and/or thriving at work, it is important that the leader models those positive affective-motivational states. If leaders lack energy in leading followers, it is likely that followers will emulate their low energy approach. Similarly if leaders lack dedication or absorption, followers will also take a more lackadaisical approach to doing their own work. In terms of thriving, if leaders themselves are not trying new things, risking failure with new approaches, it will be difficult for followers to feel psychologically safe to do so (Edmondson, 1999). Thus, leaders should act as a role model for engagement (Schaufeli & Salanova, 2007b) and thriving of their followers.

Leaders can select and develop a learning orientation in followers

Some people may have a predisposition to learning or a predisposition to positive emotions or high energy. Dweck and her colleagues (Dweck, 1986; Dweck & Leggett, 1988) identified several goal orientations. The two most relevant to engagement and thriving are orientations around performance and learning. When individuals adopt a performance-oriented goal, they strive either to demonstrate their competence via task performance to gain positive judgments or to avoid negative judgments of competence. Performance-oriented individuals, when faced with failure, often attribute failure to a fixed, poor ability, experience negative emotions, or withdraw from the activity completely. Conversely, when individuals adopt a learning-oriented goal, they strive to understand something new or to increase their level of competence for a given activity. Learning-oriented individuals like to seek out challenging tasks, believe that ability is malleable and incremental, and treat failure as a form of feedback rather than a judgment of their competence.

We suggest that if leaders can enable more learning goal-orientation in followers, they can generate more employee engagement and thriving. Employees who adopt a performance-oriented goal are more preoccupied with their own performance and how others evaluate their work. These employees therefore engage in many self-monitoring activities (How am I doing? How are others evaluating me?) that heighten a sense of conscious awareness or directed attention. As a result, energy is depleted as one becomes too preoccupied with the self and not on the task at hand (Kaplan, 1995). Therefore, adopting a performance-orientation is likely to deplete energy.

Conversely, employees who adopt a learning goal-orientation are less likely to suffer energy depletion as a resource of heightened self-monitoring. Further, seeking out challenges and engaging in explorative learning that arouses interest and curiosity further reduces self-consciousness and depletes less energy for directed attention. So leaders can enable more engagement and thriving by the energy produced from having employees who have a learning goal-orientation.

Leaders can buffer employees from job demands that are disabling rather than enabling

As described above, some kinds of job demands may prompt the learning inherent in thriving. They may provide the challenges that prod people out of their comfort zone into taking risks and trying new things (Quinn, 1996). While this may be true, some job demands may be especially detrimental for thriving and engagement because they deplete employees' energy. Role ambiguity, in particular, may be one dysfunctional job demand that leaders can address. Role ambiguity refers to the extent to which employees feel unsure about others' expectation about themselves (Rizzo, House, & Lirtzman, 1970). Role ambiguity depletes energy because when one is uncertain about one's role, it takes up individual cognitive capacity to figure out what needs to be done and who is responsible for doing it. Role ambiguity increases one's feelings of uncertainty and heightens a sense of self-awareness thereby depleting energy. To avoid undue role ambiguity, leaders should make clear each employee's roles and responsibilities so that boundaries and accountability are clear.

Leaders can build the organizational resources for engagement and thriving

Leaders create the context in which their followers work. As noted in our discussion of antecedents of work engagement, to enable employee engagement, leaders must develop a very specific context that provides job resources but moderates jobs demands (Schaufeli & Salanova, 2007b). Workers will be more engaged to the extent that they have the physical, political, financial, and social resources necessary to feel energized and dedicated to their work. Like the leader who wants to engage followers, the leader who wants to help followers thrive will also want to provide resources to help employees feel energized and be in a learning mode.

One crucial resource that leaders can provide is psychological safety. Psychological safety refers to one's belief that the environment is safe to take interpersonal risk. Accordingly, Edmondson (1999) demonstrated that team psychological safety is related to team learning behaviors such as feedback seeking, error discussion, which in turn increases team performance. She explained that when team members feel that the environment is safe to take risks, members are not preoccupied with possible embarrassment by others about their actions. Thus, we believe that psychological safety matters for engagement and thriving because it reduces the depletion of energy – a core dimension of both engagement and thriving – and learning (a key dimension of thriving).

When an environment is perceived to be psychologically unsafe, employees are more likely to be aware of the self in order to ensure that no mistake is made during the course of learning (akin to a performance-goal orientation). According to Kaplan (1995), such heightened level of conscious awareness requires directed attention and thus depletes energy, consciously or unconsciously. Conversely, by creating a psychologically safe environment, employees will be less likely to experience negative emotions associated with failure (learning or non-learning related). As failure is an expected part of risk-taking and learning behavior, employees experience fewer negative emotions. The conserved energy can then be used for subsequent resource-acquiring activities, such as learning, which contributes to a higher level of job performance. Several studies (e.g., Keith & Frese, 2005) have found that when told not to be worried about the learning outcomes or when forewarned about the negative emotions associated with failure, subjects in a learning task are better able to focus and concentrate on the task (i.e., cognitive energy), contributing to a high level of subsequent performance.

Another resource that leaders may provide to followers is individualized consideration with regard to what engages them and enables their thriving. Followers have different needs and priorities. What energizes one employee may be de-energizing to another. So to thrive, followers must have input in the development of their own work context. They must be empowered to shape and influence their work context. This may involve creating opportunities for job crafting (Wrzesniewski & Dutton, 2001), issue selling (Dutton et al., 2001) or other proactive behaviors at work (Grant & Ashford, 2008). Each of these behaviors requires autonomy which Porath et al. (2008b) have found to be related to thriving at work.

Leaders may need to regulate optimal levels of engagement and thriving

What kind of regulation of engagement or thriving is necessary? Since both constructs have an energy dimension one may ask: Is it possible to ever have too much energy? Certainly too much energy can contribute to hyperactivity or distractions. However, given how much job demands and stressors at work can deplete energy, we believe that in the real world, it would be a rare and unusual circumstance to have too much energy.

With regard to the other dimensions of engagement, it seems that too much dedication or absorption could create negative dynamics for employees as well as for work organizations. For example, too much dedication to the leader or the organization might create "yes" people who fail to question or challenge the status quo. Too much absorption might create so much intensity in the work at hand that people may fail to scan and sense changes in their work environment. The intensity can lead to mindlessness rather than

the mindfulness that is so important for high performance (Langer, 1990). In addition, too much absorption can contribute to work/family conflict because people are so absorbed in their work that they have a hard time separating at the end of the day. Thus, leaders should watch and moderate their followers' level of engagement. The decision about the right amount of engagement may vary based on the follower.

Regarding the second dimension of thriving – learning – it is also possible that too much thriving may be problematic for individuals and their organizations (Porath et al. 2008a). If people are in a constant learning mode, they may have trouble developing the competence necessary to do their normal day-to-day work. Too much learning may be over-stimulating to followers because they are always adapting to something new and never get the opportunity to become productive at work. Clearly, some people who have a stronger learning orientation (Dweck, 1986) may be able to tolerate a higher level of learning exposure. On the other hand, those with more of a performance orientation may benefit from a more moderate level of learning at work. Therefore, leaders should learn to regulate learning so that is it not overwhelming to followers.

Conclusion and directions for future research

Because both engagement and thriving are positive affective-motivational states, as we conclude, we ask, is one more important than the other? Do we need both constructs? The comparisons and contrasts described above suggest that both are important and relevant. Both constructs emphasize energy at work. Yet, each offers something unique beyond an understanding of how people are energized at work. Engagement focuses on one's connection to the present work. Beyond energy, it focuses on the dedication and absorption people have with regard to their work. It refers to building a closer connection to the work at hand in a way that builds rapt, captivated attention (i.e., absorption). Thriving, in contrast, takes the connection to work into an improvement-oriented direction. It is concerned with how people learn, grow, and develop into the

Practical implications

While much of the prior section on leadership has many practical recommendations for how leaders can facilitate more engagement and thriving, in this section, we offer a few additional practical implications for employees about how to enable more thriving and engagement at work. We focus our discussion specifically on energy because it is a core dimension of both thriving and engagement.

The literature on recovery (Sonnentag, 2003; Fritz & Sonnentag, 2005, 2006) suggests that individuals can build resources, such as energy or vigor, that have been depleted during the work day by being deliberate about how they spend their time outside of work on evenings, weekends, and vacations. For instance, non-work activities that are relaxing, that allow individuals to be both physically and cognitively detached from work, that provide individuals the opportunity to positively reflect on their work, and that create mastery can enable recovery of energy. Other recent research further suggests that: (1) regular breaks during the workday that allow the replenishment of self-regulatory energy (Trougakos, Beal, Green, & Weiss, 2008), (2) exposure to environmental scenes that capture one's interests (Kaplan, 1995, 2001), (3) access to snacks that provide glucose (Gailliot et al., 2007), especially those with a low glycemic index (Loehr & Schwartz, 2003), (4) caffeine for sustained cognitive attention (Lorist, Snel, & Kok, 1994), (5) moderate exercise (Thayer, 1987), (6) good sleep habits (Sonnentag, Binnewies, & Mojza, 2008; Zohar, Tzischinsky, Epstein, & Lavie, 2005), and (7) hydration (Loehr & Schwartz, 2003) also enable energy recovery.

Some emerging research even begins to suggest that individuals can sustain and generate energy at work. For example, having work that is meaningful and with clear purpose (Loehr & Schwartz, 2003), that matches an individual's skills with task difficulty (Quinn, 2005a), that provides positive feedback and a sense of progression (Bandura, 1997), that allows one to experience a sense of volition and autonomy (Ryan & Deci, 2000), and that involves high-quality connections (Dutton & Heaphy, 2003) are all mechanisms for enhancing energy in the doing of work.

future. In this way, the two constructs are complementary. In most cases organizations must be concerned with how to help people feel more connection (i.e., be engaged with) to work in the present situation, but also be focused on how to help people grow, develop, and learn their way (i.e., thrive). Thus, we conclude this chapter by reaffirming the relevance and necessity of both constructs and suggesting some relevant areas for future research.

We encourage future research in a number of domains related to thriving and engagement. First, we advocate the importance of studying the two in tandem to flesh out more of the distinctions proposed in this chapter. To date, these distinctions are conceptual yet speculative. We need empirical research that measures both thriving and engagement and establishes their discriminant validity through confirmatory factor analysis. We also need to demonstrate that their nomological networks, while overlapping, also offer some distinctive antecedents and outcomes (as suggested in the sections above).

Second, for thriving, we also suggest some additional research directions that may be especially fertile. Some of this agenda clearly builds on the more developed body of empirical research on engagement. While prior research demonstrates that thriving is related to outcomes including positive adaptation and job performance, it is important for researchers to develop a stronger

theoretical understanding of the contextual embeddedness of thriving at work. Such research will expand the nomological network of thriving, and strengthen the predictions and inferences made about thriving. What aspects of work design enhance thriving? As a starting point, Spreitzer et al. (2005) suggest some contextual factors at work that may enable or deplete thriving: discretion at work, broad information sharing, and a climate of trust and respect will facilitate more thriving at work. Future studies should more fully test these potential factors which have been theorized to enable the self-regulatory nature of individual thriving.

Building on the substantial body of research on recovery and engagement, future research on thriving should also examine how breaks, evenings, weekends, and other outside of work recovery activities may enable thriving at work. Winwood, Bakker, and Winefield (2007) have found that active and fulfilling non-work time activities can buffer the effects of work stress. And more directly, Sonnentag (2003) found that day-level recovery was positively related to engagement the next day.

Future research might also examine individual characteristics that may predispose some individuals to thrive more than others. Individual characteristics such as proactive personality (Bateman & Crant, 1993), growth-need-strength (Hackman & Oldham, 1980), positive affectivity

(Forgas & George, 2001), and a calling orientation (Wrzesniewski, McCauley, Rozin, & Schwartz, 1997) may be associated with greater thriving.

Another important future line of work includes the reciprocal influences and possible feedback loops that are consistent with social cognitive theory (Bandura, 1986; Wood & Bandura, 1989). Theoretical work proposed by Spreitzer et al. (2005) suggests that thriving generates resources in the system, with four kinds of resources that may be produced by those who are thriving: knowledge resources, positive meaning, positive affective resources, and relational resources. Each of these resources or assets fuels individuals and the systems in which they are embedded. Rather than simply consuming resources, thriving individuals may very well produce the resources that are likely to enhance their performance over time. Future research should be directed at better understanding the generative nature of thriving and the set of resources that may enable future thriving.

Notes

1. We thank the University of Michigan Ross School of Business and Bowling Green State University for their financial support of this research.
2. In addition, Shirom (2004) has questioned whether Schaufeli et al.'s (2002) conceptualizations of the vigor and dedication dimensions are too broad. He suggests that vigor should be distinct from resilience and that dedication should be distinct from involvement. Shirom further suggests that vigor should include cognitive, emotional, and physiological components.

References

Bakker, A. B., Demerouti, E., & Euwema, M. (2005a). Job resources buffer the impact of job demands on burnout. *Journal of Occupational Health Psychology*, *10*, 170–180.

Bakker, A. B., Demerouti, E., & Schaufeli, W. (2005b). The crossover of burnout and work engagement among working couples. *Human Relations*, *58*, 661–689.

Bakker, A. B., Hakanen, J. J., Demerouti, E., & Xanthopoulou, D. (2007). Job resources boost work engagement, particularly when job demands are high. *Journal of Educational Psychology*, *99*, 274–284.

Bakker, A., Van Emmerik, H., & Euwema, M. C. (2006). Crossover of burnout and engagement in work teams. *Work and Occupations*, *33*, 464–489.

Bandura, A. (1986). *The social foundations of thought and action*. Englewood Cliffs, NJ: Prentice-Hall.

Bandura, A. (1997). *Self-efficacy: The exercise of control*. New York: W. H. Freeman.

Bass, B. M. (2005). *Transformational leadership*. New York: Routledge.

Bateman, T., & Crant, M. (1993). The proactive component of organizational behavior. *Journal of Organizational Behavior*, *14*, 103–118.

Carmeli, A., & Spreitzer, G. (2008). *Trust, connectivity, and thriving: Implications for innovative work behavior*. Working paper.

Carver, C. S. (1998). Resilience and thriving: Issues, models, and linkages. *Journal of Social Issues*, *54*, 245–266.

Demerouti, E., Bakker, A. B., de Jonge, J., Janssen, P. P. M., & Schaufeli, W. B. (2001a). Burnout and engagement at work as a function of demands and control. *Scandinavian Journal of Work, Environment and Health*, *27*, 279–286.

Demerouti, E., Bakker, A. B., Nachreiner, F., & Schaufeli, W. B. (2001b). The job demands-resources model of burnout. *Journal of Applied Psychology*, *86*, 499–512.

Dutton, J., Ashford, S., O'Neill, O., & Lawrence, K. (2001). Moves that matter: Issue selling and organizational change. *Academy of Management Journal*, *4*, 716–737.

Dutton, J. E., & Heaphy, E. D. (2003). The power of high-quality connections. In K. S. Cameron, J. E. Dutton, & R. E., Quinn (Eds.), *Positive Organizational Scholarship: Foundations of a new discipline*. Berrett-Koehler: San Francisco.

Dweck, C. S. (1986). Motivational processes affecting learning. *American Psychologist*, *41*, 1040–1048.

Dweck, C. S., & Leggett, E. L. (1988). A social-cognitive approach to motivation and personality. *Psychological Review*, *95*, 256–273.

Edmondson, A. (1999). Psychological safety and learning behavior in work teams. *Administrative Science Quarterly*, *44*, 350–383.

Elliott, E. S., & Dweck, C. S. (1988). Goals – an approach to motivation and achievement. *Journal of Personality and Social Psychology*, *54*, 5–12.

Forgas, J. P., & George, J. M. (2001). Affective influences on judgment, decision making, and behavior in organizations: An information processing perspective. *Organizational Behavior and Human Decision Process*, *86*, 3–34.

Fritz, C., & Sonnentag, S. (2005). Recovery, health, and job performance: Effects of weekend experiences. *Journal of Occupational Health Psychology*, *10*, 187–199.

Fritz, C., & Sonnentag, S. (2006). Recovery, well-being, and performance-related outcomes: The role of work load and vacation experiences. *Journal of Applied Psychology*, *91*, 936–945.

Gailliot, M., Baumeister, R. F., DeWall, C. N., Maner, J. K., Plant, E. A., Tice, D. M., et al. (2007). Self-control relies on glucose as a limited energy source: Willingpower is more than a metaphor. *Journal of Personality and Social Psychology*, *92*, 325–336.

Gonzalez-Roma, V., Schaufeli, W. B., Bakker, A. B., & Lloret, S. (2006). Burnout and engagement: Independent factors or opposite poles. *Journal of Vocational Behavior*, *68*, 165–175.

Grant, A. M., & Ashford, S. J. (2008). The dynamics of proactivity at work. *Research in Organizational Behavior*, *28*, 3–34.

Hackman, J. R., & Oldham, G. (1980). *Work redesign*. Reading, MA: Addison-Wesley.

Hakanen, J. J., Bakker, A. B., & Demerouti, E. (2005). How dentists cope with their job demands and stay engaged: The moderating role of job resources. *European Journal of Oral Sciences*, *113*, 479–487.

Hakanen, J. J., Bakker, A. B., & Schaufeli, W. (2006). Burnout and work engagement among teachers. *Journal of School Psychology*, *43*, 495–513.

Hallberg, U. E., & Schaufeli, W. B. (2006). "Same same" but different: Can work engagement be discriminated from job involvement and organizational commitment? *European Psychologist*, *11*, 119–127.

Hobfoll, S. E. (1989). Conservation of resources: A new attempt at conceptualizing stress. *American Psychologist*, *44*, 513–524.

Ibarra, H. (2002). *Working identity*. Cambridge: Harvard Business School Press.

Jackson, S., & Dutton, J. (1988). Discerning threats and opportunities. *Administrative Science Quarterly*, *33*, 370–387.

Kahn, W. A. (1990). Psychological conditions of personal engagement and disengagement at work. *Academy of Management Journal*, *33*, 692–724.

Kaplan, S. (1995). The restorative benefits of nature: Toward an integrative framework. *Journal of Environmental Psychology*, *15*, 169–182.

Kaplan, S. (2001). Meditation, restoration, and the management of mental fatigue. *Environment and Behavior*, *33*, 480–506.

Keith, N., & Frese, M. (2005). Self-regulation in error management training: Emotion control and metacognition as mediators of performance effects. *Journal of Applied Psychology*, *90*, 677–691.

Koyuncu, M., Burke, R. J., & Fiksenbaum, L. (2006). Work engagement among women managers and professionals in a Turkish bank: Potential antecedents and consequences. *Equal Opportunities International*, *25*, 299–310.

Langelaan, S., Bakker, A. B., Van Doornen, L., & Schaufeli, W. B. (2006). Burnout and work engagement: Do individual differences make a difference? *Personality and Individual Differences*, *40*, 521–532.

Langer, E. J. (1990). *Mindfulness*. Boston, MA: Addison-Wesley.

Llorens, S., Bakker, A. B., Schaufeli, W. B., & Salanova, M. (2006). Testing the robustness of the job demands-resources model. *International Journal of Stress Management*, *13*, 378–391.

Llorens, S., Schaufeli, W., Bakker, A. B., & Salanova, M. (2007). Does a positive gain spiral of resources, efficacy beliefs and engagement exist? *Computers in Human Behavior*, *23*, 825–841.

Loehr, J., & Schwartz, T. T. (2003). *The power of full engagement*. New York: Free Press.

Lorist, M. M., Snel, M. J., & Kok, A. (1994). Influence of caffeine on information processing stage in well rested and fatigued subjects. *Psychopharmacology*, *113*, 411–421.

Mauno, S., Kinnunen, U., & Ruokolainen, M. (2007). Job demands and resources as antecedents of work engagement: A longitudinal study. *Journal of Vocational Behavior*, *70*, 149–171.

Nix, G. A., Ryan, R. M., Manly, J. B., & Deci, E. L. (1999). Revitalization through self-regulation: The effects of autonomous and controlled motivation on happiness and vitality. *Journal of Experimental Social Psychology*, *35*, 266–284.

Porath, C., Spreitzer, G., & Gibson, C. (2008a). *Social structural antecedents of thriving at work: A study of six organizations*. University of Michigan: Working paper.

Porath, C., Spreitzer, G., Gibson, C., Cobb, A., & Stevens, F. (2008b). *Construct validation of a measure of thriving at work*. University of Michigan: Working paper.

Quinn, R. (1996). *Deep change*. San Francisco: Jossey-Bass.

Quinn, R. (2005a). Flow in knowledge work: High performance experience in the design of national security technology. *Administrative Science Quarterly*, *50*, 610–641.

Quinn, R. (2005b). *Moments of greatness: Entering the fundamental state of leadership.* Harvard Business Review.

Rizzo, J. R., House, R. J., & Lirtzman, S. I. (1970). Role conflict and ambiguity in complex organizations. *Administrative Science Quarterly*, *15*, 150–163.

Rothbard, N. P. (2001). Enriching or depleting? The dynamics of engagement in work and family roles. *Administrative Science Quarterly*, *46*, 655.

Rothmann, S. & Jordaan, G. M. E. (2006). Job demands, job resources and work engagement of academic staff in South African higher education institutions. *South African Journal of Industrial Psychology*, *32*, 87–96.

Ryan, R. M., & Deci, E. L. (2000). Self-determination theory and the facilitation of intrinsic motivation, social development, and well-being. *American Psychologist*, *55*, 58–68.

Ryan, R. M., & Frederick, C. M. (1997). On energy, personality and health: Subjective vitality as a dynamic reflection of well-being. *Journal of Personality*, *65*, 529–565.

Ryff, C. D. (1989). Happiness is everything, or is it? Explorations on the meaning of psychological well-being. *Journal of Personality and Social Psychology*, *57*, 1069–1081.

Salanova, M., Agut, S., & Peiro, J. M. (2005). Linking organizational resources and work engagement to employee performance and customer loyalty: The mediation of service climate. *Journal of Applied Psychology*, *90*, 1217–1227.

Schaufeli, W. B., & Bakker, A. B. (2004). Job demands, job resources, and their relationship with burnout and engagement: a multi-sample study. *Journal of Organizational Behavior*, *25*, 293–315.

Schaufeli, W. B., Bakker, A. B., & Salanova, M. (2006a). The measurement of work engagement with a short questionnaire. *Educational and Psychological Measurement*, *66*, 701–716.

Schaufeli, W. B., Martinez, I. M., Pinto, A. M., Salanova, M., & Bakker, A. B. (2002). Burnout and engagement in university students: A cross-national study. *Journal of Cross-cultural Psychology*, *33*, 464–481.

Schaufeli, W. B, & Salanova, M. (2007a). Efficacy or inefficacy, that's the question. *Anxiety, Stress, and Coping*, *20*, 177–196.

Schaufeli, W. B., & Salanova, M. (2007b). Work engagement: An emerging psychological concept and its implications for organizations. In S. W. Gilliland, D. D. Steiner, & D. P. Skarlicki (Eds.), *Research in Social Issues in Management (Volume 5): Managing Social and Ethical Issues in Organizations* (pp. 135–177). Greenwich, CT: Information Age Publishers.

Schaufeli, W. B., Taris, T. W., & Bakker, A. B. (2006b). Dr. Jekyll or Mr. Hyde: On the differences between work engagement and workaholism. In R. J. Burke (Ed.), *Research companion to working time and work addiction* (pp. 193–220). Cheltenham, Glos, UK: Edward Elgar.

Shirom, A. (2004). Feeling vigorous at work? The construct of vigor and the study of positive affect in organizations. In D. G. P. L. Perrewe (Ed.), *Research in organizational stress and well-being* (Vol. 3, pp. 135–165). Greenwich, CN: JAI Press.

Shirom, A. (2006). Explaining vigor: On the antecedents and consequences of vigor on positive affect at work. In C. Cooper & D. Nelson (Eds.), *Positive Organizational Behavior* (pp. 86–101). Thousand Oaks, CA: Sage Publications.

Sonenshein, S., Dutton, J., Grant, A. Spreitzer, G., & Sutcliffe, K. (2005). *Narratives of thriving*. Paper presented at the Academy of Management Meeting, August 7–10, Hawaii.

Sonnentag, S. (2003). Recovery, work engagement, and proactive behavior: A new look at the interface between work and non-work. *Journal of Applied Psychology*, *88*, 518–528.

Sonnentag, S., Binnewies, C., & Mojza, E. J. (2008). Did you have a nice evening? A day-level study on recovery experiences, sleep and affect. *Journal of Applied Psychology*, *93*, 674–684.

Spreitzer, G., Sutcliffe, K., Dutton, J., Sonenshein, S., & Grant, A. M. (2005). A socially embedded model of thriving at work. *Organization Science*, *16*, 537–549.

Spreitzer, G. M. & Sutcliffe, K. (2007). Thriving in organizations. In D. Nelson & C. Cooper (Eds.), *Positive Organizational Behavior* (pp. 74–85). Thousand Oaks, CA: Sage.

Spreitzer, G. M., & Stevens, F. (2008). *Thriving at work: A construct validation.* Working paper, University of Michigan Ross School of Business.

Sutcliffe, K. M., & Vogus, T. J. (2003). Organizing for resilience. In K. S. Cameron, J. E. Dutton & R. Quinn (Eds.), *Positive organizational scholarship: Foundations of a new discipline* (pp. 94–110). San Francisco: Berrett-Koehler.

Te Brake, H., Gorter, A. M., Hoogstraten, J., & Eijkman, M. (2007). Professional burnout and work engagement among dentists. *European Journal of Oral Sciences*, *115*, 180–185.

Tedeschi, R. G., Park, C. L., & Calhoun, L. G. (1998). *Posttraumatic growth: Positive change in the aftermath of crises.* Mahwah, NJ: Lawrence Erlbaum.

Thayer, R. E. (1978). Factor analytic and reliability studies on the activation-deactiviation adjective check list. *Psychological Reports*, *43*, 747–756.

Thayer, R. E. (1987). Energy, tiredness, and tension effects of sugar snack versus moderate exercise. *Journal of Personality and Social Psychology*, *52*, 119–125.

Trougakos, J. P., Beal, D. J., Green, S. G., & Weiss, H. M. (2008). Making the break count: An episodic examination of recovery activities, emotional experiences, and positive affective displays *Academy of Management Journal*, *51*, 131–146.

Weick, K. E. (1993). *Sensemaking in organizations*. Thousand Oaks, CA: Sage.

Weick, K. E., & Sutcliffe, K. (2007). *Managing the unexpected: Resilient performance in an age of uncertainty*. San Francisco: Jossey-Bass.

Winwood, P., Bakker, A. B., & Winefield, A. (2007). An investigation of the role of non-work time behavior in buffering the effects of work stress. *Journal of Occupational and Environmental Medicine*, *29*, 862–871.

Wood, R., & Bandura, A. (1989). Social cognitive theory of organizational management. *Academy of Management Review*, *14*, 361–384.

Wrzesniewski, A., & Dutton, J. (2001). Crafting a job: Employees as active crafters of their work. *Academy of Management Review*, *26*, 179–201.

Wrzesniewski, A., McCauley, C. R., Rozin, P., & Schwartz, B. (1997). Jobs, careers, and callings: People's relations to their work. *Journal of Research in Personality*, *31*, 21–33.

Zohar, D., Tzischinsky, O., Epstein, R., & Lavie, P. (2005). The effects of sleep loss on medical residents' emotional reactions to work events: A cognitive-energy model. *Sleep*, *28*, 47–54.

11

From thought to action: Employee work engagement and job performance

Evangelia Demerouti and Russell Cropanzano

Over the past few decades, organizational scientists have shown that job performance is positively related to indicators of work adjustment, such as job satisfaction and psychological well-being. While these associations are generally consistent, however, we shall see that they are often of modest magnitude. In a like fashion, other scholars have found negative relationships between job performance and indicators of work-related health, such as burnout; once again the relationships are not large as one might intuitively expect. In this chapter, we will review this literature with a special focus on the relationship between work engagement and job performance. We argue that work engagement can be viewed as a positive indicator of work-related adjustment. Additionally, we shall also explore whether work engagement shows similar pattern of relationships with performance as its negative antipode, burnout, as well as other positive indicators like job satisfaction and happiness.

After first defining "job performance" for the purposes of this chapter, we will present the lessons that we can learn from constructs related to work engagement, namely job satisfaction (representing a broad positive work experience) and burnout (representing the negative antipode of work engagement). Next we present empirical evidence examining the predictive value for direct indicators of work engagement. Instead of simply listing studies containing relevant evidence, we pay special attention to theoretical approaches that can be used to explain the relationship between engagement and performance. More specifically we will focus on the following frameworks: Schaufeli and Bakker's (2004) three-dimensional approach to work engagement, the job demands-resources model, the conservation of resources theory, the happy productive worker thesis, and the broaden-and-build theory. We will argue that because work engagement captures both the "can do" and "will do" dimensions, it will tend to have stronger effects on job performance than other related constructs. The chapter will close with suggestions for future research in order to enhance our understanding on the relationship between work engagement and job performance.

What is job performance?

A moment's thought about the different jobs one has experienced is sufficient to illustrate how difficult it is to find an overall definition of performance that is applicable across jobs and even across situations. People work on innumerable tasks, and some of these do not even appear in formal job descriptions. When reviewing the engagement literature, the problem is magnified since different research traditions define "performance" in different ways. As we shall see, scholars exploring happy/productive workers have generally contented themselves with a single dimension of "overall" performance, whereas scholars exploring the conservation of resources (COR) model have designated three distinct performance factors. Given this theoretical complexity, it should not surprise us to find that scholars did not formulate precise definitions of performance until the 1990s (see especially, Campbell, 1990; Kanfer, 1990; Roe, 1999).

These different approaches refer to the *process* of performance, the *outcome* of performance, or both. The *process* approach focuses on the particular actions or behaviors that people undertake to achieve performance or what individuals do in their work situation (Roe, 1999). In our job as researchers, for example, a process definition would include such things as reading scientific literature, writing research proposals, and conducting studies. The *outcome* approach defines performance with respect to the products or services that are produced and whether these are consistent with the overall strategic goals of the organization (Roe, 1999). For example, an outcome important to researchers is the generation of scientific articles. In the present review, we will refer to outcome of performance, usually in the form of performance ratings. The main reason for this choice is practical. This is the way performance is defined in the literatures we examine here.

More specifically, and whenever the literature we are reviewing allows, we divide performance into its in-role and extra-role dimensions (for reviews, see Hoffman, Blair, Meriac, & Woehr, 2007; Organ, 1988). *In-role* performance is defined as those officially required outcomes and behaviors that directly serve the goals of the organization (Motowidlo & Van Scotter, 1994). In-role performance emphasizes the instrumentality of individual performance for organizational goals. While this is certainly very important, it does not describe the whole range of human performance at work. Every employee also displays (or should also display!) extra-role behaviors (Morrison, 1994). *Extra-role* or *contextual* performance is defined as discretionary behaviors on the part of an employee that are believed to directly promote the effective functioning of an organization without necessarily directly influencing an employee's productivity (MacKenzie, Podsakoff, & Fetter, 1991). Extra-role performance includes organizational citizenship behavior but also refers to such aspects as personal initiative (Frese & Fay, 2001) and the constructive exercise of voice (Van Dyne & LePine, 1998) that indicate proactive behaviors towards the organization. Moreover, citizenship behavior can be directed toward the organization and towards individuals (Dalal, 2005; Ilies, Nahrgang, & Morgeson, 2007).

There is another distinction that is worth making. Most of the studies that we review measure performance at the individual level, such as when a supervisor rates a particular employee. However, this is only part of the story. Other studies assess performance at the unit level, such as through the use of archival data collected by the organization itself.

How are constructs similar to engagement related to performance?

Since the literature on work engagement was inspired by existing constructs, it seems important to present briefly the existing insight regarding how these constructs are related to performance. More specifically we will focus on job satisfaction and burnout. Job satisfaction is a broad construct that represents a positive attitude. It has been widely researched. On the other hand, burnout is the hypothetical antipode of work engagement. As one might expect, the relationship between burnout and performance parallels that between engagement and performance, though burnout runs in the opposite direction, of course. While for the job satisfaction–job performance relationship we will restrict ourselves to results of different meta-analyses, for the burnout–job performance relationship we will particularly concentrate on studies using the conservation of resources theory. The reason is that this theory was successful in explaining the mechanism linking burnout and performance, and gaining insight into the underlying mechanisms is the ultimate aim of this chapter.

Job satisfaction

The elusive relationship between job satisfaction and job performance

Over the years, there has been considerable debate over the causal order between job satisfaction and performance and, even more fundamentally, whether a non-trivial association exists between these two variables. Scholars generally mark the start of the job satisfaction/performance debate with the publication of Brayfield and Crockett's (1955) review paper. Based on a qualitative summary of the available literature (meta-analysis was much in the future), these authors famously concluded that "satisfaction ... need not imply a strong motivation to outstanding performance" (p. 421). In fact, the reported correlation was a modest +.15. Nine years later Vroom (1964) published his own review of the literature, reporting a median job satisfaction/performance relationship of +.14.

As meta-analytic techniques became widely available, scholars were quick to make use of them. Unfortunately, they did not obtain identical results. Petty, McGee, and Cavender (1984) found a sizable corrected association, $\rho = +.31$, whereas Iaffaldano and Muchinsky's (1985) findings were less encouraging, $\rho = +.17$. Both of these meta-analyses had detractors. Organ (1988) cautioned that the Petty et al. findings might be inflated due to their flexible definition of "performance". Specifically, Petty and his colleagues may have included measures of citizenship behaviors and these, in turn, could show a stronger relationship to satisfaction than actual job performance. On the other hand, Wright (2005) pointed out that the Iaffaldano and Muchinsky results are probably conservative. He notes that the well-known +.17 relationship is actually an average that includes a number of facet measures (e.g., pay satisfaction, co-worker satisfaction, etc.). When one limits Iaffaldano and Muchinsky's findings to overall job satisfaction the correlated relationship is a respectable +.29, very close to the +.31 obtained by Petty and his colleagues.

In order to sort through these issues, a later meta-analysis was conducted by Judge, Thoresen, Bono, and Patton (2001), which paid careful attention to the earlier findings. These authors found a $\rho = +.30$. This is, of course, almost identical to the Petty et al. (1984) findings, and equally close to the Iaffaldano and Muchinsky (1985) findings for overall job satisfaction. On the basis of these considerations, the previous skepticism regarding the relationship between job satisfaction and performance has largely been overturned. It seems that satisfaction, or at least overall job satisfaction, exhibits a correlated association to job performance that is in the low .30s (Wright, 2005).

Conceptual models relating job satisfaction to performance

Scholars sometimes reflected on why satisfaction should *not* be related to performance, rather than why it should be (e.g., Fisher, 1980). As this skeptical climate was not conducive to strong theory development, conceptual progress languished (Judge et al., 2001). The solid results obtained by

Judge and his colleagues, though, should inspire future inquiry. As a guide, these authors discussed seven possible models explaining the job satisfaction/performance correlation.

- Model 1: Job satisfaction causes performance.
- Model 2: Performance causes job satisfaction.
- Model 3: Job satisfaction and performance are reciprocally related.
- Model 4: Job satisfaction and performance are both caused by a common third variable. That is, the association is spurious.
- Model 5: The relationship between job satisfaction and performance is moderated by some third variable or variables.
- Model 6: There is no relationship between job satisfaction and performance.
- Model 7: Job satisfaction and/or performance need to be reconceptualized. For example, it could be that affect causes job performance and job satisfaction is (or causes) affect.

With the likely exception of Model 6, the null association, the other six models cannot be ruled out (Judge et al., 2001). In addition, the different job satisfaction/performance models presented here are directional. They do not necessarily specify explicit and testable psychological mechanisms. For these reasons we know less about satisfaction and performance than we would like. As Judge and his colleagues observe, much work is still to be done.

A different concern has been raised by Wright (2005), Lyubomirsky, King, and Diener (2005), and Zelenski, Murphy, and Jenkins (2008). While not gainsaying the meta-analytically derived estimate of the satisfaction/performance relationship, these authors compare the size of this association with that between performance and other measures, such as psychological well-being. They argue that well-being, or simply "happiness" is a more substantial predictor. We shall return to this possibility later in the chapter.

Burnout and the conservation of resources model

The conservation of resources (COR) model (Hobfoll, 1988) is a general theoretical framework for understanding workplace stress. The COR model centers on the idea of *resources*, defined "as those objects, personal characteristics, conditions, or energies that are valued by the individual or that serve as a means for attainment of these objects" (Hobfoll, 1989, p. 516) There are a number of potential resources that can benefit an individual, including such things as social support (Halbesleben, 2006), autonomy, and involvement in decision-making. These resources are highly prized because they help individuals cope with job demands. Job demands include a number of things, such as daily hassles and role stress. To guard against resource depletion, and the resulting inability to cope with job demands, individuals seek to acquire, protect, and stockpile resources for their future needs. Stress, and more specifically burnout, results when there is a loss (or threat of loss) of one's resources or when one's resources are insufficient to cope with demands (Hobfoll & Freedy, 1993).

Early applications of the conservation of resources model to burnout

Overview of findings
In a theoretical paper, Hobfoll and Freedy (1993) argued compellingly that the conservation of resources model was a useful framework for understanding burnout (see also Halbesleben, 2006). One of the first attempts to use the COR framework to understand the burnout/performance relationship can be found in a longitudinal study conducted by Wright and Bonett (1997a). They measured Maslach and Jackson's (1986) three components of burnout: emotional exhaustion, depersonalization, and diminished personal accomplishment. Two years later they collected performance ratings. Even after the passage of time, the correlation between emotional exhaustion and performance was a healthy, $r = -.31$. Depersonalization and diminished personal accomplishment, however, were not significant predictors. Following up these findings, Wright

and Cropanzano (1998) dropped the two nonsignificant predictors – depersonalization and diminished personal accomplishment – and examined the predictive value of emotional exhaustion. As with the Wright and Bonett (1997a) study, exhaustion was significantly related to performance ($r = -.27$), though job satisfaction was not ($r = .11$). Emotional exhaustion also predicted voluntary turnover a year later ($r = .34$), but not job satisfaction ($r = -.05$). A final attempt to apply the COR model to the emotional exhaustion/performance relationship was less successful. Wright and Bonett (1997b) found that emotional exhaustion did not predict performance ratings.

This early stream of research helped establish that burnout, or at the very least emotional exhaustion, is a useful predictor of performance ratings. It may also be superior to job satisfaction, given the findings of Wright and Bonett (1997a) and Wright and Cropanzano (1998). Still, these early applications of the COR model were limited because they did little to investigate important psychological mechanisms implied by the theory. Most notably, the aforementioned work made scant effort to test process predictions. Additionally, this line of inquiry places great emphasis on emotional exhaustion but less on other more attitudinal dimensions of burnout (Wright & Bonett, 1997a, being an exception). As we shall discuss in the next section, more recent work by Halbesleben and Bowler (2005, 2007) has moved to address these issues.

Contemporary applications of the conservation of resources model

In applying the conservation of resources model to burnout, Halbesleben and Bowler (2005) began by considering their predictor (burnout) and their criterion (performance). Building on Demerouti, Bakker, Nachreiner, and Schaufeli (2001), they rejected Maslach and Jackson's (1986) three-factor structure and limited burnout to a pair of dimensions – emotional exhaustion and disengagement. They also divided job performance into three parts: in-role job performance, organizational citizenship behaviors directed toward the organization (OCB-O), and

organizational citizenship behaviors directed toward individuals (OCB-I).

Halbesleben and Bowler (2005) maintained that there is a causal path from exhaustion to disengagement, such that the former engenders the latter. Consonant with the COR framework, they then asserted that motivation is a beneficial resource. When people experience burnout they need to target their resources, including motivation, in order to get the maximal return. Thus, employees need to conserve in some areas and expand in others.

- Since individuals are exhausted, they tend to put less effort into their work. Hence, the relationship between emotional exhaustion and in-role job performance should be negative. Disengagement should be unrelated to in-role performance, as suggested by Wright and Bonett (1997a).
- Since individuals are exhausted and disengaged from the work environment they should seek to conserve energy and separate themselves from the organization. Hence, both emotional exhaustion and disengagement should be negatively related to OCB-O.
- Social support helps to reduce burnout (Halbesleben, 2006). As exhausted individuals are more in need of social support than their less exhausted counterparts, they will wish to maintain and not to jeopardize their interpersonal relationships. Thus, exhaustion should be *positively* related to OCB-I. Of course, disengaged workers are unconnected from others. Thus, disengagement should be *negatively* related OCB-I, as it is to OCB-O.

In an initial study, Halbesleben and Bowler (2005) found strong support for their model. Building upon these ideas, Halbesleben and Bowler (2007) next limited their focus to emotional exhaustion and the three productive families of behavior: in-role performance, OCB-O, and OCB-I. Dropping disengagement, they argued that there are three types of "strivings", or reasons, why individuals will work hard. *Achievement striving* pushes one to higher in-role performance, *status striving* pushes one to higher

OCB-O, and *communion striving* pushes one to higher OCB-I. All of the associations between strivings and productive work behavior are positive. Emotional exhaustion raises or lowers productivity by impacting these strivings. Thus, when exhausted workers are forced to conserve their motivational resources, they decrease their achievement and status strivings. This, in turn, lowers in-role performance and OCB-O, respectively. However, in an effort to build and maintain strong interpersonal relationships emotionally exhausted employees *increase* their communion striving. This, in turn, boosts OCB-I. Halbesleben and Bowler's empirical test was generally supportive.

How and why is engagement related to performance?

It is unfortunate for such an important topic that much of the empirical evidence on the relationship between work engagement and performance indicators is of recent vintage, often restricted, and unintegrated across conceptual traditions. The studies that we could locate are theoretically diverse, employing a number of distinct conceptual frameworks. They are also methodologically rich, several are cross-sectional but others are longitudinal and a few even use experience sampling techniques. As alluded to above, there is a good deal of variability on the criterion side as well, with some using overall measures of performance, other dividing performance into in-role and extra-role, and a few others even divided extra-role performance into subdimensions. Rather than shoehorning this work into an artificial taxonomy, we have decided to let the original scholars speak for themselves and describe each study within its own theoretical tradition. This approach should help the reader to understand the available evidence within its original context. Moreover, this narrative structure should also afford us an opportunity to sharpen the differences between the various conceptual approaches.

The Schaufeli and Bakker (2004) three-component model of engagement
Work engagement is a positive and fulfilling state of mind, which is characterized by vigor,

dedication, and absorption (Schaufeli & Bakker, 2004). *Vigor* refers to high levels of energy and mental resilience while working. *Dedication* pertains to feelings of significance, enthusiasm, inspiration, pride, and challenge. *Absorption* implies being fully immersed in one's work so that time flies and one has difficulty detaching oneself from one's work (see also May, Gilson, and Harter, 2004, for a comparable conceptualization of work engagement). Schaufeli and Bakker (2001) found that engaged employees take greater initiative and generate their own positive feedback. In short, engaged employees have high levels of energy and are enthusiastic about their work (see also May et al., 2004).

Schaufeli and Bakker developed their own instrument to measure work engagement, the Utrecht Work Engagement Scale (UWES; Schaufeli & Bakker, 2003; Schaufeli, Martinez, Marques Pinto, Salanova, & Bakker, 2002; see also Chapter 2, this volume). The UWES includes items for the assessment of the three engagement dimensions included in Schaufeli et al.'s definition: vigor, dedication, and absorption. Using this instrument, Schaufeli and colleagues tested the relationship between engagement and job performance in two studies. Schaufeli, Taris, and Bakker (2006) examined the relationship between trait work engagement and job performance. This cross-sectional study was conducted among a large and heterogeneous dataset of Dutch employees representing the Dutch workforce as a whole. In this study Schaufeli et al. found that work engagement was positively related to in-role performance ($\gamma = .37$), extra-role performance ($\gamma = .32$) and innovativeness ($\gamma = .37$) whereas workaholism was not. Interestingly, employees who work excessively hard and who work compulsively (i.e. workaholics) exhibit greater extra-role performance.

Expanding work engagement in the context of education, it has been shown that engaged students are more likely to pass their exams during subsequent semesters (Schaufeli et al., 2002). Using a sample of Spanish, Dutch, and Portuguese students, Schaufeli and his colleagues created a ratio of exams passed relative to the total number of exams taken. This ratio was higher for those reporting high levels of vigor. The ratio was also positively related to the burnout dimension of professional efficacy. Findings held irrespective of country, suggesting that that work engagement could predict academic performance of students.

The job demands-resources model

The job demands-resources model (JD-R; Demerouti et al., 2001) is a comprehensive framework for understanding the antecedents of health and motivation as well as their consequences including job performance. A unique feature of the JD-R is that it poses two parallel processes. The first is a heath-impairment process (what workers *can* do) and the second is a motivational process (what workers *will* do).

To understand these twin processes, it is helpful to distinguish between two sets of antecedents, job demands and job resources. *Job demands* are those aspects of the work that require effort on the part of the employee. Because of this effort, job demands are associated with psychophysiological costs such as exhaustion. They have the potential to impair health and thereby reduce performance. *Job resources* are those aspects of work that are functional to achieving goals, that minimize the effects of job demands, or stimulate personal growth. Because of these benefits, job resources are the hypothetical antecedents of motivation or engagement.

The JD-R model employs a two-dimensional conceptualization of burnout that is reflected in the Oldenburg Burnout Inventory (OLBI; Demerouti & Bakker, 2008). The first dimension ranges from exhaustion at the negative pole to vigor at the positive pole. The second dimension ranges from disengagement at the negative pole to engagement at the positive pole. This instrument was originally developed to assess burnout, but includes both positively and negatively phrased items, and hence, it can be used to assess work engagement and is therefore relevant to our present review (cf. González-Romá, Schaufeli, Bakker, & Lloret, 2006; Demerouti, Mostert, & Bakker, in press).

The assumptions of the JD-R model regarding these two processes have been supported

empirically. More importantly, Bakker, Demerouti, and Verbeke (2004) used the JD-R model to examine the relationship between job characteristics, burnout, and (peer-ratings of) performance. As anticipated, job demands (e.g., work pressure and emotional demands) were the most important antecedents of exhaustion. (In accordance with our earlier remarks, exhaustion was measured with vigor and exhaustion items.) In turn, exhaustion then predicted in-role performance. In contrast, job resources, such as autonomy and social support, were the most crucial predictors of disengagement. Disengagement, in turn, was a strong predictor of extra-role performance. In addition to these relationships, job demands were found to directly and positively affect in-role performance. In general, the model explained 8% of the variance in both peer-ratings of in-role and extra-role performance. These percentages are clearly higher than those reported in previous studies using other ratings of performance (about 1%, Schaufeli & Enzmann, 1998).

The importance of job and personal resources to work engagement and consequently to performance was further demonstrated through three diary studies. First, Xanthopoulou, Bakker, Demerouti, and Schaufeli (2009) investigated how daily fluctuations in job resources (autonomy, coaching, and team climate) are related to employees' work engagement and financial returns. Forty-two employees working in three branches of a fast-food company completed a questionnaire and a diary booklet over five consecutive workdays. Day-level resources had a direct positive relationship with day-level work engagement. Engagement, in turn, predicted daily financial returns – i.e. the total amount of money earned within a particular shift.

Second, Xanthopoulou, Bakker, Heuven, Demerouti, and Schaufeli (2008) examined whether daily fluctuations in colleague support predict day-levels of self-reported job performance through self-efficacy and work engagement. Forty-four flight attendants filled in a diary booklet before and after consecutive flights to three intercontinental destinations. Results of multilevel analyses revealed that work engagement mediated the relationship between self-efficacy and (in-role and extra-role) performance. In addition, colleague support had an indirect effect on in-role performance through work engagement. Interestingly, day-level work engagement showed similar positive relationships to both day-level in-role and extra-role performance.

These findings largely agree with the findings of another diary study by Sonnentag (2003) among a diverse sample of white collar workers. Specifically, she examined the relationship between day-level work engagement and two aspects of self-reported initiative: day-level personal initiative, and pursuit of learning (as two aspects of self-reported proactive behavior) over five consecutive days. It was found that work engagement helps employees in taking initiative at work and pursuing learning goals on a daily basis. In fact, work engagement mediated the relationship between recovery and proactive behavior.

To conclude, differentiating between in-role and extra-role performance as two specific performance dimensions increased the predictive value of burnout/work engagement experiences. A strength of the JD-R model is that it is relatively comprehensive, as it also explains how specific aspects of work environment, working through specific well-being indicators, influence various parameters of job performance.

Comparing the COR model to the JD-R model

Overall, Halbesleben and Bowler's COR (2005, 2007) framework shares much in common with the JD-R model. Both theories allow for an indirect path from emotional exhaustion to OCB, whereby the effect is at least partially mediated by disengagement, and both agree that disengagement is not directly related to in-role job performance. Finally, both frameworks acknowledge that physical exhaustion can lower effective work behaviors. However, the need to conserve resources appears to be more central to Halbesleben and Bowler's work, while the JD-R model posits a motivation path as well.

There are also a few differences. The COR model, and not JD-R, posits a direct path from emotional exhaustion to organizational citizenship behaviors. Another key difference lies in how the two theories think about OCB. The COR model has two types of citizenship behaviors, OCB-O and OCB-I, whereas the JD-R model has but one. Among scholars of citizenship behavior, the structure of OCB is the topic of an ongoing scholarly debate. A complete review of this literature would take us far beyond our current chapter. Suffice it to say, the distinction between OCB-O and OCB-I has been subject to a good deal of recent study, though there is not yet consensus as to whether OCB is best thought of as one variable or two (cf., Dalal, 2005; Hoffman et al., 2007; Ilies et al., 2007).

The happy/productive worker thesis

Research on the happy/productive worker thesis asserted that "happiness", although a lay concept, can be operationalized in a number of different ways (for reviews see Cropanzano & Wright, 2001; Wright, 2005; Wright & Cropanzano, 2004, 2007). The most conceptually sound approach refers to individuals who are prone to experience positive affect while also tending not to experience negative affect. This dimension has been studied under such names as subjective well-being (Diener, Suh, Lucas, & Smith, 1999), emotional well-being (Diener & Larsen, 1993), and psychological well-being (Cropanzano & Wright, 2001; Wright & Cropanzano, 2007). Wright and his colleagues argued that well-being, defined in this fashion, should be consistently related to job performance.

Evidence supported this contention. For example, among a small sample of human service workers, Wright, Bonett, and Sweeney (1993) found that employee-reported well-being predicted supervisory ratings of job performance collected a year later. This relationship was a sizable $r = +.42$. Later longitudinal studies obtained similar results, even with a range of control variables (Cropanzano & Wright, 1999; Wright & Bonett, 1997b).

The predictive value of well-being beyond job satisfaction

Wright (2005) has argued that well-being (or happiness) is a better predictor of job performance than is job satisfaction. Wright bases this conclusion on the evidence reviewed earlier. The correlation between job satisfaction and performance, even when suitably corrected via meta-analysis, is about .30. This seems to be the rough lower bound for the well-being/performance relationship, which can be in the .40s or even lower .50s. To our knowledge, there have been no meta-analyses conducted on the well-being/performance relationship. Thus, the associations cited by Wright are uncorrected for measurement error.

A number of studies have examined the incremental contribution of well-being beyond that of job performance. For example, in two field studies Wright and Cropanzano (2000) used both satisfaction and well-being to predict performance ratings; well-being was significant in both samples (ß = +.19, ß = +.20), while job satisfaction was not significant in either. In a later longitudinal study, Wright, Cropanzano, Denny, and Moline (2002) found that well-being was associated with performance ratings collected a year later. This was so even when Time 1 performance, job satisfaction, positive affectivity, and negative affectivity were included in the prediction equation. However, in the full equation the association between job satisfaction and performance dropped to nearly zero. Similar findings were also obtained in a recent experience sampling study by Zelenski et al. (2008). More research is needed on this topic, but the available evidence is consistent with Wright's (2005) suggestion that (a) happiness – defined as well-being – predicts job performance, and (b) it does so better than job satisfaction.

The predictive value of well-being beyond emotional exhaustion

A much smaller literature has compared well-being or happiness to emotional exhaustion. Wright and Bonett (1997b) compared emotional exhaustion to well-being. They found that well-being ($r = +.48$) but not emotional exhaustion ($r = -.12$) predicted job performance ratings 2 years after these measures were taken. When emotional exhaustion and psychological well-being were simultaneously used to predict performance, the relationship of well-being was significant (ß = +.24), while that of exhaustion was not (ß = −.10).

The studies reviewed here would seem to argue *for* the predictive value of psychological well-being. However, we are hesitant to say that they argue *against* the predictive value of burnout. It is dangerous to accept null results, such as those for exhaustion reported by Wright and Bonett (1997b). This is especially so, given that the sample sizes were modest, with $N = 44$ for Wright and Bonett and $N = 90$ for Wright et al. Given these considerations, it seems that more research is necessary on this topic.

The broaden-and-build model

Perhaps in response to the skeptical scholarly *zeitgeist* that surrounded early happy/productive worker research, initial investigations were more interested in establishing that a relationship did exist and less concerned with establishing why it might occur. Subsequent to this, a number of scholars (e.g., Wright, 2005; Wright & Cropanzano, 2007; Zelenski et al., 2008) have attempted to address this conceptual need. In so doing, proponents of the happy/productive worker thesis have tended to draw from Fredrickson's (2001, 2003) broaden-and-build model.

Fredrickson's (1998, 2001) work begins with the recognition that discrete emotional states automatically predispose us to certain classes of actions. For example, when embarrassed human beings tend to cover their faces, when angered we seek to attack, when frightened we attempt to withdraw from the threatening situation, and so on. The close link between emotion and action predispositions is well-documented and has long been known among emotion researchers (e.g., Ekman, 1992; Mascolo & Griffin, 1998; Mascolo & Harkins, 1998). Fredrickson's insight was to expand upon this point. As has been so often true in the history of psychological science, research on behavioral dispositions has tended to emphasize negative emotional states, such as rage, disgust, shame, and so on. Less work has emphasized the action tendencies associated with positive emotions (Fredrickson & Branigan, 2001, 2005).

According to the broaden-and-build theory of positive emotions (Fredrickson, 2001), certain positive emotions, including joy, interest, and contentment, all share the capacity to broaden people's momentary thought–action repertoires and build their personal resources (ranging from physical and intellectual resources to social and psychological) through widening the array of thoughts and actions that come to mind. For instance, joy broadens resources by creating the urge to play and be creative. Interest, another positive emotion, fosters the desire to explore, assimilate new information and experiences, and grow. Evidence for the broadening hypothesis has been reported by Fredrickson and Branigan (2005) and by Isen (2000). Accordingly, positive affect produces a broad and flexible cognitive organization as well as the ability to integrate diverse material. There are other benefits as well. Fredrickson (2003) suggests that positive emotion tends to encourage employee development, such as learning new skills and forming closer interpersonal relationships. It also fosters reasonable levels of risk taking and constructive responses to negative feedback (Wright, 2005; Wright & Cropanzano, 2007). Positive emotion also facilitates the use of cooperative interpersonal tactics and reduces workplace conflict (Barsade, Ward, Turnover, & Sonnenfeld, 2000).

The question is now whether this "broaden-and-build" effect will manifest itself in enhanced job performance, as one would assume because of the accumulation of personal resources. Fredrickson (2001, 2003) has argued that we need to investigate how (and whether) broadened thought–action repertoires are translated into decisions and actions. For example, in an organizational context, Fredrickson and Losada (2005) showed that when the ratio of managers' positive to negative emotions is relatively high, they ask more questions during business meetings, and their range between advocacy and questioning is broader (implying better performance).

Notice that the impact of emotions tends to accrue over time. Personal growth creates more positive emotion. This new wave of good feelings, in turn, produces still more efforts at individual development. In this fashion, well-being engenders a beneficial upward spiral with cumulative effects over time (Fredrickson & Branigan, 2005; Fredrickson & Joiner, 2002). The good news, of course, is that those high in well-being

tend to benefit well into the future. But there is a dark side to this analysis. Those low in well-being could tend to experience additional failures that, in turn, could cause their happiness to wane further (Wright, 2005; Wright & Cropanzano, 2004). In any case, the cumulating effects of well-being, regardless of whether they are positive or negative or both, may explain the persistent correlation between happiness and job performance obtained from a number of longitudinal studies (e.g., Cropanzano & Wright, 1999; Wright et al., 1993; Wright & Bonett, 1997b; Wright et al., 2002). This may also explain why well-being is able to predict performance even beyond the effect of daily mood states (e.g., Wright, Cropanzano, & Meyer, 2004).

While the broaden-and-build model has considerable promise, research on the happy/ productive worker thesis has seldom tested the psychological mechanisms directly. In one recent study, Wright, Cropanzano, and Bonett (2007) argued that the broaden-and-build model maintains that those who are high in well-being are better able to appreciate positive life events. If this is so, they reasoned, then having a satisfying job will do little to improve performance for those low in well-being, but will be effective in boosting performance for those high in well-being. In other words, it follows from the broaden-and-build model that happiness and job satisfaction should interact, with job satisfaction related to performance only when well-being is high. Wright and his colleagues obtained evidence in support of this contention. In a later study, Zelenski and his colleagues (2008) argued that the broaden-and-build model allowed that either positive emotion or negative emotion could predict job performance. They found that positive affect – rather than negative affect – seemed to be the more important mechanism. This is consistent with the work of Fredrickson (2003).

The recent work of Wright et al. (2007) and Zelenski et al. (2008) represents a promising effort to explore psychological mechanisms. On the whole, though, work on the happy/productive worker thesis has tended not to directly test the tenets of the broaden-and-build model (though other evidence exists, see Fredrickson &

Branigan, 2005; Fredrickson & Joiner, 2002). This paucity of theory-based research is a limitation that we hope will be addressed by future scholarship.

Self-regulation and the episodic process model

Beal, Weiss, Barros, and MacDermid (2005) provide a theoretical basis for examining the impact of state engagement on daily performance. In contrast to traditional performance models that regard within-person differences as error variance, their *performance episodes* model focuses on an individual's variability in performance over short periods of time. Their main argument is that individuals perform better when fully concentrated on the task at hand. Specifically, Beal et al. propose that resource allocation to the task is crucial for successful performance. If employees cannot allocate all of their resources to the current task, for example because they are constantly interrupted by telephone calls, they cannot perform optimally. Thus, replenishing and conserving (self-regulatory) resources is critical for successful performance during performance episodes and during a day (see Beal et al., 2005). As Beal and his colleagues suggest, tasks that are interesting to employees make it easier for them to effectively regulate their attention toward the task, while ignoring potential distractions. Because engaged employees are, virtually by definition, dedicated to their work tasks they should be intrinsically motivated to perform these tasks and thus to focus their attention. Thus according to this perspective work engagement leads to better task performance because employees will be more willing to direct their attention and other personal resources towards the task. Notice that Beal et al.'s emphasis on strategically using personal resources is conceptually similar to Halbesleben and Bowler's (2005, 2007) COR model of burnout. The difference, and it is a significant one, is that Beal et al. take a *within-persons* approach, whereas Halbesleben and Bowler take the complementary *between-persons* approach.

Although not examining particular performance episodes, Bakker and Bal (in press) concentrated on within-person performance during the working day. Bakker and Bal conducted their weekly diary study among teachers. They examined the relationship between daily job resources and day-levels of work engagement, as well as the relationship between day-level work engagement and day-level performance. Teachers were asked to fill in a diary questionnaire every Friday for five consecutive weeks. Performance represented a composite of in-role and extra-role performance as reported by each participant. Results showed that state levels of work engagement were fueled by job resources (like autonomy, exchange with the supervisor, and opportunities for development), and were predictive of in-role and extra-role performance ($\gamma = .42$, $p < .001$). These findings show how intra-individual variability in employees' work engagement can explain daily job performance.

Unit-level engagement

Thus far we have only considered engagement as an individual-level variable. However, as we discussed earlier, performance is often the result of the combined effort of many employees. It is therefore conceivable that the engagement of some team members could cross over, or impact, the engagement of others. In this way team engagement could be an emergent group-level phenomenon that has beneficial performance effects. We recognize that little research is currently available, but there are strong theoretical reasons to believe that unit-level engagement exists.

One possible mechanism is the so-called crossover or emotional contagion. Crossover or emotional contagion can be defined as the transfer of positive (or negative) experiences from one person to the other (Westman, 2001). If colleagues influence each other with their work engagement, they may perform better as a team. There is indeed some experimental evidence for such a process of emotional contagion. Barsade (2002) conducted an innovative laboratory study in which the transfer of moods among people in a group, and its influence on performance was examined. Using a trained confederate enacting mood, she showed that the pleasant mood of the confederate influenced (video coders' ratings of) the mood of the other team members during a simulated managerial exercise (leaderless group discussion). The positive mood contagion consequently resulted in more cooperative behaviour and better task performance.

In the workplace, researchers have focused on emotional contagion viewed as a reciprocal emotional reaction among employees who collaborate closely. In one field study, Totterdell, Kellet, Teuchmann, and Briner (1998) found evidence that the moods of team members were related to each other even after controlling for shared work problems. In addition, Bakker, Van Emmerik, and Euwema (2006), in their study among 2229 officers working in one of 85 teams, found that team-level work engagement was related to individual members' engagement. This was so even after controlling for individual job demands and resources. Thus, engaged workers who communicated their optimism, positive attitudes, and proactive behaviors to their colleagues thereby created a positive team climate independent of the demands and resources to which they were exposed. This suggests that engaged workers influence their colleagues. Consequently, they perform better as a team.

Recent studies have also indicated that engagement is positively related to objective performance on the department or unit level. The first study providing evidence for this relationship was conducted by Salanova, Agut, and Peiró (2005). Using a sample of contact employees from restaurant and hotel service units, they showed that levels of work engagement were positively related to customer ratings of performance, through service climate. Employees' level of work engagement had a positive impact on the service climate of hotels and restaurants, with an increase in the empathy that employees showed towards their customers as well as the service that they provided.

Using an impressive dataset of almost 8000 business units in 36 companies, Harter, Schmidt, and Hayes (2002) examined the relationship between business-unit level employee satisfaction–engagement and the business-unit outcomes of customer satisfaction, productivity, profit, employee turnover, and accidents. It should be noted, however, that the measure that Harter

et al. used captures actually satisfaction with job resources (i.e., the hypothetical antecedents of work engagement) rather than the work engagement experience itself. Using meta-analysis technique they found that the correlations for overall satisfaction as well as for employee engagement were highest for customer satisfaction–loyalty (+.32 and +.33, respectively) and employee turnover (−.36 and −.30), followed by safety (+.20 and +.32), productivity (+.20 and +.25), and profitability (+.15 and +.17). Thus, both overall satisfaction and employee engagement showed a similar pattern of relationships with several parameters of business unit performance measured on the business unit level.

What do we learn from this review?

This chapter presents a short review that covers a lot of ground. The diverse theories discussed here signify that work engagement may lead to enhanced performance, but that it does so through different mechanisms. This suggests that the link between work engagement and performance is probably not straightforward and simple. Various intervening mechanisms might be involved in explaining this relationship. Whether the relationship is due to enhancement of resources (as broaden-and-build and COR theory would suggest) or to appropriate resource allocation (as self-regulation theories would suggest) or to an appropriate team climate remains still a matter of speculation. It is therefore worthwhile to try to operationalize and empirically test the possible mechanisms. An excellent example in this direction testing the mediators of the relationship between exhaustion and job performance is the study by Halbesleben and Bowler (2007).

For all the strength of the three-part model of work engagement, it seems that the vigor aspect of work engagement is most crucial for performance. Recall that among the three burnout dimensions, exhaustion (or lack of energy) shows the more consistent pattern of (detrimental) relationships with performance. This has also been highlighted by Shirom (2006), who views work engagement as merely consisting of energy-vigor, namely physical strength, emotional energy, and cognitive liveliness. Moreover, measures of well-being include aspects of energy (or the lack of energy), alongside indicators of positive and negative feelings. Hence, measures of vigor or the absence of vigor (i.e., exhaustion) tend to be especially useful for predicting job performance. While our present case may be circumstantial, there is reason to believe that the vigor component of work engagement deserves special attention in the study of job performance.

Several of the reviewed studies applied an experience sampling design. These approaches are especially robust. Of course, they allow for the examination of differences between individuals. However, their unique strength is the ability to examine differences *within* individuals. They do so by following a set of people across days or situations or both. Evidence obtained from these studies raises the possibility that people may differ in the way in which they transform their work engagement into performance. These differences may be trait-like. Situations may have similar effects. It is also possible that different situations could transform feelings of work engagement into performance by way of different mechanisms. This would be state-like differences. For these reasons, experience sampling designs, such as diary studies, hold a special promise. Investigations employing this paradigm can allow scholars to cover trait-like and state-like differences in how engagement impacts job performance. The

studies by Xanthopoulou et al. (2008, 2009) represent excellent examples of this approach.

The role of individual characteristics, such as personality, in the engagement–performance relationship is understudied. However, it seems possible that some personality types are better able to transform their work engagement into increased performance than others. For instance, Demerouti (2006) found that flow at work (including components similar to work engagement, i.e., absorption, work enjoyment, and intrinsic work motivation) was beneficial for performance. However, this relationship only held for conscientious employees. For employees low on conscientiousness no relationship was found between flow and performance probably because they failed to invest their effort in beneficial tasks. Future studies examining the moderating effect of personality characteristics on the work engagement–performance relationship are therefore recommended.

The measurement of performance also seems to be highly relevant. As we saw, studies that succeeded in differentiating between specific performance dimensions were more successful in explaining variance in performance (examples are Bakker et al., 2004; Halbesleben & Bowler, 2007). Studies using global performance indicators (as those included in the review of Schaufeli & Enzmann, 1998) tended to do less well. This highlights that performance is not a uniform

Practical implications

An inevitable question after reviewing the relevant literature concerns the size of the relationship between engagement and job performance. It might be, for example, low and inconsistent, or perhaps no stronger than that of job satisfaction. On the other hand, the engagement–performance relationship could be stronger, perhaps as sizable as that between well-being and performance. Our impression is optimistic. It seems likely that work engagement could show relationships with performance that are similar in magnitude to those between well-being and performance. The explanation for this encouraging possibility can probably be found in the three-part configuration of work engagement, which includes energy (cf. vigor), motivational (dedication), and resource allocation (absorption) components. The additive value of these three components is greater than the independent effect of each.

This means for organizations that they should care for the work engagement of their employees. In order to create engaged and productive workforces organizations should conduct interventions focused on the empowerment of job resources because these have been found to promote personal resources and (consequently) work engagement. For instance, supervisors should provide a clear description of the tasks that the employees need to perform; they should provide employees with all the means that are necessary for achieving their tasks, and should set clear and objective standards to gauge employees' performance. In a related vein we saw in this review that the exhaustion component of burnout seems to play an antagonistic role with work engagement since it influences (in-role) performance unfavorably. Therefore, organizations should try to reduce or optimize job demands such that they do not have undesirable effects on employee health, for instance by providing ergonomic facilities for physical tasks, and variation between demanding and undemanding tasks. Thus for organizations it is important to promote work engagement and to minimize the risk for burnout such that they can obtain optimal performance from their employees.

construct and that work engagement is differentially related to different aspects of performance. Moreover, both the JD-R model and the COR model explicitly maintain that there are different psychological processes linking engagement to different performance dimensions. It is not trivial to suggest that we need more studies using objective measures of individual performance although we found several studies utilizing objective measures of unit performance.

Finally, the stimulus-organism-response explanations are inadequate to explain the relationship between work engagement and job performance. Rather, (work) environmental and individual experiences including work engagement seem to act as contingency factors affecting performance, which enhances the complexity of this phenomenon but also the challenge for both researchers and practitioners alike.

References

Bakker, A. B., & Bal, P. M. (in press). Weekly work engagement and performance: A study among starting teachers. *Journal of Occupational and Organizational Psychology.*

Bakker, A. B., Demerouti, E., & Verbeke, W. (2004). Using the job demands-resources model to predict burnout and performance. *Human Resource Management, 43,* 83–104.

Bakker, A. B., Van Emmerik, I. J. H., & Euwema, M. C. (2006). Crossover of burnout and engagement in work teams. *Work and Occupations, 33,* 464–489.

Barsade, S. G. (2002). The ripple effect: emotional contagion and its influence on group behavior. *Administrative Science Quarterly, 47,* 644–677.

Barsade, S. G., Ward, A. J., Turner, J. D. F., & Sonnenfeld, J. A. (2000). To your heart's content: A model of affective diversity in top management teams. *Administrative Science Quarterly, 45,* 802–836.

Beal, D. J., Weiss, H. M., Barros, E., & MacDermid, S. M. (2005). An episodic process model of affective influences on performance. *Journal of Applied Psychology, 90,* 1054–1068.

Brayfield, A. H., & Crockett, W. H. (1955). Employee attitudes and employee performance. *Psychological Bulletin, 52,* 396–424.

Campbell, J. P. (1990). Modeling the performance prediction problem in industrial and organizational psychology. In M. D. Dunnette & L. M. Hough (Eds.), *Handbook of Industrial and Organizational Psychology* (Vol. 1, pp. 687–732). Palo Alto: Consulting Psychologists Press.

Cropanzano, R., & Wright, T. A. (1999). A five-year study of change in the relationship between well-being and job performance. *Consulting Psychology Journal, 51,* 252–265.

Cropanzano, R., & Wright, T. A. (2001). When a "happy" worker is really a "productive" worker: A review and further refinements of the happy–productive worker thesis. *Consulting Psychology Journal, 53,* 182–199.

Dalal, R. S. (2005). A meta-analysis of the relationship between organizational citizenship behavior and counterproductive work behavior. *Journal of Applied Psychology, 90,* 1241–1255.

Demerouti, E. (2006). Job resources, work-related flow and performance. *Journal of Occupational Health Psychology, 11,* 266–280.

Demerouti, E., & Bakker, A. B. (2008). The Oldenburg Burnout Inventory: A good alternative for the assessment of burnout and engagement. In J. Halbesleben (Ed.), *Handbook of stress and burnout in health care.* New York: Nova Science.

Demerouti, E., Bakker, A. B., Nachreiner, F., & Schaufeli, W. B. (2001). The job demands-resources model of burnout. *Journal of Applied Psychology, 86,* 499–512.

Demerouti, E., Mostert, K., & Bakker, A. B. (in press). Burnout and work engagement: A thorough investigation of the independency of the constructs. *Journal of Occupational Health Psychology.*

Diener, E., & Larsen, R. J. (1993). The experience of emotional well-being. In M. Lewis & J. M. Haviland (Eds.), *Handbook of emotions* (pp. 405–415). New York: Guilford Press.

Diener, E., Suh, E. M., Lucas, R. E., & Smith, H. L. (1999). Subjective well-being: Three decades of progress. *Psychological Bulletin, 125,* 276–302.

Ekman, P. (1992). An argument for basic emotions. *Cognition and Emotion, 6,* 169–200.

Fisher, C. D. (1980). On the dubious wisdom of expecting job satisfaction to correlate with performance. *Academy of Management Review, 5,* 607–612.

Fredrickson, B. L. (1998). What good are positive emotions? *Review of General Psychology, 3,* 300–319.

Fredrickson, B. L. (2001). The role of positive emotions in positive psychology: The broaden-and-build theory of positive emotions. *American Psychologist, 56,* 218–226.

Fredrickson, B. L. (2003). Positive emotions and upward spirals in organizations. In K. S. Cameron, J. E. Dutton, & R. E. Quinn (Eds.), *Positive organiza-*

tional scholarship: Foundations of a new discipline (pp. 163–175). San Francisco, CA: Berrett-Koeler.

Fredrickson, B. L., & Branigan, C. A. (2001). Positive emotions. In T. J. Mayne & G. A. Bonnano (Eds.), *Emotion: Current issues and future directions* (pp. 123–151). New York: Guilford Press.

Fredrickson, B. L., & Branigan, C. A. (2005). Positive emotions broaden the scope of attention and thought-action repertoires. *Cognition and Emotion*, *19*, 313–332.

Fredrickson, B. L., & Joiner, T. (2002). Positive emotions trigger upward spirals toward emotional well-being. *Psychological Science*, *13*, 172–175.

Fredrickson, B. L., & Losada, M. F. (2005). Positive affect and the complex dynamics of human flourishing. *American Psychologist*, *60*, 678–686.

Frese, M., & Fay, D. (2001). Personal Initiative (PI): A concept for work in the 21st century. *Research in Organizational Behavior*, *23*, 133–188.

González-Romá, V., Schaufeli, W. B., Bakker, A. B., & Lloret, S. (2006). Burnout and work engagement: Independent factors or opposite poles? *Journal of Vocational Behavior*, *62*, 165–174.

Halbesleben, J. R. B. (2006). Sources of social support and burnout: A meta-analytic test of the conservation of resources model. *Journal of Applied Psychology*, *91*, 1134–1145.

Halbesleben, J. R. B., & Bowler, W. M. (2005). Organizational citizenship behaviors and burnout. In D. L. Turnipseed (Ed.), *Handbook of organizational citizenship behaviors: A review of good soldier activity* (pp. 399–414). Hauppauge, NY: Nova Science.

Halbesleben, J. R. B., & Bowler, W. M. (2007). Emotional exhaustion and job performance: The mediating role of motivation. *Journal of Applied Psychology*, *92*, 93–106.

Harter, J. K., Schmidt, F. L., & Hayes, T. L. (2002). Business-unit-level relationship between employee satisfaction, employee engagement, and business outcomes: A meta-analysis. *Journal of Applied Psychology*, *87*, 268–279.

Hobfoll, S. E. (1988). *The ecology of stress*. New York: Hemisphere.

Hobfoll, S. E. (1989). Conservation of resources: A new attempt at conceptualizing stress. *American Psychologist*, *44*, 513–524.

Hobfoll, S. E., & Freedy, J. (1993). Conservation of resources: A general stress theory applied to burnout. In W. B. Schaufeli, C. Maslach, & T. Marek (Eds.), *Professional burnout: Recent developments in theory and research* (pp. 115–129). New York: Taylor & Francis.

Hoffman, B. J., Blair, C. A., Meriac, J. P., & Woehr, D. J. (2007). Expanding the criterion domain? A quantitative review of the OCB literature. *Journal of Applied Psychology*, *92*, 555–566.

Iaffaldano, M. T., & Muchinsky, P. M. (1985). Job satisfaction and job performance: A meta analysis. *Psychological Bulletin*, *97*, 251–273.

Ilies, R., Nahrgang, J. D., & Morgeson, F. P. (2007). Leader-member exchange and citizenship behaviors: A meta-analysis. *Journal of Applied Psychology*, *92*, 269–277.

Isen, A. M. (2000). Positive affect and decision making. In M. Lewis & J. M. Haviland-Jones (Eds.), *Handbook of emotions* (2nd ed., pp. 417–435). New York: Guilford Press.

Judge, T. A., Thoresen, C. J., Bono, J. E., & Patton, G. K. (2001). The job satisfaction – job performance relationship: A qualitative and quantitative review. *Psychological Bulletin*, *127*, 376–407.

Kanfer, R. (1990). Motivation theory and industrial and organizational psychology. In M. D. Dunnette & L. M. Hough (Eds.), *Handbook of Industrial and Organizational Psychology* (2nd ed., Vol. 1, pp. 75–170). Palo Alto, CA: Consulting Psychologists Press.

Lee, R. T., & Ashforth, B. E. (1996). A meta-analytic examination of the correlates of the three dimensions of job burnout. *Journal of Applied Psychology*, *81*, 123–133.

Lyubomirsky, S., King, L., & Diener, E. (2005). The benefits of frequent positive affect: Does happiness lead to success? *Psychological Bulletin*, *131*, 803–855.

MacKenzie, S. B., Podsakoff, P. M., & Fetter, R. (1991). Organizational citizenship behavior and objective productivity as determinants of managerial evaluations of salespersons. *Organizational Behavior and Human Decision Processes*, *50*, 123–150.

Mascolo, M. F., & Griffin, S. (1998). Alternative trajectories in the development of anger-related appraisals. In M. F. Mascolo & S. Griffin (Eds), *What develops in emotional development?* (pp. 219–249). New York: Plenum Press.

Mascolo, M. F., & Harkins, D. (1998). Toward a component systems model of emotional development. In M. F. Mascolo & S. Griffin (Eds.), *What develops in emotional development?* (pp. 189–217). New York: Plenum Press.

Maslach, C., & Jackson, S. E. (1986). *Maslach burnout inventory manual* (2nd ed.). Palo Alto, CA: Consulting Psychologists Press.

May, D. R., Gilson, R. L., & Harter, L. M. (2004). The psychological conditions of meaningfulness, safety and availability and the engagement of the human spirit at work. *Journal of Occupational and Organizational Psychology*, *77*, 11–37.

Morrison, E. W. (1994). Role definitions and organizational citizenship behavior: The importance of employee's perspective. *Academy of Management Journal*, *37*, 1543–1567.

Motowidlo, S. J., & Van Scotter, J. R. (1994). Evidence that task performance should be distinguished from contextual performance. *Journal of Applied Psychology*, *79*, 475–480.

Organ, D. W. (1988). *Organizational citizenship behavior: The good soldier syndrome.* Lexington, MA: Lexington Books.

Petty, M. M., McGee, G. W., & Cavender, J. W. (1984). A meta-analysis of the relationships between individual job satisfaction and individual performance. *Academy of Management Review*, *9*, 712–721.

Roe, R. A. (1999). Work performance: A multiple regulation perspective. In C. L. Cooper & I. T. Robertson (Eds.), *International review of industrial and organizational psychology* (Vol. 14, pp. 231–335). Chichester: Wiley.

Salanova, M., Agut, S. & Peiró, J. M. (2005). Linking organizational resources and work engagement to employee performance and customer loyalty: The mediation of service climate. *Journal of Applied Psychology*, *90*, 1217–1227.

Schaufeli, W. B., & Bakker, A. B. (2001). Werk en welbevinden: Naar een positieve benadering in de Arbeids- en Gezondheidspsychologie [Work and well-being: Towards a positive approach of occupational health psychology]. *Gedrag & Organisatie*, *14*, 229–253.

Schaufeli, W. B., & Bakker, A. B. (2003). *UWES – Utrecht Work Engagement Scale: Test Manual.* Utrecht University, Department of Psychology (http://www.schaufeli.com).

Schaufeli, W. B., & Bakker, A. B. (2004). Job demands, job resources, and their relationship with burnout and engagement: A multi-sample study. *Journal of Organizational Behavior*, *25*, 293–315.

Schaufeli, W. B., & Enzmann, D. (1998). *The burnout companion to research and practice: A critical analysis.* London: Taylor & Francis.

Schaufeli, W. B., Martinez, I., Marques Pinto, A. Salanova, M., & Bakker, A. B. (2002). Burnout and engagement in university students: A cross national study. *Journal of Cross-Cultural Psychology*, *33*, 464–481.

Schaufeli, W. B., Taris, T. W., & Bakker, A. B. (2006). Dr. Jekyll or Mr. Hyde: On the differences between work engagement and workaholism. In R. J. Burke (Ed.), *Research companion to working time and work addiction* (pp. 193–217). Cheltenham, Glos, UK: Edward Elgar.

Shirom, A. (2006). Explaining vigor: On the antecedents and consequences of vigor as a positive affect at work. In C. L. Cooper & D. Nelson (Eds.), *Organizational behavior: Accentuating the positive at work* (pp. 86–100). Thousand Oaks, CA: Sage Publications.

Sonnentag, S. (2003). Recovery, work engagement, and proactive behavior: A new look at the interface between non-work and work. *Journal of Applied Psychology*, *88*, 518–528.

Totterdell, P. S., Kellet, K., Teuchmann, K., & Briner, R. B. (1998). Evidence of mood linkage in work groups. *Journal of Personality and Social Psychology*, *74*, 1504–1515.

Van Dyne, L., & LePine, J. A. (1998). Helping and voice extra-role behaviors: Evidence of construct and predictive validity. *Academy of Management Journal*, *41*, 108–119.

Vroom, V. H. (1964). *Work and motivation.* New York: Wiley.

Westman, M. (2001). Stress and strain crossover. *Human Relations*, *54*, 557–591.

Wright, T. A. (2005). The role of "happiness" in organizational research: Past, present and future directions. In P. L. Perrewé & D. C. Ganster (Eds.), *Research in occupational stress and well-being* (Vol. 4, pp. 221–264). Amsterdam, NL: Elsevier.

Wright, T. A., & Bonett, D. G. (1997a). The contribution of burnout to task performance. *Journal of Organizational Behavior*, *18*, 491–499.

Wright, T. A., & Bonett, D. G. (1997b). The role of pleasantness-based and activation-based well-being in performance prediction. *Journal of Occupational Health Psychology*, *2*, 212–219.

Wright, T. A., Bonett, D. G., & Sweeney, D. A. (1993). Mental health and work performance: Results of a longitudinal field study. *Journal of Occupational and Organizational Psychology*, *66*, 277–284.

Wright, T. A., & Cropanzano, R. (1998). Emotional exhaustion as a predictor of job performance and voluntary turnover. *Journal of Applied Psychology*, *83*, 486–493.

Wright, T. A., & Cropanzano, R. (2000). Psychological well-being and job satisfaction as predictors of job performance. *Journal of Occupational Health Psychology*, *5*, 84–94.

Wright, T. A., & Cropanzano, R. (2004). The role of psychological well-being in job performance: A fresh look at an age-old quest. *Organizational Dynamics, 33,* 338–351.

Wright, T. A., & Cropanzano, R. (2007). The happy/productive worker thesis revisited. In J. J. Martocchio (Ed.), *Research in personnel and human resources management* (Vol. 26, pp. 269–307). Amsterdam, NL: Elsevier.

Wright, T. A., Cropanzano, R., & Bonett, D. G. (2007). The moderating role of employee positive well-being on the relation between job satisfaction and job performance. *Journal of Occupational Health Psychology, 12,* 93–104.

Wright, T. A., Cropanzano, R., Denny, P. J., & Moline, G. L. (2002). When a happy worker is a productive worker: A preliminary examination of three models. *Canadian Journal of Behavioural Science, 34,* 146–150.

Wright, T. A., Cropanzano, R., & Meyer, D. G. (2004). State and trait correlates of job performance: A tale of two perspectives. *Journal of Business and Psychology, 18,* 365–383.

Xanthopoulou, D., Bakker, A. B., Demerouti, E., & Schaufeli, W. B. (2009). Work engagement and financial returns: A diary study on the role of job and personal resources. *Journal of Occupational and Organizational Psychology, 82,* 183–200.

Xanthopoulou, D., Bakker, A. B., Heuven, E., Demerouti, E., & Schaufeli, W. B. (2008). Working in the sky: A diary study on work engagement among flight attendants. *Journal of Occupational Health Psychology, 13,* 345–356.

Zelenski, J. M., Murphy, S. A., & Jenkins, D. A. (2008). The happy-productive worker thesis revisited. *Journal of Happiness Studies, 9,* 521–537.

12

Building engagement: The design and evaluation of interventions

Michael P. Leiter and Christina Maslach

This book makes the case for work engagement. It is a desirable state in itself and it promotes outcomes that are valuable to employees and to their companies. If positive results accrue from an engaged workforce, then the logical conclusion is that any efforts that enhance work engagement should yield important benefits. But the critical question is, what kinds of interventions will be effective in building work engagement?

Interventions may occur on the level of the individual, workgroup, or an entire organization. At each level, the number of people affected by an intervention and the potential for enduring change increases. Historically, there has been a tendency to focus on individual strategies rather than social or organizational ones. This is particularly paradoxical given that research has found

that situational and organizational factors play a bigger role in the workplace than individual ones. Also, individual strategies are less effective in the workplace, where the person has much less control of stressors than in other domains of his or her life. There are both philosophical and pragmatic reasons underlying the predominant focus on the individual, including notions of individual causality and responsibility, and the assumption that it is easier and cheaper to change people rather than organizations (Maslach & Goldberg, 1998).

However, throughout this chapter, we will focus the discussion on management interventions. We do not intend to exclude the possibility or advisability of people taking individual actions to enhance their engagement with work. Indeed, we have considered a variety of individual approaches elsewhere (Leiter & Maslach, 2005b). However, a focus on management interventions reflects a major theme in this book: the organizational context. Management interventions consider people within a social environment. They appreciate that a major part of personal identity comprises the relationships in which people participate and the roles with which they interact with others. Work organizations define relatively consistent behavior settings that have an emotional charge resonating with the importance of work to personal survival, status, achievement, and affiliation.

At this point in time, the work on designing, implementing and evaluating interventions to build engagement has barely begun. Thus, the goal of this chapter is to lay out some of the important issues for the future development of engagement interventions, and to provide a forward-looking discussion. We will begin by looking at prior work on burnout interventions, to determine if there are any valuable lessons that could be adapted to the focus on engagement. Is the goal of building engagement qualitatively different from that of reducing burnout, or are they related in some way? What are the challenges of doing applied research on the evaluation of specific interventions? We will try to illustrate some of these issues by citing a few recent examples of such intervention research. Next, we will consider the conceptual frameworks of two models of work engagement, and discuss their implications for designing and carrying out interventions to build engagement in the workplace. We hope that the guidelines that emerge from this analysis will inform future work in this area.

Lessons learned from burnout

Our view is that work engagement and burnout describe two distinct psychological relationships with work. Their defining characteristics pertain to employees' subjective experience of energy, their capacity to become involved in work, and their work-related sense of efficacy. Burnout resides on the negative end of these three interrelated qualities; work engagement on their positive pole. The most straightforward objective for intervention is moving people towards work

engagement and away from burnout. From an individual perspective, the focus would be on ways to directly influence a person's subjective experience of engagement – i.e., to have greater vigor, dedication, etc. From a management perspective, the goal would be to manipulate conditions in the work environment that would have a downstream impact on engagement – i.e., to develop work environments that are more conducive to work engagement and less conducive to burnout.

Positive versus negative conceptual frameworks

Over the initial decades of burnout research, researchers primarily posed the question from the perspective of alleviating the undesirable condition of burnout. Since the introduction of work engagement as a positive alternative to burnout (Maslach & Leiter, 1997), researchers and practitioners have also asked how to develop the positive alternative. There are clear benefits of using this positive framework of building engagement. One is motivational, in that people are often more enthusiastic about working to make things better, rather than having to deal with unpleasant problems. In a related way, an organization that is focused on engaging its employees, and becoming a workplace of choice, may have a more positive image than one that is grappling with burnout. Indeed, many organizations have found that a focus on burnout poses a liability for them, and so they have avoided acknowledging that there may be problems or that they are undertaking any efforts to deal with it. Thus the opportunity to address these issues by focusing on the positive goal of work engagement provides organizations with a less risky, and potentially more successful, process of change.

The contrast of the engagement to the burnout framework raises the question of whether interventions designed to help individuals or work groups become more positive differ qualitatively from interventions designed to alleviate people in distress. One perspective would argue that the answer is "yes", because efforts to address deficits are quite different from those that promote gains. For instance, when addressing symptoms, the ideal target is reducing their incidence to zero;

when building new capacities, the ideal target is establishing them in abundance. In a parallel way, Herzberg (1966) argued over 40 years ago that two distinct processes governed job satisfaction. Hygiene needs governed basic physiological needs, and motivator needs governed social, esteem, and actualization needs. Herzberg's approach argued that the two processes respond to distinct interventions. More recently, with regard to general emotional states, some theorists have proposed that positive and negative emotional states are independent of one another (Diener, 1999). In terms of work engagement, Schaufeli and Bakker (2004) have argued that work engagement is separate and independent of burnout, citing the independence of the negative subscales of the Maslach Burnout Inventory (MBI) from the positive subscales of the Utrecht Work Engagement Scale (UWES) (despite their strong correlations).

This "independence" perspective could be reflected in different goals for engagement and burnout interventions, and/or in different processes. With respect to goals, engagement interventions might focus on creating positive working conditions, such as new learning opportunities or sufficient resources to carry out the job. In contrast, burnout interventions might focus on alleviating negative working conditions, such as reducing conflict between co-workers or transferring an ineffective supervisor. The question with regard to processes is whether leading someone from a neutral state to work engagement uses the same processes as leading someone from burnout to a neutral state. In both cases, the shift is in a more positive direction, but the difference may lie in whether the basic approach is to correct individual flaws or organizational problems, or to promote individual self-actualization or organizational productivity. This raises the question of whether an engagement intervention is necessarily a more positive process than a burnout one.

An alternative to the "independence" perspective, however, is that reducing burnout and building engagement are essentially two sides of the same coin, and that these interventions are actually more similar than different. The theory here is that there is a continuous quality underlying interventions both to alleviate distress and to enhance positive qualities, and that any effort to address one goal will automatically have an impact on the other. A research question that would follow from this theory is whether an intervention described as a positive process to enhance work engagement would have a measurable impact on burnout as well. This would suggest that future research should include assessments of the full scope of both engagement and burnout, rather than using only one or the other.

This "linked" perspective for engagement and burnout is reflected in the connections that are fairly common between negative problems and positive solutions. It is often the presence of the former that inspires efforts to achieve the latter. This raises the question of whether a defined problem is necessary to inspire an engagement intervention; that is, can any attempts to achieve improvements or positive gains be framed without any reference to a more negative baseline or prior deficit? Furthermore, is it necessary to solve a negative problem before one can build something positive? A different question has to do with the sharper focus provided by a negative problem, as opposed to the more vague goal of something that is "better." That is, is it more noticeable to solve a problem than to establish an improvement?

Another relevant lesson from burnout research is that the managerial and organizational interventions appropriate to addressing burnout are not unique to burnout (Maslach, Schaufeli, & Leiter, 2001). Preventing burnout amounts to good management, and this could be the case with work engagement as well. It may be difficult to define an intervention to enhance work engagement that would have a unique impact on this experience without a consistent impact on the general quality of worklife.

One of the few studies on an engagement intervention illustrates a number of the issues raised here (Salanova, Cifre, & Rodriguez, 2008). An intervention process was developed for a targeted organizational unit, and its impact was compared to that of an appropriate control unit. The central problem identified in the initial diagnostic process was an inadequate innovation culture in the target unit. The team developed a strategy including three elements: job redesign, training, and supervisor replacement. For the job redesign, the department was divided into two smaller units, with the goal of increasing job control, creativity, and innovation among employees. For training, management developed a better process for conveying core job functions. The most definitive intervention was to replace the supervisor. The company relocated him to another area and to another job, which matched his technical and social competencies better. Management then promoted one of the unit members who possessed the social and technical competencies required for the job, and who had the trust of her co-workers. Following this intervention, the researchers found significant within-subject improvements from pretest to posttest in engagement (the UWES vigor and dedication scales), as well as in a measure of innovation climate, professional efficacy, and perceived competence.

This study is admirable (and rare) in both its development of a complex intervention strategy and its assessment of the impact of the intervention on engagement. However, it also demonstrates the role of negative problems within a focus on improvement, in that the impetus for the intervention was to address a problem – a poor intervention culture which was related in part to a supervisor's shortcomings. It utilizes the same kind of interventions as those used to deal with other organizational goals besides engagement, such as job redesign and personnel reassignment. The study design did not address the question of whether the intervention might have had an impact on burnout as well, but the possibility of a reduction in burnout is not excluded. The results show that the intervention had a positive effect, but its capacity to target work engagement uniquely, in either theory or practice, is not entirely clear.

Challenges of intervention research

In reviewing prior work on job burnout, a primary lesson to be learned is that there is surprisingly little published research on successful burnout strategies (see Halbesleben & Buckley, 2004; Maslach & Goldberg, 1998; Maslach,

Schaufeli, & Leiter, 2001). Many articles translate the applied implications of their studies into recommendations for intervention methods, but rarely are such interventions actually implemented or evaluated. We are convinced that this lapse, instead of reflecting a lack of interest, points towards intrinsic difficulties for exploring the essential research questions.

One challenge is the ability to do multiple, pre–post assessments of any intervention. Although some organizations are willing to participate in one assessment, those who will continue to do so, within a longitudinal design, are much fewer in number. Even when there is an initial commitment to do multiple assessments, other factors can change that (e.g., a change in organizational leadership). Many cross-sectional studies represent the first stage of a longitudinal project that was never completed.

Even when multiple assessments are possible, another challenge is the ability to link individual data over time. Employee respondents usually want to remain anonymous, so the typical procedure for linking data records rests upon codes generated by individual respondents and unknown to researchers or employers. The researchers' capacity for linking individual data depends entirely on respondents entering the codes accurately on each reassessment.

Another challenge is that any organization that is so concerned about its current problems that it is conducting assessments of them, is likely to be operating in a somewhat volatile environment. Thus, major events may occur during the span of the longitudinal study, which could have distinct effects across the organization, such that an overall assessment of change would encompass units that are increasingly distressed with units that are improving and units unaffected by events. In the field setting of organizations with demanding missions, researchers have little control over such disruptive events.

A fundamental problem in designing and implementing organizational interventions is that they require making major changes in core elements of worklife. Interventions must address substantive management processes and structures to have a consequential impact on employees' experience of worklife. Making noticeable and enduring changes in these aspects of worklife amounts to highly intrusive interventions. In changing relevant policies and procedures, the intervention requires company executives to exercise considerable organizational authority to enact these changes. This level of enthusiastic support from senior executives is rarely available to academic researchers.

Organizations are not ignoring work engagement or burnout; they are going about addressing these issues differently. Organizations, especially private sector companies, prefer to work with professional management consultants rather than with academic researchers when considering organizational development initiatives. One reason for this preference is that companies prefer strict confidentiality. They view the potential for such activity to generate published research as a problem rather than a virtue. One reason for secrecy is to avoid exposing the company's weaknesses; a related reason is to gain a competitive advantage in competitive environments. After investing the time and taking the risk of change, they do not wish to give the knowledge away, as academic researchers do.

This condition not only deprives the research literature of relevant information, it brings an opportunity cost. Consulting initiatives use the opportunity to test interventions. The program evaluations associated with such interventions are rarely as rigorous as are academic evaluations: the consultant has a clear financial and reputational interest in the results. And the outcomes are not published through peer-reviewed processes. This approach will continue to be a challenge, whether research intends to address burnout or build work engagement.

Focus on managerial interventions

Management interventions begin with changing management processes as a means of changing employees' experience of worklife. Management processes are management's direct responsibility: they have the authority and the knowledge to change them. Employees' thoughts and feelings are not under management's direct control, but are accessible indirectly through changes in the

management environment. Whether addressing burnout or building engagement, management's leverage begins with changing management processes.

An important element of management interventions is measuring these processes to ascertain both areas where change is needed, as well as the impact of any interventions. To assist organizations in this task, we developed a survey package that included measures of relevant aspects of workplace environments, key management processes, and the burnout-engagement continuum (Leiter & Maslach, 2000).[1] Many organizational risk factors have been identified in research across many occupations (see reviews by Maslach & Leiter, 2005b; Maslach et al., 2001; Schaufeli & Enzmann, 1998). These factors can be summarized within six key domains of the workplace environment: workload, control, reward, community, fairness, and values. The measure of employees' assessment of these six areas is the Areas of Worklife Scale (AWS), which includes both positively and negatively worded items, giving it a special value when considering interventions with implications for both burnout and work engagement (see Leiter & Maslach, 2004, for a more extensive presentation and analysis of the research utilizing the AWS). The measure of management processes that is used in conjunction with the AWS assesses employees' evaluation of supervision, communication, skill development, workgroup cohesion, and organizational change. Finally, the burnout–engagement continuum is assessed by the MBI-GS (Schaufeli, Leiter, Maslach, & Jackson, 1996).

This entire survey process functions as an organizational "checkup," in that it generates a profile of the strengths and strains of an organizational unit. This information guides the development of management interventions. It also provides a benchmark against which to assess further developments, as the survey can be repeated at regular intervals.

Using the checkup process for engagement intervention

This organizational checkup process was utilized by the Christian Reformed World Relief

Committee (CRWRC), a church-based organization providing community development services to distressed areas around the world (CRWRC, 2006). As a faith-based organization, CRWRC has employees with an exceptionally strong dedication to their job (Edward, 2005; Fry, 2005). They undertake demanding work requiring relocation to difficult regions for modest compensation and are highly engaged with this mission. The CRWRC did not have any indications of a widespread burnout problem among its employees, but it was concerned about the potential risk of burnout and wanted to ensure that it was providing the necessary support for its employees' energetic dedication to their work. Thus, the primary objective for the organizational checkups was to ensure and enhance work engagement among the staff.

The organization undertook the checkup survey to assure that it was supporting employees, especially those working in challenging field placements, as well as possible. In addition to the three core measures (MBI-GS, AWS, and management issues), the survey included specific assessment of field settings (infrastructure, work/family boundaries), as well as items pertaining to religious faith, health, and future plans. The survey provided an opportunity to evaluate employees' experience and determine actions that would be supportive of their continued work.

Figure 12.1 summarizes the overall findings for the core checkup survey at Time 1 (2005). The profile displays the three groups of measures, with positive scores upwards and negative scores downward. The midline of the graph represents the average score of a normative dataset ($N = 16,678$; Leiter & Maslach, 2006). The scale of the profile, based on the normative population distribution, is from one standard deviation above the normative level to one standard deviation below.

The overall impression from the profile is that the organization was doing well. The only measures below the normative level were efficacy and workload. Community and communication were only slightly above the normative line. Supervision, although positive, had only a moderate rating. All other measures were comfortably in the positive range. The overall profile defined the

challenge for this organization as building work engagement rather than alleviating burnout.

Subsequent discussions led to additional detailed analyses on issues pertaining to the social context of work including community, leadership, and communications. Together, this set of measures pointed to the organization's social environment as an area of vulnerability. The diagnosis resonated with the Director and Co-Directors. They recognized the special challenges associated with the organizational structure in which 100 employees worked in 23 countries in five continents. Increasingly, the challenge was the unreliability of communication technologies in some of the field settings. For example, in some of the remote work sites, electricity was available for only a limited time daily. The convergence of the data with their experiential knowledge confirmed the importance of addressing these challenges.

The CRWRC management team implemented a set of actions in 2006, which emphasized executive commitment to core values:

- A Co-director's Priorities Advancement Council (CPAC) was created to ensure that responsible parties followed up on decisions made at key meetings with timely implementation.
- In its semiannual meeting with regional team leaders/supervisors, the human resource department was tasked with the priority to increase supervisory skills, including the aspect of communication with staff.
- Management committed to strict attention to follow-up of leadership meetings.
- To enhance better communication, financial support was given to country field offices that were limited by low speed internet service to improve their access to higher speed technology or service and also to ensure a backup system of power.
- Central office personnel committed to improved follow-up on monthly morale reports through phone calls.

One year after the initial survey, a second survey assessed the same items. Figure 12.2 displays a combined profile for 2005 and 2006. The graphs

FIGURE 12.1

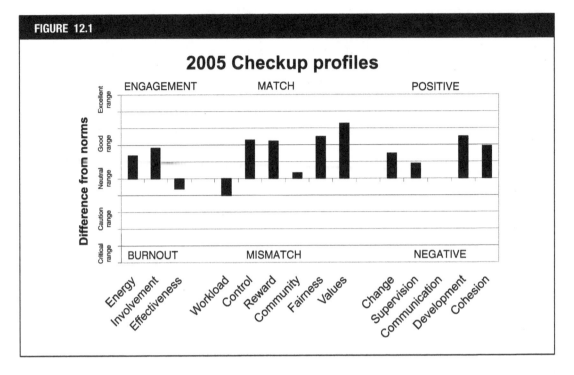

Checkup profile: Time 1.

FIGURE 12.2

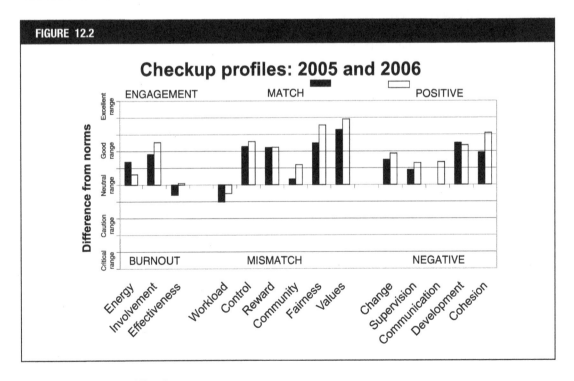

Checkup profile: Time 1 and Time 2.

indicate an overall improvement. The only score that was more negative in 2006 than in 2005 was the exhaustion–energy dimension, but this difference was small.

The focus on social environments prompted a prediction that there would be significantly more positive scores on community, communication, supervision, and workgroup cohesion. Between groups t-tests that contrasted the cohort completing the survey in 2005 with those completing the survey in 2006 confirmed significant differences on communication ($t_{(179)} = 2.88$, $p < .005$) and workgroup cohesion ($t_{(179)} = 2.46$, $p < .01$). Pairwise t-tests on the 62 individuals whose data could be linked across the two datasets found a significant difference only for communication ($t_{(61)} = 2.66$, $p < .01$). With the smaller N for this comparison, the difference for workgroup cohesion fell short of significance ($t_{(61)} = 1.76$, $p = .083$).

The professional efficacy score, which was one of the two measures below the normative level in 2005, made a modest change in the positive direction ($t_{(61)} = 1.22$, ns). Although its initial level did not indicate a problem per se, this aspect of engagement was low relative to the other two aspects, energy and involvement. A possible reason for this incongruity was that relief field work gives few opportunities for clear progress. Work on community development or disaster relief in challenging circumstances is necessarily slow. Setbacks are common, and some barriers to progress – poverty, climatic conditions, or harsh government regimes – can be impervious to influence. The professional efficacy items focus primarily on employees' sense of mastery from participating in effective, meaningful work.

The 2006 survey also included four items measuring vigor and absorption as additional aspects of work engagement (Schaufeli & Bakker, 2004). These items focus primarily on the meaningfulness of work activities themselves, without regard for their impact. Field workers in the survey scored significantly more positively on these absorption items than they scored on the efficacy subscale ($t_{(42)} = 2.81$, $p = .008$). Their colleagues who were not members of field-based teams did not differ on these two measures ($t_{(43)} = 1.76$, $p = .086$). This analysis argues for absorption and vigor as qualities of work engagement that are relevant for the specific population of field workers.

Using the checkup process for early predictors

One approach to intervention is to focus on certain targeted groups of individuals, who are in more need of some organizational attention, rather than developing a generic, "one size fits all" change program. One such target group would be those people who are showing some early signs of burnout, so that preventive interventions could occur more effectively. In a longitudinal study that utilized the organizational checkup survey (Maslach & Leiter, 2008), we found that two different patterns of scores on the survey measures were able to identify those employees who were at risk for burnout one year later. The "early warning" score occurred when employees showed only one dimension of burnout – that is, they reported either high exhaustion or high cynicism, but not both. The "tipping point" score occurred when these same employees reported a mismatch, in terms of their expectations and the workplace reality, in at least one of the six workplace areas. Those employees experiencing a negative tipping point moved towards burnout a year later; however, those employees with a positive view of these six areas were able to cope with the early signs of burnout and moved toward work engagement a year later.

The implication of this research for intervention is that the pattern of scores on the organizational checkup measures could identify in advance those employees who are especially vulnerable to change, and could help organizations determine what interventions might move to change toward engagement rather than burnout. In some cases, the necessary intervention might need to be focused on a particular individual; however, if these early predictor scores cluster within particular organizational units, then a targeted organizational strategy might be more effective.

In another longitudinal study, we found that

scores on the exhaustion dimension of the MBI-GS were predictive of injury rates a year later (Leiter & Maslach, 2009). Further, Bakker, Van Emmerik, and Van Riet (2008) found burnout to predict later performance. Again, the practical implication of such research findings is that these scores can be used as early indicators of potential problem areas and can thus guide interventions that will reduce future risk and promote a more engaged and healthy workplace environment.

Conceptual framework for engagement interventions

Having reviewed some of the lessons learned from prior research, we now turn our attention to theoretical models of engagement. These theoretical models can provide some important pragmatic guidance for interventions, by identifying the most critical goals for building engagement, and pointing to the most effective processes for achieving them.

Two models of engagement guide our consideration of intervention principles. The job demands–resources (JD-R) model (Bakker & Demerouti, 2007; Demerouti, Bakker, Nachreiner, & Schaufeli, 2001) considers burnout as resulting from a dysfunctional energy process. It builds upon the conservation of resources (COR) model (Hobfoll, 2001) that gives a central role to personal energy resources in maintaining well-being. In addition to energy, a second process in JD-R concerns motivation. An adequate or generous level of job resources motivates employees to work in ways that inspire vigor and dedication. This second process leads to work engagement. Together, the two processes describe parallel processes – energetic and motivational – that lead to distinct outcomes – burnout and work engagement.

The second model agrees that two processes influence psychological relationships with work, but has a distinct perspective on how they operate. The energy process of the mediation model of burnout and engagement (Leiter & Maslach, 2004, 2005a) focuses specifically on exhaustion rather than on burnout generally. In this model exhaustion mediates the relationship of worklife

experiences, such as work overload, on cynicism. That is, the mediation model designates a distinct role for exhaustion: it is a physical, emotional, and cognitive experience resulting from excessive demands. Exhaustion, in turn, limits employees' capacity to become involved in their work.

In contrast to the JD-R model's emphasis on resources, the mediation model considers value congruence to be the critical issue in the second process. From the perspective of the mediation model, resources are intrinsic to the first process: work overload is not simply a matter of demand; it arises from an imbalance of demands over resources. Consistent with the COR model, the mediation model proposes that the management of resources is definitive in maintaining energy at work. As such, resources *per se* are not the definitive quality of the second process.

Congruence of individual and organizational values defines the second process. The mediation model contends that employees bring personal values to work. These values are shaped by many forces, including personal experience, family dynamics, cultural background, and professional training. They may pertain to work ethic (the virtue of persistence in adversity), ethical codes (honesty versus manipulative communication), or professional roles (the primacy of customer service). Organizational values arise through an institution's history and culture. Organizations espouse values through mission statements and enact values through their allocation of time, materials, and money. The mediation model proposes that employees, as individuals and as members of workgroups, continually appraise organizational actions in terms of the actions' inherent values. They evaluate the values they perceive in an organization's actions against its espoused values to determine sincerity, and against personal values to determine congruence. For example, nurses may perceive a small hospital's purchase of expensive MRI equipment as valuing technology or revenue generation over its espoused value of adequate staffing ratios. They may interpret the purchase as indicating insincerity or even hypocrisy. Further, nurses who have a deep commitment to adequate staffing as a means of supporting high quality worklife or enabling a better standard of care will experience the equipment purchase as an indicator of value incongruity. The mediation model proposes that employees' evaluations of value congruity evolve through ongoing interactions with the organization, although it is possible that a definitive event – such as receiving or losing a promotion – may be authoritative in an individual's relationship with an organization. The model acknowledges that employees work with limited and often inaccurate information. They may perceive organizational actions through cultural, workgroup, or personal biases that incline them to view management action generously or critically. Their personal evaluations gain additional impact when they resonate with others with whom they interact at work (Leiter & Harvie, 1997).

The mediation model proposes that value congruity has a broad positive impact. Experiences that confirm value congruence empower employees by aligning their personal concerns with those of a larger social entity. Congruence is energizing in that it implies access to organizational resources to pursue objectives of personal as well as corporate importance, thereby improving the demand/resource balance. It increases involvement in work by confirming the importance of work objectives to which employees are personally attracted. It increases efficacy by providing social confirmation for the activities in which employees maintain an energetic involvement. Regardless of whether one operationalizes work engagement as energy, involvement, and efficacy, or as vigor, dedication, and absorption, the alignment of personal values with organizational values has a strong potential to improve the situation.

Guidelines for intervention goals

The views of work engagement presented by these two models have implications for assessing its development over time and designing interventions to influence that development. In particular, they point to two major foci of interventions: energy and motivation.

Energy focused interventions

The job demand-resources model and the mediation model agree on the importance of sustainable energy. Prolonged, chronic exhaustion is incompatible with an energetic, vigorous approach to worklife. Approaches to alleviating burnout have considered or tested interventions to improve employees' energy management. These approaches include maintaining a reasonable balance of demands and resources, healthy work environments, and safe working practices. When the primary focus is alleviating burnout, addressing exhaustion becomes an urgent priority. It is important to design intervention activities to be minimally intrusive because exhausted employees are concerned with minimizing demands. When the primary objective is preventing burnout or building work engagement, an intervention plan has more latitude because employees have energy to devote to the project.

Balancing demands and resources

Interventions to improve the balance of demands and resources can work on either end of the equation. They have a greater potential for success when they both increase resources and decrease demands. To avoid refusing business or client requests, demand-focused interventions repackage demands through pacing systems, such as triage. Clients have their first point of contact with an intermediary who determines the urgency of clients' needs and assigns them to the appropriate specialist. Triage systems free specialists from the personal and time demands of these initial interactions while directing their services towards those with the greatest potential for benefit. These systems seek to maintain the overall throughput of work while reducing overt pressures on service providers. Resource-based interventions can build on a wide range of resources, including improved information technology, enhanced reward systems, or additional personnel. The bottom line is that employees have more available resources to meet work demands. These interventions often require employees to learn new systems for doing work. An inherent risk with these interventions is that better control systems or enhanced resources raise expectations. If management or clients make increased demands, the intervention will only serve to maintain an imbalance between demands and resources.

Enhancing employee health

The previous section – balancing demands and resources – considered ways to reduce the rate at which work depletes employees' energy. A complementary approach is to build employees' resilience. Physical health and mental health are personal resources. Healthy people have more readily available resources to draw upon. It follows that people experiencing good physical and mental health would be less vulnerable to exhaustion than would unhealthy people (Tang, Au, Schwarzer, & Schmitz, 2001). In the most immediate sense, fatigue is a pervasive symptom of illness. People experiencing infections, poor nutrition, or drug abuse often report fatigue (Surawy, Hackmann, Hawton, & Sharpe, 1995). In contrast, people in excellent physical health have more energy at their disposal (Rozanski & Kubzansky, 2005). They have a greater capacity to persist in demanding situations.

Healthy workplace interventions are diverse. At the modest end of the scale are educational programs that provide employees with advice on managing stressors in their work or personal lives. On the other end of the scale, organizations create ongoing systems to evaluate the ergonomic qualities of office furniture, upgrade cafeteria fare, install fitness centers, and provide on-site child care. These facilities make the workplace more enjoyable and support a healthier, more sustainable lifestyle.

Improving workplace safety.

Workplace accidents have a direct impact on employee health. The immediate impact of interventions that enhance an organization's safety culture is reducing harm experienced by employees. Fewer accidents mean less time lost to injuries and less long-term disability. As mentioned earlier, our recent research has demonstrated persistent relationships of exhaustion and workplace accidents, suggesting that chronic exhaustion increases employees' vulnerability to

injury and that injuries can reduce employees' energy resources (Leiter & Maslach, 2009).

Three types of interventions

These three forms of intervention – balancing demands and resources, enhancing employee health, and improving workplace safety – have immediate implications for the energy process. When operating effectively, they all reduce the rate at which work depletes energy and increase employees' capacity to maintain a vigorous approach to work. Ideally, they not only avoid illness and distress, but support a pleasant sense of well-being.

These interventions have additional implications for the motivational process. First, through concern with the demand/resource balance, an organization can convey a non-exploitive relationship with its employees. Rather than cashing in on the energy and knowledge brought by arriving employees, it signals that it intends to sustain that capacity for the long run. As a values statement, an organizational commitment to employee health and well-being supports work engagement while avoiding health problems associated with burnout. For example, an investment of management attention, equipment, training, and other resources into supporting safe work practices confirms an organizational value: the organization cares about the well-being of employees (Hofmann, Morgeson, & Gerras, 2003; Zohar & Luria, 2004). Even when cost reduction appears to drive the safety culture, it acknowledges employees' well-being as a valuable organizational resource.

Motivational interventions

The two-process models point towards the potential of motivational interventions. As noted previously, actions aimed primarily at improving energy processes may have important implications for values and resources. Complementing these approaches are interventions focusing directly on motivation processes.

The job demands-resources model calls for enriching resources to build work engagement. The availability of job resources assists people in maintaining vigor, dedication, and absorption, especially in the face of high job demands (Bakker, Hakanen, Demerouti, & Xanthopoulou, 2007). The model contends that resources intrinsically motivate employees by enhancing their potential for growth and learning (Schaufeli & Bakker, 2004). They also provide extrinsic motivation by enabling employees' capacity to attain work objectives. Research has supported this perspective by finding work engagement to be related to a wide variety of job resources including collegial support, supervisor support, learning opportunities, variety, and autonomy (Bakker & Demerouti, 2007; Schaufeli & Salanova, 2007), as well as job control and innovation climate (Hakanen, Bakker, & Schaufeli, 2006; see also Hakanen & Roodt, Chapter 7, and Halbesleben, Chapter 8, this volume).

The most effective resource-oriented interventions go beyond a temporary infusion to an ongoing change in work processes. For example, a company redesigns its performance evaluation system away from an annual, form-based exercise to establish a continuous mentoring process focusing on employee career objectives. The process of setting objectives, developing strategies, and assessing impact become an integral part of the individual employees' worklife. It becomes as well the basis for establishing an enriched relationship with their immediate supervisors. An intervention of this scope would include the intrinsic motivational impact of personal development as well as the extrinsic rewards of bringing meaningful progress on career objectives to their supervisors' attention on a regular basis. Ideally, interventions on this scale would inspire a gain spiral (Hobfoll & Shirom, 2000; see also Salanova, Schaufeli, Xanthopoulou, & Bakker, Chapter 9, this volume) in which the greater work engagement established through introducing the revised performance evaluation system enables employees to create new resources, such as broad recognition by professional colleagues. These new resources in turn encourage more work engagement.

The JD-R model not only recognizes a wide variety of resources that are relevant to employees' work engagement, but also notes that the importance of a given resource varies across situations. That is, job autonomy may be of critical importance in one organization that places a great value on individual craft, but it may be of minor importance in another organization that emphasizes teamwork. In that latter organization, workgroup cohesion and civility may be the most relevant resources to develop.

The mediation model encompasses a similarly broad range of resources that pertain to work engagement. The example provided above about a performance mentoring system would fit equally well within this theoretical framework. The difference between the models lies in their perspectives on underlying processes. Rather than the motivational qualities of resources, which are central to the JD-R model, the mediation model emphasizes values. That is, the impact of an intervention arises largely from its confirmation of values that are shared between individuals and the organization. From this perspective, the importance of the mentoring intervention has less to do with the motivational qualities of learning opportunities and supervisor recognition. Rather, the mentoring relationship of supervisors with employees establishes a dialogue that facilitates value congruence. The relationship provides the supervisor with the opportunity to articulate organizational values and their relationship to the employees' work. The employees' focus on work objectives provides an opportunity to present their own efforts to realize important personal values through their work. An effective mentoring and performance management system is a setting in which both parties can present a distinct perspective and lead the other party to appreciate its relevance.

Guidelines for the intervention process

Building work engagement is an approach to management that is committed to helping employees maintain an energetic involvement with work that supports professional efficacy. It is our observation that such an approach is not the norm. Too many public sector institutions exhaust and discourage employees by providing inadequate resources to meet their mandated demands. Too many private sector organizations divert essential resources to profits, failing to rcinvest adequately to support their expanding scope of operations. These persistent and widespread imbalances of demands with resources deplete personal resources, impinge upon health, aggravate burnout, and discourage work engagement. Interventions to reverse these trends have to swim upstream against a torrent of socioeconomic conditions.

People are willing to put a concerted effort into something they value. In the information/service economy that is the dominant trend in the postindustrialized world, people bring a unique cluster of aspirations, values, talents, and skills that they have developed over a lifetime of enriched educational and cultural experience. As diversity becomes a valued and pervasive quality of the contemporary workplace, management cannot anticipate how individuals will fit into a set organizational structure. The challenge of providing employees with opportunities for engaged work has no ideal solution. The most effective and efficient approach to developing a supportive work environment requires a complete and ongoing assessment of employees' experience of their worklife.

Survey process

The pivotal element in including work engagement into an organization's information flow is asking people how they feel about their work. The second element is assessing their perceptions of definitive areas of worklife. Ideally, organizations establish an ongoing information flow, tracking variations in employees' experience over time to appreciate the impact of planned and unplanned changes. This information flow provides early warning signals of problems. It also signals opportunities to encourage greater work engagement. Timing can be critical.

Action planning

The research noted above and elsewhere in this book has underscored that work engagement is associated with core aspects of worklife, including decision-making involvement, professional autonomy, and core values. Changes to fundamental qualities of worklife require understanding, participation, resources, and authority. We propose that organizations establish a working group to lead work engagement initiatives. Many organizations already have a working group dedicated to quality of worklife. Updating the mandate of these existing groups may be an effective approach. The following considerations are relevant to staffing a working group and defining its mandate.

Understanding

The capacity to comprehend the diverse range of factors pertaining to work engagement requires expertise in human resource management, including performance management systems, stress management, and professional development. Another important capacity is an appreciation of survey design, analysis, and interpretations. Regardless of whether the survey function is conducted within the organization or outsourced, the committee will function more effectively with a deep appreciation of the survey research. Such understanding is valuable when assessing the quality of survey information. Some indicators have the support of converging measures that support their validity; others may appear convincing, but have little substance. Having expertise regarding psychometrics on the working group enables more effective decision-making.

Participation

People want to feel in control of important sectors of their lives. Two factors that give a sense of control are participation in decision-making and the experience of professional autonomy. To be most effective, processes to enhance work engagement invite broad participation from members of an organization. They maintain ongoing communications, informing people of their findings and plans. They develop forums that take the pulse of the organization through surveys, blogs, meetings, or dialogues. They convey respect for employees' expertise, developing strategies that will enhance individual capabilities while furthering the organization's objectives. Although the working group has the responsibility to manage confidential information carefully and to exercise a certain degree of discretion when fielding complaints about management or specific individuals, the primary posture of an effective working group is maintaining an open dialogue with the larger organization.

Resources

Building work engagement is not free. It is surely cost effective. It is an investment of the time and energy of talented people. Working groups vary in their resource requirements. They often need to delve more deeply into specific issues, requiring the resources to conduct surveys or research into documents and databases. They will require access to the organization's communication networks. There are costs involved in writing, producing printed materials, or developing electronic communications. As audiences become increasingly sophisticated in judging information on computer screens, website design makes additional demands. Beyond the operational costs associated with the working group, their recommendations for interventions will invariably require resources to implement. An environment that supports energetic, dedicated participation in work is one that provides employees with the materials, information, facilities, equipment, expertise, and support necessary to do their most effective work. Although these resources are not necessarily assigned to the working group directly, it is reasonable to expect that their deliberations will result in plans that will eventually call upon organizational resources. These expenditures become part of the organization's ongoing financial planning as it anticipates new capital and operating expenses. It shapes these plans by giving high priority to interventions and developments that have the greatest potential for enhancing work engagement.

Authority

The working group does not have direct line authority in an organization. In fact, direct authority of this sort would distract from their focus on work engagement. Maintaining focused attention on work engagement works best as a single-minded priority. Work engagement is a consideration for the long term that can be seriously diffused through the pressures of day-to-

day management concerns or the demands of budget allocations or other responsibilities. But it is essential for working groups to have access to authority to implement their plans. The most effective and meaningful format is for the working group to report directly to the senior leadership team of an organization. This connection can be strengthened by including at least one member of senior leadership on the working group. In the initial phases of a new initiative to enhance work engagement, this role could be effectively served by the CEO. The advisory role to the senior leadership team combined with a cross membership between the two groups not only assigns a route to authority, but it increases the working group's standing with employees across the organization. The process begins with a recommendation for action from the working group. Senior leadership considers this plan, approving it with appropriate modifications. The task of implementation is assigned to the appropriate component of the organization with the working group assigned to oversee, to advise, and to evaluate the intervention's effectiveness. In this way, the working group maintains an active commitment to the initiative and the capacity to assure that it pursues its intended role of furthering work engagement. At the same time, the authority structure of the organization remains intact.

Looking to the future

Enhancing work engagement is the ultimate test of theory. Identifying correlates of engagement in cross-sectional or longitudinal research begins to inform a process. Systematic interventions not only provide a way to evaluate theory; they are opportunities for research to make a meaningful contribution to participants' worklife (see Box 12.1).

Theories of work engagement suggest two distinct approaches. One general approach builds and sustains employees' energy. The second approach allocates resources in ways that confirm the organization's commitment to corporate values that inspire employee commitment. Regardless of the approach, effective change requires an enduring effort from management.

Practical implications

Six points for enhancing work engagement

1. **Collaborate.** Enhancing work engagement is something you do with someone, not to someone. Define an inclusive process that encourages the creativity and enthusiasm of everyone involved. The process of encouraging work engagement should share its core features.
2. **Establish an ongoing process.** Work engagement is not an ideal state that people attain. A company cannot conduct a limited work engagement initiative, complete the process, and move on to other things. Building work engagement is an ongoing process. It is a way of doing things in the organization that requires ongoing monitoring, adaptation, and action.
3. **Know your target.** In today's business world, the word "engagement" has taken on many meanings. For the most part, consultants use employee engagement as a synonym for job satisfaction or organizational commitment. While these are important constructs with meaningful implications for human resource management, they differ from work engagement.
4. **Be creative.** There are no hard-and-fast rules for building work engagement. First, systematic research on building work engagement is just beginning. Second, everything to date suggests that a company's specific conditions will determine to some extent what will work. The company's history, its leadership, and its position on its growth cycle may all be important. While the general principles we have presented here will be useful, they need to be adapted to the situation.
5. **Evaluate.** Good intentions do not automatically turn into effective management. It is essential to use accurate measure and a good survey process to evaluate the impact of initiatives on employees' experience of work engagement. Including reliable measures of work engagement in annual employee surveys is a good basic step. Making specific evaluations of workplace initiatives provides another vital source of information.
6. **Share.** Progress reports on work engagement are essential for the strategic planning of the company's top leadership. They also provide effective performance feedback for managers in their efforts to enhance the quality of worklife for people in their units.

An intervention to signal management commitment and train employees in new ways of working usually requires 6 months of concerted effort before employees integrate the change into their day-to-day worklife.

Enhancing work engagement defines an end in itself, but it also portends additional changes for individuals and their organizations. A thorough evaluation of interventions includes assessments of personal fulfillment at work, as well as indicators of individual and organizational performance. Assessing health indicators, including job burnout, permits a broad evaluation of an intervention's impact on employees' psychological relationships with work. We anticipate that management approaches that are sensitive to employees' aspirations and supportive of their effective contribution will alleviate burnout while enhancing engagement with work.

Note

1. Although the full package is no longer available through the publisher, researchers can access the measures from the authors. The Areas of Worklife Scale (Manageable Workload, Control, Reward, Community, Fairness, and Values) and Management Areas (Change, Supervision, Communication, Development, and Cohesion) are available through the website: http://cord.acadiau.ca/products. The MBI-GS is available through Consulting Psychologist Press (www.cpp.com).

References

Bakker, A. B., & Demerouti, E. (2007). The Job Demands-Resources model: State of the art. *Journal of Managerial Psychology*, *22*, 309–328.

Bakker, A. B., Hakanen, J. J., Demerouti, E., & Xanthopoulou, D. (2007). Job resources boost work engagement, particularly when job demands are high. *Journal of Educational Psychology*, *99*, 274–284.

Bakker, A. B., Van Emmerik, H., & Van Riet, P. (2008). How job demands, resources, and burnout predict objective performance: A constructive replication. *Anxiety, Stress, and Coping*, *21*, 309–324.

CRWRC (2006). (http://www.crwrc.org/development/index.html). Accessed 5 January 2007.

Demerouti, E., Bakker, A. B., Nachreiner, F., & Schaufeli, W. B. (2001). The Job Demands-Resources model of burnout. *Journal of Applied Psychology*, *86*, 499–512.

Diener, E. (1999). Introduction to the special section on the structure of emotion. *Journal of Personality and Social Psychology*, *76*, 803–804.

Edward, K. (2005). The phenomenon of resilience in crisis care mental health clinicians. *International Journal of Mental Health Nursing*, *14*, 142–148.

Fry, L. W. (2005). Editorial: Introduction to The Leadership Quarterly special issue: Toward a paradigm of spiritual leadership. *Leadership Quarterly*, *16*, 619–622.

Hakanen, J., Bakker, A. B., & Schaufeli, W. B. (2006). Burnout and work engagement among teachers. *Journal of School Psychology*, *43*, 495–513.

Halbesleben, J. R. B., & Buckley, M. R. (2004). Burnout in organizational life. *Journal of Management*, *30*, 859–879.

Hobfoll, S. E. (2001). The influence of culture, community, and the nested-self in the stress process: Advancing conservation of resources theory. *Applied Psychology: An International Review*, *50*, 337–421.

Hobfoll, S. E., & Shirom, A. (2000). Conservation of resources theory: Applications to stress and management in the workplace. In R. T. Golembiewski (Ed.), *Handbook of organization behavior* (2nd ed., pp. 57–81). New York: Dekker.

Herzberg, E. (1966). *Work and the nature of man*. Cleveland: World Publishing.

Hofmann, D. A, Morgeson, F. P., & Gerras, S. J. (2003). Climate as a moderator of the relationship between leader-member exchange and content specific citizenship: Safety climate as an exemplar. *Journal of Applied Psychology*, *88*, 170–178.

Leiter, M. P., & Harvie, P. (1997). The correspondence of supervisor and subordinate perspectives on major organizational change. *Journal of Occupational Health Psychology*, *2*, 343–352.

Leiter, M. P., & Maslach, C. (2000). *Preventing burnout and building engagement: A complete program for organizational renewal*. San Francisco: Jossey-Bass.

Leiter, M. P., & Maslach, C. (2004). Areas of worklife: A structured approach to organizational predictors of job burnout. In P. Perrewé & D. C. Ganster (Eds.), *Research in occupational stress and well being: Vol. 3. Emotional and physiological processes and positive intervention strategies* (pp. 91–134). Oxford, UK: JAI Press/Elsevier.

Leiter, M. P., & Maslach, C. (2005a). A mediation model of job burnout. In A. S. G. Antoniou & C. L. Cooper (Eds.), *Research companion to organizational health psychology* (pp. 544–564). Cheltenham, UK: Edward Elgar.

Leiter, M. P., & Maslach, C. (2005b). *Banishing burnout: Six strategies for improving your relationship with work*. San Francisco: Jossey-Bass.

Leiter, M. P., & Maslach, C. (2006). *Areas of Worklife Scale Manual* (4th ed.) Centre for Organizational Research & Development, Acadia University, Wolfville, NS, Canada.

Leiter, M. P., & Maslach, C. (2009). *Burnout and workplace injuries: A longitudinal analysis*. In A. M. Rossi, J. C. Quick, & P. L. Perrewe (Eds.), *Stress and quality of working life: The positive and the negative* (pp. 3–18). Grenwich, CT: Information Age.

Maslach, C., & Goldberg, J. (1998). Prevention of burnout: New perspectives. *Applied and Preventive Psychology*, *7*, 63–74.

Maslach, C., & Leiter, M. P. (1997). *The truth about burnout*. San Francisco: Jossey-Bass.

Maslach, C., & Leiter, M. P. (2005). Stress and burnout: The critical research. In C. L. Cooper (Ed.), *Handbook of stress medicine and health* (2nd ed., pp. 153–170). Boca Raton, FL: CRC Press LLC.

Maslach, C., & Leiter, M. P. (2008). Early predictors of job burnout and engagement. *Journal of Applied Psychology*, *93*, 498–512.

Maslach, C., Schaufeli, W. B., & Leiter, M. P. (2001). Job burnout. In S. T. Fiske, D. L. Schacter, & C. Zahn-Waxler (Eds.), *Annual Review of Psychology*, *52*, 397–422.

Rozanski, A., & Kubzansky, L. D. (2005). Psychologic functioning and physical health: A paradigm of flexibility. *Psychosomatic Medicine*, *67*, S47–S53.

Salanova, M., Cifre, E., & Rodriguez, A. (March, 2008). Improving work engagement through a stress management intervention: A longitudinal study. Presentation in W. B. Schaufeli & M. Salanova (Chairs), *Work engagement and vigor at work: psychological and physiological aspects*. APA/NIOSH Conference: Work, Stress, & Health, Washington, DC.

Schaufeli, W. B., & Bakker, A. B. (2004). Job demands, job resources and their relationship with burnout and engagement: A multi-sample study. *Journal of Organizational Behavior*, *25*, 293–315.

Schaufeli, W. B., & Enzmann, D. (1998). *The burnout companion to study and practice: A critical analysis*. London: Taylor & Francis.

Schaufeli, W. B., Leiter, M. P., Maslach, C., & Jackson, S. E. (1996). Maslach Burnout Inventory – General Survey (MBI-GS). In C. Maslach, S. E. Jackson, & M. P. Leiter (Eds.), *Maslach Burnout Inventory Manual* (3rd ed.). Palo Alto, CA: Consulting Psychologists Press.

Schaufeli, W. B., & Salanova, M. (2007). Work engagement: An emerging psychological concept and its implications for organizations. In S. W. Gilliland, D. D. Steiner, & D. P. Skarlicki (Eds.), *Research in Social Issues in Management (Volume 5): Managing Social and Ethical Issues in Organizations*. Greenwich, CT: Information Age Publishers.

Surawy, C., Hackmann, A., Hawton, K., & Sharpe, M.

(1995). Chronic Fatigue Syndrome: A cognitive approach. *Behaviour Research and Therapy, 33*, 535–544.

Tang, C. S., Au, W. T., Schwarzer, R., & Schmitz, G. (2001). Mental health outcomes of job stress among Chinese teachers: Role of stress resource factors and burnout. *Journal of Organizational Behavior, 22*, 887–901.

Zohar, D., & Luria, G. (2004). Climate as a social – cognitive construction of supervisory safety practices: Scripts as proxy of behavior patterns. *Journal of Applied Psychology, 89*, 322–333.

13

Where to go from here: Integration and future research on work engagement

Arnold B. Bakker and Michael P. Leiter

Modern organizations expect their employees to be proactive, show initiative, take responsibility for their own professional development and to be committed to high quality performance standards. They need employees who feel energetic and dedicated – i.e., who are engaged with their work. It is therefore not surprising that the past decade has witnessed a sharp rise in scientific studies on engagement. The work engagement research discussed in this book offers evidence for the incremental validity of engagement over and above traditional I/O concepts. Work engagement provides a distinct, valuable perspective on the experience of work.

In this final chapter, we integrate the perspectives on work engagement offered in this book and outline a research agenda. We do this by delineating a theoretical framework and by discussing seven avenues for research on work engagement. We will see that the future looks bright for engagement research. The chapter authors presented dynamic perspectives on work engagement. What we will do is try to synthesize the perspectives, and illuminate avenues for new research.

Integration

Work engagement: A unique concept
Schaufeli and Bakker (Chapter 2) review definitions of work engagement in the business context and in academia as a basis for considering the instruments assessing engagement. While the popularity of engagement in organizations

confirms the concept's practical dimension, business consultants have applied the term to a range of concepts and measures that depart from those used in scientific research. Schaufeli and Bakker's analysis shows that consultants use the word "engagement" as a novel, catchy label that covers traditional concepts, such as affective commitment (i.e., the emotional attachment to the organization), continuance commitment (i.e., the desire to stay with the organization), and extra-role behavior (i.e., discretionary behavior that promotes the effective functioning of the organization). They share our focus on the subjective experience of work, but fail to capture the distinct value added by the new concept of work engagement. Hence, the way practitioners conceptualize engagement comes close to putting old wine in new bottles (Macey & Schneider, 2008). Some consultants have even used job characteristics (i.e., job resources) as indicators of engagement (see Harter, Schmidt, & Hayes, 2002). This practice that mixes references to work conditions with references to subjective experience actually inhibits research objectives. Specifically, relinquishing a clear boundary between an experience and the environmental conditions that support that experience prevents clear analyses of the relationship between these two concepts.

In contrast, academic researchers have defined work engagement as a unique concept. Most scholars agree that engagement includes an energy dimension and an identification dimension (Bakker, Schaufeli, Leiter, & Taris, 2008). Work engagement is a positive, work-related state of well-being or fulfillment characterized by a high level of energy and strong identification with one's work. Maslach and Leiter (1997, 2008) have defined engagement as the opposite of burnout; engaged employees have a sense of energetic and effective connection with their work. Accordingly, engagement is characterized by energy, involvement, and professional efficacy – the direct opposites of the three core burnout dimensions. Schaufeli and Bakker (Chapter 2) define work engagement as "a positive, fulfilling, work-related state of mind that is characterized by vigor, dedication, and absorption" (see also Schaufeli,

Salanova, González-Romá, & Bakker, 2002, p. 74). In engagement, fulfillment exists in contrast to the voids of life that leave people feeling empty as in burnout. Vigor is characterized by high levels of energy and mental resilience while working. Dedication refers to being strongly involved in one's work, and experiencing a sense of significance and enthusiasm. Absorption is characterized by being fully concentrated and happily engrossed in one's work. Note that these definitions focus on employees' experience of work activity, and not the predictors or outcomes of these experiences. The most often used instrument to measure engagement is the Utrecht Work Engagement Scale (UWES; Schaufeli & Bakker, 2003, 2009; Schaufeli et al., 2002), which includes three subscales: vigor, dedication, and absorption.

Engagement will make a stronger contribution as a unique construct that adds unique value to the nomological network (Halbesleben & Wheeler, 2008). Research presented in this book and elsewhere supports engagement as a distinct construct. Schaufeli and Bakker (Chapter 2) discuss studies showing that work engagement differs from job involvement and organizational commitment. In addition, Halbesleben and Wheeler (2008) have provided evidence for the discriminant validity of work engagement vis-à-vis job embeddedness. Embeddedness represents the collection of forces keeping an employee on the job (i.e., links in the organization, fit with the job, and sacrifices associated with leaving the job). Their study included a sample of employees ($N = 587$), their supervisors, and their closest co-workers from a wide variety of industries and occupations. Findings showed that work engagement and job embeddedness could be empirically discriminated. Importantly, both variables made a unique contribution to explaining variance in job performance (with the exception of embeddedness and supervisor-rated performance). Only job embeddedness offered a unique prediction of turnover intention. These findings held true after controlling for the impact of job satisfaction and affective commitment (Halbesleben & Wheeler, 2008).

Taris, Schaufeli, and Shimazu (Chapter 4) discuss the similarities and differences of work engagement versus workaholism – the compulsion or the uncontrollable need to work incessantly (Oates, 1971). Compared to workaholics, engaged employees lack the typical compulsive drive that is characteristic of any addiction, including an addiction to work. For engaged workers work is fun and not a compulsion, as was concluded from a qualitative study of 15 engaged workers (Schaufeli, Taris, LeBlanc, Peeters, Bakker, & De Jonge, 2001). These workers worked hard because they liked it and not because they were driven by a strong inner urge they could not resist. Evidence from two independent Dutch studies discussed by Taris et al. (Chapter 4) revealed that workaholism (as measured in terms of working excessively and working compulsively) could clearly be distinguished from work engagement. One remarkable finding here was that the third indicator of engagement (absorption) showed a substantial loading on workaholism as well. Apart from this overlap, it appeared that workaholism and engagement are only weakly related.

The conceptual distinction between engagement and workaholism was further confirmed by inspection of the pattern of relationships between both states on the one hand, and various clusters of other concepts on the other (Taris et al., Chapter 4). Whereas both engagement and workaholism are characterized by high effort expenditure at work (in terms of the time given to working and high job demands), high scores on workaholism are generally accompanied with adverse work characteristics, lack of well-being (especially mental health), and only moderate trust in one's own job performance. Conversely, engaged workers are generally quite satisfied with their jobs and their lives, report good health, and state that they perform well.

Shirom (Chapter 6) adds an interesting view to the literature on work engagement with his elaborated concept of vigor. Accordingly, vigor refers to individuals' feelings that they possess physical strength, cognitive liveliness, and emotional energy – a set of interrelated affective states experienced at work. Feeling invigorated connotes the combined feeling of a positive energy balance and pleasantness or contentment. How is vigor related to work engagement? Wefald (2008) compared the UWES with the Shirom–Melamed Vigor Measure (SMVM) using a sample of 382 American employees and managers at a financial institution. Results showed that vigor as assessed with the SMVM is moderately high and positively related to vigor as assessed with the UWES. The correlations between physical strength, cognitive liveliness, and emotional energy on the one hand, and UWES-vigor on the other hand are .73, .57, and .43, respectively. This implies that vigor, as assessed with the UWES and integrated in our definition of engagement, is most closely related to physical strength. In addition, the vigor dimensions show positive and moderately high correlations with UWES-dedication and UWES-absorption (r's .36 to .57, p's < .01).

Within the small body of research on engagement and physical health, vigor was associated with highly important individual health outcomes. According to Shirom (Chapter 6), vigor may enhance the immune system's capacity to mount an effective response to challenges and the adoption of healthy lifestyle habits. Recent studies provide empirical support for these pathways linking vigor and health. Vigor was found to be negatively correlated with several inflammation biomarkers (Shirom, Toker, Berliner, Shapira, & Melamed, 2006), thus suggesting that they could represent possible pathways linking vigor with improved physical health. Other studies have shown that vigor is positively related to self-rated health. For example, feeling vigorous and objective physical fitness (gauged based on functional capacity) were found to interact in predicting the change over time in self-rated health (SRH) among apparently healthy employees – the higher the physical fitness, the more pronounced the effects of the initial levels of vigor on these changes in SRH (Shirom et al., 2008). Another study (Shirom, Vinokur, & Vaananen, 2008), among two samples of employees in Finland and Sweden ($N = 6188$ and $N = 3345$, respectively), found that feeling vigorous was positively associated with both SRH and subjective work capacity, controlling for socio-demographic predictors.

In conclusion, our argument for work engagement as a unique and valuable construct rests not only on its intuitive appeal, but also on empirical support for its discriminant validity. First, when contrasting work engagement with other concepts in organizational psychology, independent researchers consistently confirm its status. Second, these investigations have consistently confirmed energy and involvement or dedication as the core qualities of work engagement. Debates regarding additional qualities contribute to refinement of the construct; they do not challenge it. Together, the case for work engagement is compelling.

State work engagement

Research has generally conceptualized work engagement as a relatively stable phenomenon because of the continued presence of specific job and organizational characteristics (Macey & Schneider, 2008). Nevertheless, there is considerable interest in the short-term (i.e., daily or weekly) fluctuations in the experience of work engagement for a particular individual. In many work settings there are specific times and periods during which it is necessary that employees are highly engaged, for example when making an important presentation to a new customer or when facing other novel and challenging job requirements.

Experience sampling studies and diary studies have indeed shown that within-individual variations in work engagement do exist (e.g., Sonnentag, 2003). In Chapter 3, Sonnentag, Dormann, and Demerouti summarize existing evidence that supports a state perspective. The authors discuss quantitative diary studies demonstrating that work engagement fluctuates substantially within individuals. In a typical diary study, 30–40% of the overall variance can be found at the day (i.e., within-individual) level and 60–70% of the overall variance is at the between-individual level. Sonnentag and her colleagues claim that in order to investigate the full phenomenological experience of work engagement, one has to focus on state work engagement as a momentary and transient experience that fluctuates within individuals within short periods of time (i.e., from minute to minute or from hour to hour, perhaps from day to day).

Sonnentag et al. (Chapter 3) identify several

benefits associated with a within-person perspective. First, the within-person approach allows for a closer look at temporal patterns of work-related experiences and behaviors. Individuals are not equally engaged at work across all days. There are days (or weeks) on which employees feel more vigorous, absorbed, and dedicated than on other days (or weeks). Sonnentag and her colleagues argue that averaging across these situations by assessing a general level of work engagement (i.e., by asking individuals to provide retrospective reports over the previous months and providing summary accounts of their psychological states), ignores the dynamic and configurational part of the work engagement phenomenon.

Second, the within-person approach enables an examination of proximal predictors of work engagement. Are there specific situational features that have to be present during a specific day in order to feel engaged? For example, one may imagine that not only generally high levels of job resources such as appreciation by one's co-workers and supervisor, but also a supportive comment or encouraging feedback from one's co-workers or supervisor on a specific day increase work engagement. Xanthopoulou and her colleagues did indeed find evidence for unique effects of daily changes in social support on daily work engagement among fast-food restaurant employees (Xanthopoulou, Bakker, Demerouti, & Schaufeli, 2009b) and among flight attendants (Xanthopoulou, Bakker, Heuven, Demerouti, & Schaufeli, 2008). Similarly, there may be person-specific states that foster work engagement during a specific day or week, including daily self-efficacy, daily optimism, and daily recovery. Indeed, the studies by Xanthopoulou et al. (2008, 2009b) and Sonnentag (2003) provide evidence for this contention.

Although work engagement appears to remain relatively stable over the long term, examining the day-to-day fluctuations in its core elements of energy and dedication can clarify its underlying dynamics. The extent to which engagement responds to environmental changes is especially relevant to designing management interventions to improve work engagement among employees.

An integrative model of work engagement

Previous studies have consistently shown that job resources such as social support from colleagues and supervisors, performance feedback, skill variety, autonomy, and learning opportunities are positively associated with work engagement (Bakker & Demerouti, 2008; Schaufeli & Salanova, 2007). Job resources refer to those physical, social, or organizational aspects of the job that may: (a) reduce job demands and the associated physiological and psychological costs; (b) be functional in achieving work goals; or (c) stimulate personal growth, learning, and development (Bakker & Demerouti, 2007; Schaufeli & Bakker, 2004). Hakanen and Roodt (Chapter 7) use the JD-R model to predict engagement, and conclude that job resources are the most important predictors of engagement. For example, in a study among 2555 Finnish dentists using a two-wave cross-lagged panel design, Hakanen, Schaufeli, and Ahola (2008b) found evidence for the motivational process over a 3-year follow-up period: job resources influenced future engagement, which in turn predicted organizational commitment. Job resources seem to set in motion a motivational process through which employees satisfy their basic needs such as the needs for autonomy, competence, and relatedness (Van den Broeck, Vansteenkiste, De Witte, & Lens, 2008).

Mauno, Kinnunen, and Ruokolainen (2007) utilized a 2-year longitudinal design to investigate work engagement and its antecedents among Finnish health care personnel. Job resources predicted work engagement better than job demands. Job control and organization-based self-esteem proved to be the best lagged predictors of the three dimensions of work engagement, after controlling for T1 scores on the dimensions of engagement. In Chapter 8, Halbesleben presents the results of a meta-analysis of work engagement using different measures to operationalize the construct. Results indicate that job resources including autonomy, social support, performance feedback, and organizational climate are important predictors of engagement.

In addition to job resources, several studies have focused on state-like personal resources as predictors of work engagement (see also Halbesleben, Chapter 8). Personal resources are positive self-evaluations that are linked to resiliency and refer to individuals' sense of their ability to control and impact upon their environment successfully (Hobfoll, Johnson, Ennis, & Jackson, 2003). It has been shown that such positive self-evaluations predict goal-setting, motivation, performance, job and life satisfaction, and other desirable outcomes (for a review, see Judge, Van Vianen, & De Pater, 2004).

Sweetman and Luthans (Chapter 5) discuss why psychological capital – a concept similar to personal resources – is related to work engagement. Psychological capital (PsyCap) is defined as an individual's positive psychological state of development characterized by self-efficacy, optimism, hope, and resilience (Luthans, Youssef, & Avolio, 2007, p. 3). These characteristics facilitate work engagement. According to Sweetman and Luthans, optimism, for example, plays an influential role in one's approach to job duties, with those high in optimism expecting success when presented with a challenge. Furthermore, those high in optimism tend to attribute success to themselves, while attributing failures to external, uncontrollable circumstances (Seligman, 1998). Thus, optimists conclude success is something they can replicate and control. Finally, while high job demands may limit engagement through a decreased feeling of control, this can be counteracted through the impact of the resource of optimism offering a sense of personal control over the demands at hand (Karasek, 1979). Sweetman and Luthans (Chapter 5) explain that optimism is also related to other PsyCap constructs in that it helps people to "see adversity as a challenge, transform problems into opportunities [hope], put in hours to refine skills, persevere in finding solutions to obstacles or difficult problems [resiliency], maintain confidence [efficacy], rebound quickly after setbacks and persist [resiliency]" (Schulman, 1999, p. 32). A widening stream of research on the PsyCap construct has found support for its relation to a number of desired outcomes, including job performance (see Luthans, Avolio, Avey, & Norman, 2007).

Additionally, several authors have investigated the relationships between personal resources and work engagement. For example, Rothmann and Storm (2003) conducted a cross-sectional study among 1910 South African police officers, and found that engaged police officers have an active coping style. They are problem-focused, taking active steps to attempt to remove or rearrange stressors. Further, in their study among highly skilled Dutch technicians, Xanthopoulou, Bakker, Demerouti, and Schaufeli (2007) examined the role of three personal resources (self-efficacy, organizational-based self-esteem, and optimism) in predicting work engagement. Results showed that engaged employees are highly self-efficacious; they believe they are able to meet the demands they face in a broad array of contexts. In addition, engaged workers believe that they will generally experience good outcomes in life (optimistic), and believe they can satisfy their needs by participating in roles within the organization (organizational-based self-esteem; see also Mauno et al., 2007). These findings were replicated and expanded in a 2-year follow-up study (Xanthopoulou, Bakker, Demerouti, & Schaufeli, 2009a). The results indicated that self-efficacy, organizational-based self-esteem, and optimism make a unique contribution to explaining variance in work engagement over time, over and above the impact of job resources and previous levels of engagement. These findings substantiate Sweetman and Luthans' claim in Chapter 5 that psychological capital is an important predictor of work engagement.

In short, research shows that job and personal resources (PsyCap) are predictive of work engagement (see Halbesleben, Chapter 8). These relationships have been incorporated in an overall model of work engagement (Bakker & Demerouti, 2008; see Figure 13.1). Additionally, the model delineates that job demands moderate the resources–engagement relationship. Indeed, a central assumption in the JD-R model is that resources become more salient and gain their motivational potential when employees are confronted with high job demands (Bakker & Demerouti, 2007; Hakanen & Roodt, Chapter 7). Hakanen, Bakker, and Demerouti (2005) tested this interaction hypothesis in a sample of Finnish dentists employed in the public sector. It was hypothesized that job resources (e.g., variability in the required professional skills, peer contacts) are most beneficial in maintaining work engagement under conditions of high job demands (e.g., workload, unfavorable physical environment). The results showed clear evidence for this interaction hypothesis. For example, it was found that variability in professional skills boosted work engagement when qualitative workload was high, and mitigated the negative effect of high qualitative workload on work engagement. Conceptually similar findings have been reported by Bakker, Hakanen, Demerouti, and Xanthopoulou (2007) in their study among Finnish teachers. They found that job resources act as buffers and diminish the negative relationship between pupil misbehavior and work engagement. In addition, they found that job resources particularly influence work engagement when teachers are confronted with high levels of pupil misconduct.

The model in Figure 13.1 also proposes that engagement is positively related to performance. Demerouti and Cropanzano (Chapter 11) discuss several reasons why engaged employees perform better. One perspective taken by these authors and which holds valuable promise for future research is the broaden-and-build theory of positive emotions (Fredrickson, 2001). Accordingly, certain positive emotions, including joy, interest, and contentment, all share the capacity to broaden people's momentary thought–action repertoires and build their personal resources through widening the array of thoughts and actions that come to mind. For instance, joy broadens resources by creating the urge to play and be creative. Evidence for the broadening hypothesis has been reported in several studies (e.g., Fredrickson & Branigan, 2005; Fredrickson & Losada, 2005; Isen, 2000). Accordingly, positive affect produces a broad and flexible cognitive organization as well as the ability to integrate diverse material. Fredrickson (2003) suggests that positive emotion also tends to encourage employee development, such as learning new skills and forming closer interpersonal relationships. Demerouti and Cropanzano argue that positive emotions also facilitate the use of cooperative interpersonal tactics and reduce workplace conflict.

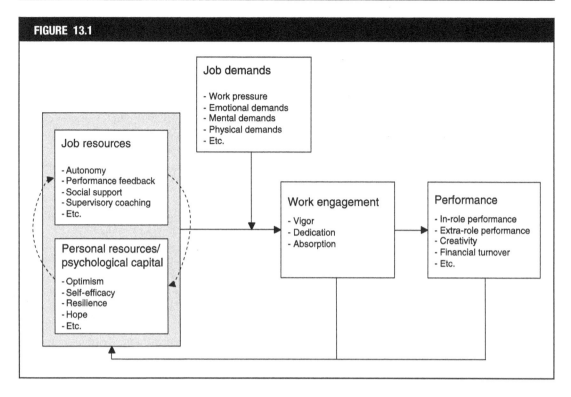

FIGURE 13.1

The JD-R model of work engagement (based on Bakker & Demerouti, 2007, 2008).

The research evidence indeed shows that engagement predicts performance. For example, Halbesleben and Wheeler (2008) found a positive relationship between engagement and other ratings (colleagues and supervisors) of performance in a study among US employees from a wide variety of industries and occupations. Demerouti and Cropanzano (Chapter 11) discuss several other studies that report evidence for a relationship between work engagement and performance. For example, Salanova, Agut, and Peiró (2005) conducted an important study among personnel working in Spanish restaurants and hotels. Contact employees from over one hundred service units (hotel front desks and restaurants) provided information about organizational resources, engagement, and service climate. Furthermore, customers from these units provided information on employee performance and customer loyalty. Structural equation modeling analyses were consistent with a full mediation model in which organizational resources and work engagement

predicted service climate, which in turn predicted employee performance and then customer loyalty. As another example, Xanthopoulou et al. (2009b) conducted a diary study among employees working in a Greek fast-food restaurant, and found that daily levels of work engagement were predictive of objective daily financial returns.

Accumulation of resources and engagement

The integrative model of work engagement in Figure 13.1 (see also Bakker & Demerouti, 2008) shows that engagement and performance have feedback loops to job resources. The model proposes that those who are highly engaged and perform well will also mobilize more personal resources or psychological capital, and more job resources like autonomy, social support, and career opportunities. In their chapter on gain spirals of resources and engagement, Salanova, Schaufeli, Xanthopoulou, and Bakker (Chapter 9) use three theories to argue that resources and work engagement may be reciprocally related.

Using conservation of resources theory (Hobfoll, 2002), Salanova and her colleagues argue that individuals strive to protect their resources, and to *accumulate* resources over time. For instance, employees learn new skills and competencies in order to increase their employability and reduce the risk of being laid off. Increased employability does not only reduce the risk of unemployment but also increases the possibility of finding a better job that offers additional opportunities for learning and development, which enhance engagement at work. Hence, gaining resources increases the resource pool, which makes it more likely that additional resources will be subsequently acquired.

Salanova et al. (Chapter 9) discuss several studies showing that resources positively affect work engagement which, in turn, positively affects resources over time. For example, Hakanen, Perhoniemi, and Toppinen-Tanner (2008a) in a 3-year panel study among 2555 Finnish dentists found evidence for positive and reciprocal cross-lagged associations between job resources and work engagement and between work engagement and personal initiative. In a similar vein, Xanthopoulou et al. (2009a) conducted a panel study (with 18 months in between the two measurement waves) among Dutch technicians, and found evidence for reciprocal associations between personal resources (i.e., self-efficacy, self-esteem, and optimism) and job resources (i.e., job autonomy, supervisory coaching, performance feedback, and opportunities for professional development), and between these resources and work engagement.

The studies discussed by Salanova et al. (Chapter 9) offer a good illustration of what Spreitzer, Lam, and Fritz (Chapter 10) mean by human thriving. Thriving is "a sense of progress or forward movement in one's self-development" (Spreitzer, Sutcliffe, Dutton, Sonenshein, & Grant, 2005, p. 538). People who thrive have a high level of vigor and bring new knowledge and skills to their work. They develop and continually improve, and look forward to each new day at work. Spreitzer et al. discuss empirical research on the role of thriving at work, and its relationship with engagement. Research has shown that thriving contributes to positive adaptation

amidst a changing work environment (Porath, Spreitzer, & Gibson, 2008). Additionally, thriving has been positively related to in-role and extra-role job performance (Porath et al., 2008) as well as to innovative behavior (Carmeli & Spreitzer, 2008).

Finally, the model in Figure 13.1 guides the design of effective organizational interventions. Whereas the work on designing, implementing, and evaluating interventions to build engagement has barely begun, Leiter and Maslach (Chapter 12) started a forward-looking discussion on the future development of engagement interventions. The perspective emphasizes enhancing the positive qualities of worklife in contrast to an exclusively problem-oriented perspective. These interventions include new learning opportunities or enhanced resources permitting employees to work more effectively. This approach strives to improve the balance of demands with resources. Its long-term goals are to foster employee health, safety, and engagement.

Future research

The work engagement studies discussed in this book offer evidence for the incremental validity of engagement over and above traditional I/O concepts. The chapters have introduced a wealth of perspectives and have posed a variety of questions regarding work engagement. Below we discuss seven avenues for research that seem highly relevant for further progress in the emerging field of work engagement.

Conceptual development

Further progress in research on work engagement would be more effective with broad agreement on the meaning of the concept. We propose to define work engagement as a subjective experience with two core dimensions: energy and involvement/identification. The inclusion of both dimensions within the UWES (Schaufeli et al., 2002), the MBI (Maslach, Jackson, & Leiter, 1996), and the OLBI (Demerouti & Bakker, 2008) supports that perspective.

The role of other constructs provides a focus for future research and conceptual development. Research could consider the absorption dimension of the UWES that its developers proposed as a core aspect of work engagement, but may on closer examination appear as an outcome of energy and identification. Another important conceptual question is the role of professional efficacy included in the MBI. Resolving these questions requires further development in theory and measurement. It may be more constructive to view efficacy as a personal resource or form of psychological capital contributing to work engagement rather than as a core dimension of engagement.

Additional empirical research can address the positioning of burnout and work engagement: are they polar opposites or neighboring or even overlapping work experiences? A recent study conducted in South Africa using the UWES, MBI, and the OLBI (Demerouti, Mostert, & Bakker, in press) suggested that the identification components of burnout and work engagement, namely cynicism/distancing and dedication, form a bipolar dimension. In addition, cynicism and dedication showed no substantial differences in the pattern of relationships with other constructs (work pressure, autonomy, and organizational commitment). In contrast, for the energy component the results suggest two distinguishable yet highly related dimensions of exhaustion and vigor. Vigor and exhaustion show a different pattern of relationships with work pressure, autonomy, organizational commitment, and mental health. Vigor is more strongly related to autonomy and commitment than is exhaustion, whereas exhaustion has stronger associations with work pressure and mental health than does vigor. These findings further substantiate the argument that vigor and exhaustion represent independent dimensions.

The finding that the distancing and dedication factors represent two ends of one construct is not very surprising because people can hold either negative or positive attitudes towards their work and it is unlikely that they can endorse both simultaneously. This is also justified by the distribution of the scores across the identification dimensions. Thus, responses to the identification items of burnout and work engagement constructs seem to follow the structure of the circumplex of emotions as suggested by Watson and

Tellegen (1985) where distancing and dedication are considered as two opposites of one continuum. However, as indicated by Demerouti et al. (in press), more research is needed on the exhaustion and vigor dimensions. Their results suggest that although employees who score low on vigor generally score high on exhaustion, other combinations are not uncommon. Future research could investigate whether the energy dimensions are more variable than the attitudinal dimensions. One could argue that even on a specific day high levels of vigor (e.g., at the start of the day) might coincide with *high* levels of exhaustion (e.g., at the end of the day).

Daily work engagement

Most previous studies on work engagement used a between-person design and cannot explain why even highly engaged employees may have an off-day and sometimes show below average or poor performance. Researchers have therefore begun to examine daily changes in work engagement. An important advantage of diary research is that it relies less on retrospective recall than regular surveys, since the questions relate to individuals' perceptions and feelings on a certain day. In addition, when daily changes in work engagement are temporarily separated from daily changes in outcomes like performance and personal initiative, state work engagement could be causally related to such outcomes. Diary research may also reveal what the day-to-day triggers are of state engagement. Sonnentag et al. (Chapter 3) summarize the existing research on state engagement, and identify avenues for future research.

Sonnentag et al. (Chapter 3) suggest intensifying conceptual development on day-specific (or even momentary) work engagement in order to arrive at a better understanding of how day-specific engagement corresponds to enduring engagement in experienced quality and configuration. In addition, they argue that it is an open question whether the scales used to assess enduring work engagement (see Schaufeli & Bakker, Chapter 2) are valid for the measurement of state work engagement. Clearly, the time anchors on the UWES and the MBI-GS (e.g., "a few times a month") do not fit with a daily reporting schedule. The appropriateness of item wording to capture the day-to-day variations in energy and dedication/involvement remains an open question. Expanding existing measures with new items or alternative response formats would help to refine critical instruments.

Until now, individual difference variables have made a minor contribution in research on state work engagement. According to Sonnentag et al (Chapter 3) personality may influence the variability of work engagement within a person, interacting between predictors and state work engagement, or between engagement and outcomes. As an example of this kind of research, Bledow and Schmitt (2008) argued that positive affectivity would make employees less dependent on positive events occurring during a work day. Consistent with this hypothesis, their diary study among German software engineers showed that positive affectivity moderated the relationship between positive events and work engagement. The positive relationship was stronger for engineers low in positive affectivity. In another diary study, Bakker and Xanthopoulou (2009) hypothesized that daily engagement would cross over from one colleague to another. In addition, since extraversion is the disposition to be sociable and cheerful, they predicted that extraverts would interact more often with their colleagues than would introverts. The frequency of daily communication was expected to moderate the crossover of daily work engagement, which in turn would determine colleagues' daily performance. Results confirmed the crossover of daily work engagement, but only on days that employees within a dyad interacted frequently. Moreover, as predicted, members of the dyad influenced each other's daily performance through a process of engagement crossover.

Engagement and job crafting
Sonnentag et al. (Chapter 3) and Salanova et al. (Chapter 9) argue that engagement is not just "happening" to employees, but rather that employees can actively create engagement experiences. As Grant and Ashford (2008) put it, "Employees do not just let life happen to them.

Rather, they try to affect, shape, curtail, expand, and temper what happens in their lives." (p. 3). Employees may actively change the design of their jobs by choosing tasks, negotiating different job content, and assigning meaning to their tasks or jobs (Parker & Ohly, 2008). It is our view that particularly engaged employees will behave in such a way.

Wrzesniewski and Dutton (2001) call the process of employees shaping their own jobs "job crafting"; this includes the physical and cognitive changes individuals make in their tasks or relational boundaries. Physical changes refer to the form, scope or number of job tasks, whereas cognitive changes refer to perception of the job. Relational boundaries include employees' discretion over their social interactions while doing the job. Job crafting has the potential to improve employees' balance of job demands with resources, increasing their person–job fit.

Wrzesniewski, McCauley, Rozin, and Schwartz (1997) suggest that employees who view their work as a calling (i.e., focus on enjoyment or fulfillment) are more likely to engage in job crafting, because work is more central to their lives. In a similar vein, engaged employees may be more inclined to proactively change their job demands and resources so that their performance is optimal. It would be interesting to examine the strategies employees use to increase their work engagement. Are engaged workers better able to mobilize their job resources? Do they search actively for feedback about their performance? Studies on engagement and job crafting may answer the question whether engaged employees really create virtuous circles (Salanova et al., Chapter 9).

Is there a dark side of engagement?
Virtually all chapters in this book offer evidence for the benefits of work engagement. Engaged employees have psychological capital, seem to create their own resources, perform better, and have happier clients. This raises the question whether there is also a dark side of work engagement. Previous research on positive organizational behavior (POB) constructs has indeed shown that there can be a dark side of POB.

For example, high self-esteem can lead to an underestimation of the time that is necessary for goal achievement (Buehler, Griffin, & Ross, 1994), and unrealistic optimism can harm individuals and organizations by promoting inappropriate persistence (Armor & Taylor, 1998). Furthermore, overconfidence has been found to hinder subsequent performance (Vancouver, Thompson, Tischner, & Putka, 2002; Vancouver, Thompson, & Williams, 2001), and creativity may lead to frustration given the unfocused effort and diminished productivity that creative individuals may experience (Ford & Sullivan, 2004).

Whereas this book has identified several of the above-mentioned qualities (e.g., self-esteem, optimism) as potential predictors of work engagement, it seems evident that "over-engagement" can also have negative consequences. For example, although engaged employees are not workaholics, they may become so engaged in their work that they take work home. Indeed, Beckers et al. (2004) conducted a survey-study among a representative sample of the Dutch workforce and found that work engagement was positively related to working overtime. The work–life balance literature has consistently shown that work–home interference undermines recovery, and may consequently lead to health problems (Geurts & Demerouti, 2003).

Furthermore, one may wonder whether work engagement may create workaholics, i.e., employees who have an inner drive to work hard, even when they no longer like working overtime. Indeed, some scholars have noted that "In order to burn out, a person needs to have been on fire at one time" (Pines, Aronson, & Kafry, 1981, p. 4). This would imply that, over time, the high arousal, positive affect (e.g., enthusiasm) of engaged workers turns into negative affect and strain. The design of future research should include ways of assessing potential long-term negative effects of high work engagement. The absorption component of work engagement seems a likely candidate for evoking unhealthy behavior. Employees may become so immersed in their work that they forget to rest or to maintain their personal relationships. A persistent pattern of excessive commitment could contribute to health or relationship problems.

Engagement and health

To date, only a handful of studies have addressed the relationship between work engagement and health. Demerouti, Bakker, De Jonge, Janssen, and Schaufeli (2001) found moderate negative correlations between engagement (particularly vigor) and psychosomatic health complaints (e.g., headaches, chest pain). In their study among four different Dutch service organizations, Schaufeli and Bakker (2004) found that engaged workers suffer less from, for instance, self-reported headaches, cardiovascular problems, and stomach aches. Similarly, Hakanen, Bakker, and Schaufeli (2006), in their study among Finnish teachers, showed that work engagement was positively related to self-rated health and workability. Peterson, Demerouti, Bergström, Samuelsson, Åsberg, & Nygren (2008) found that engaged Swedish health care workers reported fewer back pain and neck pain problems, and lower anxiety and depression. Furthermore, we have seen in Chapter 6 that vigor (physical strength, cognitive liveliness, and emotional energy) is positively related to mental and physical health. Since Wefald (2008) has shown positive relationships between the Shirom–Melamed vigor measure and work engagement, Shirom's findings can also be taken as evidence for a link between engagement and health.

However, recent research has generally failed to find evidence for a link between engagement and *physiological* indicators. Langelaan, Bakker, Schaufeli, Van Rhenen, and Van Doornen (2006, 2007) examined the relationship between burnout and work engagement on the one hand, and two physiological stress systems on the other hand, namely the hypothalamic-pituitary-adrenal (HPA) axis and the cardiac autonomic system. The HPA axis is the central mechanism in the long-term adaptation of an individual to his or her environment. The cardiac autonomic system consists of two different branches, the sympathetic system and the parasympathetic (vagal) system. The sympathetic system is involved in activity and arousal (e.g., leading to elevated blood pressure and heart rate), whereas the parasympathetic system has a prominent role in recovery and restoration (e.g., leading to a reduction in heart rate).

With respect to the HPA axis, Langelaan et al. (2006) found that their burned-out and engaged study group neither differed from each other, nor from a control group, with respect to morning cortisol levels, the cortisol awakening response (CAR), dehydroepiandrosteronesulfate (DHEAS) levels, and the cortisol/DHEAS ratio. Engaged employees only showed slightly better cortisol suppression than the burned-out and control group in response to dexamethasone, indicating a higher feedback sensitivity of their HPA axis. Furthermore, burned-out and engaged employees did not differ either from each other or from a control group with regard to cardiac autonomic (sympathetic and parasympathetic) functioning, as assessed by ambulatory measurements in their daily life (Langelaan et al., 2007). These findings were also not in line with predictions. It was hypothesized that burnout would be associated with increased sympathetic and/or reduced vagal control, whereas work engagement was expected to be associated with reduced sympathetic and/or increased vagal control.

Taken together, previous studies suggest that engagement is related to better subjectively reported health. However, engagement is not accompanied by deviances in (stress) physiological functioning. Even using a sensitive design including extreme groups (burnout versus engaged employees) did not produce the expected findings. The HPA axis and the sympathetic and parasympathetic cardiac systems did not function more optimally in engaged employees than in "normal", healthy individuals. Future studies should try to illuminate physiological processes that explain the relationship between engagement and health. What is needed is sensitive in-depth research on the psychophysiological indicators of engagement, as well as longitudinal studies on the relationship between engagement and health.

Crossover of engagement

In most organizations, performance is the result of the combined effort of individual employees. It is therefore conceivable that the crossover of engagement among members of the same work team increases performance. Crossover can be defined as the transfer of positive (or negative) experiences from one person to the other (Bakker, Westman, & Van Emmerik, 2009).

There is indeed some experimental evidence for such a crossover process. Barsade (2002) examined the transfer of moods among people in a group and its influence on performance. Using a trained confederate enacting mood, she showed that the pleasant mood of the confederate influenced (video coders' ratings of) the mood of the other team members during a simulated managerial exercise (a leaderless group discussion). The positive mood contagion consequently resulted in more cooperative behaviour and better task performance. In a similar vein, Damen (2007) asked a professional actor to show high arousal, positive emotions (e.g., enthusiasm) to business students. The students were encouraged by the actor (a presumed leader) to work on a task that asked them to process as many orders as possible relating to personal computers (including software, printers, and other hardware). Results showed that those exposed to engaged leaders were more effective and produced more. One of the reasons for this is that the emotions of the leader conveyed action readiness. The effect only worked when followers' emotions were similarly positive, suggesting that a contagion effect may have been responsible for the enthusiasm–performance link.

Future research on work engagement may focus on the crossover of engagement and performance in real-life work settings. Some researchers have started to examine reciprocal emotional reactions among employees who closely collaborate. For example, in a field setting, Totterdell, Kellet, Teuchmann, and Briner (1998) found evidence that the moods of teams of nurses and accountants were related to each other even after controlling for shared work problems. Bakker, Van Emmerik, and Euwema (2006) in their study among 2229 officers working in one of 85 teams found that team-level work engagement was related to individual team members' engagement (vigor, dedication, and absorption), after controlling for individual members' job demands and resources. Thus, engaged workers who communicated their optimism, positive attitudes, and proactive behaviors to their colleagues, created a positive team climate, independent of the demands and resources to which they were exposed. The question remains whether such a crossover of work engagement also translates into better team performance. Future studies should further illuminate the processes fostering the crossover of engagement at the workplace.

Management intervention

Intervention studies hold the greatest potential for theory, research, and practice. The process of introducing a new educational program or changing working conditions tests the limits of an idea. A serious challenge in organizational research is that researchers approach systems that maintain a certain balance between their demands, resources, and subjective experiences of employees. A single assessment in a cross-sectional survey provides a valuable snapshot, but sheds very little light on interrelationships between things. Longitudinal panel studies certainly improve the quality of information, but cannot provide definitive information on how one element has an impact on another.

Intervention studies provide a conceptual richness. They target a specific quality of the work environment, first to determine its susceptibility to change and secondly to assess downstream consequences of those changes on other aspects of worklife. In addition, from a practical perspective, intervention studies are useful. Well-informed action has the potential of contributing to the quality of life within the participating organization and beyond. Rather than just talking about work engagement, we can strive to do something about it.

The research evidence on spirals suggests that we have considerable latitude in intervention design. Studies could improve employee empowerment by improving their access to knowledge, materials, or support staff to determine its impact on work engagement. Intervention studies could examine crossover or contagion through programs that enhance the quality of collegial relationships (Leiter & Laschinger, 2008).

Overall conclusion

This book demonstrates that research on work engagement has broad and profound implications for work in the 21st century. Employees with energy and strong identification with their work access critical resources and seem to perform better. It is even conceivable that engaged workers create their own job resources over time. Our overview supports the contention that focusing on work engagement offers organizations a competitive advantage. We hope that our research agenda stimulates future research on work engagement and will be an important resource for scientists and practitioners alike.

References

Armor, D. A., & Taylor, S. E. (1998). Situated optimism: Specific outcome expectancies and selfregulation. In M. P. Zanna (Ed.), *Advances in experimental social psychology* (Vol. 30, pp. 309–379). New York: Academic Press.

Bakker, A. B., & Demerouti, E. (2007). The job demands-resources model: State of the art. *Journal of Managerial Psychology, 22*, 309–328.

Bakker, A. B., & Demerouti, E. (2008). Towards a model of work engagement. *Career Development International, 13*, 209–223.

Bakker, A. B., Hakanen, J. J., Demerouti, E., & Xanthopoulou, D. (2007). Job resources boost work engagement particularly when job demands are high. *Journal of Educational Psychology, 99*, 274–284.

Bakker, A. B., Schaufeli, W. B., Leiter, M. P., & Taris, T. W. (2008). Work engagement: An emerging concept in occupational health psychology. *Work & Stress, 22*, 187–200.

Bakker, A. B., Van Emmerik, I. J. H., & Euwema, M. C. (2006). Crossover of burnout and engagement in work teams. *Work and Occupations, 33*, 464–489.

Bakker, A. B., Westman, M., & Van Emmerik, I. J. H. (2009). Advancements in crossover theory. *Journal of Managerial Psychology, 24*, 206–219.

Bakker, A. B., & Xanthopoulou, D. (2009). The crossover of daily work engagement: Test of an actor-partner interdependence model. *Journal of Applied Psychology, 94*, 1562–1571.

Barsade, S. (2002). The ripple effect: emotional contagion and its influence on group behavior. *Administrative Science Quarterly, 47*, 644–677.

Beckers, D. G. J., Van der Linden, D., Smulders, P. G. W., Kompier, M. A. J., Van Veldhoven, M. J. P. M., & Van Yperen, N. W. (2004). Working overtime hours: relations with fatigue, work motivation, and the quality of work. *Journal of Occupational and Environmental Medicine, 46*, 1282–1289.

Bledow, R., & Schmitt, A. (2008). *Work engagement as a dynamic process: The interplay of events, emotions and resources.* Poster presented at the 2008 Conference of the Society of Industrial and Organizational Psychology, San Francisco, CA.

Buehler, R., Griffin, D., & Ross, M. (1994). Exploring the "planning fallacy": Why people underestimate their task completion times. *Journal of Personality and Social Psychology, 67*, 366–381.

Carmeli, A., & Spreitzer, G. (2008). Trust, connectivity, and thriving. Implications for innovative work behavior. *Working paper.*

Damen, F. (2007). *Taking the lead: The role of affect in leadership effectiveness.* Unpublished Doctoral Dissertation, Erasmus University Rotterdam.

Demerouti, E., & Bakker, A. B. (2008). The Oldenburg Burnout Inventory: A good alternative to measure burnout and engagement. In J. R. B. Halbesleben (Ed.), *Handbook of stress and burnout in health care.* Hauppauge, NY: Nova Science.

Demerouti, E., Bakker, A. B., De Jonge, J., Janssen, P. P. M., & Schaufeli, W. B. (2001). Burnout and engagement at work as a function of demands and control. *Scandinavian Journal of Work, Environment and Health, 27*, 279–286.

Demerouti, E., Mostert, K., & Bakker, A. B. (in press). Burnout and work engagement: A thorough investigation of the independency of the constructs. *Journal of Occupational and Health Psychology.*

Ford, C., & Sullivan, D. M. (2004). A time for everything: How timing of novel contributions influences project team outcomes. *Journal of Organizational Behavior, 21*, 163–183.

Fredrickson, B. L. (2001). The role of positive emotions in positive psychology: The broaden-and-build theory of positive emotions. *American Psychologist, 56*, 218–226.

Fredrickson, B. L. (2003). Positive emotions and upward spirals in organizations. In Cameron, K., Dutton, J., & Quinn, R. (Eds.), *Positive organizational scholarship* (pp. 163–175). San Francisco: Berrett-Koehler.

Fredrickson, B. L., & Branigan, C. A. (2005). Positive emotions broaden the scope of attention and thought–action repertoires. *Cognition and Emotion, 19*, 313–332.

Fredrickson, B. L., & Losada, M. F. (2005). Positive affect and the complex dynamics of human flourishing. *American Psychologist, 60*, 678–686.

Geurts, S. A. E., & Demerouti, E. (2003). Work/Nonwork interface: A review of theories and findings. In M. Schabracq, J. Winnubst, & C. L. Cooper (Eds.), *The handbook of work and health psychology* (2nd ed., pp. 279–312). Chichester: Wiley.

Grant, A. M., & Ashford, S. J. (2008). The dynamics of proactivity at work. *Research in Organizational Behavior, 28*, 3–34.

Hakanen, J. J., Bakker, A. B., & Demerouti, E. (2005). How dentists cope with their job demands and stay engaged: The moderating role of job resources. *European Journal of Oral Sciences, 113*, 479–487.

Hakanen, J. J., Bakker, A. B., & Schaufeli, W. B. (2006). Burnout and work engagement among teachers. *Journal of School Psychology, 43*, 495–513.

Hakanen, J. J., Perhoniemi, R., & Toppinen-Tanner, S. (2008a). Positive gain spirals at work: From job resources to work engagement, personal initiative, and work-unit innovativeness. *Journal of Vocational Behavior, 73*, 78–91.

Hakanen, J. J., Schaufeli, W. B., & Ahola, K. (2008b). The Job Demands–Resources model: A three-year cross-lagged study of burnout, depression, commitment, and work engagement. *Work & Stress, 22*, 224–241.

Halbesleben, J. R. B., & Wheeler, A. R. (2008). The relative roles of engagement and embeddedness in predicting job performance and intention to leave. *Work & Stress, 22*, 242–256.

Harter, J. K., Schmidt, F. L., & Hayes, T. L. (2002). Business-unit-level relationships between employee satisfaction, employee engagement, and business outcomes: A meta-analysis. *Journal of Applied Psychology, 87*, 268–279.

Hobfoll, S. E. (2002). Social and psychological resources and adaptation. *Review of General Psychology, 6*, 307–324.

Hobfoll, S. E., Johnson, R. J., Ennis, N., & Jackson, A. P. (2003). Resource loss, resource gain, and emotional outcomes among inner city women. *Journal of Personality and Social Psychology, 84*, 632–643.

Isen, A. M. (2000). Positive affect and decision making. In M. Lewis & J. M. Haviland-Jones (Eds.), *Handbook of emotions* (2nd ed., pp. 417–435). New York: Guilford Press.

Judge, T. A., Van Vianen, A. E. M., & De Pater, I. (2004). Emotional stability, core self-evaluations, and job outcomes: A review of the evidence and an agenda for future research. *Human Performance, 17*, 325–346.

Karasek, R. A. (1979). Job demands, job decision latitude, and mental strain: Implications for job redesign. *Administrative Science Quarterly, 24*, 285–308.

Langelaan, S., Bakker, A. B., Schaufeli, W. B., Van Rhenen, W., & Van Doornen, L. J. P. (2006). Do burned-out and work-engaged employees differ in the functioning of the hypothalamic-pituitary-adrenal axis? *Scandinavian Journal of Work, Environment, and Health, 32,* 339–348.

Langelaan, S., Bakker, A. B., Schaufeli, W. B., Van Rhenen, W., & Van Doornen, L. J. P. (2007). Is burnout related to allostatic load? *International Journal of Behavioral Medicine, 14,* 213–221.

Leiter, M. P., & Laschinger, H. S. (2008). *Civility, respect, and engagement at work: Improving collegial relationships among hospital employees.* Presentation at National Center for Organizational Development, Veterans Hospital System, Boston, MA (November).

Luthans, F., Avolio, B. J., Avey, J. B., & Norman, S. M. (2007). Psychological capital: Measurement and relationship with performance and job satisfaction. *Personnel Psychology, 60,* 541–572.

Luthans, F., Youssef, C. M., & Avolio, B. J. (2007). *Psychological capital: Developing the human competitive edge.* Oxford, UK: Oxford University Press.

Macey, W. H., & Schneider, B. (2008). The meaning of employee engagement. *Industrial and Organizational Psychology, 1,* 3–30.

Maslach, C., Jackson, S. E., & Leiter, M. (1996). *Maslach Burnout Inventory. Manual* (3rd ed.). Palo Alto, CA: Consulting Psychologists Press.

Maslach, C., & Leiter, M. P. (1997). *The truth about burnout: How organizations cause personal stress and what to do about it.* San Francisco, CA: Jossey-Bass.

Maslach, C., & Leiter, M.P. (2008). Early predictors of job burnout and engagement. *Journal of Applied Psychology, 93,* 498–512.

Mauno, S., Kinnunen, U., & Ruokolainen, M. (2007). Job demands and resources as antecedents of work engagement: A longitudinal study. *Journal of Vocational Behavior, 70,* 149–171.

Oates, W. E. (1971). *Confessions of a workaholic.* Nashville: Abingdon.

Parker, S. K., & Ohly, S. (2008). Designing motivating jobs. In R. Kanfer, G. Chen, & R. Pritchard (Eds.), *Work motivation: Past, present, and future.* SIOP Organizational Frontiers Series.

Peterson, U., Demerouti, E., Bergström, G., Samuelsson, M., Åsberg, M., & Nygren, Å. (2008). Burnout and physical and mental health among Swedish healthcare workers. *Journal of Advanced Nursing, 62,* 84–95.

Pines, A., Aronson, E., & Kafry, D. (1981). *Burnout: From tedium to personal growth.* New York: Free Press.

Porath, C., Spreitzer, G., & Gibson, C. (2008). *Social structural antecedents of thriving at work: A study of six organizations.* University of Michigan working paper.

Rothmann, S., & Storm, K. (2003). *Work engagement in the South African Police Service.* Paper presented at the 11th European Congress of Work and Organizational Psychology, 14–17 May 2003, Lisbon, Portugal.

Salanova, M., Agut, S., & Peiró, J. M. (2005). Linking organizational resources and work engagement to employee performance and customer loyalty: The mediation of service climate. *Journal of Applied Psychology, 90,* 1217–1227.

Schaufeli, W. B., & Bakker, A. B. (2003). *UWES – Utrecht Work Engagement Scale: Test Manual.* Unpublished Manuscript: Department of Psychology, Utrecht University.

Schaufeli, W. B., & Bakker, A. B. (2004). Job demands, job resources, and their relationship with burnout and engagement: A multi-sample study. *Journal of Organizational Behavior, 25,* 293–315.

Schaufeli, W. B., & Salanova, M. (2007). Work engagement: An emerging psychological concept and its implications for organizations. In S. W. Gilliland, D. D. Steiner, & D. P. Skarlicki (Eds.), *Research in social issues in management (Volume 5): Managing social and ethical issues in organizations.* Greenwich, CT: Information Age Publishers.

Schaufeli, W. B., Salanova, M., González-Romá, V., & Bakker, A. B. (2002). The measurement of engagement and burnout: A two sample confirmatory factor analytic approach. *Journal of Happiness Studies, 3,* 71–92.

Schaufeli, W. B., Taris, T. W., Le Blanc, P., Peeters, M., Bakker, A. B., & De Jonge, J. (2001). Maakt arbeid gezond? Op zoek naar de bevlogen werknemer [Does work make happy? In search of the engaged worker]. *De Psycholoog, 36,* 422–428.

Schulman, P. (1999). Applying learned optimism to increase sales productivity. *Journal of Personal Selling & Sales Management, 19,* 31–37.

Seligman, M. E. P. (1998). *Learned optimism.* New York: Pocket Books.

Shirom, A., Toker, S., Berliner, S., Shapira, I., & Melamed, S. (2008). The effects of physcial fitness and feeling vigorous on self-rated health. *Health Psychology, 27,* 567–575.

Shirom, A., Vinokur, A. D., & Vaananen, A. (2008). *Vigor and emotional exhaustion are independently associated with self-rated health and work capacity: A cross-country comparison.* Manuscript in preparation. Faculty of Management, Tel Aviv University, Tel Aviv, Israel.

Sonnentag, S. (2003). Recovery, work engagement, and proactive behavior: A new look at the interface between non-work and work. *Journal of Applied Psychology*, *88*, 518–528.

Spreitzer, G., Sutcliffe, K., Dutton, J., Sonenshein, S., & Grant, A. M. (2005). A socially embedded model of thriving at work. *Organization Science*, *16*, 537–549.

Totterdell, P. S., Kellet, K., Teuchmann, K., & Briner, R. B. (1998). Evidence of mood linkage in work groups. *Journal of Personality and Social Psychology*, *74*, 1504–1515.

Vancouver, J. B., Thompson, C. M., Tischner, E. C., & Putka, D. J. (2002). Two studies examining the negative effect of self-efficacy on performance. *Journal of Applied Psychology*, *87*, 506–516.

Vancouver, J. B., Thompson, C. M., & Williams, A. A. (2001). The changing signs in the relationships between self-efficacy, personal goals and performance. *Journal of Applied Psychology*, *86*, 605–620.

Van den Broeck, A., Vansteenkiste, M., De Witte, H., & Lens, W. (2008). Explaining the relationships between job characteristics, burnout and engagement: The role of basic psychological need satisfaction. *Work & Stress*, *22*, 277–294.

Watson, D., & Tellegen, A. (1985). Toward a consensual structure of mood. *Psychological Bulletin*, *98*, 219–235.

Wefald, A. J. (2008). *An examination of job engagement, transformational leadership, and related psychological constructs*. Unpublished doctoral dissertation, Manhattan, Kansas: Kansas State University.

Wrzesniewski, A., & Dutton, J. E. (2001). Crafting a job: Revisioning employees as active crafters of their work. *Academy of Management Review*, *26*, 179–201.

Wrzesniewski, A., McCauley, C., Rozin, P., & Schwartz, B. (1997). Jobs, careers, and callings: People's reactions to their work. *Journal of Research in Personality*, *31*, 21–33.

Xanthopoulou, D., Bakker, A. B., Demerouti, E., & Schaufeli, W. B. (2007). The role of personal resources in the job demands-resources model. *International Journal of Stress Management*, *14*, 121–141.

Xanthopoulou, D., Bakker, A. B., Demerouti, E., & Schaufeli, W. B. (2009a). Reciprocal relationships between job resources, personal resources, and work engagement. *Journal of Vocational Behavior*, *74*, 235–244.

Xanthopoulou, D., Bakker, A. B., Demerouti, E., & Schaufeli, W. B. (2009b). Work engagement and financial returns: A diary study on the role of job and personal resources. *Journal of Occupational and Organizational Psychology*, *82*, 183–200.

Xanthopoulou, D., Bakker, A. B., Heuven, E., Demerouti, E., & Schaufeli, W. B. (2008). Working in the sky: A diary study on work engagement among flight attendants. *Journal of Occupational Health Psychology*, *13*, 345–356.

Author index

Elliott, E. S., 133
Engelland, B., 76
Ennis, N., 120, 185
Enzmann, D., 18, 153, 159
Epitropaki, O., 78
Epstein, R., 142
Eriksen, H. R., 18, 19
Euwema, M. C., 5, 18, 61, 62, 65, 78, 94, 97, 128, 133, 137, 192
Extremera, N., 18

Fallon, B. J., 75
Fay, D., 14, 89, 148
Feldman Barrett, L. F., 72
Feldt, T., 16, 17, 18, 97
Fetter, R., 148
Fiksenbaum, L., 138
Finkel, S. M., 4, 125, 128
Finkenauer, C., 76
Firtko, A., 75
Fisher, C. D., 63, 70, 73, 149
Flowers, C., 43, 48
Folkman, S., 73
Foo, M. D., 78
Ford, C., 191
Forgas, J. P., 70, 143
Frederick, C., 75, 77, 118, 133
Fredrickson, B. L., 4, 31, 33, 62, 64, 71, 72, 79, 89, 96, 103, 119, 124, 125, 126, 127, 128, 155, 156, 157, 186
Freedy, J., 150
Frese, M., 14, 29, 31, 36, 64, 89, 97, 141, 148
Frijda, N. H., 71
Fritz, C., 7, 64, 75, 142, 188
Fry, L. W., 169

Gailliot, M., 142
Gan, Y., 93
Gardner, W. L., 76
Gavin, M. B., 29
Gendolla, G. H. E., 76
George, J. M., 71, 72, 74, 77, 143
Gerras, S. J., 174
Geurts, S. A. E., 30, 32, 36, 191
Ghoshal, S., 79
Giardini, A., 64
Gibson, C., 134, 135, 137, 138, 141, 188
Gillespie, J. Z., 79
Gilson, R. L., 19
Glibkowsky, B. C., 92
Goldberg, J., 164, 167
Goldman, S., 79
González-Romá, V., 13, 17, 26, 41, 43, 57, 59, 65, 75, 85, 103, 133, 153, 182, 188
Gorgievski, M. J., 103
Gorter, R. C., 17, 18, 133
Grant, A. M., 75, 133, 141, 188
Gray, J. A., 50

Green, S. G., 142
Griffin, D., 191
Griffin, S., 155
Gully, S. M., 26

Hackman, J. R., 77, 88, 103, 118, 142
Hackmann, A., 174
Hakanen, J. J., 3, 6, 16, 17, 18, 19, 22, 27, 30, 35, 75, 86, 89, 90, 91, 92, 93, 94, 95, 96, 97, 103, 121, 123, 126, 136, 137, 175, 185, 186, 188, 191
Halbesleben, J. R. B., 2, 6, 50, 91, 103, 104, 111, 113, 150, 151, 152, 154, 157, 158, 159, 167, 175, 182, 185, 186, 187
Hall, M. P., 78
Hall, S. M., 107
Hallberg, U., 17, 19, 93, 96, 133, 138
Hansen, C. J., 70
Harkins, D., 155
Harris, C., 77
Harrison, D. A., 113
Harter, J. K., 11, 12, 15, 16, 21, 54, 65, 158, 182
Harter, L. M., 19
Harvey, J., 111
Harvie, P., 173
Hawton, K., 174
Hayes, T. L., 11, 12, 15, 16, 21, 54, 65, 158, 182
Heaphy, E., 64, 142
Heller, D., 27, 30, 33
Herche, J., 76
Herring, R. A., 50
Herzberg, E., 166
Herzberg, F., 88
Heuven, E., 28, 30, 31, 122, 153, 159, 184
Higgins, E. T., 50
Hilburger, T., 89
Hobfoll, S. E., 30, 33, 62, 63, 66, 74, 76, 79, 88, 89, 93, 94, 97, 103, 119, 120, 137, 150, 175, 185, 188
Hockey, G. R. J., 87
Hoffman, B. J., 148, 154
Hofmann, D. A., 29, 174
Holman, D., 78
Hoogstraten, J., 17, 18, 133
House, R. J., 140
Howell, J. M., 123
Hox, J. J., 113
Huffcutt, A. I., 106, 108
Hunter, J. E., 106, 107, 113

Iaffaldano, M. T., 149
Ibarra, H., 136
Iida, M., 74
Ilies, R., 27, 30, 33, 148, 154
Irving, L. M., 60
Isen, A. M., 4, 156, 186

Jackson, A. P., 120, 185
Jackson, D., 75
Jackson, L. T. B., 19, 90

Subject index